T0319688

PAWNED STATES

The Princeton Economic History of the Western World

Joel Mokyr, Series Editor

A list of titles in this series appears in the back of the book.

Pawned States

State Building in the Era of International Finance

Didac Queralt

PRINCETON UNIVERSITY PRESS

PRINCETON AND OXFORD

Published by Princeton University Press
41 William Street, Princeton, New Jersey 08540
99 Banbury Road, Oxford OX2 6JX

press.princeton.edu

Library of Congress Control Number: 2022932411

All Rights Reserved
ISBN 9780691231426
ISBN (pbk.) 9780691231525
ISBN (e-book) 9780691231518

British Library Cataloging-in-Publication Data is available

Editorial: Bridget Flannery-McCoy and Alena Chekanov
Jacket/Cover Design: Lauren Smith
Production: Erin Suydam
Publicity: Kate Hensley and Charlotte Coyne
Copyeditor: Jennifer McClain

Cover image: "The London Stock Exchange—Well-Known Faces in the Consol Market," 1891, print. Lordprice Collection / Alamy Stock Photo

This book has been composed in Adobe Text and Gotham

10 9 8 7 6 5 4 3 2 1

CONTENTS

FIGURES

TABLES

ACKNOWLEDGMENTS

This book has benefited from multiple conversations and discussions with colleagues and friends. I am particularly grateful to Carles Boix, Alex Debs, Isabela Mares, Adam Przeworski, Ken Scheve, and David Stasavage for their unrelenting support and valuable suggestions. Detailed comments by Pablo Beramendi, Lisa Blaydes, Jeff Frieden, María José Hierro, Nuno Monteiro, Layna Mosley, John Roemer, Shanker Satyanath, and Andreas Wimmer also contributed to key aspects of the argument.

The project marinated in conversations—some more formal than others—with Francesc Amat, Ben Ansell, Laia Balcells, Thomas Brambor, Christian Breunig, Lawrence Broz, Allan Dafoe, Ruben Enikolopov, Rui Esteves, Marc Flandreau, Hector Galindo-Silva, Aina Gallego, Francisco Garfías, Scott Gates, Mitu Gulati, Margaret Levi, Johannes Lindvall, Debin Ma, Kris James Mitchener, Jordi Muñoz, Pilar Nogues-Marco, Maria Petrova, Giacomo Ponzetto, Leandro Prados de la Escosura, Peter Rosendorff, Pacho Sánchez-Cuenca, Peter Schram, Erik Voeten, Hans-Joachim Voth, Mark Weidemaier, Tianyang Xi, and Noam Yuchtman. I thank all of them, as well as workshop participants at the Barcelona Institute of Economics, Columbia University, Duke University, the European University Institute, the Global Research in International Political Economy webinar, the London School of Economics (LSE), Lund University, New York University (NYU), NYU–Abu Dhabi, Peking University, Sciences Po, Stanford University, University Carlos III of Madrid, University College London, the University of Manchester, the University of Notre Dame, Vanderbilt University, and Yale University, and annual meetings organized by the American Political Science Association, the European Political Science Association, the International Political Economy Society, and the International Studies Association.

The book workshop held at Yale University in fall 2019 was a turning point in the scope and ambition of the manuscript. I am indebted to workshop participants Mark Dincecco, David Lake, Helen Milner, David

Stasavage, Ken Scheve, and Mike Tomz for detailed feedback and encouragement to push the project forward. The workshop was possible thanks to the financial support of the Georg Walter Leitner Program in International and Comparative Political Economy at Yale University and the blessing (and participation) of Program Director Gerard Padró i Miquel.

My colleagues at Yale, some of them already mentioned, listened to and read multiple iterations of various chapters, contributing to what the book is today. I thank Greg Huber, Dan Mattingly, Ana L. de la O, Frances Rosenbluth, Emily Sellars, Milan Svolik, and Steven Wilkinson for that.

Parts of the manuscript were written during stays at Lund University and the STICERD Center at the LSE. I am thankful to Jan Teorell, the principal investigator of the phenomenal STANCE research group based at Lund, for his support and interest in the project over the years. I am grateful to Tim Besley for his generous invitation to the LSE and for the many conversations about the project during my visit.

The various trips to the Guildhall Library, City of London, were generously financed by the MacMillan Research Grant at Yale University. In preparation for the first visit to the archive, Toshio Suzuki shared numerous tips about where and what to look for at Guildhall and elsewhere in Europe. I thank him for his invaluable advice.

The manuscript presents original data, but it also relies on existing datasets graciously shared by Per Andersson, Francisco Comín, David Stasavage, and Ali Coşkun Tunçer. I thank Susannah Beyl, Moses Cho, Júlia Díaz Collado, Simon Cooper, Annalisa Eichholzer, Justin Jin, Yusuf Magiya, Ryan Pike, Shawn Thacker, Josh Turner, and Hikaru Yamagishi for their excellent research assistance at various stages of the project.

I am grateful to my editor at Princeton University Press, Bridget Flannery-McCoy, for her enthusiasm for the project from Day 1 and for her guidance from manuscript submission to publication. Editor Joel Mokyr believed in this project and welcomed it into a series that I always held in highest regard for its breath and erudition. Professor Mokyr's brilliant feedback and that of three anonymous referees made this a better book.

At Princeton University Press, I also thank Nathan Carr and Alena Chekanov for kindly walking me throughout the production stage and addressing the numerous questions of a first-time author. John Donohue at Westchester Publishing Services deserves recognition for his attention to detail. On my end, the production of the manuscript was smoothed by the generous financial support of the Frederick W. Hilles Publication Fund at Yale University. The earlier drafts of the manuscript were edited by Linda

Meixner, who kindly taught me how to make my writing more effective, and the final text was revised by Jennifer McClain with excellent copyediting.

Important aspects of the book borrow from my article "War, International Finance, and Fiscal Capacity in the Long Run," published in *International Organization* in 2019 by Cambridge University Press, to which I am grateful for granting permission to use some of those materials.

The book was in the making for seven years. During this period we moved four times and lived in three cities on two continents—quite a ride for a young family. Over the years, we received support and affection from friends and family. My parents, Joan and Montserrat—two role models— deserve special recognition, as do my in-laws, José Luis and Milagros, always eager to help in any capacity. My children, Eloi and Alicia, brought us happiness all along the way, and they are a constant reminder of what really matters. But this book exists only because I counted on the endless love and support of María José Hierro. Her eloquent criticism, readiness to help, and indefatigable optimism sustain every page of this book. A partner like her makes everything possible.

PAWNED STATES

1

Introduction

Societies thrive when people can depend upon a functional or "capable" state, one that monopolizes the use of force, protects property rights, and delivers extensive public goods and services from roads to public education to health care; but functional states cannot be taken for granted. State capacity, "the institutional capability of the state to carry out various policies that deliver benefits and services to households and firms,"[1] varies widely from state to state as well as within and across regions. Why do such differences exist, and why are they so persistent?

In this book, I trace differences in state capacity back to the nineteenth century. I will show that countries that then relied on domestic resource mobilization as opposed to foreign debt to fund government hold higher levels of state capacity today. Whereas tax collection compelled incumbents to invest in state strengthening institutions (from a tax agency to a universal census), external finance distorted incentives to initiate state apparatus modernization, pushing highly indebted nations into state weakening trajectories.

In the nineteenth century, recently created and traditionally isolated states floated sovereign loans in Europe to pay for war, balance the budget, and fund infrastructure projects. Rapid indebtedness of these weakly institutionalized economies often ended in external default—the suspension of debt service. In return for fresh capital, borrowers agreed to increasingly

1. Besley and Persson (2011, p. 6).

1

onerous conditions, including infrastructure concessions, the exchange of old debt for public monopolies, and leasing control over branches of the tax administration. After handing over key sources of government income to foreign bondholders, more loans were soon required to balance the budget. In anticipation of a likely default, foreign investors requested newer hypothecation of public assets, further slicing the effective tax base of the local government. By 1914, when the lending euphoria came to an end, many nations had already fallen into a debt trap, causing persistent fiscal imbalance.

Unlike one-sided theories of financial imperialism,[2] my argument also emphasizes the domestic angle to the surge of external indebtedness at early stages of state building. Foreign loans secure government funds to revenue-thirsty rulers while helping them dodge administrative reform and constraints on their power. That is, building an efficient tax bureaucracy consumes funds that incumbents cannot use for self-indulgence or nurturing patronage networks. Moreover, rulers may be obliged to share fiscal power with taxpayers to overcome hesitancy to increased taxation.[3] By relying on external debt, rulers in the global periphery can avoid the administrative and political costs of fiscal innovation, precluding advances in state capacity.

I quantify the consequences of foreign loans for state building by focusing on war finance in the nineteenth century. This decision is based on two grounds: First, war is the largest shock to any treasury[4] and the thriving force of state building throughout history.[5] Second, the euphoria in sovereign lending and the high frequency of interstate conflict concentrated between the end of the Napoleonic Wars (1815) and the onset of World War I (1914), declining dramatically thereafter. By studying the means of war finance in the so-called Bond Era, I can examine the commitment of rulers to mobilizing internal resources and whether early fiscal policy decisions pushed countries into different state building trajectories.

Addressing the usual suspects in causal inference analysis, I demonstrate that countries that relied disproportionally on foreign capital to finance war before 1914 show a lower capacity to raise taxes all the way to the present day. By contrast, countries that mobilized domestic resources to finance

---

2. Hobson (1902).
3. Levi (1988).
4. Barro (1979).
5. Boix (2015); Dal Bó, Hernández-Lagos, and Mazzuca (2015).

war show higher tax ratios and stronger tax bureaucracies today, and in some particular cases, stronger democratic institutions. The econometric evidence is accompanied by a collection of case studies that speak to different geographic areas and institutional contexts: Argentina, Chile, late-Qing China, Ethiopia, Japan, the Ottoman Empire, Peru, Siam, and South Africa. These cases illustrate the political game between foreign financiers, local incumbents, and taxpayers, and how early fiscal decisions shaped state building in the long run. In combination, the econometric analysis and qualitative accounts offer complementary evidence of the key assumptions, implications, and mechanisms of the theoretical argument.

On paper, foreign capital in the Bond Era offered an unmatched opportunity to overcome barriers to economic growth and invest in infrastructure with high social returns; however, it also weakened incentives to build capable states, pushing poor and weakly institutionalized nations into debt traps. Counterintuitively, developing nations might have benefited from tighter access to external capital at early stages of state building, which would have strengthened rulers' incentives to expand state capacity on a permanent basis. My conclusions have implications for the study of international finance, state building, and political reform, as I outline below.

The Globalization of Finance

The argument of the book builds on the assumption that countries in the Global South or periphery had access to relatively cheap external credit during the Bond Era;[6] however, sovereign borrowers outside Europe had weak fundamentals and little or poor reputation in capital markets, and they experienced regular episodes of default.[7] I shed light on this apparent contradiction by introducing the concept of *extreme conditionality*: the hypothecation of local assets (e.g., state monopolies, railroads, and customs houses) for fresh foreign loans.

The ability of foreign bondholders to gain new concessions and take control over collateralized assets in the case of default heightened as the interests of financiers and creditor governments grew closer, a phenomenon accelerating in the last decades of the nineteenth century. In Britain— the leader of capital exports—the gradual alignment between financial and government interests resulted from three interrelated factors: elite replacement, bondholders' coordination, and imperial competition. The

---

6. I use the terms *Global South* and *periphery* interchangeably to refer to countries in Asia, Africa, Central and South America, and Southern and Eastern Europe.

7. Reinhart and Rogoff (2009).

new "gentlemanly class"[8]—the marriage of banking families and landed elites—assumed leading positions in the Foreign Office, the Bank of England, and consular service. Meanwhile, foreign bondholders inaugurated the Corporation of Foreign Bondholders (CFB), an encompassing organization representing big and small investors that perfected the art of requesting diplomatic assistance in sovereign debt crises. Initially hesitant, the British government grew receptive to such demands, incorporating finance into the set of imperialist policies, a practice that France and Germany had been open about since the 1870s.

Mitchener and Weidenmier have shown that "supersanctions" involving foreign financial control and gunboat diplomacy were regularly imposed on *embarrassed governments*—as countries that suspended debt service were referred to. Forty-eight percent of the countries that had defaulted between 1870 and 1914 were supersanctioned. Borrowers that defaulted more than once were supersanctioned 70 percent of the time.[9] Mitchener and Weidenmier argue that supersanctions were imposed on a case-by-case basis and upon manifest bad behavior, namely, *ex post*. I argue instead that severe sanctions gradually became part of the lending business model, a generally recognized practice of debt collection. The possibility of imposing supersanctions following debt service interruption was increasingly agreed upon at time of issue, or *ex ante*, thus my preference for the term *extreme conditionality*. Seizure prioritized pledged assets—state monopolies and tax sources that had been hypothecated in the original loan contracts.[10] Coding the presence of pledges out of 700+ sovereign bond prospectuses in 1858–1914, I show that the expectation of taking control of local public assets decreased the premium paid by countries with poor or no reputation in international markets. For one, extreme conditionality offers an original explanation of the secular decrease of the spread (the interest rate difference between wealthy and poor nations) in the Bond Era despite the high frequency of sovereign default.

My treatment of international lending resonates with the *Hobson-Lenin hypothesis*, according to which European powers used international finance as an instrument of imperial domination.[11] Extreme conditionality can be

---

8. Cain and Hopkins (2016).

9. Mitchener and Weidenmier (2010, p. 27). As I discuss in chapter 4, this is only a lower-bound estimate of the frequency of supersanctions.

10. Until the mid-twentieth century, the terms *loan* and *bond* were used interchangeably. I follow that convention throughout the book.

11. Hobson (1902) and Lenin (1934), and Frieden (1994) for a concise review.

interpreted as a microfoundation of financial imperialism, a nonviolent policy to gain control over foreign assets. However, unlike the Hobson-Lenin hypothesis, I emphasize the domestic angle to the surge of external finance in the Bond Era: foreign loans secured government funds while helping rulers postpone administrative reform and constraints on their power.

War and State Making

The argument in this book revisits the connection between war and state making in the era of international finance. Contrary to the unconditional characterization of the so-called bellicist hypothesis, that is, *more war, more state*, I argue—very much alongside Tilly's original work—that the effect of war on state building ultimately depends on how warfare is paid for: financing war with taxes (or domestic credit) is conducive to state making, whereas financing wars with external loans may not be similarly conducive because rulers may dodge the long-term equivalence between loans and taxes if war debt is repaid in specie.[12] When this equivalence holds—when rulers repay war debt with tax money—positive institutional transformations associated with the bellicist hypothesis can be expected. That is, war makes states because rulers are compelled to expand tax capacity to repay war debt. If rulers find ways to minimize the war bill or manage to service war debt in specie rather than tax money, war will not make stronger states, unraveling the equivalence of debt and tax for the purpose of state building.

The importance of external finance of war for state making has been emphasized by the institutional sociologist Miguel Angel Centeno.[13] I advance our understanding of external finance on state building in two ways: First, I put forward a political explanation for the preference of external finance over taxation. I argue that the possibility of bypassing administrative costs and tax bargaining with domestic constituency can preempt investment in tax modernization and political reform, impeding the growth of state capacity over time. The new theoretical predictions shed light on which countries are likely to be negatively affected by external finance and why those effects are long-lasting. Second, by introducing the

---

12. In the economic literature, this equivalence is referred to as *Ricardian equivalence*. My argument suggests that the Ricardian equivalence was largely met for lenders because they recovered their investment one way or another, hence their willingness to lend; but the equivalence does not necessarily apply for the purpose of state building if rulers repay foreign debt with equity instead of tax money, avoiding gains in tax capacity.

13. Centeno (1997, 2002).

concept of extreme conditionality into sovereign borrowing, I elucidate the reasons that weakly institutionalized countries were allowed to float loans even after recent default and despite showing an eroding tax base.

Public Finance and Limited Government

The argument and evidence advanced in this book speak to the relationship between state finance and political reform. Public credit in Europe gave rise to a key political institution: limited government, the constitutional right of a parliament to control the national budget on an annual basis.[14] To prevent monarchs from reneging on war debt, the Crown's lenders demanded veto power over spending decisions.[15] This compromise secured war funds for the Crown and enabled taxpayers and creditors—often the same individuals—to hold the monarch accountable. Mutual gain transformed taxation into a nonzero-sum game—the ruler secured funds for war and the taxpayers protection from foreign aggression—enabling sustained investment in state capacity.[16] State building in Europe, in sum, brought together public credit and political development.

In this book, I reexamine contractual theories of public finance and representation in light of the first globalization of credit markets. Cheap external capital may strengthen incentives to finance externally while preempting tax bargaining with domestic constituents and the development of *domestic* credit markets, thus the formation of a mass of domestic lenders with whom to strike bargains conducive to limited government. In other words, the internationalization of credit may work against the spread of democracy, a key driver of strong, capable states.[17]

1.1 External Public Finance and State Building

Before I delve into historical evidence, let me anticipate the main logic of the argument in chapter 2, where I advance a political economy of public finance and delineate fiscal consequences of early policy decisions. Although I focus on war financing—a paramount fiscal shock often related to state building—I envision the argument to apply to other policy realms that require substantial revenue mobilization in a relatively short period of

14. Dincecco (2009, p. 95).
15. Bates and Lien (1985); North and Weingast (1989).
16. Levi (1988); Besley and Persson (2009).
17. Acemoglu and Robinson (2019); Stasavage (2020).

time: for example, combating a pandemic, building critical infrastructure, and recovering from a natural disaster.

Suppose there is an incumbent or ruler who must finance a given exogenous war. To simplify the analysis, I assume two funding options, taxes or loans, ruling out intermediate combinations. Likewise, I consider only *external* loans because domestic credit markets outside Europe were largely tight or nonexistent before the twentieth century.[18] The ruler, motivated only by individual gain, seeks to maximize private income by keeping a cut of total government funds (i.e., rents). Taxpayers, by contrast, prefer all their tax money to be spent on public goods, whereas government lenders—private individuals based overseas—want to recover their investment (the principal and interest) within a stipulated time (or maturity).

To discipline the ruler, taxpayers demand some institutionalized say in how public moneys are spent, that is, power-sharing institutions. If these are granted, the ruler secures war funds at the cost of limiting his discretion over fiscal policy, hence rents from office. Once power-sharing institutions are in place, they are likely to stay for two reasons: First, taxation can become a win-win for the ruler and taxpayers: the former secures a stable stream of funds, and the latter hold the ruler accountable while benefiting from public goods. Second, power-sharing institutions help taxpayers overcome collective action problems in disciplining the ruler, hence their bargaining power.[19] Foreign private investors have market-based means to discipline the ruler: they compensate the risk of default ex ante by charging a higher interest rate (or premium) and ex post by imposing a default sanction: for instance, denying new loans if debt service is interrupted (also known as *capital exclusion*).

The ruler decides which principal to serve: taxpayers or foreign financiers. On the one hand, taxes strengthen power-sharing institutions, thus reducing the share of public funds the ruler can retain for self-consumption. But the capacity of the state to tax improves by exercising it, expanding future tax revenue and the size of the pie the ruler can partially appropriate. On the other hand, external finance secures funds for war today while saving the costs of administering taxes and postponing constraints on the ruler's power. In the future—once the war is over—the ruler will decide whether to assume the cost of taxation to repay war debt with tax money (i.e., funneling resources to enhance tax capacity and sharing

---

18. Japan is an outlier and because of that it is one of the few successful cases of state building.
19. Stasavage (2011).

fiscal power with taxpayers)—or to suspend debt service and deal with the consequences of default.

The incentives of a ruler to finance war with external loans instead of taxes depend on three domestic factors—the initial strength of power-sharing institutions, the initial strength of the tax administration (or fiscal capacity), and the ruler's time horizons—plus two external factors—the liquidity of international capital markets and the size of the default sanction.

If the war bill is to be paid tomorrow, rulers with short time horizons—for instance, in polities with political instability—might find external war finance preferable even at the cost of future default sanctions. Arguably, those costs are the problem of some future leader. Initial fiscal capacity and political conditions matter, too: If the state has high tax capacity and strong limited government to begin with, preference for financing the war with taxation will strengthen, all else constant. By contrast, rulers in countries with weak executive constraints and low fiscal capacity will find taxation disproportionately burdensome because they need to relinquish political power for relatively small increases in tax capacity.

International factors interact with domestic institutions—a leitmotif in the book. As the liquidity of international finance grows, interest rates decrease for both unseasoned and seasoned borrowers, diminishing the future tax cost of war. This effect is particularly relevant to the Bond Era, when capital surplus from the Industrial Revolution was poured into global financial markets, fueling a culture of cheap credit.

The ruler honors debt in the future only if the cost of interrupting service, namely, the external default sanction, is higher than the cost of building up tax administration and sharing power with domestic taxpayers. The ability of external default sanctions to discipline borrowers depends on its severity and credibility.[20] Foreign bondholders devised in the Bond Era a mechanism that met both properties: extreme conditionality. This involved the hypothecation of public assets (e.g., state monopolies, customs houses, land) as a precondition of new loan issues. In case of default, pledges would be seized or managed by foreign bondholders until debt was liquidated.

Confiscation of national assets, or *debt-equity swaps*, and foreign control of local tax administration, known as *receiverships*, were perceived unpopular enough to preempt the temptation to default. The key for extreme conditionality to work was the enforcement mechanism. Seizure of national

---

20. Bulow and Rogoff (1989); Schultz and Weingast (1998).

assets, which was impossible if borrowers did not agree to it, occurred only under the veil of coercion. Although bondholders lacked military capacity, they sought diplomatic help from their government.

Officially, the British government resisted involvement in private disputes between bondholders and embarrassed governments. Unofficially, British ambassadors would exert good offices on behalf of home creditors if only to counterbalance the growing and open interventionism of the French and German governments in private credit markets. At other times, the Foreign Office would be as blatantly interventionist as its continental counterparts. Elite replacement within the British government greased the alignment between financial and national interest. In nineteenth-century Britain, landed elites and big merchant families merged into a gentlemanly class that assumed key positions in government and the Bank of England, the pillar of British public credit. Public and private interest became intertwined. International lenders took advantage of this and geostrategic competition between the Great Powers to request of emerging economies the hypothecation of national assets and sources of revenue as a precondition of fresh loans. This had two substantive effects—one of interest for public finance historians and the other for students of state building.

First, extreme conditionality sheds light on the causes of the secular reduction of the spread in the Bond Era. By raising the credibility of default sanctions—the confiscation of national assets—the risk and premium levied on developing nations declined over time despite repeated episodes of default. Second, extreme conditionality was a double-edged sword for state building. By pawning national assets, rulers secured cheap cash without having to assume administrative costs of taxation or sharing power with taxpayers—the hook—but they opened the door to financial control by foreign private investors—the catch. By "agreeing" to debt-equity swaps and installment of receiverships, emerging economies regained access to international markets after default without having strengthened their capacity to tax. If anything, default sanctions shrank the tax base in the hands of the government, leaving the local treasury in a precarious position.

1.2 The Rise of External Public Credit

A key assumption in the argument of this book is that the Global South had access to cheap credit overseas. International capital markets were not invented in the nineteenth century; however, they acquired an entirely new dimension at that time.[21] Following the Napoleonic Wars, first Britain and later France and Germany pushed surplus capital emanating from the Industrial Revolution into the developing world in the form of sovereign loans. Recipients were a combination of previously closed economies (e.g., China, Japan, Siam), newly independent states (mostly in Latin America, Southern and Eastern Europe, and Northern Africa), and colonial dominions. Borrowers used foreign capital to wage war, balance the budget, and invest in large infrastructure.

The nineteenth century was exceptional for many reasons: First, the magnitude of international lending was unprecedented, and unseen until the turn of the twentieth century. Relative to world GDP, international capital flows in 1980 were still three times smaller than a hundred years earlier.[22] Second, sovereign loans were private contracts between European financiers and foreign governments. Official lending (bilateral or multilateral) played a residual role, the opposite of the modern day.[23] Third, and perhaps most surprisingly, capital was cheap.

Figure 1.1 plots interest rates of an original dataset of 900+ sovereign loans floated in the London Stock Exchange (LSE) between 1816 and 1913. The vertical distance between the two superimposed curves shows the time-varying average spread between emerging economies and European countries, that is, the premium levied on developing nations. The spread remained around 100 basis points until 1860 and gradually vanished thereafter.

I elaborate on the conditions of external public credit in chapters 3 and 4. Here it suffices to say that the modest spread between advanced and developing economies remained for effective interest rates, and that risk was not compensated with shorter maturities. I argue that extreme conditionality—the hypothecation of public assets—helps explain the secular reduction of the spread in the Bond Era. I examine this hypothesis by analyzing the effect of bond securities (also known as pledges, collateral, and hypothecation) on effective interest rates of 700+ newly digitized sovereign loans floated in London. The evidence indicates that the credibility of pledges, hence their capacity to reduce risk, increased as private financial interests and British national interests grew closer in the later decades of

21. Eichengreen, El-Ganainy, Esteves, and Mitchener (2019).

22. Eichengreen (1991, p. 150).

23. Stallings (1972, pp. 13–26) for evidence of this switch following World War II, and Bunte (2019) for continuation of that pattern until the present day.

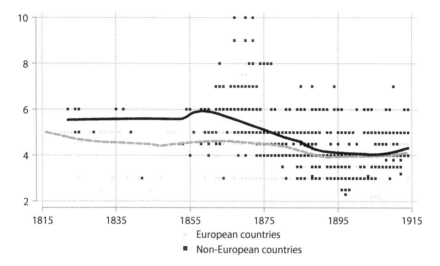

FIGURE 1.1. Nominal Interest Rates in the Bond Era: European vs. non-European Countries. A dashed lowess line is superimposed for the European sample and a solid line for the non-European sample. Compiled by author from multiple sources (see chapter 3).

the nineteenth century. This result contributes to the theories of the spread while revisiting the principle of absolute sovereign immunity in the era of high imperialism.[24]

1.3 State Building and Fiscal Capacity

To quantify the consequences of cheap capital on state building, I focus on the capacity of the state to tax, also known as *fiscal capacity*. This involves the state's ability to assess wealth, monitor compliance, and secure a stable stream of government funds. Taxes are one of the three pillars of the modern state, the others being the monopoly of coercion and the enforcement of property rights or *legal capacity*.[25] Because neither of the other two key functions of the state can be implemented without funds, "the history of the state revenue production is the history of the evolution of the state."[26] For the sake of illustration, figure 1.2 shows the modern-day relationship between tax capacity, measured by income tax ratios, and a general proxy of state capacity produced by the Fund for Peace, the *Fragile States Index*.

24. Verdier and Voeten (2015) for the standard interpretation.
25. Besley and Persson (2011).
26. Levi (1988, p. 1).

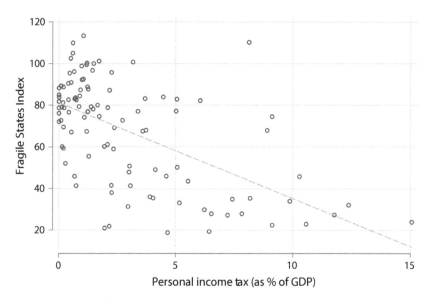

FIGURE 1.2. State Fragility and Fiscal Capacity. This figure plots the Fragile States Index for 2010 on average income tax ratios from 1995 to 2005, drawn from the IMF's government financial statistics and augmented by the author with information from national treasuries (N = 102). The Fragile States Index (Fund for Peace, 2020) triangulates news content analysis with economic, political, and institutional indicators plus qualitative review.

One thing remains clear: a state that underperforms in tax capacity is not a strong state.

Building fiscal capacity requires tax harmonization across the territory and the establishment of a professionalized tax apparatus endowed with extensive powers to assess wealth, collect taxes, and sanction noncompliers. In recent decades, a burgeoning group of scholars has addressed different aspects of fiscal capacity building. A consensus exists about the key role of war in growing the state capacity to tax. Raising an army; buying firearms, cannons, and equipment; transporting troops; feeding soldiers at the front; treating the wounded—all consume vast resources. The fiscal effort required by war is expected to strengthen the capacity of the state to penetrate all layers of society and extract resources in the form of taxes.[27] To implement this in an expedited, orderly, and systematized fashion, rulers may apply a series of "self-strengthening reforms,"[28] including fiscal centralization and the introduction of budgets,[29] the pro-

27. Mann (1984).
28. Hui (2004).
29. Dincecco (2011) and Cox and Dincecco (2021), respectively.

fessionalization of the tax administration,[30] and the adoption of modern forms of taxation—from excises[31] to progressive income taxes.[32] Far from disappearing, the financial innovations that fund the means of war are expected to exert lasting effects on the extractive capacity of the state;[33] or, as Charles Tilly famously put it, "war made the state, and the state made war."[34]

The foregoing argument, known as the *bellicist theory of state formation*, draws heavily from the history of state building in Western Europe.[35] Evidence of the bellicist hypothesis outside Western Europe is mixed. Some point to dissimilar initial conditions: non-European societies were too fragmented and ethnically heterogeneous to capitalize war efforts.[36] Others to the type of war waged in the Global South: short and small.[37] I deviate from this interpretation by showing in chapter 6 that war in the nineteenth century in the global periphery was bigger, longer, and more frequent than usually understood. A key reason it did not translate into stronger states is because it was disproportionally financed with external capital. Rulers in the Global South waged war without having to put forward the institutional transformation and agree to political innovations that European monarchs were compelled to before 1815, simply because the international credit market was too small and expensive at that time.

The reexamination of the bellicist hypothesis in the era of international finance reveals ways in which the joint consideration of debt and taxes can expand the study of fiscal capacity. To date, major contributions focus on one of these two instruments, keeping the other constant.[38] The results in this book indicate that our understanding of the political dilemmas of public finance can benefit from examining the opportunities and trade-offs between taxation and credit, internal and external revenue mobilization.

---

30. Ardant (1975).

31. Brewer (1988).

32. Scheve and Stasavage (2010, 2016).

33. Besley and Persson (2011); Brewer (1988); Dincecco and Prado (2012).

34. Tilly (1990, p. 42).

35. Seminal contributions can be found in Downing (1993), Ertman (1997), Hintze (1975), Mann (1984), and Tilly (1990).

36. See, for instance, Centeno (2002) and López-Alves (2000) for Latin America and Taylor and Botea (2008) for Asia and Africa.

37. See Centeno (2002, ch. 2) and Soifer (2015, ch. 6) for war and state building in Latin America.

38. See Besley and Persson (2011), Dincecco (2011), and Stasavage (2011).

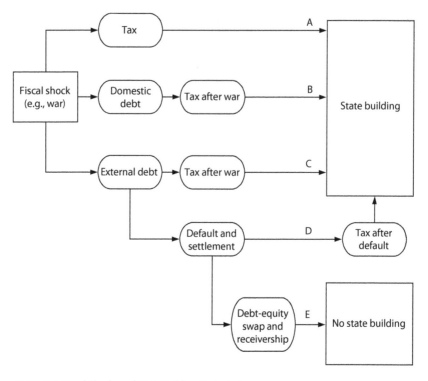

FIGURE 1.3. Fiscal Shocks and State Building Trajectories.

1.3.1 STATE BUILDING TRAJECTORIES

The means to fund government in the Bond Era had lasting consequences because they compromised future policy options. To explain why, I need to expand the time frame to early-modern times as well as the set of revenue-generating policies by considering domestic credit. In this stylized setup, a ruler decides how to secure funds to address a major fiscal shock—and I stick with war. I consider five possible responses, A through E, in figure 1.3.

Paths A and B imply domestic resource mobilization in the form of taxes and domestic debt. Following paths A and B, monarchs in early-modern Europe secured funds for war by relinquishing fiscal power over national elites in return for taxation, domestic credit, or both. Power-sharing institutions materialized into constitutional monarchies (e.g., Britain) or oligarchic regimes in which tax farmers and regional parliaments kept the Crown in check (e.g., France).[39] Because monarchs depended on domestic resources, they were compelled to build large tax bureaucracies to honor

---

39. For France, see Johnson and Koyama (2014) and Mousnier (1974).

debt after war. Repudiation was political suicide because it implied the loss of political and financial support of big taxpayers and Crown lenders.[40] By making debt repayment self-enforcing, military expenses grew fiscal capacity over time.

European monarchs were compelled to mobilize domestic resources because international markets were tight before the Bond Era.[41] The few who managed to finance war externally (e.g., Spanish monarchs relied on Genoese bankers) were not compelled to invest in state institutions, leading their countries into decay.[42]

After 1815, external loans emerged as a widespread option to fund public spending. Emerging economies could follow path A (taxation) or C–E (external finance in its different trajectories). B was off the table because of the low levels of capital accumulation outside Western Europe, a requirement for domestic credit markets.

Resorting to taxation to finance the means of war (path A) could be a matter of luck—for instance, having skilled politicians in office capable of seeing down the path as Ethiopia and Siam once had—or imposition by circumstances—for example, having to wage war while being excluded from international markets as had once occurred in Spain and Chile.

Statistically, most countries in the periphery during the Bond Era took paths C–E, consistent with the theoretical argument: when the initial stock of fiscal capacity was low and power-sharing institutions were weak—conditions common in the Global South—the administrative and political costs of taxation trumped those of external finance even if it opened the door to foreign control in the (distant) future.

Japan exemplifies path C to state building. This country raised numerous external loans yet never defaulted.[43] Compared to Siam (a relatively similar case[44]), Japan built a stronger bureaucratic state because it assumed the political cost of taxation—power-sharing institutions—as part of the Meiji Restoration. Compared to Argentina, the poster child of international economic integration in the Bond Era, Meiji Japan borrowed less overseas because it inherited a stronger domestic credit market, a rarity (and a blessing) in the Global South. Joint external and domestic resource mobilization

40. Saylor and Wheeler (2017).

41. Homer and Sylla (2005).

42. Drelichman and Voth (2014).

43. Suzuki (1994).

44. See Paik and Vechbanyongratana (2019) for a comparison of state building in Japan and Siam.

pushed Japan down the same path of state building that Western European powers jumped into before 1800.

Japan was unique. The vast majority of countries lacked a domestic credit market to work with and financed externally, taking paths D and E freely or by force. Path D is not necessarily bad for state building, but it can retard it. Arguably, it describes the cycle followed today by countries in financial hardship; for example, Greece after 2010. In the modern day, external default is a relatively ordered process led by multilateral organizations that condition financial support on austerity programs that combine spending cuts and tax reform intended to improve local capacity. For instance, the "first memorandum" between Greece and the troika (the EC, IMF, and ECB) conditioned bailout on an increase in the value added tax (VAT); taxes on corporate profits, real estate, luxury goods, and imported cars; and excises on alcohol, cigarettes, and fuel.

The absence of multilateral organizations in the Bond Era, combined with geostrategic competition of the Great Powers, allowed bondholders to push emerging economies onto path E. Hypothecation of national assets gradually became required to access external capital—extreme conditionality. When default happened—and it often did—foreign control followed. Debt-equity swaps were not intended to produce improvements in tax capacity, nor were receiverships. These parastate organizations took control of entire branches of the local tax administration and were installed for one purpose only: the repatriation of private capital. Receiverships were managed by foreign bondholders or their representatives and operated under European (and American) standards. They might have brought in new tax technologies and created positive externalities in the local administration, but evidence in chapter 5 suggests otherwise. In the Bond Era, receiverships were installed to make profit, not to build capacity.

In sum, unlike paths A–D, E does not satisfy the long-term equivalence between debt and taxes. Quite the opposite, debt-equity swaps and receiverships erode the local tax base and require fresh securitized loans to balance the budget, creating endemic fiscal deficits.

1.3.2 CHANGE AND CONTINUITY

The political dilemmas of public finance shed light on the reasons that fiscal policy in the nineteenth century could affect long-term state capacity. External finance, which allowed rulers to dodge political compromise with taxpayers and investment in tax capacity, was not always available. Countries could be excluded from fresh loans but nevertheless need funds, for instance, to wage international warfare. Warring states could also be in good standing with foreign creditors but happen to wage a war in the midst of an international financial crisis, when credit was tight.

As speculative as it was, the Bond Era was characterized by ups and downs, lending euphoria followed by "sudden stops"[45] of credit, freezing capital flows around the world on a temporary basis—usually four years. I take advantage of these exogenous episodes to examine whether incentives to enhance taxation strengthened when rulers needed funds for war but could not count on foreign credit. Pursuing this path, rulers would be putting in motion two mechanisms that connected fiscal efforts in the past to state capacity in the future. First, to foster compliance with higher taxes, rulers would be compelled to articulate power-sharing institutions over fiscal policy to overcome taxpayers' hesitancy to further taxation. Once in place, taxation would become a self-sustaining compromise: the rulers would secure funds while taxpayers would hold them accountable for their fiscal decisions, expanding the capacity to tax in the long run. I refer to this as the *political mechanism* of transmission.

Students of democracy agree that power-sharing institutions are actionable when taxpayers face low coordination costs and easy ways to escape taxation—conditions harder to meet in large-scale and poor economies.[46] Negotiating power-sharing institutions in return for tax increases was also off the table for most countries under colonial rule. In response, I consider a second mechanism of transmission that is independent of political status, geographic scale, and capital mobility. I call it the *bureaucratic mechanism*, which refers to the efforts against fiscal capacity disinvestment that tax bureaucracies exert to safeguard organizational survival.[47]

In chapters 8 and 9, I evaluate the effect of external finance on fiscal capacity and the plausibility of the two mechanisms of transmission. A battery of statistical analyses involving advanced and developing nations suggests that access to external finance distorted incentives to invest in fiscal capacity, preventing state building. By contrast, waging war excluded from capital markets expanded the capacity of the state to tax in the short and long run. Resorting to taxation contributed to the expansion of power-sharing institutions, particularly in smaller and wealthier countries, and the growth of the state bureaucracy in sovereign states and colonial dependencies.

45. Catão (2006).
46. Bates and Lien (1985); Boix (2003); Stasavage (2011).
47. Schumpeter (1991).

1.4 Why Europe and Not the Global South?

Ultimately, the theoretical argument and empirical evidence in this book seek to shed light on the broader question that gives this section its name. It is common knowledge among economic historians that states in Europe were made by war *and public credit.* Then why did war make states in Europe but not elsewhere? In short, European monarchs borrowed from domestic sources, guaranteeing efforts in fiscal capacity building to repay debt after war.

Before 1800, international capital markets were limited at best.[48] Lacking access to cheap foreign capital, European monarchs were compelled to mobilize domestic resources to pay for war. Following the military revolution in the mid-sixteenth century, military outlays grew at a faster pace than tax revenue, requiring new forms of government funding. Monarchs then borrowed heavily from merchants and landed elites, but loans came at a price. To convince elites that debt would be repaid, monarchs shared power over fiscal policy with the Crown lenders. Organized into parliaments or lending cartels, the Crown lenders would deny the monarch new funds if debt service was interrupted and withdraw political support if necessary. To avoid the consequences of domestic default, monarchs invested in modernizing the tax administration and secured proceeds to meet domestic debt obligations. By 1815, most European powers had already achieved relatively high levels of fiscal capacity.[49] Securing high tax yields, they could benefit from international liquidity in the Bond Era without having to compromise national sovereignty.

The globalization of public credit in the nineteenth century changed all that. Recently independent states and semiautonomous countries that came to exist outside Europe only in the nineteenth century faced starkly different initial conditions to build states. While European monarchs lacked external options but counted on domestic creditors, rulers in the global periphery lacked home lenders but had access to foreign capital. Emperors, presidents, and sultans outside Europe contracted loans to finance war, budget deficits, and infrastructural investment while postponing key administrative and political reform. External debt soon piled up, consuming vast foreign reserves. When debt service was interrupted, severe conditions were imposed for fresh funds, including receiverships and debt-equity swaps, further eroding the tax base. Many emerging

48. Homer and Sylla (2005).
49. Dincecco (2011).

economies fell into debt traps, causing detrimental long-term consequences for state building and political reform.

Why Europe and not the Global South? One thing is clear: European monarchs before 1800 were hardly more public spirited than leaders of emerging states after 1800—they simply faced a different international context, and state building benefited from it.

1.5 Competing Arguments

States are weak when government cannot accomplish the tasks it intends to do: economic, social, or political. Next, I discuss three widely accepted causes of state weakness: access to natural resources, ethnic division, and colonialism. The argument I advance in this book is not meant to substitute or falsify any of these three hypotheses. I interpret external finance as an additional cause of state weakness, which nevertheless has connections to existing accounts; for instance, natural resources were used as collateral in international loans, and colonial rule was partially articulated via financial control. After briefly addressing these debates, I comment on productive uses of foreign capital, also known as *developmental finance*,[50] and ways to fund government other than tax and debt.

1.5.1 FACTOR ENDOWMENT AND RESOURCE CURSE

Engerman and Sokoloff emphasize the role of factor endowment in explaining the divergence in economic growth, inequality, and political institutions within the American continent. Climate and soil conditions supporting slave-plantation economies and an abundance of natural resources highly valued on world markets led to political institutions that exacerbated long-term inequality and state weakness in Latin America.[51]

In the modern day, institutional quality is eroded by rents from oil and gas. The availability of nontax revenue weakens incentives to initiate tax bargaining with taxpayers[52] and to invest in the bureaucratic apparatus of the state.[53] In rentier states, patronage becomes the means to rule.[54] Corruption trickles down from the political to the bureaucratic

---

50. Fishlow (1985).

51. Engerman and Sokoloff (2002). See Coatsworth (2005) for a competing argument.

52. Brautigam, Fjeldstad, and Moore (2008); Morrison (2009); Prichard (2015); Ross (2004).

53. Besley and Persson (2011).

54. Beblawi (1987).

arena, reducing professionalism, neutrality, and independence of public administration.[55] The voracity to seize rents from natural resources can destabilize resource-rich states and make civil war endemic.[56] Building capable states under such conditions is extraordinarily difficult.

Foreign aid also allows autocrats to cultivate patronage,[57] dilute accountability mechanisms, and abandon the search for legitimacy,[58] leading to perverse effects not different from those of oil.[59] Instead of a competing hypothesis, external finance can be understood as an alternative form of "easy money," carrying dilemmas similar to foreign aid. Once aid or loans are disbursed, donors and lenders experience similar difficulty disciplining recipient governments.[60] In addition, in the case of loans, rulers may decide to interrupt debt service in anticipation of debt relief or some form of foreign financial intervention or both, relaxing present-day efforts to expand tax capacity and pushing the cost of default onto future generations.

1.5.2 SOCIAL DIVISIONS

Ethnic heterogeneity is a common deterrent to the provision of public goods,[61] chief among them state bureaucracies.[62] Countries outside Europe are said to be highly diverse or ethnically fractionalized, hence their weaker state capacity, a point often made to explain state fragility in Latin America[63] and Asia.[64] This argument might raise issues of reverse causality: states become strong by substituting preexisting social divisions—ethnic, religious, linguistic—for one national identity. Social homogenization is achieved in multiple ways, from indoctrination to mass expulsion to ethnic cleansing.[65] Take France, for instance: exploiting within-country variation, Johnson shows that at the turn of the eighteenth century those parts of France with higher state capacity (measured via

---

55. Ross (2001); Vandewalle (1998).

56. Collier and Sambanis (2005); Tornell and Lane (1999).

57. Ahmed (2012); Bueno de Mesquita and Smith (2009); Smith (2008).

58. de la Cuesta et al. (2021); Moss, Pettersson Gelander, and van de Walle (2006).

59. Easterly (2006).

60. Collier (2006).

61. Alesina, Baqir, and Easterly (1999); Baldwin and Huber (2010); Easterly and Levine (1997); Habyarimana, Humphreys, Posner, and Weinstein (2007).

62. Besley and Persson (2011); Lieberman (2003).

63. Centeno (2002); López-Alves (2000).

64. Taylor and Botea (2008).

65. Alesina, Reich, and Riboni (2017); Sambanis, Skaperdas, and Wohlforth (2015); Wimmer (2013).

tax receipts) showed higher identification with the French nation.[66] The French state manufactured the French nation, not the other way around. This process continued after the Revolution with state-led cultural assimilation.[67] Contemporary examples outside Western Europe can be found in China, where the state uses the public education system to build national identity,[68] and Africa, where state capacity leads to lower levels of ethnic-based contestation.[69]

Social divisions may also be exacerbated by having access to international capital. To fund the central government, rulers in the capital may be compelled to negotiate institutional design and grant policy concessions to territorially concentrated minorities, building robust federal states.[70] Access to external capital can discourage the central government from reaching out to regional elites, abandoning nation building projects and intensifying territorial divisions.[71]

1.5.3 COLONIALISM

Colonialism is a key cause of state weakness. "Extractive institutions" imposed by Western powers in nonsettler colonies deprived the periphery of its main sources of wealth.[72] The lack of self-determination, the continuation of slavery in the form of forced labor,[73] and arbitrary border design[74] raised tremendous obstacles to state building.[75] This is a compelling explanation with little to add.

I interpret external finance as a complementary hypothesis that amplifies the negative effects of colonial subjugation. In chapter 3, I show that colonies were allowed to borrow from international markets—a widely known result in economic history—and in chapter 6, I show that colonies participated in war, regional and colonial, and were expected to be financially self-sufficient, hence to build fiscal capacity. If colonies met all

---

66. Johnson (2015).

67. Weber (1978); Zhang and Lee (2020).

68. Cantoni, Chen, Yang, Yuchtman, and Zhang (2017).

69. Müller-Crepon, Hunziker, and Cederman (2021).

70. Alesina and Spolaore (1997); Sambanis and Milanovic (2014).

71. Bormann et al. (2019); Hierro and Queralt (2021).

72. Acemoglu and Robinson (2012).

73. Mamdani (1996).

74. Herbst (2000).

75. See Michalopoulos and Papaioannou (2018) for a detailed and fascinating review of mechanisms linking colonial rule and long-term state weakness.

criteria for war to make states, why did they not build stronger states? Although colonies financed virtually all domestic expenses, including policing and public administration,[76] the lion's share of interstate war was assumed—reluctantly—by the metropole, in the form of either grants-in-aid or heavily discounted loans; hence, the weak connection between colonial war and state making.

1.5.4 DEVELOPMENTAL FINANCE

Developmental finance refers to investment in projects with high social returns. Railroads, accounting for a third of all international capital flows in the Bond Era, were the paramount example of developmental finance at the time.[77] Railroad investment, for instance, grew the US economy[78] and helped irradiate state power in Sweden.[79] The success stories of developmental finance, however, tend to concentrate on a handful of relatively wealthy economies with robust institutions. In large parts of the Global South, railroads reduced dramatically the cost of internal transportation, hence the price of export staples, but did little to stimulate local industry. Or, as Coatsworth put it, railroads brought growth *and* underdevelopment.[80]

The mixed record of developmental finance reflects the international and domestic politics at the time, and it transpires the theoretical argument. The search for yield and strong bargaining power of foreign investors combined with corrupt and opportunist politicians often led to irrational network planning, external dependence for capital and inputs, and budget deficits caused by profit guarantees. The book offers various examples of aggressive foreign lending (e.g., the imperial railroad guaranteed bonds in China) and the conditions under which investors competed for new concessions and seized existing lines. But embezzlement,[81] delusional greatness,[82]

---

76. Frankema (2011).

77. Suter (1992).

78. But see Fogel (1963) for a restrained assessment.

79. Cermeño, Enflo, and Lindvall (2018).

80. Coatsworth (1981).

81. Claudio Bruzual Serra, the Venezuelan delegate who negotiated the largest and most ruinous foreign loan in the nineteenth century, pocketed Bs.114,000. Venezuela's president, Joaquin Crespo, kept a larger cut, Bs.2 million (4% of loan total). Back to Venezuela, Bruzual Serra was appointed Minister of Finance. The person who brought the scandal to light, Federico Bauder, was put in jail (Harwich Vallenilla, 1976, p. 225). Not surprisingly, the economic record of railroad investment in Venezuela is poor.

82. In 1910, the Cuban president, José Miguel Gómez, negotiated a new foreign loan in Britain to build a new presidential palace and other buildings. President Gómez was willing to

and short-sighted policy[83] on the side of local governments also played a part. My reading of international lending is that more often than not, both developmental and nondevelopmental finance in the Global South during the Bond Era exacerbated external dependence and eroded the effective tax base, causing persistent fiscal disequilibria—the opposite of state building.

My focus on war finance—a form of nondevelopmental investment—is based on two factors: First, increased demand of foreign capital caused by war is easier to date thanks to existing war datasets. Second, the analysis of the effect of war allows me to pin down the scope conditions under which the bellicist hypothesis holds, clarifying the important relationship between military competition and state building from the military revolution in the late sixteenth century to the present.

1.5.5 OTHER FORMS OF PUBLIC FINANCE

Debt and taxes constituted two prominent ways to fund governments in the Bond Era, but there were others, including monetary expansion. This policy often led to price instability, a decline in real tax receipts, and currency depreciation, contravening the mandate of the gold standard. While money printing addressed the liquidity shortage, it created problems larger than those it was intended to solve. In general, this policy was to be avoided to finance fiscal shocks.[84]

Rulers could also exert financial repression,[85] expropriate the Church,[86] sell offices,[87] trade slaves,[88] or rely on intraempire transfers[89] to secure public funds. Choosing taxation instead of any of these measures is, again, a matter of capacity and political calculus. Notably, in terms of state building, any alternative path to taxation would be expected to exert effects

---

surrender to British investors a public railroad with its connection to the waterfront of the port of Havana, granting de facto control over Cuban exports. President Gómez accepted the conditions despite the outcry from the opposition and local press. The loan did not move forward only because the US Department of State stepped in to protect American interests in the island (Zanetti and García, 1998, pp. 245–251).

83. The search for short-term popularity gains derived from inaugurating major infrastructure played a key role in the poor performance of road investment in the second half of the nineteenth century in Spain (Curto-Grau, Herranz-Loncán, and Solé-Ollé, 2012).

84. Cappella Zielinski (2016); Fujihira (2000); Sprague (1917).

85. Calomiris and Haber (2014); Menaldo (2016).

86. Comín (2012).

87. Hoffman (1994).

88. Herbst (2000).

89. Grafe and Irigoin (2012); Davis and Huttenback (1986).

similar to those of external finance because it would not require building a tax apparatus capable of assessing wealth and securing a steady stream of revenue—namely, enhancing fiscal capacity—nor would it activate key mechanisms of transmission of the ratchet effect of war—that is, strengthening power-sharing institutions and bureaucratic capacity. The scope conditions for state building are somewhat narrow. Easy access to foreign credit following the globalization of capital in the nineteenth century narrowed them further.

1.6 Plan of the Book

In the next chapter, I advance the theory of the book by articulating a political economy of public finance. Although the discussion can be generalized to other major fiscal shocks, I focus attention on military expenses because war was a major and clearly identifiable reason to tax and issue debt before 1914. I pin down a series of domestic and external factors shaping the ruler's preferences for loans vs. taxes, including initial levels of tax capacity and power-sharing institutions, default sanctions, and liquidity in international markets. The discussion leads to the notion of extreme conditionality because it helps us understand why countries with weak fundamentals accessed capital at favorable terms. The case of Peru is examined in brief to illustrate the logic of conditionality. I conclude chapter 2 by formulating the reasons that war finance exerted long-term effects on state building, or mechanisms of transmission.

The remainder of the book is organized into two parts: "The Rise of Global Finance" (chapters 3–5) and "The Consequences of Global Finance for State Building" (chapters 6–9). Chapters 3–5 may be of particular interest to economic historians and international relations scholars inasmuch as I focus on the rise of global finance, test for extreme conditionality, and elaborate on the causes of the low spread between advanced economies and the periphery. Chapters 6–9 may be of interest to students of state capacity building from the Industrial Revolution onward as well as to students interested in historical origins of democratic politics.

In chapter 3, I articulate the main characteristics of the Bond Era—who lent, who borrowed, and how capital was invested—and elaborate on my skepticism about the difference between "developmental" and "revenue" finance for the purpose of state building at that particular time.[90] I then

90. Fishlow (1985).

review standard *push* or supply explanations for the lending euphoria in the long nineteenth century. To this end, I document the rise of public finance by introducing an original dataset of interest rates for 92 countries from 1816 to 1913. The data show clear evidence of the favorable terms of access to capital offered to emerging economies compared to those offered in early-modern Europe and to those offered today.

Chapter 4 sheds light on the *pull* or demand determinants of the lending euphoria, namely, which country-specific characteristics predict low interest rates. Along with standard theories—the gold standard, reputation, and empire membership—I test the notion of extreme conditionality, that is, the hypothecation of public assets for the purpose of external finance. Law scholars have found that asset seizure was grounded in previously pledged assets. To assess the effect of hypothecation, I coded pledges among 700+ original loan prospectuses issued in London between 1858 and 1913 and examined whether pledging decreased effective interest rates. The statistical analysis, which exploits within-country longitudinal variation, shows that pledging reduced the spread when both bondholder coordination and geostrategic competition intensified—in other words, when the capacity to confiscate foreign assets gained credibility.

Default sanctions derived from extreme conditionality included asset seizure and receiverships. The latter were debt collection agencies that took over the local tax administration for the purpose of debt liquidation. In principle, receiverships could be advantageous for local tax capacity if they incorporated know-how and new tax technologies. I review secondary evidence of the performance of receiverships in chapter 5 and complement it with an in-depth analysis of the Ottoman Public Debt Administration (1881–1914), the most ambitious receivership ever run based on the outstanding debt it was meant to liquidate. Results are pessimistic throughout, in line with modern experiences of foreign-led state building.[91] Receiverships were profitable for bondholders because debt was liquidated; however, local tax ratios and administrative performance did not improve relative to preintervention years. The last part of chapter 5 brings us to late-Qing China, where foreign financial control was installed in 1911 after two decades of trying. This case illustrates, first, that the Qing's reluctance to share power with provincial leaders paved the road to foreign intervention; and second, that bondholders took control of an institution, the Maritime Customs Service, which was *already* proficient in tax collection.

91. Lake (2016).

The findings in chapter 5 illuminate the reasons that external finance rarely translated into state building in the Bond Era. Cheap capital often led to high indebtedness and default. Debt restructuring included a mix of new concessions and receiverships, softened with some debt relief. By agreeing to those conditions, countries were readmitted to capital markets without having improved their capacity to tax. If anything, their fiscal position was weakened because foreign control shrank the tax base left for local authorities. New loans and debt suspension loomed on the horizon. In the second part of the book, "The Consequences of Global Finance for State Building," I show that states that relied heavily on external finance to secure government funds did not build state capacity. Because military expenses were a key reason to float loans, I examine the consequences of war finance for short- and long-run state building, with a focus on taxation.

In chapter 6, I elaborate on the nature of war outside Europe and how it was financed in the nineteenth century. First, I revisit historical statistics of war. Based on duration, intensity, and frequency, war in the periphery in the nineteenth century was not different from the average war in the formative period of state building in Europe in the fifteenth to seventeenth centuries. Along with statistical evidence, I rely on war historiographies to shed light on the characteristics of interstate warfare outside Western Europe. Second, I show statistical evidence to document the use of external finance for war purposes, a result that allows me to revisit Polanyi's haute finance hypothesis.[92] Last, I reflect on colonial war finance by studying the effect of war, access to foreign funds, and fiscal performance with a paired comparison between the Cape of Good Hope and the Transvaal in South Africa.

Having shown that war was pervasive around the globe and that it was commonly funded with external capital, I examine the consequences for state building in chapter 7. Some tests focus on short-term effects of war on taxation, others on its long-term repercussions. The study of war finance on state capacity raises questions of reverse causality and selection. I gain leverage on endogeneity issues by exploiting exogenous shocks in international credit markets and focusing on ongoing wars, namely, those initiated while capital flowed but that were eventually hit by a global credit crunch. The chapter also addresses issues of what historians refer to as *history compression*[93] in the study of legacy effects. Overall, the evidence in chapter 7

92. Polanyi (2001).
93. Austin (2008).

suggests that war funded primarily with external debt did not make states in the short or long run; by contrast, war funded by taxation did.

Whereas chapter 7 shows that war finance is consequential for state building, chapter 8 examines why. To that end, I elaborate on the political and bureaucratic mechanisms of transmission introduced in chapter 2. The discussion identifies key differences in war finance before and after 1815, shedding light on the reasons that Europe built strong states and constitutional monarchies while most emerging economies did not. The historical comparison motivates an empirical test of the political channel of transmission from 1815 to date. I show evidence that war finance in the Bond Era shaped the strength of power-sharing institutions by 1914, particularly in small and densely populated polities, and that those effects, although attenuated, persist until the present day. The bureaucratic mechanism of transmission, namely, the idea that tax bureaucracies made by and for war seek organizational survival, also receives support once tested against historical data. Results in chapter 8 emphasize the importance of the study of history to understand political, economic, and bureaucratic characteristics of modern-day states.

In chapter 9, I illustrate the book's argument by studying state building trajectories in five sovereign countries of varied geographic and institutional extraction: Argentina, Chile, Ethiopia, Japan, and Thailand. To assess the different paths in figure 1.3, I divide the exercise into two paired comparisons, Japan–Argentina and Siam–Ethiopia, and a longitudinal analysis for Chile. The comparison between Japan and Argentina sheds light on the importance of domestic credit markets (strong in Japan, weak in Argentina) to keep foreign dependence under control and prevent falling into a debt trap. The Siam-Ethiopia comparison exemplifies the perils and limits of bureaucratic strengthening in the absence of political reform and how access to external funds can undo state strengthening efforts, causing stagnation (Siam) and decline (Ethiopia). Finally, Chile illustrates opposite incentives to mobilize domestic resources depending on access to foreign capital. The War of the Pacific (1879–1883), waged under capital exclusion, activated both the bureaucratic and political mechanisms of transmission. Advances in fiscal capacity were followed by stronger parliamentary power to hold the executive accountable for the growing funds it was to manage.

I conclude in chapter 10 by reflecting on the effects of external public finance on state building, and why interstate competition helped build strong states in Europe but seldom elsewhere. Then I look at the similarities and differences between external finance in the Bond Era and today.

Much has changed: The weight of private loans has declined dramatically in favor of official lending, switching the priority of conditionality from debt collection to capacity building. Relatedly, extreme conditionality is no longer practiced, perhaps with the exception of China. And yet, some problems persist. First, external finance allows rulers to escape politically costly reform and to postpone state capacity building, feeding all sorts of perverse incentives and attracting vulture investors. And second, when default comes, the foreign enforcers today (e.g., IMF inspectors) face legitimacy barriers similar to those that receiverships did a hundred years ago despite their different mandates. Directed state building, now and then, might just be an impossible enterprise.

2

A Political Economy of External Finance

Why do some countries articulate strong and inclusive states while others end up with ineffective bureaucracies, irresponsive government, and a pile of external debt? What prevents rulers—monarchs, emperors, presidents—from building capable states? And why is state weakness a highly persistent phenomenon? In this chapter, I shed light on these important questions by examining new political dilemmas that came to exist once external finance became a widespread option to fund government. I argue that foreign interference and myopic domestic policy hold responsibility—arguably to different degrees—for the abuse of foreign borrowing and underinvestment in state capacity in the Global South during key stages of state formation.

To come to this conclusion, I elaborate on the political motives that made rulers prefer foreign loans over taxes, and I advance a mechanism devised by foreign investors to minimize risk: *extreme conditionality*, the exchange of distressed debt for control over local assets. Access to cheap credit at the price of foreign foreclosure led to debt traps and fiscal erosion in large parts of the developing world, the opposite of state building. Although the perverse effects of external finance carried lasting consequences, history is not deterministic. Investment in tax capacity, which might occur by conviction or for exogenous (unplanned) circumstances, can push countries into a path of sustained state building. The theoretical discussion in this chapter informs the empirical design in the second part of the book, where I examine conditions under which war makes states and mechanisms that connect early fiscal decisions to long-run state capacity.

2.1 Public Finance Dilemmas

In examining the dilemmas of public finance, I focus on the costs and benefits accrued by a sitting incumbent at the time of financing war with domestic or external funds—taxes and foreign debt, respectively. Although the focus is on war—the prototypical example of a financial shock conducive to state building—the discussion is intended to apply to other situations in which a ruler is compelled to mobilize significant resources to fund government in a relatively short period of time: for example, critical infrastructure, health crises, or natural disasters.

The decision to finance war with taxes or debt depends on both domestic and international factors. First, I examine the advantages and disadvantages of each financial mechanism separately, and then the conditions under which one is preferred to another. The second part of the discussion articulates ways in which foreign lenders can discipline borrowers while not discouraging them from issuing external debt. I conclude by examining how early decisions about war finance affect long-term state building. The interested reader can refer to the appendix (section 2.7) for a simple formalization of the argument.

2.1.1 DOMESTIC RESOURCE MOBILIZATION

How do rulers secure funds to finance war? I focus on two common options—taxes and loans—which I assume to be mutually exclusive, (i.e., if one is used the other is not). Certainly, this is a simplification. War can be financed with a mix of taxes and loans plus other instruments, including inflation, confiscation, and natural resource royalties. But this assumption suffices to identify administrative and political obstacles to domestic resource mobilization via taxation.[1]

The literature on state building emphasizes the lasting fiscal consequences of war. Building on this intuition, I assume that the financial instrument to fund war today carries fiscal consequences—positive or

---

1. Any funding alternative to taxation will weaken further the connection between war and state making. Refer to chapter 1 for details.

negative—beyond wartime, namely, tomorrow. By establishing a time frame, we can examine intertemporal dilemmas of public finance for a sitting ruler and shed light on the persistence of weak states.

Throughout, I assume that the ruler is a revenue maximizer who cares only about rents from office. Perhaps exaggerated, this assumption allows us to investigate the conditions under which institutions limit predation.[2] The share (or cut) of government revenue that the ruler can pocket is inversely proportional to the level of executive constraints. That is, the stronger the monitoring power taxpayers have over the public purse, the less the ruler can steal from the national treasury.

Taxpayers are wary that rulers use their tax money unwisely—from building a new presidential palace to waging war for personal aggrandizement.[3] Central to the problem of taxation is that rulers cannot credibly commit to spending tax money wisely if they cannot be sanctioned for fiscal misbehavior. To solve credibility issues, rulers may be compelled to grant taxpayers veto power over spending decisions. Consistently, increases in taxation for the purpose of war yielded major advances in power-sharing institutions in early-modern Europe (1500–1800).[4] Power sharing took the form of representative parliaments (e.g., Britain) or oligopolistic arrangements between rulers and domestic economic elites (e.g., France).[5] In either form, big taxpayers and Crown lenders—often the same individuals—gained monitoring power over fiscal policy.

Once political power is shared with taxpayers, retracting the privilege might be difficult precisely because the new institutions strengthen the organizational capacity of taxpayers and their bargaining power vis-à-vis the ruler.[6] From the point of view of sitting rulers, power-sharing institutions secure funds to wage war at the cost of losing fiscal autonomy vis-à-vis taxpayers on a lasting (even permanent) basis. In Charles Tilly's words,

> [Power-sharing institutions] were the price and outcome of bargaining with different members of the subject population for the wherewithal of state activity, especially the means of war.[7]

2. Levi (1988).

3. Gennaioli and Voth (2015); Hoffman (2015).

4. Ferejohn and Rosenbluth (2016); Hintze (1975); Spruyt (1994); Stasavage (2016). See Downing (1993) for a competing view.

5. The British case is treated by Bates and Lien (1985) and North and Weingast (1989), and the French case by Mousnier (1974) and Johnson and Koyama (2014). I return to them below.

6. Stasavage (2011); and Greif, Milgrom, and Weingast (1994) for a micro-foundation.

7. Tilly (1990, p. 64).

The implementation of taxes requires some bureaucratic infrastructure, or *fiscal capacity*. This refers to the technical capabilities to assess private wealth and monitor compliance. The *stock* of fiscal capacity establishes an upper bound to the total tax revenue that can be raised today. The stock can expand over time as a result of purposeful investment and learning by doing. When rulers invest a portion of government income in expanding tax capacity (e.g., building regional delegations of the tax agency), there are fewer government funds left to seize, decreasing the ruler's present consumption or rents.[8]

The stock of fiscal capacity also expands by practicing taxation. Brewer shows an extremely detailed account of how excise inspectors in seventeenth-century England learned common avoidance and evasion techniques, turning beer excises into a major source of government revenue.[9] Via investment or know-how accumulation, war in Europe acted as a catalyst of fiscal capacity expansion. Crucially, tax pressure seldom came back to prewar levels, a phenomenon known as the *ratchet* or *displacement effect* of war,[10] growing the scope of the state as time passed.

The discussion above posits a key trade-off in financing government with taxation: tax efforts expand future fiscal capacity, hence the size of total government income, but they also limit the ruler's discretion over tax yields going forward and reduce short-term rents in light of increased administrative expenses—the political and administrative costs of taxation, respectively. Whether rulers are willing to assume these costs depends on how much they value enhanced tax capacity in the future vis-à-vis rents today. The so-called time horizons of the ruler might reflect personal characteristics or be determined by the political context: for example, a history of rapid turnover in office may discourage forward-looking policy decisions. In principle, rulers with shorter time horizons will be less attracted by the future gains in fiscal capacity, thus less inclined to assume the political and administrative costs of financing war with taxes.

2.1.2 EXTERNAL RESOURCE MOBILIZATION

Loans are logical substitutes for taxation. Public credit comes with multiple benefits: At wartime, it allows states to outspend their rivals.[11] More

---

8. This type of intertemporal dilemma in fiscal capacity building is treated in detail in Besley and Persson (2011) and my earlier work, Queralt (2015).

9. Brewer (1988).

10. Peacock and Wiseman (1961).

11. Schultz and Weingast (1998); Slantchev (2012).

generally, loans help smooth tax pressure over time, minimizing negative effects on the aggregate demand while the war is ongoing.[12]

Before the nineteenth century, European powers had borrowed massively to finance war.[13] Monarchs issued short- and long-term loans from local merchants and tax farmers, and sometimes from abroad too, although external finance played a subsidiary role before 1800.[14] After the Napoleonic Wars, the newly created and historically isolated countries were compelled to invest in their military and infrastructure to maintain their sovereignty; however, most local capital markets were tight[15] or collapsed in the presence of Western competitors.[16] Low levels of capital accumulation caused interest rates of government bonds to skyrocket. Take the case of the Mexican War of Independence: Domestic loans in 1824 fluctuated between 10 and 50 percent, compared to the 5 percent nominal (8.6 percent effective) loan floated by the same country in London that year.[17] Because domestic credit was scarce, governments in the periphery turned to foreign capital markets.

International lending is plagued with credibility issues. Rulers might finance their way out of a fiscal shock with foreign capital and renege on it later. To discipline rulers, international lenders may threaten borrowers with international sanctions, which can take various forms, including credit exclusion and trade embargoes.[18] By the logic of credit exclusion, countries that default on their external debt are denied further issue until they resume debt service.[19] For countries needing external capital to balance their budgets, credit exclusion might be highly problematic.

External default may also damage bilateral trade relations. Trade partners in countries where debt is held might refrain from trading with the country in default. In practice, credit exclusion and trade embargo are not independent. Exporters need short-term loans to conduct business, the "lifeblood of international trade."[20] Credit exclusion precludes these

---

12. Barro (1979).

13. The edited volume by Yun-Casalilla and O'Brien (2012) offers an excellent survey of the use of domestic debt to finance war in Europe.

14. Refer to chapter 3.

15. Michie (2006, p. 101). See Calomiris and Haber (2014) and Summerhill (2015) for case-specific accounts.

16. Austin and Sugihara (1993, p. 19).

17. Bazant (1995, pp. 45–46).

18. Refer to Panizza, Sturzenegger, and Zettelmeyer (2009) for a comprehensive review.

19. Eaton and Gersovitz (1981).

20. Rogoff (1999, p. 31).

types of commercial loans, penalizing further the balance of payments of the embarrassed government.

By accepting the risk of international sanctions in case of default, rulers using external finance gain access to virtually unlimited resources to navigate a fiscal shock: war finance. In contrast to taxation, rulers do not have to concede political rights to international lenders to secure public funds—a good margin suffices. In addition, loans come with low public visibility, which preempts political scrutiny and social contestation during wartime. If only in the short run, external finance secures government funds while relaxing political constraints on the rulers' actions.[21]

After war ends, the rulers decide whether to raise taxes in order to honor war debt or suspend debt service and assume the consequences of default. In honoring debt, rulers repay the principal plus an interest rate that, in principle, reflects market reputation: that is, countries with a history of default are expected to pay a premium to compensate for anticipated risks.[22] Servicing debt carries the same political and administrative consequences as taxation: Politically, rulers are compelled to grant political rights to taxpayers in order to secure compliance with the tax code. Administratively, rulers need to strengthen tax capacity to secure enough funds for repayment. Together, the political and administrative costs of debt service limit executive discretion over government funds, thus the rents from office. Alternatively, rulers may prefer to dodge that bullet by suspending debt service after war and assuming the sanctions of default, a decision that affects the rulers' future utility and, as it will become clear, shapes the best response of international lenders.

2.1.3 WHEN ARE EXTERNAL RESOURCES PREFERRED?

When do rulers prefer to finance war with external loans? Intuitively, they do so whenever the expected payoff of borrowing is greater than that of taxing. That depends on three elements: the initial conditions (political and administrative), the liquidity of capital markets, and the severity of the default sanction. Let me elaborate in order.

Initial Conditions
To overcome credibility issues in taxation, rulers may grant monitoring power to taxpayers, hence limiting the slice of total revenue the rulers

---

21. Cappella Zielinski (2016); Flores-Macías and Kreps (2017); Fujihira (2000); McDonald (2011); Shea (2013).

22. Tomz (2007).

can keep for themselves. It is not hard to imagine that the opportunity cost of taxation is bigger for rulers who face weaker executive constraints before war. That is, largely unconstrained rulers must forgo a disproportionally larger share of private consumption to overcome credibility issues in taxation, decreasing the attractiveness of this policy choice over external borrowing.[23]

The effect of fiscal capacity is rather similar. Intuitively, low initial levels of fiscal capacity are a disincentive to finance war with taxation because there is little revenue surplus (if any) that the ruler can seize for self-consumption. The main obstacle to taxation, however, may come from an anticipated small expansion in fiscal capacity, or ratchet effect. In Europe, the "tax state" was built over centuries by marginal increments in capacity.[24] The large gains in tax progressivity found by Scheve and Stasavage during World War I built upon modern tax apparatuses that had been developed over decades, crucially after the adoption of income taxes as early as 1842.[25] More generally, we can expect the marginal gains in fiscal capacity at times of war to be proportional to its initial stock: substantial when the stock is high, modest otherwise.

Anticipating strong resistance to taxation and little progress in mobilizing tax revenue, rulers of low-capacity states may forge weak preference for funding war with taxation, everything else being constant. This brings us to time horizons. When rulers do not care about the future consequences of their actions, no default sanction can stop them from financing war externally. Time horizons may reflect individual time preferences, general political instability, or the importance of winning a war for political survival. Either way,

> borrowing provides the current leader with resources today, while repayment typically has to be made by a future government. From the national perspective, loans are not free resources, but unless the leader is fortunate enough to have a long tenure, they are from the leader's perspective.[26]

Presumably, time horizons correlate with the type and stability of the regime: Elected officials who are held accountable for their decisions on a regular basis may be dissuaded from floating a loan that cannot be repaid.

23. See the chapter appendix for a formal discussion.
24. Schumpeter (1991). See Dincecco (2011) for historical evidence.
25. Scheve and Stasavage (2010, 2016) for progressivity, and Aidt and Jensen (2009) and Mares and Queralt (2015, 2020) for origins of the modern income tax.
26. Bueno de Mesquita and Smith (2013, p. 527).

By constrast, rulers in countries with high turnover in government and weak executive constraints are likely to finance war externally and push the repayment dilemma to a future leader. This is to say, countries that would disproportionally benefit from administrative and political reform offer rulers the weakest incentives to put them in motion. Weak institutions call for bad policy. We can find a good example of this in late-Qing China, where a precarious fiscal structure and distaste for power-sharing institutions led the emperor to accept increasingly onerous conditions from predatory foreign investors, causing the demise of the dynasty and foreign financial control in 1911. I return to this case in chapter 5.

Liquidity in Credit Markets

Capital markets experience regular expansions and contractions, known as "boom-and-bust" cycles.[27] In expansive times, more and cheaper credit is available across the board, also for countries with a history of default.[28] Ballard-Rosa, Mosley, and Wellhausen show evidence of this in modern day.[29] Exploiting cross-national data from 1990 to 2016, they find that investors are less averse to lend to weakly institutionalized and autocratic countries in boom times.

Rulers' preference for external finance also covaries with international liquidity: it strengthens when capital is abundant (because credit is cheaper) and weakens otherwise. External finance is most expensive during global credit crunches, like the 2008 financial meltdown. Far from anecdotal, international financial shocks might be highly consequential for understanding why some rulers take the first steps toward tax reform. If they lack access to external funds because international lending is tight, incentives to finance war with taxes are likely to strengthen, leading to gains in fiscal capacity and power-sharing institutions. Simply put, state building can occur when rulers run out of alternatives to taxation.

Default Sanctions

Trade embargoes and capital exclusion are said to weaken incentives to suspend debt service, but the evidence of their effectiveness is mixed.[30] The credibility of sanctions hinges on two conditions:[31] First, creditors must

---

27. Eichengreen (1990); Neal (2015); Reinhart and Rogoff (2009).

28. Frieden (1991a, p. 54); Panizza, Sturzenegger, and Zettelmeyer (2009, p. 676).

29. Ballard-Rosa, Mosley, and Wellhausen (2021).

30. See Panizza, Sturzenegger, and Zettelmeyer (2009) for an exhaustive review.

31. Bulow and Rogoff (1989); Schultz and Weingast (1998).

overcome collective action problems in punishing the embarrassed government. Second, once coordination obstacles are overcome, creditors must
still benefit from executing the sanction. Unless both conditions are met,
default sanctions lack credibility and cannot prevent debt suspension.[32]

For credit exclusion and trade embargoes to be effective, the embarrassed government should not be able to shop around and pit one issue
house against another. That is why market exclusion requires investors'
coordination and unity of action. The practice of market exclusion was
adopted in London as early as 1826, and it was generally effective from the
very outset in denying new credit to countries in default.[33] Credit rationing
is still applied today when countries show no willingness to repay.[34]

Even when creditors are able to overcome collective action problems,
sanctioning defaulters with trade embargoes or lengthy exclusion might
not be in the lenders' best interest. Sanctions damage the export sector
of the borrower, the main channel used to accumulate foreign reserves.
Because debt is often denominated in foreign currency (in the Bond Era,
British pounds sterling and French francs), harsh sanctions can make debt
service next to impossible. To recover investment, foreign investors may
prefer to impose mild sanctions on borrowers even if coordination issues
are overcome.[35]

In the Bond Era, default generally carried transient penalties, casting
doubt on the effectiveness of international sanctions. Flandreau and Zumer
show that interruption of debt service increased the spread by 500 basis
points in the short term; however, within 12 months the spread would
be about 90 basis points and descend continuously thereafter.[36] These
scholars conclude the following:

> While there is indeed a penalty for defaulting, this penalty turns out
> to be, over the medium run, of a smaller order of magnitude than the
> savings associated with the amount of debt that has been repudiated.
> Governments had a clear incentive for not repudiating their debt, but it
> was too small to act as a systematic deterrent.[37]

32. Schultz and Weingast (1998, pp. 21–22).

33. Flandreau (2020). A few exceptions, such as the independence war bonds of Greece,
are noteworthy. Despite interrupting service of these loans, Greece was able to float fresh loans
(Tomz, 2007, p. 228).

34. Frieden (1991a, p. 55).

35. Bulow and Rogoff (1989).

36. Flandreau and Zumer (2004, p. 39).

37. Flandreau and Zumer (2004, p. 39).

If threats of long-term exclusion and trade embargoes were not necessarily credible, how could international lenders discipline borrowers? Why would they lend them any money? To address this question, I introduce the notion of extreme conditionality.

2.2 Extreme Conditionality

Mitchener and Weidenmier define "supersanctions" as instances where external military pressure or political and financial control was imposed on defaulting nations.[38] They contemplate two types of supersanctions: foreign financial control and gunboat diplomacy. Foreign financial control, also known as fiscal house arrest or receivership, put foreigners in charge of local tax collection until the debt was liquidated. Receiverships could be managed directly by bondholders (e.g., Serbia, Tunis, Turkey) or by the creditors' governments (e.g., Egypt, Liberia, Nicaragua). Gunboat diplomacy, much less common, involved direct military repression. For instance, on behalf of private bondholders, Great Britain, Germany, and Italy imposed a naval blockade in 1902 to force Venezuela to resume debt service.

Mitchener and Weidenmier find that 28 percent of default episodes between 1870 and 1914 carried a supersanction. Forty-eight percent of countries that defaulted were supersanctioned; 70 percent if default happened more than once. And these estimates are only a lower bound because they do not include debt-equity swaps—the exchange of sovereign debt for control of public assets, such as railways, tobacco monopolies, and land. For instance, in 1906 a committee of external creditors based in London took control over coffee sales of Brazil to secure funds for debt service. With this operation, Brazil lost control over its major export staple.[39] Swaps were frequent and affected all kinds of countries—big, small, friendly, and unfriendly.

Despite the frequency of use, Mitchener and Weidenmier argue that supersanctions were decided case by case and upon manifested bad behavior, that is, ex post. I argue that supersanctions gradually became part of the lending business model as a generally accepted and recognized mechanism for loan contract enforcement. As such, the possibility of imposing a supersanction to prevent or follow a service interruption was increasingly

38. Mitchener and Weidenmier (2010).
39. Cain and Hopkins (2016, p. 284).

14th. To insure the prompt remittance of the sinking fund and interest, and in order to give efficacy to the special guarantees affected to this Loan, the Government of Costa Rica hereby specially agrees that in case of default in the punctual payment, in the manner hereinbefore stipulated of any one of the half yearly instalments for the payment of the interest and amortisation of the Bonds, and so from time to time, when any such default shall be made, the holders for the time being of the said Bonds, or of such portion thereof as shall not then have been redeemed, shall have the right, and they are hereby specially empowered, to appoint one or more agent or agents to enter into the actual collection from the fiscal agents of the Republic of the produce of the branches of the revenue which form the special guarantees for this Loan as above mentioned; and if the encashment from those sources shall not be sufficient, such agent or agents shall have the right to take the administration of the said Railways, and to receive in the same manner the net produce thereof until the sums received by such agent or agents amount to the sum requisite, not only for the payment of the interest and sinking fund due, but also sufficient to cover all the charges and expenses incurred by such agent or agents.

FIGURE 2.1. Article 14 of the 1872 Loan to Costa Rica. *Source: The Stock Exchange Loan and Company Prospectuses.* Adaptation of image digitized at the Guildhall Library, City of London.

confirmed at the time of issue, or ex ante. Because access to cheap capital gradually required the hypothecation of national assets, I coined the expression *extreme conditionality* to describe the situation. That is to say, loans were conditioned to the extreme of losing national sovereignty in case of default.

The 7 percent loan to Costa Rica in 1872 is a good example of this phenomenon. This Central American republic floated in London a bond of £2.4 million, ten times the size of its three largest sources of revenue combined (coffee, tobacco, and liquor). The loan was meant to finance the construction of two new railways plus other works of the republic and repayment of a small debt with Peru dating back to the war of independence. Capital inflows were conditioned on a battery of severe sanctions in case of default: The government pawned its three largest branches of revenue. If insufficient, the railway to be built was also hypothecated, the estimated revenue of which accounted for £320,000 per year. If Costa Rica suspended debt service, bondholders were legally allowed to take control of tax collection and the railroad to be built, as described by article 14 of the loan contract (see figure 2.1).

The provisions of the 1872 Costa Rica loan mirror an extended practice in the Bond Era. By hypothecating (or pledging) key assets and sources of revenue, sovereign borrowers gained access to external capital even when they had a murky reputation in international markets. Now, for extreme conditionality to be credible, it had to be enforceable and profitable. How did private investors manage to take control of foreign assets? And conditional on enforceability, did they benefit from taking control of local assets?

Enforceability strengthened over time for three reasons (fully articulated in chapter 4): First, investors in London, the world financial capital, created in 1868 an encompassing organization known as the Corporation of Foreign Bondholders (CFB), which perfected collective action in negotiating debt settlements with embarrassed governments and lobbying for diplomatic assistance. Second, the new "gentlemanly class"[40]—the fusion of landed aristocracy and big banking families—assumed high-ranking positions in the British government, the diplomatic service, and the Bank of England, the pillar of British public credit. Third, in the era of high imperialism, finance became another fundamental aspect of foreign policy (coupled with colonialism and commerce). To balance the open interference of French and German governments in private capital markets, the Foreign Office often found itself interceding on behalf of its nationals in default and concession negotiations with foreign governments. Officially, the British government interfered only when "national interest" was at stake, as some have claimed.[41] But that consideration grew in scope and frequency with the intensification of imperial competition and elite replacement in government.

Gunboat diplomacy—the use of military means to solve debt disputes—was the most punitive supersanction. If diplomatic pressures were effectively exerted, however, gunboat diplomacy would be observed only in cases where borrowers miscalculated the consequences of their actions.[42] The rare possibility of using military resources to solve debt disputes had a more far-reaching consequence: It "influenced how policy makers perceived their choice set";[43] that is, it shaped expectations about how the loan market operated and what the consequences were if debt service were interrupted. When a country pledged key assets as part of a loan contract, both lenders and borrowers had an expectation of its enforceability.

Was extreme conditionality profitable for foreign investors? Surrendering assets to foreign investors was interpreted as a national humiliation, something any incumbent would like to avoid. But the credibility of

40. Cain and Hopkins (2016).
41. Fishlow (1985); Platt (1968); Tomz (2007).
42. Consistently, Tomz (2007) shows that gunboat diplomacy was infrequent.
43. Mitchener and Weidenmier (2010, p. 120).

extreme conditionality required that investors would benefit from executing the supersanction, be it in the form of receivership or asset foreclosure. Although no systematic study has been conducted on the profitability of foreign control, indirect evidence reviewed in chapter 5 suggests private investors fared well. In negotiating the terms of loan contracts, investors prioritized liquid assets, including but not limited to state monopolies, infrastructure, and customs offices of international ports, for which valuation data were readily available. These securities often were known pockets of revenue whose yields were included in previous budgets or loan prospectuses; other times, the very same projects financed with external capital were used as security, reducing information asymmetries and allowing for an accurate assessment of the returns of foreclosure.

To support that extreme conditionality was credible, hence enforceable and profitable, I provide two pieces of evidence: In chapter 4, I show that the inclusion of specific pledges in loan contracts reduced the premium paid at issue, holding time-invariant characteristics and secular trends constant. In chapter 5, I review qualitative evidence of the profitability of receiverships for foreign private investors.

2.2.1   WHY ACCEPT EXTREME CONDITIONALITY?

In the presence of extreme conditionality, sovereign default was intended to inflict substantial damage on the popularity of the local incumbent.[44] Foreclosure of national assets in the form of receiverships and swaps was perceived as a national humiliation, and these episodes were instrumented by local opposition to erode the popularity of the incumbent.[45] To minimize public contestation, local governments did everything to the best of their ability to keep these clauses secret. In Uruguay, for instance, port and banking concessions to British investors in 1883 were passed in secret sessions in the legislature to avoid alienating public opinion, already suspicious of British stakes in the country.[46]

Large popularity shocks may be counterproductive for investors if they weaken the borrower's preference for external finance. After all, why would a ruler swallow such a bitter pill? The reason lies in the effect of extreme

---

44. Ahmed, Alfaro, and Maurer (2010); Borensztein and Panizza (2010); Panizza, Sturzenegger, and Zettelmeyer (2009).

45. Examples can be found in Cuba (Zanetti and García, 1998, pp. 244–246), Egypt (Hyde, 1922, pp. 535–536), Mexico (Wynne, 1951, pp. 38–39), and Greece (Wynne, 1951, p. 305).

46. Winn (1976, p. 112).

conditionality on interest rates, which reflect the perceived risk of an investment. The popularity shock of foreign control was deemed so damaging that investors anticipated low probability of default when extreme conditionality clauses were included in loan contracts.[47] By agreeing to them, the ruler traded access to cheap external capital—the hook—for the possibility of foreclosure in the future—the catch.[48]

Although extreme conditionality reduced the cost of capital, it would be naive to expect rulers to eagerly accept the strings attached. Here is where financial markets were (and are) like no other: They "operate on the basis of both price and control by lenders of the supply of funds offered to borrowers."[49] If the borrower does not accept the conditions, creditors can simply negate capital. Credit rationing provides unmatched bargaining power to international lenders. A good example can be found in the negotiation of the 1891 Portuguese loan. A syndicate of French bankers wanted the concession of the public tobacco monopoly in Portugal for 35 years as a condition for a new loan. Despite initial opposition by Portuguese authorities, the deal was accepted. Why? The words of the Portuguese minister of finance in presenting the budget are self-explanatory:

> "The last loan, besides being on very onerous terms, could not be obtained without security, and this security [the tobacco monopoly], which was the principal revenue of the country, had to be put into the hands of the creditor who paid himself with his own hands, delivering the excess to the government."[50]

2.3 External Finance and State Unmaking

War makes states if the long-run equivalence between debt and taxes holds, that is, when rulers enhance the tax administration to honor war debt with tax money. Externally financed war may not translate into state building in these scenarios: (1) a country defaults on its external obligations and the debt relief or "haircut" is substantial; or (2) a country defaults and swaps war debt for foreign control of national assets. Either solution disconnects

---

47. Refer to chapter 4 for evidence of this.

48. I formalize this argument in the chapter appendix by endogenizing the probability of default in the presence of extreme conditionality. There I show that the relationship between the severity of supersanctions and preference for external finance is U-shaped.

49. Frieden (1991a, p. 55).

50. Annual Report of the Corporation of Foreign Bondholders 1893, p. 202.

war efforts from state building by weakening incentives to revamp the tax administration to liquidate war debt.

In the Bond Era, debt relief could be substantial, reaching as high as 50 percent of outstanding debt;[51] however, it was seldom pro bono. Debt relief was generally conditional on issuance of new loans with which to wash old debt.[52] The fresh capital allowed old creditors to recover part of their initial investment while imposing newer debt obligations and harsher conditions on borrowers—key among them, foreign control over local assets.[53]

The hypothecation of national assets allowed countries to access credit at lower rates and avoid credit rationing, but exposed borrowers to financial control and debt-equity swaps, which if executed shrank the tax base—the opposite of a ratchet effect. By agreeing upon (or not opposing) a super-sanction after default, embarrassed governments were again in compliance with international law and regained access to international markets;[54] however, they did so with a smaller tax base and without having improved their tax capacity with respect to prewar years.

Suppose that the borrowing-default-foreclosure cycle repeats. Because debt obligations are now higher and the tax base narrower, creditors will likely require new hypothecation of assets for fresh loans, further eroding the effective tax base available to the local government. Intuitively, a couple of cycles like this can push any country into a debt trap—a steady state characterized by high indebtedness and low tax capacity, the opposite of state building. The history of foreign debt in Peru is a prototypical example of this slippery slope.

2.4 Foreign Finance and State Unmaking: The Case of Peru

Peru floated its first two foreign loans in the early 1820s in London to pay for the war of independence against Spain. The loans, secured by the net revenue of both the mint and customs, were defaulted in 1826.[55] Two decades of internal instability followed. During this time, guano deposits in the

---

51. Lindert and Morton (1989); Jorgensen and Sachs (1988).

52. See, for instance, the default settlements in Latin America (Rippy, 1959, pp. 26–28).

53. Suter and Stamm (1992).

54. Notice that foreign bondholders running receiverships were also highly interested in returning the embarrassed government to capital markets because doing so would resume trade, replenish foreign reserves, and expand the tax base with which to service old debt. See, for example, the Ottoman Public Debt Administration in chapter 5.

55. Wynne (1951, p. 109).

Chincha Islands were discovered and nationalized in 1842. Revenue from guano rapidly became the first source of government funding.

A default settlement with foreign bondholders was accepted in 1849. The outstanding principal was refinanced with a new loan, secured by one-half of the proceeds derived from the sale of guano to Great Britain. Three new loans were floated in London in 1853, 1862, and 1865, all of them secured by guano deposits. The last loan included an explicit provision for a debt-equity swap in article 12:

> Art 12. Should the declaration respecting the stocks of guano, not have been made during two consecutive half-years, the representatives of the Bondholders of this Loan are authorized to take possession, at any time, of the quantity of guano in the deposits of the Chincha Islands and of other places in Peru which may be required to complete the provision for three half-years' service.[56]

The loan of 1865, the largest at £10 million, was issued to finance war against Spain. This loan was equivalent to 250 percent of annual revenue.[57] Military expenses continued to increase, and one year later a new loan was floated in New York. "While loan after loan was contracted, the public finances were conducted with a reckless disregard of all sound fiscal principles. No attempt was made to develop a proper system of taxation."[58] The last two loans were ultimately insufficient to balance the budget.

Peru avoided default in 1869 by signing a contract with Dreyfus Brothers & Co. of Paris, which acquired the monopoly of the sale of guano to Europe and its colonies in return for advance payments to service external debt. For the duration of the contract (renewed in 1874), Messrs. Dreyfus were appointed the financial agents of the government abroad.

Motivated by increased liquidity, Peru regained access to credit markets and raised in 1872 the largest loan to date, £37 million, seven times its total annual revenue (£4.49 million in 1872).[59] Two-thirds of the fresh capital was spent in refinancing old debt, and the remainder on railways. The loan was secured by the guano and customs revenues plus the two new railway lines. The financial situation deteriorated shortly thereafter, and debt service was interrupted in 1876.

56. Wynne (1951, fn.12).
57. Vizcarra (2009, table 4).
58. Wynne (1951, p. 114).
59. Vizcarra (2009, table 4).

The president of Peru, General Mariano Ignacio Prado, and bondholders in London negotiated a new settlement known as the Raphael Contract. A company formed by bondholders' representatives, the Peruvian Guano Company, Ltd., was created and granted the sole right to sell guano in all markets of the world for a period of four years. This agreement, however, did not cancel the concession to Dreyfus, which had preferential access to the guano. The new company raised little revenue, and Peru remained banned from international markets.

In 1879, a new international military conflict arose—the War of the Pacific. The Peruvian government approved a loan to be floated in London, but exclusion held. The government turned inward, printing paper money, contracting some internal loans from Lima bankers, and raising some taxes, most notably an export tax on sugar.[60] The bulk of tax revenue, however, was in the hands of foreigners. Peru lost the war and control of the main guano deposits. A new debt settlement with foreign bondholders was reached in 1889, years after the war had ended. Under the Grace Contract of 1889,

> Peru was released absolutely by her foreign bondholders from all responsibility for the loans of 1869, 1870, and 1872. In return for this cancellation of the debt she ceded to them for a term of 66 years the state railways [seven lines]; assigned to them all the guano in Peru up to 2 million tons ... gave them the franchise for the operation of steamers of Lake Titicaca.... In addition ... the bondholders were empowered to select as a free grant unappropriated land to the extent of 5 million acres upon conditions of development and colonization ... and certain concessions relating to the Cerro de Pasco mines.[61]

In sum, the 1869 loan had been collateralized with the guano deposits; the 1870 and 1872 loans, with railways. Peru lost control over these resources to bondholders in 1889. As part of the default settlement, Peru was readmitted to international markets despite not having put forward any meaningful fiscal reform. External finance in the nineteenth century distorted incentives to build a state in Peru and, arguably, ended in foreign looting.

60. Sicotte, Vizcarra, and Wandschneider (2010, p. 299).
61. Wynne (1951, p. 171).

2.5 Opportunities of State Building in the Era of International Finance

Although the case of Peru does not invite optimism, external finance does not necessarily cause debt traps. Some rulers are arguably more public spirited or forward looking than others and are committed to service debt—the Meiji Restoration comes to mind. Others might call the bluff of financial colonialism and opt for fiscal austerity, as Ethiopian and Siamese rulers arguably did.[62]

More generally, I expect opportunities to strengthen fiscal capacity and avoid debt traps to arise under imposed (or "exogenous") circumstances, in particular, exclusion from international capital markets. If rulers need to fund government but lack access to external capital, their incentives to enhance taxation may strengthen, everything else constant. To mobilize domestic resources for war, the ruler may be compelled to grant taxpayers power over fiscal policy and reshuffle the tax administration, activating the political and bureaucratic mechanisms of transmission.

2.5.1 THE POLITICAL MECHANISM OF TRANSMISSION

The political consequences associated with taxation cannot be overemphasized. Power-sharing institutions are crucial to understanding the persistence of the fiscal effects of war mobilization, or why the effects of past warfare are felt today. By sharing power with taxpayers, rulers enable an accountability mechanism that helps them overcome credibility issues. Ironically, the ability of rulers to raise taxes grows by tying their hands.

The reinforcing effect of power-sharing institutions on taxation has been widely examined in the social sciences. Margaret Levi argues that limited government is conducive to "quasi-voluntary compliance" by taxpayers precisely because political accountability grants credibility to the promised returns for taxes.[63] Besley and Persson formalize the opportunities for sustained cooperation in tax policy created by power-sharing institutions. In "common-interest states"—where government revenue is used to fund public goods (e.g., national defense)—taxation becomes a self-enforcing game: the ruler secures a constant stream of funds to enhance

---

62. Refer to chapter 9 for a brief history of public finance and state building in Japan, Ethiopia, and Siam.

63. Levi (1988).

the public good while taxpayers are protected from arbitrary use of tax monies.[64] Recently, Acemoglu and Robinson coined the term *shackled Leviathan* to characterize the complementarities emerging from a "powerful state" and a "powerful society." The former involves high tax capacity (although not exclusively); the latter, taxpayers' ability to hold government accountable.[65] Meanwhile, David Stasavage emphasizes the stickiness of power-sharing institutions in Europe and beyond. Representative assemblies, which may have a marked oligarchic character, solve collective action problems of taxpayers to keep the ruler in check. Once summoned, the practices and the coordination gains they facilitate may be difficult to erase.[66] Power-sharing institutions, in sum, propagate revenue mobilization efforts in the long run. This I call the *political channel of persistence*.

Under what conditions is taxation more likely to activate the political mechanism? The students of democratization suggest that the exchange of political rights for tax compliance happens when at least one of two conditions is met: small geographic scale and high capital mobility. Stasavage shows that the capacity of representative assemblies to monitor fiscal policy in early-modern Europe depended on the size of the polity.[67] Poor technologies of communications and transportation limited the ability of distant elites to coordinate their monitoring of the Crown. French kings, for instance, exploited geographic scale by arranging separate tax contracts with different regional powers, limiting advances in executive constraints. Although their power was never absolute—tax farmers and regional assemblies exerted significant influence in fiscal policy—French monarchs had more leeway than their counterparts in smaller polities. In the Bond Era, Siamese kings took advantage of geographic scale to raise taxation while limiting power-sharing concessions.

Low levels of capital mobility are a second obstacle to the activation of the political mechanism of transmission. Bates and Lien, as well as Boix, argue that owners of mobile capital have a comparative advantage

---

64. Besley and Persson (2011).

65. Acemoglu and Robinson (2019, p. 65).

66. Stasavage (2020). In addition, Fujihira (2000) points out the role of two modern power-sharing institutions—representative parliaments and political parties—in facilitating sustained levels of taxation. These institutions aggregate competing tax preferences of capital and labor, facilitating compromise and sustained cooperation after war.

67. Stasavage (2011).

at extracting political concessions from the ruler because they can credibly threaten to withdraw tax payments or flee to other jurisdictions.[68] When fiscal capacity is limited, rulers are compelled to grant owners of mobile capital some say in policy making to secure their tax compliance. Capital mobility increases with levels of monetization of the economy, which results from economic growth and international trade.

The foregoing discussion suggests that poor and geographically large countries are at a disadvantage in experiencing the activation of the political mechanism of transmission following an increase in the tax burden. For such countries, I expect the ratchet effect of war finance to be channeled through the bureaucratic mechanism.

2.5.2 THE BUREAUCRATIC MECHANISM OF TRANSMISSION

Professional tax administrations in Europe were created by and for war, completing a long and complex process of fiscal centralization.[69] To secure bigger and more stable tax revenue inflows, central governments gradually substituted tax farms and locally appointed tax collectors (e.g., the *landräte* in German principalities) by professionally trained tax officials. Over time and not without setbacks, government-paid inspectors gained new monitoring powers, resources, and legal provisions to do their job.

There are at least two reasons why we can expect bureaucratic efforts to finance war to persist: First, tax administrations operate in the best interest of a revenue-maximizing ruler. Second, bureaucracies are "among those social structures which are the hardest to destroy."[70] In Europe, the same administrations once created to finance war gave rise to a class of state bureaucrats who safeguarded organization survival, carrying on the effect of war finance in the long run.[71] This I call the *bureaucratic channel of persistence*.

Unlike the political mechanism, reserved for sovereign countries,[72] the bureaucratic mechanism is meant to apply to both sovereign and non-sovereign entities. Colonies in the nineteenth century were expected to

---

68. Bates and Lien (1985); Boix (2003).

69. Ardant (1975); Dincecco (2011); Ertman (1997).

70. Weber (1978, p. 987).

71. Schumpeter (1991).

72. Self-government colonies in the British Empire were allowed to elect local parliaments, as was French Algeria, but these were exceptions.

secure resources to fund local expenses.[73] To finance infrastructure projects, colonies issued loans in European markets on a regular basis. Colonies were also expected to contribute to imperial and local war finance, but incentives to mobilize resources were weak because local governments relied on imperial bailouts.[74] Keeping in mind this important difference with sovereign nations, tight capital markets were likely to strengthen the incentives to enhance local bureaucracies to fund colonial expenses, plausibly activating the bureaucratic mechanism of taxation.

2.5.3   THE LEGACY OF WAR FINANCE ON STATE BUILDING

The foregoing discussion suggests that rulers generally prefer to finance war externally because doing so minimizes short-term political and administrative costs. If, however, they resort to taxation—a decision that might be guided by exogenous circumstances—war finance might activate one or two mechanisms of transmission depending on scope conditions (i.e., geographic scale and income), raising the state's capacity to collect taxes on a permanent basis.

In chapter 7, I examine long-run effects of war finance by taking advantage of global financial crises in the nineteenth century. These unanticipated and exogenous shocks in access to capital limited opportunities to finance war externally. I show that waging war while being exogenously excluded from international credit markets exerted positive effects on fiscal capacity in the short and long run. External finance, on the other hand, could easily lead to debt traps, particularly if they involved foreign control.

One may argue that debt-equity swaps and receiverships are positive for state capacity, particularly when they involve putting local tax administrations under the control of skilled foreigners. Potentially, European and American administrators could incorporate modern managerial techniques and know-how, but evidence of foreign financial control in the Bond Era does not support this claim. Gardner, Maurer and Arroyo Abad, and Reinhart and Trebesch, among others, find that foreign receiverships

---

73. Berman (1984); Frankema (2011).

74. Davis and Huttenback (1986) show that self-governing colonies were better at resisting contributions to imperial war finance than Crown colonies. For details, refer to the paired comparison of South African republics in chapter 6.

in Latin America, Africa, and Europe had detrimental effects on local taxation.[75] Foreign financial control in Egypt may be an important exception;[76] however, the expansion of fiscal capacity in that country was accompanied by the loss of political sovereignty.[77] I resume this debate in chapter 5.

If war is financed domestically and the political and bureaucratic mechanisms are activated, I expect early fiscal efforts to last. In chapter 8, I show evidence of the activation of these mechanisms and subsequent endurance. In chapter 9, I submerge into a case study, Chile 1816–1913, to investigate the changing political calculus of war finance depending on access to external capital. Together, chapters 7–9 suggest that early decisions about war finance pushed countries onto starkly diverging paths—one characterized by endemic indebtedness and weak state capacity, the other by sustained state building and political reform.

2.6 Conclusion

I suggest that having access to external credit is consequential to understanding the conditions under which war makes states precisely because taxes and loans may not exert the same transformative effects on fiscal capacity. A key implicit assumption underlying the bellicist theory of state building—the workhorse model of this book—is the long-run equivalence between debt and taxes, namely, that loans operate as deferred taxes. According to this model, lenders recover their investment plus interest while borrowers assume full responsibility for war debt by enhancing the tax system, thus elevating fiscal capacity in the long run.

Although no scholar would defend a strict reading of the so-called Ricardian equivalence between debt and taxes, a general understanding holds that loans and taxes operate in roughly similar ways. The argument made in this chapter is that the conditions under which the debt-tax equivalence holds for sovereign borrowers may be narrower than previously thought. Whereas international investors in the Bond Era recovered their investment one way or another—in tax money or specie—the equivalence did not necessarily hold for local treasuries. Generalized debt relief coupled

---

75. Gardner (2017); Maurer and Arroyo Abad (2017); Reinhart and Trebesch (2015).
76. Owen (1981, ch. 9).
77. Cromer (1908); Owen (1981).

with foreign control short-circuited the long-run relationship between debt and taxes, shedding light on the perverse consequences of early access to external finance for state building.

The discussion in this chapter resonates with the dilemmas derived from investing in good (liberal) institutions in Acemoglu, as well as Besley and Persson.[78] These scholars argue that political motives are responsible for underdevelopment in state capacity. The fear of future extraction via taxation by the opposition precludes investment in fiscal capacity despite the potential benefits for both parties. In the presence of external finance, the political dilemmas of state building identified by these scholars only amplify. Resorting to foreign loans, rulers secure government funds while dodging political compromise and fiscal efforts required to establish "good institutions."

2.7 Appendix

In this appendix, I advance a simple decision-theoretical model to formalize the political dilemmas of public finance and extreme conditionality presented in this chapter. Consistent with the preceding discussion, I focus on the political calculus of war finance by a revenue-maximizing ruler. The world exists in two periods—today and tomorrow—and war begins and ends in period 1. I make two assumptions about war finance. First, war is paid with tax revenue or loans; intermediate combinations are ruled out. Wars are rarely funded with tax revenue alone because they are too expensive; however, this assumption allows me to explore the political calculus at stake (i.e., the exchange of taxation for political rights) with the simplest possible model. Second, I assume that the cost of war, W, is fixed. Endogenizing the size of war would be an interesting approach but is beyond the scope of the book. Combined, the two assumptions reduce the attractiveness of loans relative to taxes, expanding the states of the world in which war leads to higher fiscal capacity. That is, the assumptions are most favorable to the bellicist hypothesis.

The ruler can raise a finite amount of revenue via taxation, $\kappa T > W$, where κ denotes the stock of fiscal capacity in period 1 and T the tax base. The ruler seeks to maximize private consumption, financed by the share of public funds $(1 - \alpha)$, $\alpha \in [0, 1]$, the ruler can keep (i.e., the rents from

78. Acemoglu (2003); Besley and Persson (2011).

office). The more closely α approaches 1, the stronger the power taxpayers have over fiscal policy (or the less the ruler can appropriate from the treasury's coffers). The fiscal contract derived from taxation limits the share of total revenue that the ruler can use for private consumption to $(1 - \alpha)/2$. Later I consider a more general expression.

For the sake of simplicity, I assume that tax capacity expands over time as a result of know-how accumulation. That is, tax collectors learn over time common avoidance schemes. This assumption suffices to capture one of the key dilemmas of fiscal capacity building: the exchange of tax revenue for political rights. Forgone consumption derived from pecuniary investment in capacity could be considered, but it would complicate the analysis unnecessarily.[79] I assume that know-how expands fiscal capacity by $\eta < 1$ units, $\kappa + \eta \leq 1$, between periods 1 and 2, capturing the ratchet effect of taxation in a simple reduced form.

The ruler's payoff in period 2 is discounted at a rate $\delta \in [0, 1]$, hence the expected value of financing war with taxes is

$$\frac{1-\alpha}{2}(\kappa T - W) + \delta\left[\frac{1-\alpha}{2}(\kappa + \eta)T\right] \tag{2.1}$$

Expression 2.1 captures in a stylized fashion an intrinsic dilemma in fiscal capacity building. The new tax expands the long-run volume of resources that can be mobilized via taxation in period 2, $(\kappa + \eta)T$, but it does so at the cost of granting taxpayers power over fiscal policy, hence limiting the share of tax revenue that the ruler can accrue from the national budget to $(1 - \alpha)/2$. Because of credibility issues, higher taxation cannot be achieved without the ruler relinquishing fiscal powers in period 1. Once political power is shared with taxpayers, retracting the privilege might be difficult precisely because the new institutions strengthen their tax bargaining power vis-à-vis the ruler, hence the persistence of strong executive constraints in period 2.

Alternatively, the ruler may float a loan $L > W$ to finance war. Servicing debt implies paying back the standing principal L plus interest i, that is, $(1 + i)L$. The interest rate is set in the international capital market, where loans are floated. The country-specific interest rate is broken down into two parts: $i = r + p$, where $r < 1$ is the interest rate of a risk-free sovereign bond (e.g., the British consol), and premium $p = (1 + r)d/(1 - d)$. The

---

79. See examples of such models in Besley and Persson (2011) and Queralt (2015).

latter is strictly increasing in the probability of default, d, which encapsulates the reputation of the borrower in international markets. The premium p is derived by setting the international investors' profit when lending is risk free, $L(1+r) - L$, equal to the international investors' profit when the probability of default is nonzero, $d \times 0 + (1 - d) \times (1 + r + p)L - L$, and solving for p. Intuitively, lenders charge a premium to countries with a history of default to bring the expected value of lending to a potential lemon equal to the expected value of lending to a seasoned borrower. The interest rate of the risk-free asset, r, is set in the international market. For the sake of simplicity, capital supply is defined by the inverse linear function $r_s = \alpha_s + \phi_s q_s$, where q_s denotes the global supply of capital and $\phi_s > 0$. Global capital demand is given by the inverse function $r_d = \alpha_d - \phi_d q_d$, $\alpha_d = 1$, $\phi_d > 0$. The international market clears at $r^* = 1 - (\phi_d(1 - \alpha_s)/(\phi_d + \phi_s))$.

Together, the ruler's expected value of financing war externally is

$$(1 - \alpha)(L - W) + \delta\left[(1 - d)\left(\frac{1 - \alpha}{2}(\kappa T - (1 + r^* + p)L)\right) - dS\right] \quad (2.2)$$

where default carries a sanction $S \in [0, 1]$. Notice that by borrowing in period 1, rulers can keep loose executive constraints, meaning that in the short run they retain a larger share of the national budget for self-consumption, $(1 - \alpha)$. If they decide to service debt in period 2, they will need to share fiscal power with taxpayers in return for tax compliance. As a direct consequence, the share of the budget they can appropriate will reduce to $(1 - \alpha)/2$.

When does a risk-neutral ruler prefer to finance war with external loans? Whenever the expected payoff of lending is greater than that of taxing, or

$$L \geq \frac{\frac{1 - \alpha}{2}(\kappa T + W) + \delta\left[\frac{1 - \alpha}{2}\eta T + d(\frac{1 - \alpha}{2}\kappa T + S)\right]}{(1 - \alpha)(1 - \delta\frac{1 + r^*}{2})} \quad (2.3)$$

Let me comment on the various parts of expression 2.3.

Fiscal Capacity

Preference for loans is a function of the stock of fiscal capacity κ and the anticipated ratchet effect η. External loans are preferred when either of these parameters are low. That is easy to see. Historical accounts suggest that significant advances in tax capacity occur when rulers build on preexisting fiscal infrastructure. If the ratchet effect of taxation is lower at lower levels of capacity (i.e., the relationship between η and τ is convex or, more reasonably, S-shaped), then preference for taxation will be twice weakened when the initial stock is low.

Executive Constraints

Preference for external finance is a function of initial executive constraints and forgone consumption. When initial constraints α are weak, financing war with taxes reduces considerably the ruler's private consumption, hence weakening preference for taxes. But as executive constraints increase, preference for taxation strengthens:

$$\partial RHS/\partial \alpha = \frac{-2\beta d\delta}{(-1+\alpha)^2(-2+\delta(1+r^*))} > 0$$

everything else being constant.

Notice that in expression 2.1 I assumed private consumption was sliced by half if the ruler opted for taxation. Forgone consumption can be generalized to $(1-\alpha)/\psi$, $\psi > 1$. That is, larger ψ makes war taxes less attractive relative to external finance. We may expect the relationship between initial constraints and forgone consumption to be concave rather than linear. That is, to overcome credibility issues, largely unaccountable rulers might be compelled to reduce their cut from the national budget more than other rulers who are already constrained. If that is the case, autocrats will disproportionally disfavor taxation because forgone consumption will be greatest for them.

The discussion about initial capacity and political conditions suggests that weakly institutionalized countries will be unlikely to finance war with taxation when external finance is available. In addition, the preference of loans over taxation will be strengthened in the presence of low discount rates, δ. Although these appear in both the numerator and denominator of expression 2.3, the effect is unambiguous. As δ decreases, the numerator decreases and the denominator increases, hence the stronger preference for loans.

Market Liquidity

The lower the liquidity in the capital market (higher r), the more taxation is preferred, everything else being constant. That is easy to see. When international capital markets experience a positive shock—for instance, following a capital surplus in a major economy—the international credit supply shifts to $r_s = \alpha'_s + \phi_s q$, $\alpha'_s < \alpha_s$, and a new equilibrium is reached,

$(r', q')^*$, characterized by lower interest rates $(r')^* < r^*$ and more trading $(q')^* > q^*$.

Recall that the interest paid by a borrower with a shaky reputation is given by $i = r + p$, the baseline rate plus a premium. Because both i and p are a function of the baseline rate, an increase (decrease) in liquidity brings down (up) the price that a lemon pays for external capital. For a large enough negative shock, $\alpha_s'' > 1$, international lending ceases, strengthening incentives to finance war with taxes. I build on this intuition in chapter 7, where I exploit credit crunches in international capital markets to identify periods in which rulers are most compelled to raise taxes to fund war.

Extreme Conditionality

In expression 2.3, preference for loans weakens as the magnitude of default sanction S increases, discouraging indebtedness. That outcome is not good for international lenders. Extreme conditionality can simultaneously facilitate cheaper credit while solving credibility issues. To see this point, assume that the probability of default d is a negative function of default sanction S. In other words, the bigger the anticipated sanctions are, the lower the probability of default is, everything else being constant. Clearly, this is a simplification. Default is a function of the capacity to pay, war outcome, and "political willingness."[80] With this in mind, this assumption facilitates understanding what lenders can do to secure debt service while not discouraging borrowing.

To make things as simple as possible, I assume that the relationship between the probability of default and default sanctions is linear, $d = 1 - S$. Define

$$\bar{S} = \frac{1}{2}(1 - \frac{1-\alpha}{2}\kappa T) \tag{2.4}$$

with $\bar{S}$ solving the first-order condition in the right-hand side of expression 2.3. Then we can divide the state of the world in two: For any $S \leq \bar{S}$, preference for taxation strengthens in proportion to the size of default sanctions; that is, in expectation of default sanctions, rulers prefer to tax instead of borrow. Although this might be good for building states and striking political bargains with taxpayers, it is bad business for international creditors. For $S > \bar{S}$, as the magnitude of default sanctions increases, preference for borrowing strengthens. The lower probability of default when sanctions

---

80. Reinhart and Rogoff (2009).

are high reduces the price of external finance, $\partial p / \partial d > 0$, making loans preferable over taxation for the sitting ruler.

By requiring the hypothecation of national assets, lenders in the Bond Era were able to push the cost of default to levels satisfying $S > \bar{S}$. Extreme conditionality facilitated cheap credit access to lenders with weak fundamentals but opened the door to high indebtedness, default, and foreign control.

## PART I

The Rise of
Global Finance

The next three chapters offer an introduction to the globalization of public credit, namely, the regular use of external finance for the purpose of government funding. Chapter 3 characterizes the first global financial market, 1816–1914, by documenting the expansion of capital exports and the secular decline of interest rates in sovereign lending. For the first time ever, countries in the core and the periphery, rich or poor, sovereign or dependent, had access to virtually unlimited cheap capital. In chapter 4, I investigate country-specific policy and institutions that contributed to the secular decline of the spread. After confirming the leverage of existing explanations with a multivariate regression analysis, I advance the extreme conditionality hypothesis to explain why countries with weak fundamentals and a history of default secured external capital at relatively favorable rates. After discussing enforceability issues, I show statistical evidence that pledges in sovereign bonds decreased interest rates of borrowed capital. The consequences of pledging and financial control for state building are discussed in chapter 5. Secondary sources and a case study of the Ottoman Public Debt Administration show that foreign management of state monopolies and tax administration did not improve state capacity. Last, I elaborate on the international *and domestic* causes leading to the scramble for concessions in late-Qing China, including the foreclosure of the most efficient tax administration in the country.

In sum, part I shows evidence of the globalization of public credit, the effect of extreme conditionality on the spread, and the fiscal consequences of foreign financial control. Building on this evidence, part II includes an assessment of the consequences of early access to cheap capital for short- and long-term state building and political reform.

3

The Globalization of Public Credit

> Any government which claimed sovereignty over a bit of the earth's surface and a fraction of its inhabitants could find a financial agent in London and purchasers of her bonds.
>
> —JENKS (1927, P. 282)

A primary argument of this book is that easy access to external finance at early stages of development can distort rulers' incentives to undertake state-strengthening efforts, causing persistent fiscal weakness. In this chapter, I review key stages in the formation of the first *global* market of public credit and examine a key assumption in the argument: that new and old-but-traditionally-isolated states accessed European capital at relatively favorable terms. To support this claim, I put together an original dataset about the conditions of external finance in the Bond Era, expanding time coverage and country samples and almost tripling the number of sovereign loans recorded in existing datasets. In this chapter, I show aggregate characteristics of the "lending frenzy,"[1] and in chapter 4 I discuss country-specific *pull factors*. The perverse effects of easy money for state building are examined starting in chapter 5.

---

1. Taylor (2006).

3.1 The First Globalization of Capital

The modern state, which is the most sophisticated organization ever put in place, provides security, regulates markets, enforces contracts, and redistributes income; it participates in space programs, leads cancer research, and secures mass public education among endless other contributions. This massive intervention of the state in the economy and society is relatively recent: before World War I, the scope of the state was significantly narrower, as were the types of expenses funded by the public.

One may safely say that before 1914, military expenses represented the lion's share of government spending. Rulers (monarchs, princes, sultans, chiefs) resorted to a plethora of options to finance war from tributes to expropriation to the slave trade. War expenses, however, were often larger than the immediate revenue possibilities of the state. Commencing in the late medieval period (1250–1500), commercial city-states in Europe established the foundations of modern public credit, allowing rulers to accrue future taxes that could be paid gradually once war had come to an end. This was a major advancement in war policy inasmuch as it allowed city-states to outspend larger military rivals. Initially, territorial states relied on foreign commercial cities to issue public credit. Conditions were far from favorable, and monarchs paid high premiums for short-term loans.[2]

Beginning in the sixteenth century and compelled by the rising costs of military technology, territorial states switched focus to domestic lenders, often merchants and tax farmers and sometimes landed aristocracy as well.[3] Although external finance never disappeared,[4] it became marginal until the eighteenth century, when the British Crown floated new loans in Amsterdam to fund growing war expenses. This was, however, a somewhat limited international credit market, both in magnitude and geographic scope. The heyday of Dutch foreign lending was confined to the last decades of the eighteenth century and involved eight countries (compared to 90+ sovereign and colonial borrowers in nineteenth-century London). Dutch lending was also barely diversified: Roughly three out of four loans floated in Amsterdam went to the British Crown, and average maturities were 12 years

---

2. See Stasavage (2011) for a seminal account of the origins of public credit in Europe and the evolution of city- and territorial-states' public credit.

3. Tracy (2014) for an overview.

4. Philip II of Spain (r. 1556–1598) and before Edward III of England (r. 1327–1377) borrowed from Italian bankers, but those operations remained fairly uncommon.

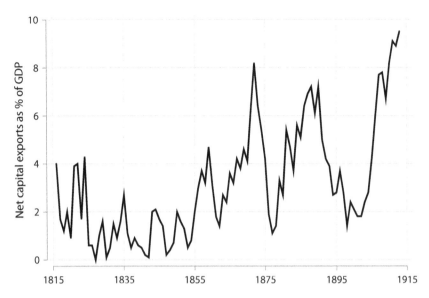

FIGURE 3.1. Net Capital Exports as Percentage of British GDP, 1816–1913. This figure shows the current account balance for Britain during the Bond Era. *Sources*: Imlah (1958) for net current account (nominal); Broadberry et al. (2012) for nominal GDP between 1816 and 1829; and Mitchell (2005) for nominal GDP between 1830 and 1913.

long, indicating high aversion to international lending.[5] Dutch capital dried up under French occupation in 1795, and England, which had enhanced its capacity to mobilize revenue since the Nine Years' War (1689–1698),[6] became the new and only financial capital of Europe and the world.

3.1.1 LONDON, THE WORLD'S BANKER

Having financed successive coalitions against Napoleon and improved its capacity to push capital overseas, London seized momentum to funnel surplus capital derived from the Industrial Revolution to the rest of the world.[7] The openness of the British savings market was incremental and not exempt from boom-and-bust cycles caused by investment euphoria followed by a sudden collapse of lending. The setbacks did not stop the frenzy. In a matter of years, trading resumed and gave way to new and more expansive cycles.

Figure 3.1 plots the current account balance for Britain between 1816 and 1913. Between 1820 and 1850, approximately 1.5 percent of British GDP

---

5. Loan operations and maturity in Riley (1980, pp. 84 and 35, respectively).

6. See Brewer (1988) for the expansion of fiscal capacity in eighteenth-century England.

7. Hobson (1914); Jenks (1927); Obstfeld and Taylor (2004); Rippy (1959).

TABLE 3.1. External Capital Stock by Country in the Long Nineteenth Century

	1825	1855	1870	1890	1914
Great Britain	0.5	0.7	4.9	12.1	19.5
France	0.1	—	2.5	5.2	8.6
Germany	—	—	—	4.8	6.7
Netherlands	0.3	0.2	0.3	1.1	1.2
United States	0.0	0.0	0.0	0.5	2.5
Canada	—	—	—	0.1	0.2
All	0.9	0.9	7.7	23.8	38.7
UK/All	0.56	0.78	0.64	0.51	0.50
World GDP	—	—	111	128	221

Source: Table 2.1 in Obstfeld and Taylor (2004).
Note: Values represent gross foreign assets in current USD billion.

was invested overseas. External capital flows increased to 3 percent in the 1850s and 1860s and thereafter averaged 4.5 percent, peaking at 9 percent on the verge of WWI.[8] These figures stand in clear contrast to 1990–2010, when the UK remained a net receiver of foreign capital.[9]

Back in the nineteenth century, London was the undisputed financial capital of the world. Despite the existence of other financial centers, the vast majority of foreign securities were channeled through the London Stock Exchange (LSE).[10] "Whoever the capitalists engaged in government loan business and from whatever source their initial capital was derived, they did not long delay in establishing financial residence in London."[11]

Table 3.1 reports the gross value of foreign assets for major capital exporters in the nineteenth century. At its peak, the British share of total global foreign investment was almost 80 percent, far exceeding the combined capital exports of its nearest competitors.[12] In order to appreciate the high leverage of British finance in the world, these figures should be compared to the United States' share of global assets in 2000 at 25 percent or with its maximum share of 50 percent circa 1960. That Britain was known as the "world's banker" in the nineteenth century should come as no surprise.

8. Although the current account pools public and private capital, its evolution is "closely tied to the trends and cycles of foreign lending" (Taylor, 2002, p. 726).
9. OECD (2017).
10. Michie (2006).
11. Jenks (1927, p. 267).
12. Clemens and Williamson (2004).

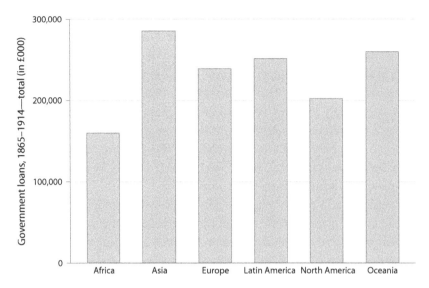

FIGURE 3.2. Government Loans by Region from 1865 to 1914. These data show the regional breakdown of total government loans issued in Britain as they appear in Stone (1992).

Paris and Berlin joined the money market decisively in the last decades of the nineteenth century.[13] Whereas British financiers invested in both government securities and private projects, French and German investors specialized in sovereign loans to Southern and Eastern Europe plus North Africa.[14] In total, France and Germany invested 2.5 and 1 percent, respectively, of their GDP overseas, still a remarkable figure.[15]

Quantitatively, capital flows from the three European financial capitals to the rest of the world were unprecedented and remained unseen until after the end of the Cold War.[16] On average, between 1816 and 1913 4 percent of world GDP crossed borders in the form of capital investment, twice the levels for 1945–1995.[17] And relative to world GDP, the volume of cross-border loans was still three times smaller in 1980 than in 1880, a hundred years earlier.[18]

In terms of geographic specialization, British capital diversified the most. Data collected by Irving Stone and reproduced in figure 3.2 show that

13. Feis (1930) for an overview, and Esteves (2008, 2011) for a disaggregated list of French (2011) and German (2008) investment overseas.

14. Feis (1930); Fishlow (1985); White (1933).

15. Edelstein (1982, p. 3).

16. Bordo, Eichengreen, and Kim (1998, pp. 3–4).

17. Estimates computed with Jordà, Schularick, and Taylor's (2016) data.

18. Eichengreen (1991, p. 150).

British capital in the form of government loans reached all continents. These loans were issued by sovereign states and colonial subjects, British or not. Relative to other financial capitals, British investment dominated French and German capital in North and South America, Asia, and North and South Africa; that is, everywhere except Southern and Eastern Europe.[19] By 1914, 64 percent of total foreign investments in North America emanated from Britain (Germany was the runner-up with 10.4 percent); 42 percent in Latin America (US, 18.5 percent), 96 percent in Oceania (France, 4 percent), 50 percent in Asia (France, 17.6 percent), and 60.5 percent in Africa (France, 22.2 percent).[20]

Lending was a private business despite growing diplomatic interference in capital markets. Government-to-government loans were rare, and multilateral official lending nonexistent. Until the 1860s, much of the lending business was in the hands of a group of selected underwriters, key among them the Rothschilds and the Barings.[21] Large underwriters negotiated loans on behalf of foreign governments, and tender was bought by a relatively small group of investors, only in the hundreds, mostly based in London.[22] Sovereign loans were then sold to atomized, inexperienced investors in secondary markets. The small investors numbered in the tens of thousands and occasionally in the millions (e.g., Russia's loans in the early twentieth century were owned by 1.6 million Frenchmen).[23] The acceleration of foreign lending in the second half of the nineteenth century offered new opportunities to lesser underwriters to broker sovereign loans.[24] Some of them specialized in governments with weaker fundamentals and shaky debt records, a risky business that major houses preferred to avoid.[25]

3.1.2 WHO BORROWED?

As the opening quotation in this chapter suggests, all nations were welcome to float loans in the London Stock Exchange (LSE), sovereign or not. France and Germany, the main rivals to British hegemony, would market

19. Esteves (2011, table 1).

20. Woodruff (1966, table IV/3, p. 154).

21. Flandreau and Flores (2009).

22. Mauro, Sussman, and Yafeh (2006, p. 136).

23. Suter (1992, p. 45).

24. Flandreau (2020). The market share of big merchant houses declined from 53% in the 1870s to 35% in the 1910s (Cottrell, 1976, p. 30).

25. Flandreau, Flores, Gaillard, and Nieto-Parra (2009).

sovereign bonds in London too, normally as part of larger issues floated simultaneously in other capitals. However, the vast majority of loans went to new and old-but-traditionally-isolated sovereign states in North and South America, Southern and Eastern Europe, East and Southeast Asia, the Middle East, and Northern and Southern Africa. British capital also flowed into Spanish, Dutch, Turkish, French, and German colonies, but only occasionally.

British colonies floated loans in the LSE on a regular basis, and they did so on favorable terms because of the so-called empire effect. Accominotti, Flandreau, and Rezzik argue that colonies were treated as de facto British "provinces," implying that the metropole would do everything in its capacity to avoid default, hence the perceived lower risk of this venture.[26] Ferguson and Schularick concur, while claiming that colonies were also more likely to implement *Gladstonian* economic policy—namely, favoring sound money, balanced budgets, and openness to trade.[27] Consistently, most colonies were considered a fiscal drain and were subjected to tight fiscal supervision.[28]

By the late 1870s, most of the self-governing colonies or "dominions" (all territories in modern-day Australia, Canada, New Zealand, and South Africa) were able to borrow on the open market without the direct support of the British government. From 1881 onward, the dominions were declared fiscally autonomous and deprived of imperial guarantees except for emergencies. The larger group of colonies, including the Crown colonies, protectorates, and India, were deemed "dependent," that is, without real autonomy to issue debt because they required the explicit approval of the British government.

All colonial stock was originally managed by the Crown agents. Based in London, the agents acted as plenipotentiary finance ministers—both bankers and national debt commissioners of the colony.[29] They decided when and how much debt to issue and how to pay it back. They worked with local governments but were not accountable to them.[30]

Colonies were generally poor. To overcome investors' reluctance to underwrite them, colonial governors may have been tempted to float loans at excessively low prices, leading to fiscal imbalances and ultimately to

26. Accominotti, Flandreau, and Rezzik (2011).
27. Ferguson and Schularick (2006).
28. Frankema and van Waijenburg (2014); Gardner (2012); Herbst (2000).
29. Kesner (1977, p. 314).
30. Davis and Huttenback (1986).

default. The Crown agents, drawing from experience and reputation, were expected to overcome low demand for colonial stock and avoid moral hazard due to temptation by colonial governors, hence their key role in colonial investment.[31]

From 1881 onward, the Crown agents represented dependent colonies only. The colonial authority "established the highest permissible rate of interest, fixed the amount desired, and set what other conditions it saw fit. The secretary of state then authorized the Crown agents to see the loan on the best terms possible."[32] On behalf of the colony, the agents shopped for underwriters in the LSE and hired individuals they trusted. The agents were considered truthful representatives of the colonies.[33] In fact, the terms that agents were able to negotiate on behalf of colonies were so attractive that self-governing colonies requested to work with them after 1881. The British treasury objected—"fiscal autonomy came with responsibility."

After the Colonial Loans Act of 1899 and the Colonial Stock Act of 1900, the dependent colonies gained the same trustee status as the benchmark British government perpetual bond, the consol, hence virtually free access to funds at highly subsidized rates.[34] Loans floated by dependent colonies almost tripled within 10 years, from £7.4 million from 1890 to 1899 to £18.4 million from 1900 to 1909.[35]

In the French Empire, colonial stock was closely monitored by the Ministry of Finance, and new issues required the approval of the French Parliament. Representation of colonial interest, however, was decentralized to currency boards and commercial banks, which also served as underwriters of colonial issues.[36] Because colonial loans were tightly monitored, French colonies borrowed extensively and at favorable terms, generally under 4 percent.[37]

The relationship between international finance and imperialism intensified in the last decades of the nineteenth century. But the globalization of credit was not a by-product of colonial lending. Capital flows

---

31. Sunderland (2004, p. 150).
32. Davis and Huttenback (1986, p. 185).
33. Davis and Huttenback (1986); Kesner (1981); refer to Sunderland (1999) for a competing view.
34. Ferguson and Schularick (2006, p. 286).
35. Davis and Huttenback (1986, p. 168).
36. Flandreau (2006).
37. Feis (1930, p. 143).

to colonies represented a small proportion of total international lending.[38] Based on my calculations, British capital exports within the British Empire between 1816 and 1913 (measured as issue amount spent on sovereign debt) were three times smaller than capital exports out of the empire.[39] In France, investment in colonial securities represented 4.3 percent of all French foreign investments from 1852 to 1881, and 9 percent in 1913.[40]

Most international lending in the Bond Era went to sovereign countries, newly created (e.g., Peru) or recently integrated into the Western sphere (e.g., Japan). As is made clear in chapter 4, the conditions accepted by (or imposed on) sovereign states grew favorable to European lenders over time as a result of imperial competition between the Great Powers, among other reasons.

The Bond Era came to a halt with WWI. The surge in demand for liquidity to finance the Great War caused a series of financial disturbances that permanently disrupted global financial markets.[41] The concatenation of WWI with the Great Depression and World War II prevented international markets from stabilizing during those years. After 1945, however, the market specialized in private debt, specifically foreign direct investment (FDI). The euphoria over foreign bonds stopped in 1914, but its consequences are still felt.

3.1.3 BORROW FOR WHAT?

Public external finance in the Bond Era served three purposes: defense expenditure, debt conversion (i.e., refinancing old debt with new debt), and major infrastructure projects. External finance for military expenses and debt conversion falls within the category of "revenue finance" and in principle does not grow the local economy.[42] The long-term consequences of revenue finance for state building are discussed in detail in part II of the book. Here I reflect upon the third leg of foreign loans, that is, capital borrowed for productive uses, or "developmental

38. Kesner (1981, p. 44).

39. Calculations draw from the newly collected data for this book, presented later in this chapter. The anticolonial bias in international lending is corroborated by Davis and Huttenback (1986).

40. Cameron (1966, tables 3 and 4).

41. Neal (1990, ch. 11).

42. Fishlow (1985).

finance."[43] Foreign investment can help developing economies over-come barriers to economic growth caused by market failures and local capital shortage. In the nineteenth century, railroad investment was the paramount example of developmental finance, consuming a third of total British investment overseas and reaching more than 70 countries and colonies.[44]

At least on paper, railroads had it all. First, they connected produc-tion sites to trade ports, reduced transportation costs, and increased export competitiveness. Second, railroads created a demand for labor, coal, steel, and financial services. Third, by growing the economy, railroads stim-ulated consumption of imported goods and increased tariff receipts. At its best, steam locomotion was good for both the local economy and the treasury.[45]

Railroad construction exceeded the financial means of the periph-ery. Governments in the Global South actively sought to attract foreign capital to finance the construction of this revolutionary technology.[46] Demand met supply. In Latin America, for instance, 75 percent open railway miles in 1900 were owned by foreign firms, 70 percent of them British.[47]

To attract capital, governments in the periphery were compelled to offer European investors a plethora of preferential provisions, including but not limited to profit guarantees, tariff exemptions for construction materials,[48] ease in expropriating land,[49] and network monopolies. These clauses increased the expected return of investment and served to attract foreign capital, but carried perverse effects too. For instance, profit guar-antees, the meaning of which is self-explanatory, created serious stress on the local treasuries, requiring the issue of *revenue loans* to meet the

43. The distinction between revenue and developmental finance is somewhat exaggerated because military considerations played a key role in the construction and nationalization of railroads in the Bond Era (Bogart, 2009; Onorato, Scheve, and Stasavage, 2014; Pratt, 1916). The argument here omits this important nuance.

44. Stone (1992, pp. 13–14).

45. Bignon, Esteves, and Herranz-Loncán (2015).

46. Lewis (1983).

47. Sanz Fernández (1998, p. 377).

48. For instance, tariff exemptions were incorporated into foreign loans to the Spanish gov-ernment. The exemptions were applied to railroad investment in both the Spanish peninsula and colonial Cuba (Comín, 2012, pp. 170–171).

49. During the Porfiriato (1876–1910), nearly 11% of Mexican territory was given over to the land survey companies in compensation (Salvucci, 2006, p. 273).

conditions of developmental finance.[50] Guarantees also weakened incentives of foreign concessionaires to construct and maintain high-quality railroads, accelerating their obsolescence.[51] Network monopolies, another common clause in railroad loan contracts, sought to limit competition as a means to secure profits; however, they also prevented the design of a nationwide rational network, reinforcing economic *and* political fragmentation, which was bad for the economy and state building.[52]

The overall economic impact of railroad investment should be assessed in light of its *forward* and *backward linkages*. The former point to the contribution of railroads to lowering costs of transportation and commodity exports, whereas the latter focus on new industrial and financial sectors derived from railroad investment. Forward linkages are often sized by their *social savings*, namely, the resources that reductions in transportation costs free up relative to alternative means of transportation.[53] In some peripheral countries, social savings were vast—equivalent to 26 percent of GDP in Argentina,[54] 18 percent in Brazil,[55] 38 percent in Mexico,[56] and 16 percent in India.[57] However, forward linkages were modest (or null) in many other economies, including Colombia,[58] Peru,[59] Uruguay,[60]

50. The largest external loan floated in Venezuela in the nineteenth century sought to secure the profit guarantees of the largest investor of the *Gran Ferrocarril de Venezuela*, the *Disconto Gessellschaft*, a Germany-based bank. This 1896 loan increased the outstanding external debt of Venezuela by 70% (Harwich Vallenilla, 1976, pp. 222–227). Refer to chapter 9 for profit guarantees in the case of Argentina.

51. The F. C. Central del Norte in Argentina is a good example. After being sold to foreign investors in 1888, no additional tracks were built in the next five decades (Scalabrini Ortíz, 1972, p. 230). In Venezuela, only 20% of the 7% guaranteed projects were put in motion (Santamaría García, 1998, p. 481).

52. The persistence of fragmentation in the presence of railroads is found in small and large economies: from Cuba (Zanetti and García, 1998, ch. 5) to China (Köll, 2019, ch. 3).

53. Fogel (1963). See Chaves, Engerman, and Robinson (2014) for a concise critical assessment of the assumptions under social savings estimates. Notice also that social savings calculations do not account for investment costs.

54. Summerhill (2001).

55. Summerhill (2003).

56. Coatsworth (1981).

57. Donaldson (2018).

58. McGreevey (1971, p. 266) estimates social savings in Colombia in 1924 on the order of 3.2% of gross domestic product. Ramírez (2001) finds virtually identical estimates.

59. The most favorable estimate of social savings by 1914 in Peru is in the range of 2% to 7% (Zegarra, 2013). Passenger savings were under 0.5%. Refer to Bonilla (1972) for similar conclusions.

60. Herranz-Loncán (2011) estimates are on the order of 3.8% of GDP for freight and 1.9% for passenger transportation.

and Venezuela in Latin America,[61] and Spain,[62] China,[63] and Turkey elsewhere.[64]

For state building, backward linkages may be even more important. In Britain, France, Germany, and the United States, railroad expansion had positive externalities on other sectors of the economy.[65] Demand for finance, steel, engineering, and fuel was largely met locally, fostering innovation and growing the economy and the tax base. The railroad networks connected economic sectors and distant regions, enabling the central government to extend its reach beyond the capital, hence increasing the effective tax base.[66]

In the periphery, backward linkages were largely absent, even in countries experiencing record social savings.[67] Railroads inputs (financial and material) were regularly imported from Europe and the US. This had a direct negative effect on the balance of payments. The rapid generation of foreign exchange generated by foreign capital inflows drove the overvaluation of the exchange rate, adding another hurdle to industrial development (i.e., backward linkages).[68] Because tariff exemptions to intermediate inputs were necessary to attract foreign finance for railroad construction, the imports of highly valuable goods (locomotives, wagons, steel) did not yield tariff revenue, which was key to servicing foreign debt.[69] Overall,

---

61. Although no social savings estimate exists for Venezuela, Harwich Vallenilla (1976), Santamaría García (1998), and Polo Muriel (1998) conclude that railroads did not foster economic growth in Venezuela. General surveys of uneven economic returns of railways in Latin America can be found in the edited volumes by Kuntz Ficker (2015) and Sanz Fernández (1998).

62. Herranz-Loncán (2003, 2006) shows that the average social savings of railroad development in Spain was not statistically different from zero. This type of investment experienced strong heterogeneity in performance: the earlier lines connecting preexisting industrial areas did well, whereas later lines built for political reasons (and possibly speculation) were economically inefficient, pushing the average social savings to zero.

63. Huenemann (1984) estimates social savings as low as 0.5% of GDP.

64. Quataert (1977). Sub-Saharan countries, independent or colonial, barely attracted railroad investment in the Bond Era.

65. See Hawke (1970, p. 211) for Britain; Fishlow (1965, ch. 3) for the United States; Caron (1983) for France; and Fremdling (1983) for Germany.

66. See Mann (1984) for the role of railroads in articulating the "infrastructural powers" of the state in Europe; and Cermeño, Enflo, and Lindvall (2018) for a recent application in Sweden.

67. Refer to Summerhill (2005) and Coatsworth (1979) for the absence of backward linkages in Brazil and Mexico, respectively.

68. Salvucci (2006, p. 288) for the Dutch disease preventing industrialization in Argentina.

69. Tax leaks were magnified when investors built railroads on privately owned land. That was the case, for instance, of foreign-owned sugar monopolies in Cuba (Zanetti and García, 1998, p. 404).

large shares of railroad social savings were "leaked" overseas in the form of input imports and interest rates, and with them the capacity to diversify the economy and expand the tax base. In Mexico, for instance, roughly a quarter of total export earnings were lost to European financiers in the form of railroad operations, imports, and debt service.[70]

The absence of backward linkages led to an export-led growth model with little diversification, exposing developing nations to "commodity lotteries," namely, abrupt changes in the international price of export staples, which regularly hurt economic and fiscal performance.[71] Railroads, the quintessence of developmental finance, brought economic growth to the periphery but also underdevelopment.[72]

More generally, the perils of external finance for state building that I advance in this book are not limited to *revenue finance* (i.e., war and debt consolidation). Developmental loans in the periphery often generated perverse economic and political incentives, the consequences of which limited, or even canceled, their potential contribution to economic growth *and* state building.

3.2 Causes of Lending Frenzy

Sovereign lending (i.e., loans to foreign government) played a crucial role in the rise of global finance. Wars of independence in Latin America in the 1810s and 1820s set the stage for the century to come. Brazil, the province of Buenos Aires, Chile, Colombia, Mexico, Peru, and smaller countries in Central America floated loans in London to equip their armies and terminate colonial rule.[73] Loans were easy to market. The first foreign security mania—to which loans to Austria, Denmark, Greece, Naples, Portugal, Prussia, and Spain contributed[74]—ended within years, when many of these countries interrupted debt service.[75] Foreign government securities regained momentum in the mid-1830s and grew thereafter.

---

70. Coatsworth (1981, p. 181).

71. Blattman, Hwang, and Williamson (2007). Fluctuations in global capital markets remain a major hurdle to the consolidation of social benefits in modern-day Latin America (Wibbels 2006).

72. This conclusion is shared by Coatsworth (1981), Kaur (1980, p. 698), and Zanetti and García (1998, pp. 99–100), among others.

73. Marichal (1989).

74. Flandreau and Flores (2009).

75. Reinhart and Rogoff (2009, p. 91).

FIGURE 3.3. Share of Countries in Default from 1800 to 1913. Only independent nations at the time of default are considered. *Source*: Reinhart and Rogoff (2009).

In 1853, foreign government bonds accounted for 6 percent of all listed securities on the LSE; by 1913, they represented an unprecedented 21 percent.[76]

The lending frenzy in the nineteenth century might be surprising in light of the global cycles of sovereign default that characterize that era. Figure 3.3 shows that the proportion of countries in default during any given year in the nineteenth century was over 20 percent, with peaks as high as 45 percent. How are both phenomena compatible? Some suggest irrational behavior on the lenders' side; others, informational asymmetries between investors and borrowers; and still others, market-based explanations. Next, I briefly survey these explanations and then introduce an original dataset on long-term sovereign loan rates with two goals in mind: the new data documents the lending euphoria in an unprecedented way (based on the sample size and time coverage), and it allows me to test the notion of extreme conditionality, which sheds light on the apparent paradox in the continuation of sovereign lending despite massive default episodes.

76. Michie (2006, table 3.3). These estimates do not include government-guaranteed railroad bonds, hence they are a lower-bound estimate of total sovereign lending.

3.2.1 IRRATIONAL AND FRAUDULENT BEHAVIOR

Charles Kindleberger is a leading proponent of irrational behavior as an explanation for the first financial globalization. Speculation and manias "close to mass hysteria and insanity" distorted interest rates, driving a wedge between prices and economic fundamentals.[77] Some accounts are indeed compatible with the notion of irrational lending. For instance, Feis refers to reckless loans in the 1860s to the Khedive, as the Egyptian government was known at the time. This country lacked an annual budget, an official register, and an ordered tax apparatus; however, the Khedive quintupled external debt between 1863 and 1879.

> The ordinary [European] investor did not realize the financial state of the country. Banks were willing to take the risk of loss for larger return and special pledges.... When one banking group retired, another entered the field.[78]

This quotation leads to a related cause of the lending frenzy: blatant fraud. Floating a foreign bond involved three players: borrowers (countries), private investors, and issue houses or underwriters. The latter played a key role in the Bond Era, negotiating the bond covenant on behalf of borrowers, circulating the prospectus that stipulated the terms of the loan, advancing funds to the borrower, and selling the bonds to individual private investors.[79] Borrowers paid underwriters large commissions for their service; indeed, Jenks came to the conclusion that "the real profits of the loan business went to the[se] contractors."[80]

Large underwriters were careful and cultivated a reputation for marketing safe products, but second-tier underwriters and promoters took advantage of information asymmetries to trade lemons.[81] The "art of puffing"—the promotion of bubbles—was a general practice in the LSE well into the 1870s.[82] Taking advantage of the unscrupulous economic press (more below), promoters engineered loans to make them look like safe bets. Flandreau offers various textbook examples of "white-collar

77. Kindleberger (1996, p. 20).
78. Feis (1930, p. 383).
79. Eichengreen (1991, p. 151).
80. Jenks (1927, p. 49).
81. See Flandreau and Flores (2009) and Flandreau, Flores, Gaillard, and Nieto-Parra (2009) for extensive research on issuing houses' prestige.
82. Flandreau (2016, p. 8).

criminality" occurring in the LSE—ponzi schemes benefiting promoters and vulture investors specializing in sovereign debt restructuring, often the same individuals.[83]

In the early 1870s, a parliamentary investigation took place in Westminster to address the blatant fraud and disastrous outcomes of sovereign loans to smaller Central American countries.[84] This report revealed the unscrupulous practices that issue houses pursued to market their products; however, foreign rulers might have seen this as an opportunity, too:

> So governments quite unacquainted with the mysteries of finance, like Morocco in 1860, learned from roving agents how easy it was to arrange loans in London or in Paris. Politicians desirous of looting their country's treasury decently and without ostentation discovered how readily the matter could be arranged by way of a floating debt.[85]

In the same vein, Rippy concludes that British bankers and more than a few Latin American governments alike were "scandalously dishonest."[86] They all profited "at the expense of [small] British investors." Fraud was an extended problem because it benefited foreign investors *and* irresponsible local rulers, as discussed in chapter 2.

3.2.2 INFORMATION ASYMMETRIES

Fraud was possible because investors had limited access to real-time unbiased information.[87] The submarine cable across the English Channel, that is, between the two world financial capitals, arrived only in 1851, thirty years into the Bond Era. The telegraph reached key overseas markets only in the late nineteenth century: Buenos Aires in 1878, Tokyo in 1900. In the meantime, investors based their decisions on the economic press published in London; however, this press did not establish full-time correspondents overseas until late in the game.[88] For example, the *Times*, one of the most respected publications of the day, did not deploy a permanent

---

83. Flandreau (2016, chs. 4–5).

84. Select Committee on Loans to Foreign States, *Report from the Select Committee on Loans to Foreign States: With the Proceedings of the Committee*, House of Commons, London, 1875.

85. Jenks (1927, p. 273).

86. Rippy (1959, p. 32).

87. Neal (2015, pp. 166–167). See Mauro, Sussman, and Yafeh (2006, ch. 2) for a competing view.

88. Jones (1979).

correspondent in Argentina until the 1890s. In the meantime, the financial press relied for information on local investors who often had conflicts of interest.[89]

Information issues did not end there. Flandreau, Nye, and Taylor write of the structural capture of journalism by promoters: During the railway mania in the 1840s, for instance, specialized journals distorted information in return for advertising revenues.[90] In 1872, the 28-year editor of the *Times* faced charges of fallibility and corruption originating in blatant conflict of interest. He happened to own shares of products his journal advertised.[91] These scandals undermined the credibility of the financial press as a whole.[92]

Biased information was not only published regularly in the specialized press, but it was also present in the prospectuses circulated by issue houses on behalf of borrowers. Some prospectuses were blatant fabrications, chief among them the bond scheme of Poyais, a fictitious country in Central America that happened to quote two bonds in London in the 1820s secured upon all the revenues of the nonexistent government of Poyais. Other prospectuses were misleading or contained falsehoods about the record of debt service of countries in the past. Issue houses failed to disclose information in their possession that would have warned investors that the borrowing government was highly unstable and doomed to default.[93] Winkler finds various examples of this when examining the fine print of prospectuses circulated among American investors during the first decades of the twentieth century.[94] In the 1920s, for instance, prospectuses of Chilean national debt claimed falsely and repeatedly that "Chile had been borrowing for 95 years and has never defaulted on its loans." In reality, Chile had defaulted twice in the nineteenth century—first in the 1820s and later in the late 1870s—accumulating a total of 26 years of exclusion. Regardless, Chilean loans were successfully quoted in 1921 and 1922 only to be defaulted eight years later.

89. Jones (1979).

90. Flandreau (2016), Nye (2015), and Taylor (2015).

91. The management of the 1890 financial crisis is illuminating. Despite having inside information on Barings' and Argentina's imminent bankruptcy, the *Times* and the *Economist* retained that information and called instead for plans for an orderly rearrangement of Argentina's finances (Nye 2015, p. 217). Substantial losses followed.

92. Nye (2015); Taylor (2015).

93. Borchard (1951, pp. 143–144).

94. Winkler (1933, ch. 5).

3.2.3 SEARCH FOR YIELD

Some authors argue that the lending euphoria can be explained by market forces. On one hand, in the absence of local credit markets, emerging markets required strong inflows of foreign capital to finance basic government operation.[95] On the other hand, investment overseas resulted (and was perceived as) more profitable than domestic investment. The unusually high profits of railroads and other social overhead investments in the emerging primary product economy in the Americas (but also South Africa and Australasia) pushed British savings overseas.[96] In a recent piece, Meyer, Reinhart, and Trebesch show that the real return of external sovereign bonds was 7.87 percent in 1815–1869 and 6.19 percent in 1870–1914, surpassed only in 1995–2016 at 9.12 percent.[97] The highest return was for bonds of serial defaulters, which yielded 3.4 percent excess return relative to the British consol in 1815–1869 and 4.2 percent in 1870–1913.[98]

To secure profits, British lenders invested in export-related infrastructure and natural resource projects (e.g., railways and mines). These investments were meant to grow the local economy, tax receipts, and exports, hence foreign reserves with which to serve external debt.[99] Investment in foreign government loans was risky business, however: Lindert and Morton compute the spread relative to the British consol for 10 emerging economies from 1850 to 1914 and find that nominal rates were clearly larger than home government bonds, but bonds issued between 1850 and 1914 barely broke even with British consols.[100] This is, however, an average for a sample of countries with starkly different experiences with sovereign lending; whereas Japan, Australia, Canada, and Egypt (only after financial intervention) always repaid, others like Mexico and Russia interrupted debt service after the revolutions, lowering the average aggregate return.

All things considered, the frenzy in capital markets is probably explained by a combination of all three factors: poor information, fraud, and higher margins overseas. An additional reason for the lending euphoria may be the bondholders' ability to seize assets and sources of revenue in

---

95. Mauro, Sussman, and Yafeh (2006, p. 11).

96. Edelstein (1982, p. 7) and Neal (2015, p. 155).

97. Meyer, Reinhart, and Trebesch (2019, table 3).

98. Meyer, Reinhart, and Trebesch (2019, table 5).

99. Fishlow (1985). This is consistent with Flandreau and Zumer (2004), who show that local economic growth decreased the spread of peripheral countries.

100. Lindert and Morton (1989).

case of default, hence limiting risk. In the next two chapters, I articulate this argument, test for it, and discuss the implications of foreign financial control for long-term state building. In the remainder of this chapter, I introduce an original interest rate dataset to quantify the breadth of international lending and the relatively low price of credit in the long nineteenth century.

3.3 Access to International Finance

To shed light on the favorable terms of external finance in the Bond Era, I put together an original dataset of international loans or bonds—until the mid-twentieth century both terms were used interchangeably—floated between 1816 and 1914 in London, the world's banker. Existing datasets are limited to a subset of countries and specific decades of the nineteenth century or both. Two of the three most ambitious datasets assembled to date by Accominotti, Flandreau, and Rezzik and Ferguson and Schularick list the spread of 32 and 57 countries, respectively, in secondary markets in London from 1880 to 1913.[101] Of extreme value for the study of the spread in the most intense era of lending, these datasets cannot characterize the first 65 years of the Bond Era, 1815–1880. A third dataset, and closest to the one I put together, is assembled by Suzuki, who records new quotations (or *primary market*) data for 53 countries from 1870 to 1913.[102] In total, Suzuki's dataset lists 329 loans issued in London.

Guided by Suzuki's example, I collected primary market data from primary and secondary sources for a larger number of countries, 92 in total, as early as 1816 and up to 1914. I considered all central government and government-guaranteed loans irrespective of their purpose (e.g., war, debt refinancing, and infrastructure).[103] In all, the new dataset includes 944 loans, virtually tripling Suzuki's collection. For each bond, I collected data on nominal interest rate, price of quotation, maturity, purpose, and name of the underwriter.[104] With the new dataset, I seek to advance understanding of the first globalization of capital and simultaneously solidify a key

101. Accominotti, Flandreau, and Rezzik (2011); Ferguson and Schularick (2006).

102. Suzuki (1994).

103. In chapter 6, I elaborate on the fungibility of external capital in the national budget, and why for the study of state building we should contemplate all sovereign bonds regardless of their official use.

104. I stop data collection for a given territory as soon as it integrates into a larger sovereign jurisdiction, for example, the province of Buenos Aires after reuniting with Argentina in 1861.

assumption of the main argument of this book: capital was abundant and relatively cheap for both consolidated and new economies.

3.3.1 DESCRIPTIVES

Key primary sources of the dataset are *The Stock Exchange Loan and Company Prospectuses* and *Wetenhall's Course of the Exchange* (first day of quotation of calendar years from 1825 to 1871), both kept at the archives of the London Stock Exchange, now held at the Guildhall Library, City of London. Secondary sources are Dawson; Hobson; Jenks; Marichal; Mauro, Sussman, and Yafeh; and Suzuki. In addition, I draw from Ayer, from *Fenn's Compendium of the English and Foreign Funds, Debts and Revenues . . .* (1838, 1855, 1869, 1883, 1898),[105] and selectively from the *Annual Reports of the Council of the Corporation of Foreign Bondholders*, vol. 1 (1874)–vol. 45 (1917).

Table 3.2 shows some descriptive statistics to illustrate the spread of British capital exports, followed by a breakdown of the number of loans per country. The total amount issued in loans was almost £4 billion, equivalent to $600 billion in today's dollars but in a world economy one-tenth as large. Capital flowed to every continent, beginning with Europe and the Americas, and eventually Africa, Asia, and Oceania. Issue amount in Europe may seem disproportionally large, but that reflects varying income levels. Relative to local economies, borrowed quantities were substantial in Latin America, Asia, and Africa.

3.3.2 NOMINAL INTEREST RATES IN HISTORICAL PERSPECTIVE

David Stasavage has produced the most ambitious deep-historical dataset to date of sovereign borrowing in early-modern Europe.[106] He shows that public credit in that continent followed two tracks.

The city-states took the faster route. Venice and Siena, for instance, were able to issue long-term debt at low interest rates as early as the thirteenth century. Commercial city-states lived on long-distance trade and banking. Medieval European merchants had made their initial fortunes in risky activities like long-distance trade; once established, they became rentiers by shifting their fortunes into fixed income, either public or private.

---

105. Ayer (1905); Dawson (1990); Fenn (1838, 1855, 1869, 1883, 1898); Hobson (1914); Jenks (1927); Marichal (1989); Mauro, Sussman, and Yafeh (2006); Suzuki (1994).

106. Stasavage (2011). This paragraph follows chapter 2 in that work.

TABLE 3.2. Descriptive Statistics of Sovereign Bonds, 1816–1913

Region	Countries	Loans	Issue amount in million £ (% of total)	Earliest loan
Africa	15	102	301 (8%)	1860
Americas	33	279	1,100 (28%)	1822
Asia	10	128	544 (14%)	1854
Europe	25	252	1,700 (43%)	1816
Oceania	9	183	285 (7%)	1859
Total	92	944	3,940	

Note: Countries in the sample with number of loans in the sample in parentheses: Antigua and Barbuda (1), Argentina (41), Austria (10), Bahamas (1), Barbados (1), Belgium (7), Bolivia (2), Brazil (31), Bulgaria (4), Canada (30), Cape of Good Hope (27), Chile (30), China (30), Colombia (6), Confederate States of America (1), Costa Rica (6), Cuba (8), Denmark (15), Dominican Republic (7), Ecuador (2), Egypt (20), El Salvador (3), Fiji (1), Finland (1), France (9), Germany (5), Ghana (3), Greece (22), Grenada (2), Guatemala (6), Guyana (4), Haiti (2), Hawaii (1), Hesse (1), Honduras (5), Hong Kong (2), Hungary (13), India (28), Iran (2), Ireland (5), Isle of Man (1), Italy (12), Jamaica (8), Japan (13), Liberia (4), Mauritius (7), Mexico (17), Montenegro (1), Morocco (1), Naples (4), Natal (21), Netherlands (8), New South Wales (30), New Zealand (29), Newfoundland (13), Nicaragua (2), Niger (1), Nigeria (3), Norway (8), Orange Free State (1), Paraguay (4), Peru (11), Portugal (20), Poyais (1), Prussia (6), Puerto Rico (1), Queensland (29), Romania (9), Russia (44), Saint Lucia (2), Serbia (3), Sierra Leone (4), Singapore (4), South Africa (3), South Australia (30), Spain (16), Sri Lanka (Ceylon) (10), Sweden (16), Switzerland (2), Tanzania (1), Tasmania (18), Thailand (2), Tonkin (1), Transvaal (4), Trinidad and Tobago (10), Tunisia (2), Turkey (36), Great Britain (10), United States of America (7), Uruguay (9), Venezuela (5), Victoria (23), and Western Australia (22). See text for sources.

Territorial states took the slower track. Long-term debt appeared only in the early sixteenth century; until then, English, French, or Castilian monarchs relied on short-term debt (usually one or two years) and paid higher interest to their lenders, often Jewish or Italian bankers (e.g., the English monarch Edward III issued loans in Florence and Genoa to finance the Hundred Years' War, 1337–1453). Only in the early sixteenth century, pushed by pressing costs derived from the military revolution, did territorial states issue long-term loans.[107]

Figure 3.4 plots Stasavage's data from 1250 to 1800.[108] The pattern speaks for itself: a secular decline occurred in nominal rates over five centuries; however, differences between territorial states and city-states were lasting. Average nominal rates in the seventeenth century in France and England were 6.14 and 7.78 percent, respectively, compared to 4.5 and 2.6 percent in Barcelona and Genoa, respectively. It took an additional

107. Public credit took the form of annuities (e.g., the French *rentes*) to evade usury laws.
108. Stasavage (2011).

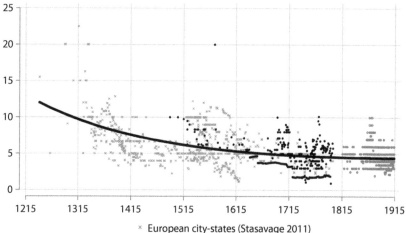

FIGURE 3.4. Nominal Interest Rates before and after 1800. This figure plots nominal interest rates for 1,198 sovereign bonds from 1200 to 1800 for 31 polities (light gray Xs for city-states, dark dots for territorial states) as drawn from Stasavage (2011), and newly collected nominal interest rates for 944 bonds in the period from 1816 to 1913 for 92 countries (light gray circles). A lowess line is superimposed.

century for nominal rates to converge around 5 percent. In figure 3.4, I plot the newly collected interest rates for the long nineteenth century. Far from a structural break, the secular decline continued after 1815 despite entry of unseasoned countries in capital markets and repeated default episodes.

Low interest rates in the nineteenth century are not a statistical artifact derived from pooling seasoned and unseasoned countries into the same chart. Figure 1.1 shows that the nominal spread between European and non-European countries was under 100 basis points at the beginning of the nineteenth century and converged to 0 by the turn of the century.

British colonies were favorably treated in capital markets because they were perceived by investors as British provinces—the empire effect discussed earlier. The low spread in figure 1.1, however, is not a by-product of having British colonies in the non-European sample. Figure 3.5 shows that when dependent colonies and self-governing colonies before 1881 (when they lose access to colonial agents) are excluded, the results are qualitatively similar. The near convergence between European and non-European countries happens later, but the spread remains under 100 basis points throughout—a quantity substantially lower than that between territorial

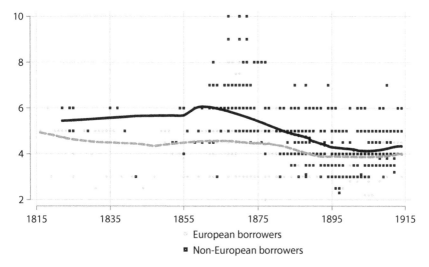

FIGURE 3.5. Comparison of Nominal Interest Rates Excluding British Dependencies. In this test, Crown colonies are excluded from the non-Europe sample. Self-government colonies before 1881 are also excluded because their loans were marketed by Crown agents (see text for details). After 1881, self-governing colonies are considered financially independent and listed along other non-European borrowers. Squares are used to indicate loans of non-European countries and circles those of European countries. A dashed lowess line is superimposed for the European sample and a solid line for the non-European sample. Compiled by author from multiple sources.

states and city-states a hundred years earlier. Did emerging economies bear very short maturities in return for relatively inexpensive credit?

3.3.3 MATURITY EXTENSION

Short maturities allow lenders to discipline borrowers: the threat of exclusion is expected to incentivize borrowers to enact prudent macroeconomic policy, hence debt service.[109] Long maturities express confidence in the borrowers' ability and willingness to repay. Because credibility issues were rampant in territorial states in medieval Europe, loans matured after one or two years.[110] Repeated defaults by unseasoned and politically unstable polities occurred in the nineteenth century; however, maturities were long and remained so until World War I, 31 years on average before 1870 and 38 years afterward.[111] These figures are high relative to early-modern Europe

109. See Diamond and Rajan (2001) and Jeanne (2009) for a formal treatment.

110. Stasavage (2011, p. 34).

111. I collected maturity extensions for 496 loans. My estimates are between those in Mauro, Sussman, and Yafeh (2006), who argue that maturities were around 20 years in the period from

as well as current times. Responding to the massive defaults in the 1980s and 1990s, maturities for emerging economies were between 5 and 10 years in the early 2000s.[112]

3.3.4 EFFECTIVE INTEREST RATES

The lending frenzy was manifested in historically low nominal interest rates and long maturities. Now I focus on *effective* interest rates. These can be measured in various ways: I follow Mauro, Sussman, and Yafeh and use the ratio of the coupon to the price, or *yield at issue*, which measures the income an investor receives on a bond as a percentage of the price of the bond.[113] Importantly, this ratio emulates the way investors regarded bond profitability.[114]

In order to compute the yield at issue, I was able to compile the price at issue for 803 bonds, 87 percent of the sample.[115] Using the price at issue has advantages and disadvantages: On the positive side I can analyze loans issued before standardized series were published in economic journals, hence the entire nineteenth century instead of only its final three decades, the period analyzed in virtually all existing research. The disadvantage is that the data generation process is endogenous: borrowers may issue a new loan when conditions are favorable and they anticipate cheaper credit. As a method of validation, I correlate the yield at issue in the primary market with yield in secondary markets, which operates continuously between new quotations. To implement this test, I draw yield in secondary markets from Ferguson and Schularick, who gathered data on the spread over British consols for securities from 57 independent countries, colonies, and self-governing territories of the British Empire from 1880 to 1913.[116]

1870 to 1913, and those of Meyer, Reinhart, and Trebesch (2019), who estimate average maturity between 1815 and 1869 in 46 years (30 countries) and in 42 years (45 countries) for 1870–1913.

112. Borensztein et al. (2004); Mauro, Sussman, and Yafeh (2006).

113. Mauro, Sussman, and Yafeh (2006). The assumption underlying this ratio is that interest rates will remain at the current rate and do not allow for any appreciation or depreciation that an investor receives at disposal (Brown, 1998, p. 23).

114. Mauro, Sussman, and Yafeh (2006, p. 41). Traders today apply sophisticated formulas for the valuation of bonds, one reason being the quality of information at hand.

115. Missing observations come mainly from bonds collected from secondary sources. In subsequent analyses, I dropped two bonds, one for Spain and another for Puerto Rico, due to abnormal yield values: 19.2 and 33.3, respectively.

116. Ferguson and Schularick (2006).

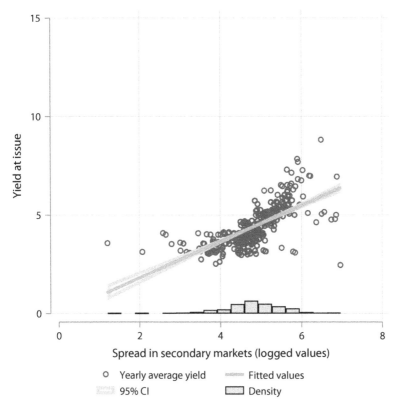

FIGURE 3.6. Primary and Secondary Bond Markets Compared, 1880–1913. Secondary market values, which are yearly averages, are log-transformed to cope with abnormal observations. Primary market data compiled by author. Secondary market data from Ferguson and Schularick (2006).

The distribution of prices in the secondary market has a long tail due to anomalous values. The linear correlation of yield at issue in primary markets and the original and log-transformed yield in secondary markets are 0.6 and 0.7, respectively, suggesting that the ratio of the coupon to the price—the contemporary investors' shortcut—is genuinely informative of the future valuation of the bond in secondary markets. For reference, figure 3.6 plots the primary against the log-transformed secondary market yield.

To conclude the descriptive characterization of the Bond Era, I investigate regional differences of yield at issue. The horizontal dotted line in figure 3.7 shows that the average yield at issue between 1816 and 1913 was at 5.19 percent. All regions except Oceania, which had disproportional representation of British colonies, experienced effective rates within

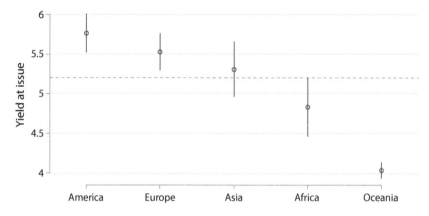

FIGURE 3.7. Average Yield at Issue by Region, 1816–1913. Yield at issue available for 803 bonds. Sample average represented with dashed line. Primary market data coded by author.

1 percentage point of the sample average, consistent with the convergence of nominal rates in figures 1.1 and 3.5.[117]

Figure 3.7 suggests that economies around the world paid modest premiums relative to the very seasoned economies in Europe. The spread of emerging economies in the Bond Era contrasts with the spread charged in secondary markets in the 1990s and early 2000s, which went as high as 800 basis points in times of crisis, or relative to the 300 basis points between 2002 and 2008, the most liquid and stable financial period since 1914.[118] The long-term consequences of early access to cheap capital for state building are the focus of later chapters in the book.

3.4 Conclusion

This chapter offers an original quantification of the first globalization of capital, one that includes the largest number of polities and longest period of time to date. The descriptive statistics indicate that the lending frenzy in the Bond Era was manifested in historically low nominal and effective interest rates and long maturities, all of which contributed to a culture of cheap money. In the next chapter, I study country-specific determinants of

117. These results are consistent with Bordo and Rockoff (1996). They size the spread of emerging economies between 1870 and 1914 between 200 and 300 basis points relative to British consols; for reference, the spread of the United States was 100 points.

118. Cruces and Trebesch (2013) for the 1900s to the early 2000s; Özmen and Doğanay Yaşar (2016) for 2002–2008 data.

the spread by testing existing models and advancing an original hypothesis: the ability to impose financial control over countries in case of default, or extreme conditionality. This hypothesis sheds light on the puzzling coexistence of regular, massive defaults and the rapid recovery of capital exports that followed and illuminates the perverse effects of cheap external capital on long-term state building.

4

Extreme Conditionality in International Lending

The previous chapter argued that the price of external capital in the Bond Era responded to supply or "push factors": capital surplus in Europe, fraud, and low domestic returns. In this chapter, I revisit demand or "pull factors," namely, country-specific characteristics that attracted foreign capital. Along with standard explanations—the gold standard, reputation, and empire—I articulate a complementary hypothesis; that is, foreign financial control by bondholders in case of default, or *extreme conditionality*. I elaborate on the conditions under which private bondholders took over local assets and test the hypothesis against an augmented version of the historical interest rate data that includes newly collected information on loan pledges.[1] Results suggest that pledging public assets reduced interest rates of emerging economies but exposed them to foreign financial control. The chapter is organized in three parts: I begin by reviewing leading explanations of the spread in the nineteenth century. Then I articulate the extreme conditionality hypothesis and test some of its empirical implications. Finally, I discuss the risks of pledging national assets for long-term state building.

---

1. I use interchangeably the expressions *pledge, hypothecation, security,* and *collateral.*

4.1 Bond Yield in the Nineteenth Century

The expansion of European capital exports in the nineteenth century is responsible for the drop in the average cost of external finance, especially for countries with weak fundamentals. Push factors are not unique to the nineteenth century: Frieden and Mosley find similar results in studying external finance of emerging economies from World War II to the present.[2] When capital is abundant, even borrowers with weak and undemocratic institutions access international finance at favorable terms; in other words, in good credit cycles, investors are risk tolerant.[3]

A long tradition of economists and economic historians shows that country-specific characteristics also shape the terms of external finance: that is, demand matters. Existing accounts specific to the Bond Era focus on the borrower's record of default, institution-induced credibility, and empire membership.[4] I review these explanations before introducing the notion of extreme conditionality.

4.1.1 REPUTATION

Why do countries service debt? They might do so because they want to cultivate a good reputation[5] or because they want to avoid credit exclusion.[6] The notion of reputation incorporates the beliefs that bondholders have about the type of government they are dealing with. Governments (countries) with good reputations are expected to do everything in their power to service debt in good or bad times (e.g., implement an austerity policy if needed). Default, although occasionally justified from the investor's point of view, tends to hurt the country's reputation and thus is to be avoided. Good reputation is rewarded by investors with easier access to credit because they perceive the borrower as reliable.[7]

2. Frieden (1991b) and Mosley (2003).

3. Ballard-Rosa, Mosley, and Wellhausen (2021).

4. This list does not exhaust all explanations: some emphasize local economic conditions (Flandreau and Zumer, 2004), issue linkage (Lipson, 1985; Kelly, 1998), and central banks (Poast, 2015). The analysis of these hypotheses requires macroeconomic and institutional data that exist only for a selected group of countries or only for the later decades of the nineteenth century.

5. Tomz (2007).

6. Eaton and Gersovitz (1981).

7. Tomz (2007).

Tomz's cooperative theory of lending through reputation contrasts with Eaton and Gersovitz's noncooperative version.[8] According to this model, lenders compel countries to cultivate their reputations—hence service debt—by threatening them with *credit exclusion*, the practice of refusing quotations of securities to governments that fail to fulfill their obligations or come to terms with their creditors.[9] The principle of exclusion was enshrined in the rules of the London Stock Exchange (LSE) as early as 1826.[10]

Figure 3.3 shows that massive defaults occurred with regularity in the Bond Era, yet effective interest rates decreased over time, bringing some scholars to question the notion of reputation. Lindert and Morton study the conditions of access to capital from 1850 to 1985. Drawing on a sample of 10 emerging economies, they find that countries in default are not systematically punished by international lenders.[11] In some cases, Lindert and Morton claim, the prospect of continued business with large borrowers is enough to regain market access in a short period of time.[12] Eichengreen as well as Jorgensen and Sachs find that countries interrupting debt service during the interwar period were not excluded or penalized in the postwar era because markets attributed default to unforeseen external shocks and rendered the debtor's abrogation of contracts excusable.[13] Instead of initiating an arduous negotiation, investors understood that a quick settlement would ultimately benefit them because it would accelerate the borrower's recovery. Reinhart and Trebesch find support for this conjecture by analyzing forms of debt relief between 1920 and the 2000s.[14]

If countries can default without cost, why would they ever service? Tomz addresses this puzzle by advancing a dynamic model of reputation that relaxes the assumption of complete information about the preferences

---

8. Eaton and Gersovitz (1981).

9. Jenks (1927, p. 284).

10. Article 62 of the rules of the LSE reads as follows: "The Committee will not recognize new bonds, stock, or other securities, issued by any foreign government that has violated the conditions of any previous public loan raised in this country, unless it shall appear to the Committee that a settlement of existing claims has been assented to by the general body of bondholders. Companies issuing such securities will be liable to be excluded from the official list" (Melsheimer and Gardner, 1891, p. 164).

11. Lindert and Morton (1989).

12. This argument is similar to the one made by Drelichman and Voth (2014) for Spain during the reign of Philip II.

13. Eichengreen (1987); Jorgensen and Sachs (1988).

14. Reinhart and Trebesch (2016).

of foreign governments and that allows preferences to vary over time, resulting from a change in an incumbent or in the populace.[15] In this model, investors continually update their beliefs about the type of government they are confronting. Analyzing bond yields in secondary markets at different points in time as early as 1770, Tomz shows that investors offered worse credit to unproven governments than to better-known or "seasoned" countries, that reputation was built by servicing debt punctually over a number of years, and that regular defaulters struggled to raise new capital in international markets. To date, Tomz offers the strongest evidence for the argument of reputation.

4.1.2   THE GOLD STANDARD

The incentive to cultivate a reputation might conflict with short-term political survival. Opportunistic policy (e.g., printing money to cover a budget deficit) might damage the macroeconomy and put debt service in jeopardy. To credibly commit to honor debt, rulers might peg currency to a precious metal or major currency. In a world of open capital markets, the adoption of a fixed exchange rate puts monetary and fiscal policy at the service of the exchange rate.[16] This policy bundle is expected to preclude political-business cycles and secure debt service.

Bordo and Kydland argue that adherence to the gold standard sent a strong signal of resolve to international markets, serving as a "good housekeeping seal of approval."[17] Drawing on secondary market bond yields from 1870 to 1914, Bordo and Rockoff show that the terms of access to external finance fared better among gold standard adopters.[18] To their surprise, Bordo, Edelstein, and Rockoff find supportive evidence for the gold standard in the interwar period despite the turbulence in international markets.[19] Obstfeld and Taylor size adherence to the gold standard at about 30 basis points before 1914, but they find no effect during the interwar period.[20]

Other scholars are more critical of the gold standard. Ferguson and Schularick argue that gold was insufficient to credibly commit to stable

---

15. Tomz (2007).

16. This trade-off is known as the Mundell-Fleming trilemma.

17. Bordo and Kydland (1995).

18. Bordo and Rockoff (1996).

19. Bordo, Edelstein, and Rockoff (1999).

20. Obstfeld and Taylor (2004).

macroeconomic policy and debt service.[21] Some countries adopted the gold standard only de jure. Far from blind, international investors looked "behind the thin film of gold," penalizing defectors with higher premiums. Comparing spreads five years into adherence between 1880 and 1914, Mitchener and Weidenmier find that emerging markets in which the gold standard had been adopted still paid a 285-basis-point premium.[22]

4.1.3 THE EMPIRE EFFECT

Grants-in-aid from the metropole were uncommon in the nineteenth century. Instead, British, French, Ottoman, and Spanish colonies floated loans in international capital markets on a regular basis. These loans were marketed in the metropole and occasionally in other financial capitals; for example, Tonkin, a French colony, floated a loan in London in 1896 to finance the construction of a new railway. Private investors did not discriminate in favor of contracting public debt from the empire.[23] Actually, most of the lending went to sovereign nations (refer to chapter 3).

Most research on colonial loans has focused on the British Empire, the largest and best documented and the only one hosting the financial capital of the world.[24] The empire effect—the notion that colonies are treated favorably by investors—was challenged by Obstfeld and Taylor as well as Flandreau and Zumer.[25] By assembling a substantially larger dataset, Ferguson and Schularick revived the empire effect, estimating that membership in the British Empire decreased the spread by 150 basis points between 1880 and 1914.[26] Accominotti, Flandreau, and Rezzik confirm Ferguson and Schularick's results while articulating a novel causal mechanism: British colonies were neither better run nor enjoyed better macroeconomic stability. Simply put, investors anticipated that "strategic default would not be an option because underlying assets could be seized with support of imperial courts."[27]

---

21. Ferguson and Schularick (2006, 2012).
22. Mitchener and Weidenmier (2009).
23. Davis and Huttenback (1986); Feis (1930); Platt (1968).
24. French (2011) and German (2008) capital flows to colonial dominions have been recently examined by Esteves.
25. Obstfeld and Taylor (2004); Flandreau and Zumer (2004).
26. Ferguson and Schularick (2006).
27. Accominotti, Flandreau, and Rezzik (2011, p. 402).

4.2 Empirical Validation of Existing Explanations

In light of the mixed results from existing hypotheses of the bond spread, I seek to test them anew by exploiting a novel dataset that includes more political units than any previous test—as many as 92 and extending back to 1816.[28] For reference, Ferguson and Schularick, the most comprehensive dataset to date, sample 62 political units from 1880 onward.[29]

The outcome variable in this analysis is the effective interest rate at issue ($N = 803$), and the unit of observation is the country-year.[30] Some countries issued more than one loan in a given year. For these cases, I compute the average yield per year, reducing the sample size from 803 to 693 country-year observations between 1816 to 1914.

I draw on conventional measures of the three explanations of the spread. For adherence to the gold standard, I include a time-varying indicator variable drawn from Meissner.[31] I completed this variable with data collected by Officer as well as Reinhart, Rogoff, Trebesch, and Reinhart.[32] Note that the gold standard was adopted by both sovereign and nonsovereign states. For reference, 30 percent of loans in the sample were floated while the local currency was pegged to gold.

I account for reputation arguments in two ways: The most common measure is the record of external default, information drawn from Reinhart and Rogoff.[33] The original variable indicates the onset of default and the restructuring years that followed. Chile, for instance, interrupted debt service between 1826 and 1842 and between 1880 and 1884. The default indicator is 1 for every year in both intervals, and 0 otherwise. To test for reputation, I establish whether an external default took place in the last 10 years, a strategy borrowed from Ferguson and Schularick.[34] Tomz shows that countries borrowing from international markets for the first time paid a premium for lacking a reputation. The indicator variable Unseasoned

28. Refer to chapter 3 for further details about this original dataset.

29. Ferguson and Schularick (2006).

30. The effective interest rate at issue is measured as the ratio of the coupon to the price. See chapter 3 for details.

31. Meissner (2005).

32. Officer (2008); Reinhart et al. (2018).

33. Reinhart and Rogoff (2009).

34. Ferguson and Schularick (2006).

Borrower takes the value 1 for the first loan issued by any given country after 1816.[35]

Finally, I produce a time-variant categorical variable, Empire, to indicate the colonial status of any given territory: for instance, Morocco is treated as an independent country until 1912 and as a (French) colony in 1913–1914.[36] To account for the loss of access to Crown agents, self-governing territories in the British Empire are treated as independent borrowers after 1881.[37] With these data at hand, I model the effective interest rate at issue with an ordinary least squares (OLS) model:

$$\text{Yield at Issue}_{it} = \alpha + \beta_1 \text{Gold Standard}_{it} + \beta_2 \text{Reputation}_{it}$$
$$+ \beta_3 \text{Colonial Status}_{it} + \epsilon_{it} \tag{4.1}$$

Results plotted in figure 4.1 confirm the three hypotheses in the existing literature while extending the sample size in both geographic and temporal scope. Data availability for covariates slightly reduces the sample size; nevertheless, with 95 percent confidence, adherence to the gold standard decreases premiums by 155 basis points, twice the effect of membership in the British Empire. Non-British colonies (the dataset includes French, Ottoman, and Spanish colonies) were levied somewhere between 216 and 157 additional points than independent countries. Results suggest also that reputation matters. Countries in default at least one year during the previous ten were charged a 136-basis-point premium when they issued a new loan in London. First-time borrowers were charged an additional 89 basis points, everything else held constant.

The magnitude of the point estimates in figure 4.1 is arguably modest. Take the worst-case scenario: a non-British colony off gold, recently experiencing default. The predicted premium is 501 basis points, a number far from trivial yet significantly below modern-day premiums.[38] Why were embarrassed governments not penalized by private investors at higher rates? To address this question, we should pay attention to the fine print of loan contracts and what was negotiated in default settlements.

---

35. Tomz (2007).

36. No territory floated a loan in London while a part of the Dutch or German empire, but some did so after gaining independence, for example, Belgium and Tasmania, respectively.

37. The colonial status coefficient is virtually identical if self-governing territories are treated as dependent colonies after 1881.

38. In July 2011, the Greek, Irish, and Portuguese spreads were 1,600, 1,200, and 1,100 basis points, respectively, relative to the German bond (De Santis, 2012, p. 6).

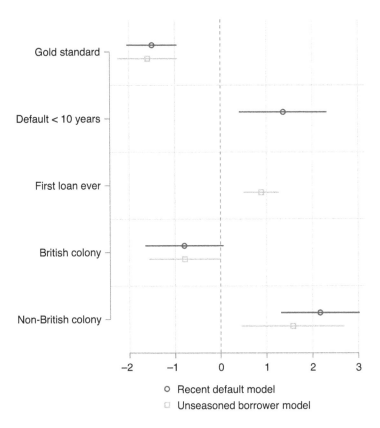

FIGURE 4.1. Test of Existing Explanations of the Bond Spread: Reputation, the Gold Standard, and the Empire Effect. Period covered: 1816–1914. The recent default model samples 69 countries and the unseasoned borrower 82. The reduction in the sample size is attributable to data availability for two controls: default history and the gold standard. Effective interest rate calculated by author. Sources for gold standard: Meissner (2005), Officer (2008), Reinhart et al (2018); for default during the previous 10 years: Reinhart and Rogoff (2009); colonial status: Hensel (2018) and author.

4.3 Loan Contracts and Default Settlements in the Bond Era

International lending in the nineteenth century took place almost exclusively under municipal law, that is, the law of that land where the loan was floated (e.g., London if a bond was quoted at the London Stock Exchange).[39] Until the passage of the Foreign Sovereign Immunity Act in the United States in 1973, countries in default invoked the principle of sovereign immunity to escape municipal jurisdiction. Before the restriction

---

39. See Waibel (2011) for an illuminating treatment of international private law.

imposed by this principle, to sue a sovereign debtor was almost impossible for individual investors.[40] In the absence of a clear legal framework, other mechanisms were necessary to protect bondholders' interests. Overt military coercion, commonly known as gunboat diplomacy, was exceptional.[41] Most often the resolution of default involved ad hoc negotiation and compromise between bondholders and debtors.[42] Default settlements in the Bond Era included debt relief, fresh loans to refinance old debt, and eventually foreign financial control in the form of debt-equity swaps and receiverships.[43] Foreclosure of national assets did not take place in the abstract, but it prioritized state monopolies, land, railroads, and branches of the tax administration hypothecated in previous loan contracts.

4.3.1 DEBT RELIEF

A standard default settlement in the Bond Era was accompanied by a cut in the outstanding debt, a reduction in the interest rate, and the conversion of arrears of interest to new debts.[44] From 1821 to 1871, reduction of standing debt was small, 3 percent of face value on average, but increased to 23 percent in the period from 1870 to 1925. Interest rate cuts were frequent and in the range of 15 percent during both periods.[45] Because settlement could take years to materialize, arrears of interest frequently exceeded the face value of defaulted bonds and often became the lion's share of settlement negotiations. On average, arrears were converted at 75 percent into new bonds issued at low interest rates; the remaining 25 percent was written off by the bondholders. Debt relief, in other words, was substantial in the Bond Era.

4.3.2 FOREIGN FINANCIAL CONTROL

Even if desirable, debt write-offs weakened incentives to enact fiscal reform to service external debt, precluding the equivalence between debt and taxes crucial for state building. But debt condonation was not the main obstacle to state strengthening reform. Debt relief had more important

---

40. Mauro, Sussman, and Yafeh (2006, p. 132). See Verdier and Voeten (2015) and Weide-maier and Gulati (2018) for competing interpretations of the evolution of sovereign immunity.

41. Three prominent episodes of debt-related gunboat diplomacy happened in Mexico in the 1860s, Venezuela in 1902, and Egypt in 1882.

42. Frieden (1994).

43. See Krasner (1999, ch. 5) for an overview.

44. The content of this paragraph borrows from Suter (1992, pp. 94–95).

45. See Borchard (1951, pp. 326–328) for a detailed list of interest rate cuts.

strings attached: it was often granted as part of a larger debt readjustment that included foreign financial control—that is, the exchange of external debt for equity and receiverships.[46]

Debt-Equity Swaps

In order to regain access to international capital markets without paying back loans with tax money, borrowers may lease state-owned monopolies (e.g., a copper mine), key infrastructure (e.g., a railway), and land to foreign bondholders, who exploit the asset until the debt is liquidated. Exchanges of debt for assets are nowadays known as debt-equity swaps.

A textbook example of a debt-equity swap is Peru in 1886. In a default settlement negotiation with British bondholders, Peru exchanged its extant debt for the creation of the Peruvian Corporation, owned and managed by the foreign bondholders. Under the Grace Contract, Peru ceded its state railways to this private company for a period of 66 years, turned over its guano deposits up to a maximum of two million tons, guaranteed the company a subsidy from customs revenue, and endowed it with a land grant of five million acres. In return, Peru regained access to capital markets without having expanded its capacity to tax. Unsurprisingly, dependence on external finance persisted.[47]

Debt-equity swaps were a fairly common practice in loan negotiations in Latin America as well as in Eastern and Southern Europe: They had occurred earlier in Peru (1865, guano), and also in Brazil (1906, coffee), Bulgaria (1904, tobacco), Colombia (1861, land), Costa Rica (1871 and 1885, railways), the Dominican Republic (1893, railways), Ecuador (1855, land; 1895, railways), El Salvador (1899, railways), Greece (1893, salt, petroleum, and cigarette paper, among others commodities), Paraguay (1855, land; 1877, railways and land), Portugal (1891, tobacco), Serbia (1881, railroads, salt, and tobacco), Spain (1835, mercury), and Venezuela (1886, railways), among others.[48]

Receiverships

Instead of state-owned monopolies, borrowers could lease parts of the tax administration to foreign investors, often customshouses in key ports. Setting up a receivership required the creation of a parallel bureaucracy

---

46. Suter and Stamm (1992, p. 659). The Ottoman case, elaborated in chapter 5, offers a specific example.

47. Further details about external finance of Peru in chapter 2.

48. Borchard (1951); Gnjatović (2009); Mauro and Yafeh (2003); Nadal (1975); Suter (1992); Wynne (1951).

or debt administration council to monitor or take control of tax collection. Receiverships could be operated by private foreign investors (e.g., the Ottoman Public Debt Administration) or be under the direct supervision of a foreign power (e.g., the US in the Dominican Republic). By creating a receivership, borrowers surrendered power over the portion of revenue that became the property of the bondholders or the collecting agency and distributed it in accordance with the loan agreement.[49] The receivership was terminated when external debt was liquidated.

Receiverships were relatively frequent despite the obvious breach in national sovereignty. They were established in China (1911), Costa Rica (1911), the Dominican Republic (1905–1913), Egypt (1881–1913), Greece (1898–1913), Liberia (1912–1913), Morocco (1905–1911), Nicaragua (1912), Serbia (1895–1913), Tunisia (1870–1881), Turkey (1882–1913), Uruguay (1903), and Venezuela (1902–1903), among others.

Mitchener and Weidenmier find that 28% of default episodes ended up in receivership, which they refer to as "fiscal house arrest."[50] As valuable and meaningful as this estimate is, Mitchener and Weidenmier's data do not account for preemptive revenue control clauses like the one imposed in Portugal in 1892,[51] or in the 1902, 1904, and 1907 French loans to Bulgaria,[52] or in China in 1898, when European bondholders gained monitoring power over customs revenue as a precondition to issue three new loans to pay war indemnities to Japan.[53] Mitchener and Weidenmier's estimate does not include debt-equity swaps either. This is meant not as a criticism but as a call to attention to the underestimated ability of bondholders to seize foreign assets upon sovereign default. Next, I offer a framework for the study of foreign financial control and its implications for both the spread and state capacity building in the Bond Era and beyond.

4.4 Extreme Conditionality and Enforcement

In chapter 2, I introduced the notion of extreme conditionality—that is, severe sanctions resulting from interrupting debt service, including

---

49. Borchard (1951, p. 93).

50. Mitchener and Weidenmier (2010). Properly, Mitchener and Weidenmier's estimate includes receiverships and military intervention, but the latter is anecdotal.

51. Wynne (1951, pp. 371–382).

52. Tooze and Ivanov (2011).

53. Feis (1930) and van de Ven (2014). Foreign direct control of Chinese customs would arrive in 1911.

debt-equity swaps and receiverships. The concept of extreme conditionality resonates with the notion of supersanctions in Mitchener and Weidenmier, under whose framework supersanctions were imposed on borrowing nations manifesting bad behavior ex post, and on a case-by-case basis.[54] I conjecture that the possibility of imposing foreign financial control was gradually enshrined in the norms of international lending. It became a practice of debt collection mutually recognized by investors and borrowers and agreed upon at time of issue, or ex ante. Access to foreign funds was conditional on the hypothecation of public assets, which were the focal point of foreign control in case of default. By pledging key sources of revenue, emerging countries accessed international credit markets at unprecedented low rates.

Handing over domestic assets to foreign bondholders was considered a national humiliation. By raising the domestic cost of default for a given sitting incumbent, extreme conditionality was meant to minimize the likelihood of default. However, it did not always prevent default; and when that happened, a supersanction followed in the form of a debt-equity swap and/or receivership. This sequence of events is far more common than is generally understood: supersanctions were imposed on at least half of countries that defaulted between 1870 and 1913, and on 70 percent of those that suspended debt service more than once.[55] How were private bondholders capable of imposing and executing extreme conditionality on sovereign states?

Far from easy tasks, seizing assets and establishing receiverships required first and foremost the approval of the local government. Receiverships were often unpopular with governments because they were interpreted as an improper delegation of power.[56] The first impulse of an embarrassed government was to oppose seizure and invoke the principle of sovereign immunity to prevent investors from suing them.

In the first half of the nineteenth century, foreign bondholders organized into ad hoc committees to negotiate settlements bilaterally with governments in default.[57] In order to extract favorable concessions, bondholders would deny new bonds to countries in default, a practice known as *credit exclusion*. This practice was officially adopted at the LSE soon after

---

54. Mitchener and Weidenmier (2010).

55. Mitchener and Weidenmier (2010, p. 27).

56. Hyde (1922, p. 535). In some instances, receiverships were welcomed by local authorities, for instance, in Santo Domingo (Maurer, 2013, ch. 3). One may safely count that as an exception.

57. Flandreau (2013).

the 1820s debt crises.[58] Chabot and Santarosa argue that the hypothecation of national assets and sources of revenue perfected credit exclusion because they simplified the interpretation of a breach of contract.[59] If a borrower secured two loans on the same asset or used pledged revenue streams for purposes other than those stipulated in the loan contract, the LSE would consider that as clear evidence of bad faith and deny fresh capital. In anticipation, borrowers would be cautious about pledging assets and using them for spurious ends. In this way, pledges strengthened the logic of reputation in external finance.

Although credit exclusion allowed bondholders to negotiate favorable terms in default settlements, it was hardly enough to enforce swaps and receiverships. These required coercive power, which bondholders lacked. There is little discussion in the literature about the eagerness of French and German governments to intercede in favor of their investors.[60] The French government exerted tight control on the loans floated at the Paris Bourse and refused a quotation when disapproving the nature or direction of a loan.[61] Often, French and German governments brokered loans on behalf of private investors, particularly in the arms trade,[62] and exerted diplomatic pressure on default settlement negotiations.[63] Diplomatic pressure could end up in economic concessions, financial control, and even occupation, like the French did in Tunisia (1881) and Morocco (1912) to "safeguard the claims of French bondholders."[64]

The United States also grew more interventionist in the negotiations of loans and default settlement.[65] Following the Monroe Doctrine, the US pursued a "debt-enforcement empire" in Central and South America and sponsored "controlled loans," by which the debtor country agreed to allow the US or a US appointee to take over tariff or internal tax collection in the event of default—an example of extreme conditionality.[66] *Dollar diplomacy* reached its zenith under President Taft (1909–1913), when the US administration brokered loan contracts in China, Argentina, and Mexico on behalf

58. Neal and Davis (2006, p. 288).
59. Chabot and Santarosa (2017).
60. Feis (1930); Rich (1992); Stern (1977); Viner (1929).
61. Platt (1968, p. 7).
62. Grant (2007).
63. Feis (1930, chs. 5 and 6).
64. Cohen (1986, p. 107).
65. Maurer (2013); Mitchener and Weidenmier (2005); Perez and Weissman (2006).
66. Ahmed, Alfaro, and Maurer (2010, p. 40).

of major bankers (including the Morgan firms, now JP Morgan), blurring the line between national and private interests.[67]

In the later decades of the nineteenth century, the French, German, and US governments resorted to financial diplomacy to advance their economic and geostrategic interests. Foreign policy involved interfering in otherwise private contracts between domestic merchant banks and foreign governments. Many have argued that Britain did not follow that path, standing for free and open markets. I argue instead that Britain's laissez-faire policy in the Bond Era was gradually abandoned for three reasons: First, a process of elite replacement within the British state apparatus placed financial interests at the vanguard of foreign policy priorities. Second, private bondholders perfected the art of lobbying for diplomatic assistance at the time of contracting new loans and negotiating default settlements with foreign nations. Third, in the "age of empire,"[68] the Foreign Office was compelled to counter competing powers' open interventionism in financial markets. Under these conditions, bondholders grew their ability to insert extreme conditionality clauses in private loan contracts and execute them in case of default. Next, I elaborate on these circumstances.

4.4.1 ELITE REPLACEMENT

The second half of the nineteenth century witnessed the birth of the "gentlemanly class" in Britain, a coalition between landed aristocracy and new banking elites.[69] The British aristocracy found in finance an opportunity to maintain its status and lifestyle in times of land decline. For financial elites, this coalition offered a fast track to high social status and political access. The gentlemanly class specialized in commercial activities (finance, shipping, and insurance) and civil service (government and military).

This new coalition knitted a tight and closed network. They attended the same public schools (e.g., Eton) and universities (Oxford and Cambridge), were members of the same London clubs, and married within one another's families.[70] A famous example is the foreign secretary and later prime minister, the 5th Earl of Rosebery, married to Hannah de Rothschild

---

67. Carosso (1987, p. 594).
68. Hobsbawm (1987).
69. Cain and Hopkins (2016).
70. Cassis (1994) and Scott (2003) for in-depth anthropologies of the gentlemanly class.

and criticized for "fail[ing] to achieve the complete separation of his private and public interest."[71]

The gentlemanly class assumed a high profile in public office. The Conservative party represented their general interest, and occasionally banking families held parliamentary seats themselves.[72] However, foreign policy was largely decided by the executive branch of government, where patronage appointments remained fairly common. Taking advantage of aristocratic dominance of the state bureaucracy, the new gentlemanly class secured a disproportional presence in the Treasury, the Foreign Office, and the Colonial Office, as well as in the British administration in India, Southeast Asia, Africa, and diplomatic positions in Latin America.[73]

Meanwhile, the big banking families held seats on the board of the Bank of England, a quasi-state apparatus that managed the gold standard mechanism, hence the solvency and prestige of issue houses and, by extension, the health of British and colonial public credit.[74] Almost organically, the fates of the old landed elites, the new financial sector, and the British Empire grew tightly connected. Securing fair treatment to foreign investors overseas became a matter of national interest rather naturally.[75]

"This degree of coherence or like-mindedness [between state officials and international bankers] explains why, at the top of the gentlemanly order, the barriers between business and government were no more than mobile Chinese walls."[76] In other words, the weight that finance gained in foreign policy during the Bond Era resulted from preference alignment, not nefarious practices (e.g., bribing). Alignment should not be confounded either with blind support or capture, a thesis defended by Hobson and popularized by Vladimir Lenin.[77] The British government represented various interests and remained accountable to Parliament, where industrial interests—who opposed imperialism, the gold standard, and foreign investment—were also represented.[78]

71. Ferguson (2004, p. 286).

72. See Cassis (1994, table 8.3) for members of Parliament of high-finance extraction.

73. Cain and Hopkins (2016, p. 125); Ingham (1984, p. 151); Smith (1979, p. 5).

74. Keeping prestige was of outmost importance to issue houses because they lived by their reputation (Flandreau and Flores, 2009).

75. Green (1992, p. 203); Ingham (1984, p. 131).

76. Cain and Hopkins (2016, p. 50).

77. Hobson (1902); Lenin (1934).

78. In contemporary debate, imperialism was associated with higher taxes (to fund military spending) and underinvestment in local productive development (Daunton, 2002, p. 129). Actually, less than 10 percent of British industrial development in 1907 received capital from London

Before granting government support, bondholders were expected to exhaust all legal means in the borrowing country and show that the latter had breached international law, for instance, "in instances where specific revenues that had been pledged as collateral to bondholders were willfully diverted for other purposes. Such behavior, to the Victorian mind, was simply bad faith."[79] The Foreign Office was strict in its reading of the situation because of potential perverse incentives that intervention could create, namely, imprudent lending in expectation of diplomatic assistance.[80] And yet, government intervention grew fairly common in the last decades of the nineteenth century.

4.4.2   FOREIGN BONDHOLDERS' COORDINATION

Small investors were left out of the gentlemanly class, but purchased government securities from them—namely, merchant banks, issue houses, or underwriters (I use the three expressions interchangeably). The underwriters could market sovereign bonds in primary markets or buy all of them outright and sell them in secondary markets.[81] Although underwriters kept a residual share of the bonds they marketed to cultivate confidence in their product, small investors were the ultimate buyers of sovereign bonds.

In case of default, issue houses and small investors did not necessarily share strategy. Issue houses tended to favor faster settlements to

---

(Ingham, 1984, p. 146). A good example of Liberal opposition to government support to foreign bondholders can be found in Sir Campbell-Bannerman's speech in a parliamentary debate about a famous episode of gunboat diplomacy in Venezuela (1902–1903): "Behind these poor fishermen [the pretext to gunboat Venezuela], who were so convenient for the noble Lord and the [Conservative] Government, there lies the great body of financial claims culminating in the claims of the bondholders. I venture to say that nothing could be more mischievous than that we should even seem to accept the doctrine, if it deserves to be called a doctrine, that when our countrymen invest in risky enterprises in foreign countries and default follows, it is a public duty to rescue them. Every man who invests money in a country like Venezuela knows what he is doing. It would, I suppose, not be quite accurate to say that great risks always mean high dividends, but it is more nearly accurate if you put it the other way about—that high dividends generally involve great risks; but if the whole power of the British Empire is to be put behind the investor, his risk vanishes, and the dividends ought to be reduced accordingly" (Hansard's Parliamentary Debates, Session February 17, 1903, 4th series, vol. 118, p. 71).

79. Cohen (1986, p. 104).

80. Fears of moral hazard are described in Cain and Hopkins (2016, p. 340) and Smith (1979, p. 17) and more generally in Platt (1968) and Lipson (1985).

81. For an extraordinarily clear explanation of how bonds were floated, see Mosley (2003, pp. 256–257).

resume lending and minimize damage to their reputation. Small bondholders tended to be more aggressive in their demands, preferring better to faster settlements—after all, their modest savings were at stake.[82] The creation in 1868 of the Corporation of Foreign Bondholders (CFB) mitigated preference misalignment by putting issue houses and small investors under the same roof.

The CFB was a nongovernmental organization representing private holders of foreign securities quoted in the LSE that specialized in negotiating default settlements.[83] Before its creation, small investors organized in self-constituted ad hoc committees to negotiate bilaterally with delinquent payers. There existed no institutionalized structure to coordinate action and share information with other bondholders or to represent their claims to the British government.[84]

Both small investors and loan contracting houses were represented in the governing body of the CFB—the Council—facilitating compromise and unity of action in default negotiations.[85] The CFB was organized into permanent and country-specific committees, which reported to the Council on a regular basis. The Council disseminated this information[86] and shamed members who defected from credit exclusion.[87] The CFB was involved in the negotiation of every single settlement involving British capital.[88] Advances in bondholders' coordination and specialization help explain why the number and rapidity of default settlements were highest after the inauguration of the CFB.[89]

---

82. Flandreau and Flores (2012a) show that the misalignment between bondholders and prestigious underwriters was smaller because the latter had strong incentives to demand tougher restructuring conditions to preserve their reputation.

83. Similar associations were formed in other financial capitals: the Vereeniging voor den Effecthandel was founded in Amsterdam in 1876, the Association Nationale des Porteurs Francais de Valeurs Mobilières in Paris in 1898, the Association Belge pour la Défense des Détenteurs de Fonds Publics in Belgium in 1903, and the Spezial-Organisation zur Vertretung der Schweizerischen Finanzinteressen im Ausland in Switzerland in 1913.

84. Wynne and Borchard (1933, p. 285).

85. Disagreements between small and big investors did not vanish after 1868 and were a subject of regular discussion. A CFB reorganization in 1898 gave further leverage to small bondholders.

86. Mauro, Sussman, and Yafeh (2006).

87. Wright (2005).

88. The one exception was the negotiation of the Brazilian default of 1898 (Esteves, 2007, p. 25).

89. Suter (1992, ch. 6). For in-depth analysis of CFB effectiveness, see Eichengreen and Portes (1986, 1989), Kelly (1998), and Mauro, Sussman, and Yafeh (2006).

The degree of governmental involvement in loan and default negotiations was the subject of heated debate in the early years of the CFB. Although government intervention could help solve default crises (to the liking of small investors), it could also scare away borrowers and hurt the business model (which merchant banks feared). Both positions were heard as early as the first general meeting in 1873. The low-interventionism position prevailed in that inaugural meeting, but the relationship between the CFB and the government grew stronger shortly thereafter.[90]

Indeed, as early as 1876, the CFB sought government support following Egypt's external default. British bondholders were the main creditors to the Khedive, as the Egyptian government was known at the time, and the CFB requested government support and the use of force if necessary. For that, the CFB hired top negotiators and organized public gatherings to gain the sympathy of the financial press and prominent conservative politicians, including Lord Salisbury, then secretary of state for India, and Sir Stafford Northcote, chancellor of the Exchequer.[91] If there was any doubt, "there has never been a time when our commercial and financial interests have been so eager to embark in costly military operations as they are now," the *Economist* wrote.[92]

Lobbying efforts succeeded. Foreign financial control and gunboat diplomacy followed and Egypt became a British protectorate in 1882. Although multiple economic considerations were at play—the Suez Canal was critical to secure trade flux with India[93]—the CFB shares responsibility for the loss of Egyptian sovereignty.[94] Importantly, foreign financial control of Egypt helped bondholders recover their investment and expand their business in the region.[95]

The CFB also sought support of British officials overseas. "From the earliest [annual] report to the latest it is clear that the diplomatic agents of Great Britain acted on behalf of the bondholders in their respective countries and thereby rendered invaluable service which no organization without quasi-official standing could have commanded."[96] For instance,

---

90. Ronald (1935, pp. 424–426).

91. Meszaros (1973, p. 429).

92. *Economist*, XL (July 29, 1882), pp. 936–937.

93. Kohli (2019, ch. 2) for the importance of Egypt for trade with India.

94. Meszaros (1973, p. 438). For additional discussion on lobbying by bondholders in Great Britain, see Smith (1979, pp. 16–24).

95. Hansen (1983).

96. Ronald (1935, p. 425). The first annual report dates as of 1873.

in 1884, the CFB requested the assistance of the British representative in Paraguay, Sir Edmund John Monson—of gentlemanly extraction—in the negotiations of a default settlement, upheld since 1874. Although we can only speculate about what was discussed in those meetings, within months Paraguay agreed to the bond conversion suggested by the bondholders. Diplomatic support was duly acknowledged: "The thanks of the Bondholders are due to Mr. Monson for the assistance he has rendered to Dr. Stewart [the CFB agent in Paraguay] in obtaining this result."[97]

In sum, concerted action between big and small bondholders perfected the art of credit exclusion and enhanced the CFB's capacity to reach for government assistance. Combined with preference alignment between high finance and high politics—reproduced also within the original CFB Council, where 9 of the 29 members were members of Parliament[98]—the Corporation elevated qualitatively the bondholder's bargaining power vis-à-vis embarrassed governments. Next, I assess the third and last ingredient for the enforceability of extreme conditionality—the international context under which sovereign loans were contracted.

4.4.3   THE AGE OF EMPIRE

Officially, the British government in the Bond Era interpreted defaults as the consequence of imprudent investment and preferred to stay away from what was considered a private matter.[99] Over time, the principle of nonintervention was relaxed because of the imperialistic ambitions of Great Britain coupled with that of competing powers: France, Russia, and later Germany and the United States.[100]

In the absence of international law that supported government intervention on behalf of private matters, British government action was initially guided by the Palmerston Doctrine of 1849. Responding to bondholders' supplication for assistance, Foreign Secretary Palmerston issued a circular to the House of Commons on March 2, 1849, in which he enshrined the British government policy upon sovereign default of private capital. The spirit of this policy may be summarized in one paragraph:

> It is simply therefore a question of discretion with the British Government whether this matter should or should not be taken up by

97. *Annual Report of Foreign Bondholders*, vol. 12 (1885, p. 95).
98. Ronald (1935, fn. 31).
99. Lipson (1985, p. 187).
100. Cain and Hopkins (2016); Feis (1930).

diplomatic negotiation and the decision of that question of discretion turns entirely upon British and domestic considerations.[101]

This circular was "sufficiently broad to permit the British Government to justify any course it chose to take."[102] In a now classic text, D.C.M. Platt argues that the British government intervened on behalf of British investors only when preexisting geostrategic considerations were at stake.[103] Cain and Hopkins suspect that Platt's own readings of official intervention "follow the workings of the official mind rather too closely,"[104] an interpretation I generally share.

Platt concedes a change in approach to foreign defaults after 1870, when other Great Powers were pushing for empire: "It proved impossible [for the Foreign Office] to remain entirely inflexible on non-intervention, especially in cases where political interests were likely to be damaged."[105] Under this international context, "the Foreign Office invariably felt obliged at least to make sure that British bondholders received treatment parallel to that obtained by other nationalities."[106] From Platt's point of view, British interventionism in financial markets was reactive, that is, a response to that of other European powers on behalf of their bondholders.

The revised doctrine of British diplomacy by the turn of the nineteenth century was enshrined in 1889 in an interview with Lord Salisbury (three times prime minister):

The Foreign Office judged each case on its particular circumstance. In cases of simple default due to misfortune or necessity, it would be improper for H. M. Government to exact payment; but where unfair discrimination had been exercised between equal creditors, or where the

101. House of Commons, *State Papers British and Foreign* XLII, March 2, 1849, p. 385.

102. Feis (1930, p. 103).

103. Platt (1968), and Lipson (1985) and Tomz (2007) for concurrent opinion.

104. Cain and Hopkins (2016, p. 265), and Gallagher and Robinson (1953) for concurrent opinion. Notice that Cain and Hopkins and Gallagher and Robinson disagree on the identity of the domestic interest prioritized by the British diplomacy. Cain and Hopkins argue that foreign policy pursued the interest of financial elites, whereas Gallagher and Robinson claim that the Foreign Office chased the interests of manufacturing. My own reading is that those interests often coincided. Take the case of railroad investment overseas: Its expansion was good for steel and locomotive exporters in Britain and that of manufactured goods, which gained new markets to sell their products and import raw materials. At the same time, railroad investment overseas was financed with British capital, benefiting merchant houses in London. Once built, commodity exports were shipped and insured by the same financial circles in London. The empire often advanced both the manufacturing and financial interests at once.

105. Platt (1968, p. 17).

106. Platt (1968, pp. 46–47).

preferential rights and securities of British subjects [read bondholders] were unjustly denied, ground would exist for special sympathy from the Foreign Office.[107]

The new doctrine broadened the set of scenarios in which government intervention was justified while emphasizing refusal to discriminatory treatment relative to creditors from other Great Powers. In a context of imperial competition, however, allegations of discrimination grew fairly common and motivated government intervention. The "scramble for concessions" in late-Qing China, which I return to in chapter 5, is a good example of that.[108]

In general, the Foreign Office would limit diplomatic intervention to "good offices." These, "when exercised by such men as Consul-General Chatfield in Central America or Consul-General Wilson in Chile, must have been difficult indeed to distinguish from unqualified diplomatic intervention."[109] When major economic or geostrategic considerations were at play, the Foreign Office would manage loan contracts and default settlement negotiations firsthand. British diplomacy played a leading role in negotiating loans, securities, and receiverships in Brazil (1913), China (1898–1911), Egypt (1876), Greece (1898), Persia (1889), and Turkey (1875), among others.[110] These negotiations were carried out by state officials—usually of gentlemanly extraction—or hand-picked representatives, like Ernest Cassell, an independent financier who led loan negotiations with Egypt, China, and the Ottoman Empire outside official channels but under the auspices of the Foreign Office.[111]

Military intervention, or gunboat diplomacy, was used as a last resort and employed surgically because it conflicted with the official laissez-faire policy. Famous episodes include military intervention in Egypt (1882), Guatemala (1913), Mexico (1861), Morocco (1910), and Venezuela

---

107. Quoted in Platt (1968, pp. 39–41).

108. Here it suffices to say that British involvement in loan negotiations is consistent with existing models of Great Power competition (e.g., Gent 2007). Protection of bondholders could not have been externalized to other Great Powers as these would have advanced the interests of their nationals. Whenever other powers were involved, the Foreign Office was compelled to abandon laissez-faire politics and prevent discrimination against British bondholders in loan concessions and default settlements.

109. Platt (1968, p. 42).

110. See surveys by Cain and Hopkins (2016), Peterson (2002, pp. 106–111), and Wynne (1951).

111. Thane (1986).

(1902).[112] More importantly, in the age of empire the threat of military intervention shaped expectations about costs of noncompliance with debt obligations.[113] Bear in mind that military intervention was considered an accepted practice of debt collection by the international community until the early part of the twentieth century. In 1902, "at arbitration the Hague Tribunal found not only that Germany and Britain were justified in intervening [militarily in Venezuela for the purpose of debt collection] but also that, because of their willingness to use force to secure justice, they had a right to payment ahead of the powers who had been content with a peaceful solution."[114]

Merchant banks built on those fears to include harsh conditions in loan contracts. For instance, in the late 1890s, the Rothschilds agreed to bail out Brazil at the price of extreme conditionality.[115] The £10 million funding loan floated in London in 1898 required the hypothecation of all federal receipts from customs duties and imposed severe deflationary measures.[116] Why did Brazil accept these terms?

> The Rothschilds simply employed the gentle tools of logical persuasion, conjecturing "that besides the complete loss of the country's credit the measure [i.e., default] could greatly affect Brazil's sovereignty, provoking complaints that could arrive at the extreme of foreign intervention." With contemporary examples of the United States in Cuba, Puerto Rico, and the Philippines, and, even more germane, Great Britain in Egypt, Brazilian politicians took the Rothschilds' threat seriously.[117]

The veiled threat of military intervention, "which was unauthorized but managed to sound authoritative,"[118] speaks to the international context of the time and the expectations that came with external finance and debt

112. Tomz (2007, p. 145) shows evidence that in the first half of the nineteenth century the British government refused to use force on behalf of bondholders as a general rule.

113. Mitchener and Weidenmier (2010, p. 156).

114. Finnemore (2003, p. 28). The Great Powers only renounced military means for debt collection in 1907, when they signed Convention II of the Treaty of the Hague. And even then, it is hard to believe that loan-related concessions in China and elsewhere would have taken place absent the clout of military coercion.

115. At that time, Brazil was experiencing economic hardship, and debt service consumed half of the federal budget. Rothschilds had been the official banker of Brazil since 1855.

116. Cain and Hopkins (2016, p. 283).

117. Topik (1979, p. 331) quoting Manoel Ferraz de Campos Salles, the president of Brazil between 1898 and 1902.

118. Cain and Hopkins (2016, p. 283).

suspension. Atul Kohli summarizes this position as compellingly as English allows:

> It is not surprising that Platt and others searching official records do not find explicit orders, say, from a Palmerston, to the British navy to go secure the Barings loan in Argentina. That is not how power operates. . . . When pressure was needed, the sigh of naval vessels and whispers from proconsuls were often enough to bend the will of rulers on the periphery.[119]

Such whispers carried weight. Take Venezuela: In 1849, Congress passed the *Ley de Espera y Quita*, which extended the maturity of loan contracts up to nine years.[120] Outraged by this unilateral move, British bondholders sought diplomatic assistance from the Chargé d'Affairs, Belford H. Wilson, who petitioned backup from the Royal Navy. Wilson's request received support from Thomas Cochrane, then commander-in-chief of the North America and West Indies Station of the British Navy, who in correspondence with Wilson confirmed that he "was assembling [in Trinidad] a force sufficient to effect whatever is necessary to the accomplishment of Her Majesty's command."[121] When Wilson presented a copy of Mr. Cochrane's note to the Venezuelan government, the foreign minister agreed to discuss the settlement of the claims. Within weeks, the controversial law was abolished and the rights of foreign bondholders were reinstated.[122] No display of military force was necessary. A note sufficed.[123]

Driven by conviction, dragged by other Great Powers' desires for empire, and possibly both, British diplomatic intervention accelerated in the 1870s. The British government openly interfered in loan contracts

119. Kohli (2019, p. 74).

120. Banko (1995).

121. The quoted text was pronounced by Thomas Cochrane—not coincidentally, of gentlemanly extraction—and was referenced by Wilson in his correspondence with Lord Palmerston (Carl, 1980, pp. 109–110).

122. The Venezuelan government accused Wilson of colluding at a profit with the board of investors of the British Colonial Bank, inaugurated in 1839 to manage the liquidation of foreign debt contracted to finance the war of independence from Spain. The allegations were denied by the British creditors and Mr. Wilson (Carl, 1980, p. 111).

123. This example sheds light on the empirical challenge of testing gunboat diplomacy with hard data. The best test to date is offered by Tomz (2007), who concludes that gunboat diplomacy was not regularly used for the purpose of debt collection. That analysis draws from military interstate dispute data (Jones, Bremer, and Singer, 1996), which lists threats, naval display, and overt military action, but does not account for much of the opaque yet key diplomatic back channels like the one employed by Mr. Wilson in 1850.

and default settlements in Latin America, West Africa, Zanzibar, Burma, Malaya, Persia, China, and the Ottoman Empire, among others.[124] By the early 1900s, there was little doubt about the advantages of loan diplomacy, as the British minister to Persia reminded the Foreign Office:

> The more we get [Persia] into our debt, the greater will be our hold and our political influence over her government. Once the day of liquidation comes, the greater Persia's financial obligation to us . . . the stronger will be our moral claim to an authoritative voice in the settlement.[125]

The risks associated with external finance were also felt by sovereign borrowers. The so-called Drago Doctrine, which considers military means for the purpose of debt repayment unlawful, originated in the early twentieth century in Latin America as a response to European gunboat diplomacy in Venezuela. Luis M. Drago, lawyer, journalist, and minister of foreign affairs of Argentina (in office 1902–1903), denounced the "subordination . . . of the local government to the creditor nation so frequently repeated in recent history."[126] Drago's writing eloquently reflects how the Palmerston and Salisbury doctrines were understood in the Global South:

> Many hold to the circular of Lord Palmerston of 1848, confirmed in 1880 by Lord Salisbury, according to which the right of military intervention is indisputable, it to be decided in each case whether it is advisable or not from simple considerations of expediency of purely national and domestic character.[127]

The Drago Doctrine was incorporated into international law only after 1907, and it applied to cases of insolvency, not fraud, leaving room for interpretation.[128] Fears of military coercion in the age of empire were shared beyond Latin America, and I illustrate that in chapter 9 when I examine the relationship between external finance and state building in Thailand, Ethiopia, and Japan.

To recapitulate, the bargaining power of British investors vis-à-vis peripheral economies grew over time as a result of elite replacement within the British government, bondholders' organizational gains, and Great

---

124. McLean (1976, p. 305).

125. A. Hardinge to Lansdowne, July 18, 1903, C.P. [8399] cited in McLean (1976, pp. 297–298).

126. Drago (1907, p. 725).

127. Drago (1907, pp. 697–698).

128. Drago (1907, p. 704).

Power rivalries for territorial and economic concessions. Under such conditions, investors were able to insert extreme conditionality clauses in loan contracts and have them enforced in case of default thanks to implicit or explicit governmental support.

The language of loan contracts gradually reflected the increased bargaining power of bondholders. Most often, loans required the hypothecation of assets with the understanding that these would be subject to foreign confiscation in case of default. At other times, loan contracts explicitly incorporated debt-equity swaps and receiverships if service was interrupted, solidifying investors' expectations. For instance, Bulgaria secured a new loan in 1892 for a mortgage on the Kaspitshan-Sofia-Kyustendil and Rustchuk-Varna railways plus the revenues and dues of the two harbors. In case of default, foreign bondholders were entitled after six months to take over the railroads and to sell them if necessary after two years. Explicit references to swaps and receiverships in case of debt suspension were introduced in the loan contracts of China (1898, 1911, 1913), Costa Rica (1911), El Salvador (1922), Liberia (1906), Morocco (1904), Poland (1920), Portugal (1891), and Serbia (1902, 1906, 1909, 1913), to name a few examples.

4.5 An Empirical Investigation of Extreme Conditionality

In this section, I assess a key aspect of extreme conditionality: the relationship between pledges and the spread. If pledges are credible—read seizable—collateralized bonds should be rewarded by investors with a lower premium. Asset seizure did not occur in the abstract. The legal basis for debt-equity swaps and receiverships comprised pledges made at the time of contracting a new loan. Law scholars recognize that pledges in the Bond Era had intrinsic legal value: First, collateralized loans received priority in the negotiation of default settlements. Loans with pledges would be repaid first and subject to lower interest reduction and principal haircuts.[129] Second, lenders of loans that were pledged had priority in the control or administration of those resources in case of financial intervention.[130] If investors anticipated the ability to enforce swaps or receiverships in case of default, and collateralized assets served as focal points in default

---

129. Irmscher (2007).
130. Borchard (1951, pp. 98–100).

settlements, then loans containing pledges would be expected to carry a lower interest rate.

Chabot and Santarosa have shown the impact of pledges on bond prices in secondary markets by comparing the bond price of collateralized and noncollateralized loans in two important cases: Spain (1870–1874) and Argentina (1887–1899).[131] Their research design focuses on loans that were virtually equivalent except for the presence of pledges, showing a cleanly identified negative effect of collateral on bond prices. In the empirical exercise that follows, I take a different and complementary route by examining under a regression framework the effect of pledges on interest rates in primary markets for as many as 88 countries from 1858 to 1914. Unlike Chabot and Santarosa, my analysis emphasizes the importance of imperial competition between Great Powers for the credibility of loan pledges.

4.5.1 CODING PLEDGES

To test the effect of pledging on the price of capital, I digitized the *Stock Exchange Loan and Company Prospectuses* collection held by the Guildhall Library, City of London, where the archives of the LSE are currently stored. This collection includes 707 bond prospectuses for 88 countries floated or marketed in London between 1858 and 1914 (earliest and latest entry).[132] I considered all government and government-guaranteed loans regardless of their official use: war, debt conversion, and infrastructure.[133] In coding pledges out of the prospectuses, I dismissed general statements—for example, loans secured upon the "general revenue of the country," a frequent rhetorical recourse—and focused on specific pledges—for instance, a tobacco monopoly or the customs receipts in a major port.

Specific pledges reduced asymmetric information about the value of the collateral. Prospectuses often included information about the yearly income generated by the specific pledge (see, for instance, figure 4.4a); other times, loans were collateralized against the very same infrastructure to be financed by external capital (for instance, a new railroad; see

131. Chabot and Santarosa (2017).

132. The collection lists company prospectuses before 1858, but the first sovereign loan is dated as of that year.

133. For fungibility of government income, refer to chapter 6.

£600,000, or Fcs. 15,000,000, or 4,000,000 Thalers.

ROUMANIAN STATE RAILWAY
L O A N,
WITH GOVERNMENT GUARANTEE.

Being balance of a Loan of £4,800,000, issued in Berlin, and authorized by the Act of Concession voted by the Legislative Bodies and sanctioned by Decree (No. 1,516) of His Highness Prince Charles I., of Roumania, dated September 21st (October 3rd), 1868.

To be issued in Bonds to Bearer of £15 each, or in multiples of Four, Eight, or Ten Bonds respectively, bearing Interest at 7½ per cent. per Annum.

The Interest to commence from the 1st January, 1870, and to be payable half-yearly on the 1st January and 1st July in each year.

The Bonds to be Redeemed at par, by the operation of an accumulating Sinking Fund, in yearly drawings. The first drawing to take place on the 1st March following the completion of the Line, from Galatz to Roman.

Messrs. GLYN, MILLS, CURRIE & Co. are authorised by the Contractors of the Loan to receive subscriptions for the above Bonds, which are issued by virtue of a Concession granted by His Highness Prince Charles I., of Roumania, and approved by the Roumanian Chambers, on the 3rd of October, 1868, to provide the requisite capital for the construction of Railways in the Principalities. A portion of the contemplated lines has already been opened, and a further section is expected to be opened in the course of two or three weeks, and the remaining lines by the end of August, and before October, 1870, and only for a small portion of the lines, the latest time is stipulated to be in the course of 1871. The present issue of the Bonds is designed for the works and purchases executed, and all particulars will be found in the Report of the Special Commissary of the Roumanian Government, appended to this Prospectus. In the same official document, a literal translation of which is annexed, will be found in detail the various terms and conditions of the issue. The Loan bears the immediate and unconditional guarantee of the Roumanian Government for the due payment of interest, and is moreover secured on the entire property of all the conceded Railways.

FIGURE 4.2. Example 1: Pledge in the 1870 Romanian Bond. Excerpt of original prospectus. *Source: The Stock Exchange Loan and Company Prospectuses.* Adaptation of image digitized at the Guildhall Library, City of London.

figure 4.2). Those prospectuses detailed expected returns of the project, including operational expenses and yearly income.[134] All this information

---

134. In the Romanian railroad loan just mentioned, the prospectus was followed by a one-page note specifying the route of the railroad, locomotives, passenger carriages, and expected

REPUBLIC OF SAN DOMINGO.

ISSUE OF £1,500,000 DOMINICAN UNIFIED DEBT 4 PER CENT. BONDS.

Being part of a total of £4,236,750 authorized by Law of August 9th, 1897, and created for the purpose of discharging all the Bonded and Floating Debts of the Republic, all of which have separate special securities attached to them, and of unifying and applying all those securities to this new Debt.

The remainder of the creation under the denomination of "Obligations Or de St. Domingue," bearing $2\frac{3}{4}$ per cent. interest and redeemable in 1999, out of surplus revenue, has been applied to the conversion at par of the Gold Bonds of 1893 (chiefly held in Belgium) in accordance with arrangements made between the Government and the **Committees of Bondholders in Belgium** which have been submitted to and approved by the **London Committee of Bondholders**, acting in conjunction with the **Council of Foreign Bondholders** in London.

(a) Title page

of the "Caisse de la Regie" will hereafter be made under the advice and approval of the Council of Foreign Bondholders in London. It is also provided by Law, and will be a term of the contract with the Bondholders, that in case of any default in the payment of Coupon or Sinking Fund, or in case of "other manifest necessity," the Improvement Company under its powers as their Trustee shall call upon the Governments of the United States, Great Britain, Belgium, Holland and France to each name a Commissioner, and the Dominican Government consents that the person or persons so appointed shall constitute a "**Financial Commission**" for the purpose of collecting directly the Revenues of the Republic and exercising the functions of the "Caisse de la Regie."

(b) Pledge clause

FIGURE 4.3. Example 2: Pledges in the 1897 Dominican Bond. Excerpts of original prospectus. *Source*: *The Stock Exchange Loan and Company Prospectuses.* Adaptation of image digitized at the Guildhall Library, City of London.

was meant to attract the attention of investors while helping them calibrate the expected return in case of default.

A total of 175 prospectuses, or 29.8 percent of the sample, include one or more specific pledges, with the vast majority of bonds with pledges involving sovereign countries, not colonial dependencies. To minimize coding assumptions, I set Pledge to 1 whenever a country includes one or more specific pledges in a loan contract and 0 otherwise. I offer three examples in figures 4.2–4.4. The first is from 1870, when the Romanian government issued a loan in various financial capitals of Europe to build a state railway (figure 4.2). This particular loan was "secured on the entire property of all the conceded Railways," as stated in the last line of the excerpt in figure 4.2.

---

income: "Exports c[ould] be effected [by the railroad] in a safe and comparatively cheap way—the above figures [200 million francs of export value yearly] will be doubled."

IMPERIAL CHINESE GOVERNMENT
5% TIENTSIN-PUKOW RAILWAY SUPPLEMENTARY LOAN

FOR

£4,800,000 STERLING.
Present Issue £3,000,000.

AUTHORISED BY IMPERIAL EDICT,

WHICH HAS BEEN COMMUNICATED TO THE MINISTERS OF GREAT BRITAIN AND GERMANY IN PEKING.

This Loan which is the direct obligation of the Imperial Chinese Government for principal and interest is specifically secured by a first charge upon the Provincial Revenues specified herein to the aggregate amount of 3,600,000 Haikuan Taels (say £500,000) per annum, and by a second charge upon the Provincial Revenues referred to herein to the aggregate amount of 3,800,000 Haikuan Taels (say £528,000) per annum.

Principal and Interest free from Chinese Taxes and Imposts.

ISSUE IN LONDON OF £1,110,000 5% STERLING BONDS,

BEING PART OF THE

above ISSUE of £3,000,000, of which the remaining £1,890,000 is offered for subscription in Germany upon similar terms.

(a) Title page

So long as principal and interest of the Loan are regularly paid, there is to be no interference with these provincial revenues; but if principal or interest of the Loan be in default at due date, then, after a reasonable period of grace, likin and suitable internal revenues of the four provinces sufficient to provide the amount above stated are to be forthwith transferred to, and administered by, the Imperial Maritime Customs, in the interest of the Bondholders. And so long as this Loan or any part thereof shall remain unredeemed, it is to have priority both as regards principal and interest, subject to the obligations created by Article 9 of the Loan Agreement of 13th January, 1908, over all future Loans, charges and mortgages charged on the above-mentioned revenues of the four Provinces.

(b) Pledge clause

FIGURE 4.4. Example 3: Pledges in the 1910 Chinese Bond. Excerpts of original prospectus. *Source*: *The Stock Exchange Loan and Company Prospectuses.* Adaptation of image digitized at the Guildhall Library, City of London.

Figure 4.3 shows a second type of security: control over the tax administration in case of default, the so-called receivership. In this example, the government of Santo Domingo (modern-day Dominican Republic) agreed to hand over the tax administration to the Corporation of Foreign Bondholders (CFB) in London in case of default. As reflected in the loan, tax collection had already been externalized to an American firm a few years earlier—a sign of low fiscal capacity.[135] The loan required the agreement of Santo Domingo, the CFB, the American firm, and the American government. The effective rate at issue for this loan was 6.1 percent, 230 basis points above the average rate in 1897—a nontrivial yet modest premium considering the dire fiscal position of the country. Unsurprisingly, Santo Domingo suspended debt service two years later. As part of the default settlement negotiations, an American receivership was installed in Santo Domingo (1905–1941), railways were put in the hands of American bondholders, and a monthly installment by the Treasury to an agent nominated by the European bondholders based in Santo Domingo was to be deposited until the debt was liquidated.[136]

The third example, in figure 4.4, shows that foreign intervention clauses were agreed upon with large countries as well—China in this case. The loan of 1910, for instance, allowed foreign bondholders to seize key sources of revenue in case of default. To float that loan, the Chinese government hypothecated the *likin* (internal toll and most lucrative tax in the empire) plus the internal revenues of four provinces: Zhili, Shantung, Kiangsu, and Anhui. If China defaulted, the collection of these revenues would be transferred to the Imperial Maritime Customs Service, a tax agency that was effectively seized by European investors only one year later.[137]

Assessing the £25 million reorganization loan to China in 1913,[138] van de Ven offers an illuminating description of how pledges were perceived by European investors in the era of high imperialism:

> [John] Jordan [the British envoy to China] believed that the [European] banks . . . rel[ied] on the belief that the powers were prepared to

135. Santo Domingo's government had defaulted on a loan floated in 1869 to purchase munitions and new equipment for a cruiser (Wynne, 1951, p. 207). In 1888, the American firm had replaced a Dutch *régie* created for the purpose of debt collection.

136. Wynne (1951, pp. 224–269).

137. Find details of foreign financial control in China in chapter 5.

138. This loan was secured with further *likin*, all the maritime customs revenue, and the Salt Tax Administration. In the event of default, the salt tax was to be put under the management of the Maritime Customs Administration, as occurred with the 1910 loan (Feis, 1930, p. 450).

use gunboat diplomacy to recover their money. He wrote that "lending money to China is a mild form of gambling. The lenders trust to her great natural resources and to political pressure or intervention," adding, "the recovery of all this money will be an unpleasant task for our successors."[139]

This example sheds light on the investors' calculations at the time and the anticipated diplomatic (when not military) intervention of European governments on their behalf. Pledges were not mere scraps of paper: they shaped expectations, and these were reflected in the price of capital.

4.5.2 ANALYSIS

The ability of investors to seize pledged assets grew over time as a result of gentlemanly representation in key government offices, advances in bondholders' organizational capacity, and Great Powers' imperial ambitions. To account for the the time-varying credibility of pledges, I first run a linear interaction between pledging and time:

$$\text{Yield at Issue}_{it} = \alpha + \beta_1 \text{Pledge}_{it} + \beta_2 \text{Year}_t + \beta_3 \text{Pledge}_{it} \times \text{Year}_t$$

$$+ X\beta_4 + \eta_i + \epsilon_{it} \tag{4.2}$$

where X denotes a vector of time-varying country-level controls. I expect β_1 to be positive and β_3 negative. At the beginning of the nineteenth century, the expectation of asset seizure in case of default was remote. Bondholders were good at denying credit if needed but government interventionism on behalf of private investors was unlikely. In those times, the presence of a pledge in a loan contract could reveal a lemon; that is, only countries that anticipated difficulty paying back their debt would have pledged their assets to overcome creditors' doubts, hence $\beta_1 > 0$.

As time passed, bondholders became better organized. By creating encompassing investors' organizations, lenders improved their ability to negotiate with embarrassed governments and to lobby their home government for diplomatic support. By then, European governments were themselves involved in a colonial-imperial race, making them more receptive to bondholders' requests. In that context, I expect pledges to be deemed credible, that is, seizable in case of default. Accordingly, investors would

---

139. van de Ven (2014, p. 170).

revise downward their prior beliefs about the risk of lending to an emerging economy. Empirically, I expect interest rates to decrease in the presence of pledges, $\beta_3 < 0$.

Pledges are not randomly assigned. To minimize selection, I include a battery of country fixed effects η_i. These capture unobserved characteristics (e.g., weak economic fundamentals, strong military, or diplomatic relations with Britain) that affect yield and the need to pledge.[140] Substantially, the "within estimator" captures the effect of pledging relative to not pledging for the same country.

The analysis is limited to loans for which I can compute the effective yield at issue. This brings the sample size from 707 to 643 units. As I did for the analysis in figure 3.6, I compute the average yield at issue for any year in which a given country floated more than one loan. Within the same year some loans might come with a pledge, but others do not. I compute the share of the total issue amount for any given year. If 50 percent or more derives from a pledged loan, I assign value 1 to Pledge for that country-year observation. The final sample size comes down from 643 to 567 country-year observations.

Column 1 in table 4.1 reports results for the simplest specification, including country fixed effects and no other covariates. The estimates are consistent with expectations: by the mid-nineteenth century, pledges were hardly seizable. Collateral was read by investors as a signal of poor macroeconomic performance, hence $\hat{\beta}_1 > 0$. As time passed, pledges became credible and interest rate premiums decreased accordingly, $\hat{\beta}_3 < 0$.

Figure 4.5 offers a visual representation of the main result. Two patterns are worth mentioning. First, observe a secular decline in effective interest rates. Despite repeated episodes of default in this period,[141] markets offered credit at increasingly lower rates as years passed. Second, one way lemons' rates converged with those of seasoned borrowers, I argue, was by pledging precious public assets and sources of revenue. At the outset of the period of study, pledges were interpreted as empty promises, hence they led to no premium cut. As time passed and bondholders became more effective in negotiating settlements and seizing collateral, the gap between

---

140. Arguably, when borrowers have a strong military (e.g., Russia), asset seizure is less likely, decreasing the credibility of pledges. If any, this issue adds a downward bias, that is, it pushes β_3 toward zero.

141. Reinhart and Rogoff (2009).

TABLE 4.1. Bond Yield and Pledging, 1858–1914

	(1)	(2)	(3)	(4)	(5)	(6)
Pledge × Year	−0.039***	−0.030***	−0.025***	−0.033***		
	(0.012)	(0.009)	(0.009)	(0.012)		
Pledge × After CFB					−0.732*	−0.781*
					(0.420)	(0.439)
Pledge	74.056***	56.336***	48.109***	62.293***	0.773**	0.726*
	(22.833)	(17.840)	(16.234)	(22.854)	(0.381)	(0.374)
Year	−0.030***	0.046***	0.048***	−0.013**		
	(0.005)	(0.004)	(0.007)	(0.006)		
After CFB					2.544***	2.649***
					(0.250)	(0.387)
Gold standard			−0.257			−0.269
			(0.266)			(0.290)
Default within the last			0.356**			0.404**
10 years			(0.163)			(0.197)
Public debt/Revenue				0.027		
				(0.034)		
ln(per capita exports)				0.183		
				(0.153)		
Fiscal deficit/Revenue				0.037		
				(0.049)		
Intercept	62.075***	−82.391***	−86.283***	28.644**	2.180***	2.263***
	(8.828)	(8.304)	(12.223)	(12.005)	(0.149)	(0.157)
Country FE	Yes	Yes	Yes	Yes	Yes	Yes
Year FE	No	Yes	Yes	Yes	Yes	Yes
Colonial status	No	No	Yes	No	No	Yes
Observations	567	567	492	286	567	492
R-squared	0.888	0.938	0.918	0.873	0.934	0.914

Note: Bond yield is measured at issue. Pledges coded by the author. See chapter 3 for sources for the gold standard and external default. Country-clustered standard errors in parentheses. *** $p < 0.01$, ** $p < 0.05$, * $p < 0.1$.

these curves narrowed. The spread at issue vanished in approximately 1880, soon after the establishment of the CFB.

Thus far, I have assumed that the ability of foreign bondholders to seize pledged assets grew over time because they gained bargaining power, preferences of high politics and finance aligned, and imperial competition intensified; however, the secular decrease of interest rates could coincide with other unobserved trends (e.g., a sustained expansion of capital supply), making the relationship in column 1 in table 4.1 biased if not spurious. In order to account for any secular trends in international capital markets, I fit a battery of year fixed effects in column 2. As expected, the effect of

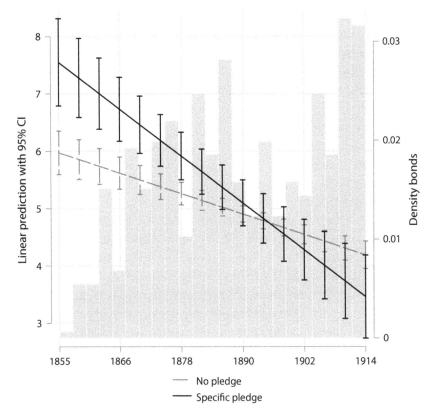

FIGURE 4.5. Effect of Pledges on Bond Yield Over Time. Bond yield is computed at issue (refer to chapter 3 for details). Dark solid lines and gray long-dash lines show predictions for pledged and nonpledged loans, respectively. 95% CI reported. The density superimposed shows the distribution of bonds issued over time.

pledges over time weakens once we control for the common secular trend; however, it does not vanish.

Column 3 adds controls for standard explanations of the spread examined earlier in this chapter: the gold standard, recent default, and colonial status.[142] Including these covariates decreases the magnitude of the pledging, as expected, but the effect is still negative and is statistically different from zero.

142. I do not include an indicator for "first loan ever" because it is collinear with country fixed effect. For consistency with previous analysis, self-governing territories after 1881 are considered financially independent, but results hold if they are considered colonial dependencies until 1914.

In column 4, I add a series of economic controls that guide investors' decisions in the Bond Era:[143] public debt as a proportion of revenue, fiscal deficit as a proportion of revenue, and trade openness (measured as logged per capita exports).[144] These controls, drawn from Ferguson and Schularick, are available only for 1880 onward.[145] Despite the significant reduction in sample size, results for the interaction terms in column 4 are similar to previous specifications.

Thus far, I have assumed that the ability to seize pledged assets increased linearly over time; however, the creation of the CFB in 1868 was arguably a game changer in debt renegotiation. In column 5, I interact the pledge variable with a time indicator, "after CFB," which equals 0 until 1868 and 1 afterward. This indicator is meant to estimate any significant change in the effect of pledging on the effective interest rate before and after the official creation of the CFB—a difference-in-difference estimator. Because the dataset begins in 1858, little statistical power exists before the 1868 cutoff; and results may be assessed accordingly. The interaction Pledge × After CFB in column 5 is negative and statistically significant at 90 percent. This coefficient means that, everything else constant, a loan including a pledge would have an effective interest rate 0.73 points lower after the CFB was established (a 15 percent decrease relative to the average interest rate in the sample), arguably because of the heightened capacity of bondholders to execute asset seizure in case of default. In column 6, I repeat the exercise by adding institutional controls. Results, if any, strengthen the working hypothesis. Because macroeconomic data are available only after 1880 (after the CFB was created), I cannot include those controls in this specification.

Accominotti, Flandreau, and Rezzik as well as Ferguson and Schularick show abundant evidence of the so-called empire effect, that is, the systematic lower spread for colonies relative to other economies with similar fundamentals.[146] Accominotti et al. argue that investors perceived colonies as an extension of the national territory—namely, provinces. If colonies defaulted, investors could resolve the dispute under imperial jurisdiction; that is, investors could bring the embarrassed colonial government to (British) court. If this is true, we should observe few pledges in colonial

143. Accominotti, Flandreau, and Rezzik (2011, p. 392).

144. Interest services as a proportion of revenue is also an important control (Flandreau and Zumer, 2004); however, this variable has many missing values. Because it correlates strongly with debt as a proportion of revenue, I choose the latter. Results are identical nonetheless.

145. Ferguson and Schularick (2006).

146. Accominotti, Flandreau, and Rezzik (2011); Ferguson and Schularick (2006).

TABLE 4.2. Pledging and the Empire Effect

	(1)	(2)
Pledge × Year × Independent	−0.028***	
	(0.011)	
Pledge × Year × Empire	0.021	
	(0.015)	
Pledge × After CFB × Independent		−0.898*
		(0.477)
Pledge × After CFB × Empire		1.213
		(0.784)
Observations	567	567
R-squared	0.938	0.936

Note: Empire and Independent are mutually exclusive. Empire = 1 if unit is a dependent colony in the British Empire. Independent = 1 if unit is not a dependent colony of the British Empire: i.e., sovereign nations, colonies of other sovereign nations, and self-governing British dependencies after 1881 (see text for discussion). All models include all constituent parts of the three-way interaction, but only selected coefficients are reported. Country-clustered standard errors in parentheses. *** $p < 0.01$, ** $p < 0.05$, * $p < 0.1$.

bonds to begin with. By the same token, pledges should help reduce the spread among foreign countries, not colonial dependencies. Imagining that the British government would allow a debt-equity swap in any given colony is difficult because doing so would reduce the empire tax base.

Pledges were uncommon among colonies: only 6 percent of colonial bonds had one compared to 50 percent outside the empire.[147] Indeed, as many as 35 (or 70 percent) of the independent countries in the Bond Era collateralized a specific national asset at some point between 1850 and 1914. The few countries that never did include Great Powers and self-governing British territories. In order to test the differential effect of pledges in and outside the empire and over time, a three-way interaction is required. Table 4.2 reports the results. For ease of interpretation, I report two-paired comparisons, namely, the effect of pledges over time for the British Empire and sovereign countries, separately. In column 1, I report the interaction with Year (following expression 4.2) and in column 2 with the indicator variable After CFB. Results confirm that pledges reduced the price of external finance for sovereign countries, not colonies, but they did so only once

147. Weidemaier, Scott, and Gulati (2013) find similar numbers in pre-WWII bonds (N = 493).

bondholders gained the ability to seize pledged assets in case of default, that is, in the final decades of the nineteenth century.[148]

Before I conclude this section, let me entertain an alternative hypothesis, by which pledges decreased the interest rate because they conveyed information about the financial health of the borrower.[149] As I mentioned earlier, prospectuses with pledges enclosed key data about the yearly income of the collateral and, when the loan was developmental, how it would contribute to commercial activity. The disclosure of this information could have been interpreted as a sign of government transparency, which tends to correlate with "good institutions" and be rewarded by capital markets.[150] Were this the case, the mere presence of pledges (regardless of any gains in bondholders' ability to seize assets) should decrease the yield at issue. I assess this possibility later in table 4.3 by examining the bivariate relationship between pledges and yield (see section 4.9). Results are null, contravening this alternative hypothesis.

4.6 Extreme Conditionality and State Building

In 1951, Borchard argued that pledges had "intrinsic value" and "legal significance," enabling foreign financial control in case of default.[151] The statistical evidence above is consistent with Borchard's diagnosis. In the later decades of the nineteenth century, the presence of specific collateral in loan contracts decreased the interest rates at issue, arguably because anticipated swaps and receiverships reduced the risk of lending to economies with weak economic fundamentals. Lower interest rates poured much needed capital into the Global South, but pledges did not stop default. Supersanctions often followed, and local assets and streams of revenue were put in the hands of foreign investors in at least 28 percent of default episodes

---

148. To be consistent with previous specifications, self-governing colonies are considered financially independent after 1881. If any, this biases results against finding an effect because self-governing colonies were less likely to pledge assets than sovereign countries or colonies of other powers. Results hold if self-governing territories are considered dependent colonies all the way to 1914.

149. I thank an anonymous reviewer for pointing out this possibility.

150. Hollyer, Rosendorff, and Vreeland (2018) for the relationship between transparency and governance quality, and Schultz and Weingast (2003) for the democratic advantage in capital markets.

151. Borchard (1951, p. 99).

and 48 percent of sovereign defaulters,[152] completing the circle of extreme conditionality.

The prevalence of foreign financial control in the Bond Era is critical to understanding why external finance was unlikely to contribute to state building. By surrendering assets and sections of the tax apparatus to bondholders, the tax base available to the local government shrank, leaving emerging economies in precarious fiscal positions. Revenue shortages would soon require new loans, possibly agreed upon as part of foreign financial control. This stylized sequence of events (i.e., trajectory E in figure 1.3) pushed many emerging economies into a "debt trap,"[153] characterized by high indebtedness and persistence of low state capacity.

Why would incumbents of emerging economies assume such a big risk? Why would they float loans if swaps and receiverships in case of default were anticipated? One reason, elaborated in chapter 2, is that external finance allowed rulers to dodge the immediate costs of alternative sources of revenue, key among them taxation. Higher or new taxes may give rise to demands for power sharing over fiscal policy by taxpayers—namely, having a say about how tax revenue is spent. Alternatively, power-sharing institutions may be required to induce quasi-voluntary compliance from taxpayers. Either way, tax reform was likely to limit the incumbent's discretion over spending decisions. By contrast, foreign loans allowed rulers to accumulate power in the short run while shifting the political costs of servicing external finance (either power-sharing institutions or foreign control) to future leaders.

The search for yield by foreign investors combined with myopic political calculations of unconstrained rulers was responsible for high indebtedness, default, and foreign financial control—the opposite of state building.

4.7   Betting on Default?

Was confiscation of public assets the ultimate goal of international finance? Did investors bet on default? Fishlow admits that

> default could become for [European investors] a source of gain rather than of loss, but only when some implicit guarantee of intervention

---

152. Mitchener and Weidenmier (2010). Recall these statistics are a lower bound because they do not include debt-equity swaps.

153. Fishlow (1985, p. 400).

[i.e., financial control] promised to bring order to the financial chaos of mismanaged states and lead to refunding of prior debt.[154]

Flandreau suggests that British investors entertained the idea a "default-colonization nexus," and to that effect, requested the hypothecation of land in expectation of debt interruption.[155] The "scramble for concessions" in loans to China could be interpreted under this lens.[156]

Loan contracts often included pledges as well as *sinking funds*, which forced borrowers to set aside capital periodically to repurchase a portion of the existing bonds and gradually reduce the face value of the loan. Sinking funds were created to dissuade borrowers from reneging on the outstanding principal at the end of the credit term. Before 1914, debtor countries could pay the sinking fund to an agent, usually the underwriter of the bond, instead of the creditors directly.[157] From the investors' point of view, the presence of sinking funds reduced risk and translated into lower interest rates. A sinking fund, however, did not secure a stream of future income, unlike taking control of a state monopoly or a receivership.

Along with pledges, I coded sinking funds from every loan in the Guildhall prospectus series: 52 percent of loans floated in the LSE had a sinking fund. In table 4.4 in the chapter appendix, I report results for expression 4.2 once pledges are replaced by the presence of a sinking fund in a loan contract. The effect of the interaction coefficient is zero no matter the specification. A benevolent interpretation of this result is that sinking funds were not strong enough risk reduction mechanisms compared to pledges. A not-so-benevolent interpretation is that sinking funds were not as profitable for investors as was foreclosing foreign assets; hence their null effect on the price of capital.

More generally, the use of international lending for political and economic advantage resonates with the Hobson-Lenin hypothesis of financial imperialism;[158] however, my reading of extreme conditionality is that the confiscation of assets was a second-best outcome for private investors, not a deliberate goal. Bondholders gained leverage vis-à-vis sovereign borrowers in the second half of the nineteenth century, and they profited from

154. Fishlow (1985, p. 401).
155. Flandreau (2016, pp. 93–101).
156. Cain and Hopkins (2016).
157. Tunçer (2015, p. 20).
158. See Frieden (1994) for a phenomenal treatment.

regular debt service and also default; however, to date I have found insufficient direct evidence to sustain that default and foreign control were the ultimate drivers of international lending, maybe with the exception of late-Qing China. Hopefully, new archival discoveries will shed light on this old but important question.

Departing from the Hobson-Lenin hypothesis, this book brings attention to the domestic causes of foreign financial control and state weakness. My argument attributes shared (although arguably asymmetric) responsibility to foreign investors and local rulers, who often preferred to assume the risks of external finance to the certainty of political and administrative costs associated with tax reform.

4.8   Summary and Implications

This and the previous chapter show evidence of the relatively favorable terms of external finance for economies with weak fundamentals in the Bond Era. Standard explanations of the spread have been tested and confirmed with an original dataset that covers the longest period and largest number of political units to date. Along with standard explanations, I argue that the low spread resulted from foreign bondholders' ability to seize key assets and sources of revenue in case of default. Foreign financial control did not take place in the abstract: it often built on previously pledged assets and sources of revenue. Consistently, I show that pledges decreased the spread conditional on bondholders gaining organizational capacity and creditors' governments becoming more interventionist in lending markets. The role of pledges in shaping investors' beliefs is novel because collateral is often considered "irrelevant."[159]

The conditions under which developing nations accessed (cheap) external finance are crucial to understanding the persistence of limited state capacity in emerging economies. The expectation of foreclosure and preemptive appropriation of foreign assets help explain the historically low spread for emerging economies despite repeated default episodes in the Bond Era. Incumbents in the borrowing countries, far from victims, might have preferred to push war bills (and other major expenses) to future generations while gaining access to cheap credit in the short run and bypassing the political costs of taxation. In the case of default, responsibility fell to

159. Bulow and Rogoff (1989, p. 156). See Weidemaier and Gulati (2017) for a survey of recent work by international law scholars showing that "contract terms mattered" even in the age of "absolute" sovereign immunity.

some future leader to raise new taxes to service debt, negotiate debt relief, or agree upon a debt-equity swap or receivership.

For the purpose of state building, default and foreign control of domestic assets—possibly sweetened with some haircut—contributed to break the connection between fiscal shocks (e.g., war) and state making. Instead of expanding fiscal capacity to service debt after the fiscal shock, emerging economies often canceled public debt by requesting relief and leasing their assets to foreign powers. Under such conditions, even interstate war fiscal efforts eroded or *unmade* state capacity, carrying on long-term consequences for institutional development. I show statistical evidence of that in chapters 7 and 8.

An important caveat accompanies the above interpretation: bondholders' temporary control of local tax administrations may be good for state building. Well-designed foreign financial control could exert positive influence and externalities over the local bureaucratic apparatus. In the next chapter, I evaluate this possibility. The evidence suggests, however, that the tax administrations did not improve under the control of foreign bondholders.

4.9 Appendix

This appendix examines an alternative hypothesis for the effect of pledges and reports a test for sinking funds. First, do pledges signal government transparency and good governance? Were this the case, the mere presence of pledges should *decrease* the interest rate charged at issue *regardless of when loans were floated*. I assess this alternative hypothesis in table 4.3. In column 1, I report the bivariate relationship between pledges and yield at issue. The relationship is positive and statistically different from zero, and resonates with Mosley's bivariate analysis of 70 loans floated by 22 states during the 1880–1914 period.[160] However, the positive sign of the coefficient is inconsistent with the alternative hypothesis.

Pledges are not randomly assigned. There are country-level unobserved characteristics that likely correlate with the presence of pledges and yield at issue. Column 2 shows that once we account for country fixed effects, the effect of Pledge is a third of the original size, and still positive. Now we need to account for any secular trend that could have affected pledging and yield, for instance, imperial competition. Once we include a battery of

160. Mosley (2003, pp. 289–291).

TABLE 4.3. Bivariate Relationship between Pledges and Yield at Issue

	(1)	(2)	(3)	(4)
Pledge	2.117***	0.642*	0.148	0.059
	(0.293)	(0.329)	(0.241)	(0.217)
Country FE	No	Yes	Yes	Yes
Year FE	No	No	Yes	Yes
Controls	No	No	No	Yes
Observations	567	567	567	492
R-squared	0.200	0.818	0.932	0.912

Note: Bond yield is measured at issue. Pledges coded by the author. Controls are gold standard, external default in the last 10 years, and time-varying colonial status. Intercept not reported. Country-clustered standard errors in parentheses. $*** p < 0.01, ** p < 0.05, * p < 0.1$.

TABLE 4.4. Sinking Funds and Yield at Issue

	(1)	(2)	(3)
Sinking Fund	−0.036	−11.131	−0.073
	(0.089)	(12.554)	(0.540)
Sinking Fund × Year		0.006	
		(0.007)	
Sinking Fund × After CFB			0.040
			(0.554)
Year		0.041***	
		(0.007)	
After CFB			2.695***
			(0.597)
Country FE	Yes	Yes	Yes
Year FE	Yes	Yes	Yes
Controls	Yes	Yes	Yes
Observations	492	492	492
R-squared	0.912	0.912	0.912

Note: Bond yield is measured at issue. Sinking funds coded by the author. Controls are gold standard, external default in the last 10 years, and time-varying colonial status. Country-clustered standard errors in parentheses. Intercept not reported. $*** p < 0.01, ** p < 0.05, * p < 0.1$.

year fixed effects in column 3, the effect of Pledge vanishes. In column 4, I add other relevant controls and the effect of Pledge remains null. In sum, table 4.3 suggests that the *average* effect of pledges on the spread between 1850 and 1914 is zero. Pledges reduced the interest rate only when imperial competition intensified, as indicated in figure 4.1.

Second, I examine the effect of sinking funds. These were meant to reduce risk, but they did not bring to investors the profits associated with seizing foreign assets and tax branches. In table 4.4, I examine whether sinking funds decreased the yield at issue. I report three models: Because sinking funds were easily enforceable—at least relative to asset seizure—I report a model without a time interaction in column 1. Immediately after, I report an interaction with Year and After CFB in columns 2 and 3, respectively. Results are null across specifications. That is, sinking funds did not reduce interest rates.

5
Debt Traps and Foreign Financial Control

Foreign financial control (FFC) following default may exert positive effects on fiscal capacity if foreign administrators reshuffle the local bureaucracy and incorporate new tax technologies and managerial standards.[1] If this is the case, borrowing overseas to finance a major fiscal shock (e.g., war), even if followed by default and FFC, would be beneficial for long-term state building. In this chapter, I cast doubt on this possibility and argue instead that FFC played a key role in pushing countries into a debt trap, or trajectory E in figure 1.3.

I first elaborate on various modalities of financial control and review existing evidence of its performance in Asia, Latin America, Africa, and peripheral Europe. Second, I examine the most ambitious FFC ever attempted in this period, the one imposed on the Ottoman Empire from 1881 to 1914. This case illustrates the risks of easy access to external finance—rapid indebtedness, pledging, and default—and the consequences of losing financial sovereignty. My assessment of FFC in the Ottoman Empire suggests that it was profitable for foreign bondholders but had no quantifiable effect on local tax capacity. Improvements in fiscal performance in the early 1900s in the Ottoman Empire resulted from domestic elite replacement, not foreign control.

---

1. For the sake of language efficiency, in this chapter I use the acronym FFC.

FFC is sometimes seen as the culmination of "financial imperialism," a reflection of the bargaining power of private lenders vis-à-vis vulnerable nations.[2] That picture is only partial. Foreign control also resulted from poor decisions by local rulers, who preferred to serve a foreign master than sharing powers with taxpayers. The *political* costs of financial reform proved too big for many rulers in the Global South, who preferred to assume the risks of FFC attached to external finance. This remains clear in the Ottoman case but also in China. In section 5.4, I shed light on the domestic politics underneath the installment of FFC in the East Asian giant in 1911. I conclude by drawing implications of FFC for long-term state building.

5.1 Goal and Types of Financial Control

Foreign control over the finances of a sovereign nation was never taken lightly in the Bond Era.[3] Because these interventions could otherwise be interpreted as a form of colonialism, FFC often required a concerted action on the part of European powers.

Implemented by bondholder representatives, foreign states, or agencies acting on behalf of both the bondholders and their governments, FFC occurred in differing degrees, the mildest form of which was the inspection of books and accounts kept by the agency in charge of securing local revenue to service debt. This was, for instance, the option chosen by the British in the negotiation of the 1861 default settlement in Mexico, where direct foreign intervention was regarded as a "national humiliation."[4] An intermediate form was participation in receiverships (locally known as *régie* or *caja de recaudación*), state banks, and monopoly companies in charge of revenue collection for debt service purposes. This was the model used in Greece after 1893 with the establishment of the Société de Régie des Revenues Affectés au Service de la Dette Hellénique, with which foreign officials monitored the collection of revenue from state monopolies for the purpose of debt service. The strictest form of control involved surrendering to bondholders the power to raise taxes directly in the debtor country until the debt was liquidated. This form of intervention required the establishment of a permanent administration with powers to assess

---

2. See Hobson (1902) for the strongest defense of this argument.
3. Material in this paragraph is borrowed partly from Borchard (1951, ch. 18).
4. Wynne (1951, p. 25, fn. 29).

wealth as well as monitor and collect taxes without the intermediation of the local government. The daily operation of financial control was exercised by bondholders' representatives, who often allowed delegates of the local government to participate on the board of the debt administration council without veto power.

Revenues that had been pledged in defaulted bonds—most often customs and state monopolies—were prioritized in the establishment of FFC. Under unilateral or multilateral European command, this happened in Bulgaria (1904), China (1911), Egypt (1880), Greece (1893), Morocco (1902), Serbia (1895), Tunisia (1869), Turkey (1881), and Uruguay (1903), among others. The United States began exerting FFC in the first decades of the twentieth century. Under the Monroe Doctrine, the US took control over pledged customs receipts in eight Latin American economies as well as in Liberia. Orchestrated directly by the White House, American intervention had an intense political component.[5]

After World War I, the League of Nations (1920–1946) exerted financial control over countries in default. Although financial control before the Great War was primarily designed to protect holders of bonds in default, the measures put forward by the League were meant to reactivate economies and stabilize prices as a means to regain access to the credit market. International control by the League was indeed the closest predecessor of the stabilization programs implemented by the IMF in the second half of the twentieth century (more in chapter 10). Next, I assess the type of intervention implemented by European powers and the United States before WWI.

5.2 Did Foreign Financial Control Build States?

FFC is an invasive policy that may nevertheless produce positive results for local state capacity. Foreign administrators might incorporate new budget and tax technologies that spread beyond the revenues under their control (e.g., double-entry bookkeeping for national budgets). Well managed, these reforms might expand the capacity of the state and persist after the council terminates its activity once debt is liquidated. In other fields, foreign intervention has proved successful, for example, in election monitoring and international peace missions.[6]

---

5. Maurer (2013).
6. Hyde (2007) and Fortna (2004), respectively.

Not so well managed, financial control might serve as a mechanism of extraction that leaves the country in worse condition, similar to what occurred under colonial rule.[7] Krasner and Weinstein argue that foreign intervention must be voluntary (or "contractual") in order to succeed: if financial control is coerced by bondholders with the support of the creditor governments—as was often the case in the Bond Era—poor performance may be expected.[8] Even if local elites perceive foreign control as a constrained best, the local populace and political opposition might be reluctant to cooperate with a foreign administration. This constant friction can inhibit transmission of know-how and genuine administrative reform. Recent attempts to induce state building with foreign intervention in the Middle East have failed precisely for the lack of legitimacy of the international mission in the host societies.[9]

In assessing the effect of financial control in the Bond Era, we should recall that one and only one mandate was pursued: mobilizing local resources for debt service. In other words, advancing the bondholders' interests was the top priority.[10] Improving local conditions was important as long as resource mobilization was facilitated. The order of priorities is well exemplified in the US-Haiti Convention of 1915. Receipts from the American customs receivership on the island were to be allocated in the following order: first, administrative expenses of the receiver (an American national appointed by the US president) and the staff; second, debt service; third, police; and finally, Haiti's current expenses.[11]

Existing evidence of the performance of financial control is at best inconclusive: China lost control of its customs receipts in 1911, when the Maritime Customs Service (MCS) became a debt collection agency for European bondholders. Foreign control of customs enhanced fiscal capacity and secured external finance at favorable terms. The success of the MCS, however, predated direct foreign control. By 1911, this agency had a record of 50+ years of professionalism and efficient bureaucratization (I return to the MCS below).

Egypt is another example of "successful" financial control. The British took over its tax administration in 1882 to secure debt service. The Khedivate (as this tributary state of the Ottoman Empire was known) repaid all

---

7. Acemoglu and Robinson (2012); Easterly (2006).
8. Krasner and Weinstein (2014).
9. Lake (2016).
10. Borchard (1951); Feis (1930); Fishlow (1985); Wynne (1951).
11. Waibel (2011, p. 47).

outstanding debt in decades and quickly regained access to international markets under quite favorable conditions;[12] however, financial control went hand in hand with the loss of political sovereignty, and Egypt became a de facto protectorate of the British government.[13]

The French installed a receivership in Bulgaria in the early 1900s. In 1930, when war reparations represented twice its GDP, Bulgaria implemented a series of fiscal reforms intended to strengthen fiscal capacity. As a result, the budget deficit was drastically reduced; however, these reforms were not dictated or inspired by the French receivership administrators. Efforts to build the state in Bulgaria were implemented precisely to avoid further concessions to French bondholders in return for new debt relief.[14] Still, this could be interpreted as an indirect positive effect of foreign financial control.

Fishlow, Maurer and Arroyo Abad, Reinhart, and Trebesch investigate changes in tax capacity before and after financial intervention with hard data. Fishlow studies the performance of tax revenue among emerging economies that defaulted on their sovereign debt in the nineteenth century, computing the rate of annual revenue growth before and after the settlement. His sample includes ten countries, but only four of them were subject to financial control: Turkey, Egypt, Peru, and Greece. On average, revenue growth dropped from 6.4 percent to −0.2 percent in Turkey, from 9.0 percent to 4.0 percent in Peru, and from 5.1 percent to 2.0 percent in Greece. Only in Egypt, a country that had also lost its political sovereignty, did revenue growth increase, from 1.4 percent to 2.0 percent (a difference not statistically significant).[15]

Reinhart and Trebesch, who investigate cycles of indebtedness, default, and settlement in Greece over the last 200 years, discover a recurring pattern of bailout lending that accompanies financial control: "While the foreign creditors succeeded in enforcing debt repayment . . . , the state of Greek finances remained problematic and the economic conditions unfavorable."[16] Borrowing from Levandis, they conclude:

> Instead of considering the debt problem in broad aspects and of adopting measures to eradicate the endemic disease with which Greek

12. Hansen (1983); Lindert and Morton (1989).
13. Kelly (1998, pp. 42–43).
14. Tooze and Ivanov (2011).
15. Fishlow (1985).
16. Reinhart and Trebesch (2015, p. 16).

finances were perennially afflicted, they [the bondholder and creditor government representatives] introduced half measures, inadequate to remedy the situation.[17]

Reinhart and Trebesch's critical assessment resonates with Wynne's evaluation of foreign intervention in that country: the *régie* put in place to secure tax revenue from state monopolies succeeded in securing debt service but lacked the capacity (or interest) to fight rampant corruption within the tax administration.[18]

Maurer and Arroyo Abad study the performance of eight customs receiverships set up by the United States in Latin America: Bolivia, Cuba, Santo Domingo, Ecuador, Haiti, Nicaragua, Panama, and Peru. American intervention was comprehensive: besides customhouses, the Americans had a say in economic policy, internal taxation, debt ceilings, and expenditures.[19] This was a matchless opportunity to implement ambitious reforms and enhance fiscal capacity permanently. Examining customs revenue performance from 1900 to 1931, Maurer and Arroyo Abad show that American receiverships in Latin America failed in "every single case" to raise revenues relative to preintervention times.[20] The US did not incorporate newer technologies, raise the salaries of public officials, or introduce a proper sanctioning system for corrupt bureaucrats.[21]

In sum, existing work on FFC casts doubt on its effectiveness. Contributing to this body of work, I evaluate the effect of financial control by studying one intervention in detail—the Ottoman Public Debt Administration, the most ambitious receivership ever run based on the outstanding debt it was meant to liquidate. This case exemplifies key aspects of the argument laid down in chapters 2–4: An economy with weak fundamentals and military needs was presented with an opportunity to access virtually unlimited external capital. As its credit rating deteriorated, it hypothecated multiple assets in issuing new loans. After 20 years of uninterrupted borrowing, it suspended debt service in 1876. Foreign financial intervention and debt-equity swaps were imposed as part of the 1881 default settlement.

---

17. Levandis (1944, p. 102).

18. Wynne (1951, pp. 344–335).

19. For instance, the American administrators had veto power over customs rates in Santo Domingo, Haiti, and Nicaragua; in the latter two cases, the US also supervised internal taxes. In Cuba, Santo Domingo, and Haiti, the US established debt ceilings; in Cuba, Haiti, Nicaragua, and Panama, the US put limits on how the receipts could be spent (Borchard, 1951, p. 294).

20. Maurer and Arroyo Abad (2017, p. 33).

21. Maurer (2013) for an extended treatment.

Tax capacity did not improve under external financial control. It did only after the Young Turks assumed power in the early twentieth century, a process unrelated to the receivership.

5.3 Foreign Financial Control in the Late Ottoman Empire

The Ottoman Empire participated in ten interstate wars and experienced nine large domestic revolts between 1816 and 1913. Continuous military conflict stimulated tax reform, but receipts remained insufficient to pay war expenses. Access to international credit markets allowed sultans to finance war externally and avoid the large interest rates of domestic bankers. The Sublime Porte, as the Turkish government was known, floated its first foreign bond in 1854. Twenty years later the Porte accumulated debt equivalent to 10 times its total annual tax receipts. International financial control was established in the Ottoman Empire in 1881 as part of a default settlement that involved over 50 percent of debt relief.

The account that follows suggests that foreign intervention advanced the interests of bondholders, first and foremost. Foreign control added positive externalities to the local economy because it modernized the sectors under its supervision. In terms of state building, however, tax capacity did not substantially change relative to preintervention years. In other words, although foreign intervention expanded the size of the pie, the state did not improve the capacity to tax a larger portion to fund basic goods and services. Chronic budget deficits and high indebtedness persisted.

5.3.1 THE LONG ROAD TO HIGH INDEBTEDNESS

For the Ottoman Empire, the nineteenth century was one of economic and financial reform necessitated by the accumulation of military defeats in the late eighteenth century—first to Russia, then to Napoleon.[22] Catching up with military technology employed by Western powers—or "defensive developmentalism"[23]—required funds; however, the tax system in the Ottoman Empire was highly decentralized. Provincial notables controlled taxation and acted independently of the central government. Sultan Mahmud II (r. 1808–1839) initiated a battery of military and financial reforms inspired by Western economies. In the mid-1820s, the sultan dissolved

22. Material in this paragraph is borrowed partly from Pamuk (2018, ch. 4).
23. Gelvin (2005).

the Jannisaries—by then an obsolete elite army—and replaced them with a modern civil army of 75,000 men. He also withdrew (with limited success) the local nobles' authority to tax. Reforms regained impetus with the proclamation of the Tanzimat Decree in 1839, which sought to put an end to religion-based legal discrimination, strengthen property rights protection, and end abuses in tax collection by local tax farmers.

Sultan Abdulmejid (r. 1839–1861) continued the reforms initiated by his father. The central administration was reorganized to mirror ministries and departments in European bureaucracies. In the 1840s, an attempt was made to end tax farming definitively by replacing provincial nobles with central government bureaucrats. When this reform failed, tax farming was reestablished, but conditions thereafter were more favorable for the Porte. Reforms continued over the entire nineteenth century. Pamuk estimates central government revenue increased from 3 to 12 percent of GDP between 1808 and 1914. This was a substantial increase;[24] however, expressed in grams of gold, tax revenue per capita in the first decade of the twentieth century was between four and five times smaller in Turkey than in France, England, or Prussia.[25]

The Ottoman Empire went to war frequently in the long nineteenth century. Major internal and external conflicts occurring during this period appear in table 5.1. Military spending constituted the largest outlay of the imperial budget. According to the earliest data available in the 1840s, it represented 46 percent of expenditures; by 1905, it still represented 36 percent of a budget three and a half times larger than that of the 1840s.[26]

War finance changed over time. In the first half of the nineteenth century, war was financed by debasement—the specie content of gold coins was changed 35 times during the reign of Mahmud II.[27] The sultan also borrowed from local financiers, known as the Galata bankers, who made short-term loans. Named after the neighborhood in Constantinople in which they were based, Galata bankers acquired capital in London and profited from the difference between the commercial market rate in London and the 12 percentage points they charged the sultan.[28] Debasement, which led to frequent monetary instability and high rates of inflation, was abandoned in the 1840s, when a bimetallic system was adopted. This reform,

24. Pamuk (2018, p. 102).
25. Karaman and Pamuk (2010).
26. Güran (2003).
27. Pamuk (1987, p. 57).
28. Jenks (1927, pp. 305–306).

TABLE 5.1. The Ottoman Empire (O.E.) at War

Interstate war	Years	Intrastate war	Years
Turko-Persian	1821–1823	O.E. vs. Greeks	1821–1828
Russo-Turkish	1828–1829	O.E. vs. Montenegrins of 1852	1852–1853
O.E. vs. Egyptians	1831–1832	O.E. vs. Montenegrins of 1858	1858–1859
O.E. vs. Mehmet Ali	1839–1840	Turkey vs. Montenegro	1862–1862
Crimean	1853–1856	O.E. vs. Cretans of 1866	1866–1867
Russo-Turkish	1877–1878	O.E. vs. Christian Bosnians	1875–1877
Greco-Turkish	1897–1897	O.E. vs. Cretans of 1888	1888–1889
Italo-Turkish	1911–1912	O.E. vs. Cretans of 1896	1896–1897
First Balkan	1912–1913	O.E. vs. VMRO Rebels	1903–1903
Second Balkan	1913–1913		

Source: Wimmer and Min (2009).
Note: This table lists military conflicts with 1,000+ casualties.

however, was not enough to stabilize the economy and secure sufficient revenue for war.[29] From the 1850s, Turkey looked outside for capital to balance its budget and finance military expenditures, a decision with lasting consequences.

The first foreign loan was contracted by Turkey in 1854. The impetus? War with Russia in Crimea. In the 1850s, Turkey was still a "mysterious entity to Western Europe,"[30] so the first attempt to float the loan in March 1854 failed. Later that year, the second attempt came with the hypothecation of the Egyptian tribute—the annual contribution of the Egyptian Khedive to the Sublime Porte. Once collateralized, the loan was subscribed successfully, raising £3 million and carrying 6 percent interest; the issuance price was 80 percent. External funds were exhausted almost immediately, and another war loan was necessary within the year. This new loan of £5 million was guaranteed by the British government, which had a strong interest in stopping Russian influence in the Black Sea. This very popular loan, carrying a 4 percent nominal interest rate and sold at 103 percent, helped Turkey win the war. This was the first and last loan guaranteed by a European power. From that moment the Turks were on their own.

In order to alleviate concerns about the state of Turkish finances, the Porte announced a battery of fiscal reforms in the early 1860s. First, it revised the charter of the Imperial Ottoman Bank (IOB) to consolidate

29. Pamuk (2018, p. 103).
30. Wynne (1951, p. 393).

monetary policy and centralize tax collection and debt service. The IOB, originally established in 1856 under a royal charter by a group of London bankers—hence Ottoman in name only—acquired a monopoly on the note issues and became the de facto Turkish central bank.[31] To signal credibility in debt service, the Porte made the IOB the "treasurer-paymaster of the empire." In other words, all the revenue of the empire was paid into and disbursed through the IOB. Finally, in 1861 the Porte introduced a new budgetary system, which allowed publication of the estimated revenue and expenses on an annual basis.[32]

Despite carrying on fiscal reform, budget deficits remained and investors lent on gradually stricter terms.[33] New loans were spent in servicing old debt and new military expenditures. Formally, only four loans were meant to finance war before 1876;[34] however, loans were floated for war purposes even if they were not identified as such. For instance, the £22 million floated in Paris in 1869 to officially "balance the budget" was partly used to buy war materials to quash a rebellion in Crete.[35] The quotation of new loans for war purposes appears in figure 5.1, in which the occurrence of warfare is plotted against the stock of outstanding debt from 1841 to 1913.

Loans during wartime were followed by new quotations to purchase vessels, equipment, and armaments from Europe. By 1876, the sultan had assembled the third largest navy in the world, much of it imported from British shipyards.[36] Military expenses did not help balance the budget. Far from halting the expenditures for military buildup, European ambassadors

31. With the 1863 reorganization, control was placed in the hands of a joint Anglo-French directorate. Ten of the 20 members were French and resided in Paris; the remainder were English and resided in London (Blaisdell, 1929, p. 219).

32. The figures presented in this chapter are drawn from the data compiled in these budgets and systematized by Güran (2003).

33. Wynne (1951, p. 416).

34. Suvla (1966).

35. Blaisdell (1929, p. 37).

36. Davison (1963, p. 266). Specifically, Turkey put together 185 vessels carrying 2,370 guns, including four line-of-battle ships, five first-class mailed frigates, twelve corvettes, and five gunboats of modern construction (Farley, 1872, ch. 9). Keeping the fleet up to date, Turkey acquired 20 ironclads from British builders from 1864 to 1871 and introduced submarine mines and torpedo technology, adopting a novel technology used earlier only in the American Civil War. The army was also modernized: the Porte purchased new guns and munitions from Krupp (Prussia) and Armstrong (Britain), including new fortress and siege guns. The carriage department was enlarged, and it replaced wooden gun carriages with wrought iron ones. Quick-firing rifles were also purchased from the British only one year after these rifles were adopted by the British army.

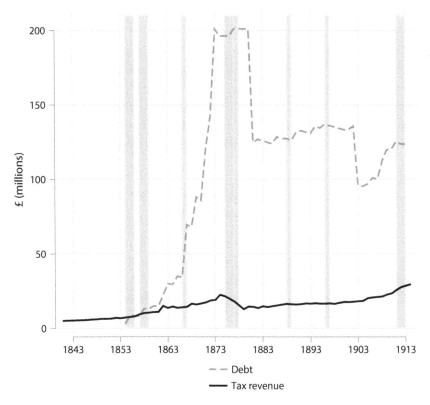

FIGURE 5.1. External Debt vs. Tax Revenue in the Ottoman Empire. War data drawn from Wimmer and Min (2009) and tax and debt series from Güran (2003) and Tunçer (2015), respectively.

in Constantinople agreed that the sultan should further equip his army and navy.[37] Demand met supply.

External debt escalated rapidly. Between 1854 and 1874, Turkey floated 16 loans in total,[38] Britain being the first market, followed by France, Austria, Germany, and Italy. Debt grew from £3 million in 1854 to over £200 million in 1871. To overcome investors' growing reluctance to issue new capital, the Sublime Porte collateralized customs, municipal taxes, tributes from provinces, and state monopolies, some of which would eventually be seized by bondholders—for example, the tobacco monopoly, pledged in the 6 percent imperial loan of 1873.[39] By 1876, outstanding debt was

37. Jenks (1927, p. 309).

38. Birdal (2010, table 2.1).

39. Article 7 of the loan contract hypothecated the "surplus of the produce of the Tobacco Monopoly of Constantinople," which was put into the hands of foreign bondholders as part of the 1881 default settlement.

one order of magnitude larger than annual government revenue, which was slightly over £20 million (see figure 5.1).

High indebtedness (the largest in the region), a series of bad harvests starting in 1872, and growing military expenditures made debt service almost impossible. The Porte renewed the charter of the IOB for 20 more years and even accepted the creation of an international financial commission to supervise the imperial budget in 1874. All efforts were hopeless. The Porte reduced debt payments in 1875 and announced default in 1876.

5.3.2 DEFAULT AND THE ESTABLISHMENT OF THE OTTOMAN PUBLIC DEBT ADMINISTRATION (OPDA)

Economic mismanagement led to default and a political crisis. The sultan was deposed by his own cabinet in 1876. A nationalist Muslim faction in the state bureaucracy made Abdülhamid II the new sultan and forced him to accept a constitution and to establish a parliament. The First Constitutional Era lasted two years. Coinciding with the Ottoman defeat in the Russo-Turkish War of 1878, the new sultan ended parliamentary rule and concentrated all power around him.[40]

Renegotiation of default was not easy. Meetings were intermittent and extended over six years. While in default, Turkey fought the second Russo-Turkish War. In order to raise funds for it, Turkish delegates returned to London to float a new bond called the Ottoman defense loan, which required arduous negotiation with British bondholders but was ultimately accepted.[41] The new loan did not bring victory. Turkey lost to Russia. In 1878, the Congress of Berlin agreed upon war indemnity and territorial cessions. The British and French governments participated actively in this treaty because they wanted to keep Russia in check while advancing the interests of the bondholders of Turkish public debt. Russia accepted that Turkish bonds hypothecated prior to the war would receive priority once debt service resumed. In return, Russia gained territorial concessions.

Negotiations to settle the defaulted bonds held by British and French investors continued after the Congress of Berlin. A syndicate of French banks invited French bondholders (somewhere between 30,000 and 50,000) to appoint a delegate to negotiate the resolution of the default on their behalf. They chose M. Valfrey, a French diplomat, who traveled to England

40. Devereux (1963, ch. 10).
41. Birdal (2010, pp. 39–43).

to request that British bondholders follow suit. The Corporation of Foreign Bondholders (CFB) appointed the Right Honorable Robert Bourke, a member of Parliament and of gentlemanly extraction, as its delegate to negotiate on their behalf. Once organized, the settlement was sealed within months and signed by the Sublime Porte and the bondholders' representatives in November 1881. The agreement was called the Decree of Muharrem (after the month in which it was drafted).

The Porte agreed to create an independent council run by bondholders' representatives, who collected tax revenue and serviced the outstanding debt. In return, the Porte regained access to new credit thanks to a sizable debt conversion that included an escalating interest rate from 1 to 4 percent.[42] Based in Constantinople, the Ottoman Public Debt Administration (OPDA) had seven members on the board: six representing the English, Dutch, French, German, Austro-Hungarian, and Italian bondholders plus one representing the local (i.e., Galata) bankers. The Turkish government had a representative with advisory powers and access to all books, but he could not intervene in the works of the administration.[43] The Ottoman Public Debt Administration (OPDA) was granted powers to collect revenue directly from taxpayers without interference of the local government and to redirect tax receipts to debt service.

A bilateral agreement between bondholders and the Turkish government, the OPDA represented first and foremost the interests of the holders of defaulted bonds and as such was committed to safeguarding the investments in Ottoman securities made by private foreign investors in continental Europe and Britain.[44] All representatives of the French and British bondholders in the settlement negotiations as well as the other members of the board of the OPDA had political experience and maintained tight connections with their embassies.[45] Despite the potential conflict of interest, the OPDA agreed to remain generally independent from governmental pressure.[46]

In 1907, however, the OPDA assumed a different role, one that advanced not only the interests of bondholders but also—and explicitly—that of their home governments: the OPDA was assigned the responsibility of collecting a 3 percent customs surtax on European imports. This

42. Feis (1930, p. 315).
43. Feis (1930, p. 334).
44. Birdal (2010).
45. Blaisdell (1929); Feis (1930).
46. Birdal (2010); Wynne (1951).

responsibility was never part of the Decree of Muharrem. In the past, the Great Powers had acquired the capacity to limit duties on goods of foreign origin entering the Ottoman Empire.[47] Negotiations to update the rates began in the 1880s at the request of the Porte, which needed the additional import tariff revenue. Rates were increased by three points, but receipts were to be redirected to bail out Macedonia as originally stated in the Treaty of Berlin of 1878. The powers did not trust that the Porte would channel receipts to the Balkans and requested the OPDA to collect the surtax on its behalf. This task changed the nature of the OPDA and the perception that locals had of the institution. From 1907 onward, the administration was considered an "agent of the powers"[48] instead of a representative of private bondholders.

5.3.3 THE TERMS OF FINANCIAL CONTROL

As part of the Decree of Muharrem, the Sublime Porte agreed to cede the following revenues to the OPDA: first, indirect taxes from spirits, stamps, fish, and silk and from the tobacco and salt monopolies; second, a battery of "political taxes," including the tribute of Bulgaria, the annuity of Eastern Roumelia (modern Bulgaria), and the surplus revenues of Cyprus; and third, the product of any increase in the customs revenue resulting from the revision of existing commercial treaties (that happened in 1907) or resulting from the increase of the *temettu*, or business tax (that never happened).

The decree provided that four-fifths of the tax receipts collected by the OPDA were to be used for payment of interest and the rest in amortization. It had the power to appoint and dismiss its own officials without interference from the Ottoman government. Any change in the tax code that affected the ceded revenues required an absolute majority of its members. In return for the cession of sovereignty, the bondholders' representatives agreed not to request repayment of the nominal capital stated on the prospectuses—a total of £210 million, £191 million of which was outstanding—but on the contracted loans—namely, the monies that the Turkish government had received net of intermediaries' commissions and issuance

47. For France, this capacity originated in the treaty signed by Suleiman the Magnificent and Francis I of France in 1534 and was confirmed by later treaties with France (Blaisdell, 1929, p. 24). For Britain, the capacity originated in the Trade Treaty of Balta Liman of 1838, by which customs duties for imports were fixed at 3% (Pamuk, 2018, pp. 97–98).

48. Blaisdell (1929, p. 174).

prices below par.[49] Together, the outstanding debt was reduced by over 50 percent—from £191 million to £97 million. Arrears were also reduced by 85 percent—from £62 million to £9 million—making a total of £106 million in debt to be liquidated by the OPDA. Based on the calculations made at the time, the OPDA was expected to reduce outstanding debt by £1.3 million a year—hence it was meant to stay.

Loans were divided into four groups, and they were to be repaid in order. The loans to be paid last, group 4, were those with no specific pledge. Were the Porte to dishonor the terms of the settlement, "the original rights, positions, and securities were to be restored." The OPDA would cease its activities when all debts contracted before 1876 were liquidated.

5.3.4 DID THE OPDA IMPROVE FISCAL CAPACITY?

The OPDA had control over three types of revenue. The "political taxes" from Bulgaria, Eastern Roumelia, and Cyprus were fixed contributions agreed upon in international treaties. The OPDA had little room to maneuver to improve the efficiency of these revenues; moreover, these tributes represented small quantities relative to the Turkish budget, and they decreased over time.[50]

The Decree of Muharrem also established that any increase in customs and income tax receipts should be delivered to the OPDA. The customs duties were not increased until 1907, and then they were funneled to Macedonia. The renewed tariff treaty excluded the bondholders from any share in the additional revenue, hence the OPDA had little incentive to change the existing structure of customs receipt collection.[51] The rate of the *temettu*, a premodern form of business tax levied on shops and stores, remained the same until 1914; hence no additional yield was transferred to the OPDA.

The performance of foreign control should be assessed relative to the management of indirect contributions, the third and largest revenue source administered by the OPDA. The latter farmed out the tobacco monopoly to

---

49. Feis (1930, p. 313).

50. Bulgaria never paid the tribute, which was eventually replaced by a tithe on tobacco. In 1885, Eastern Roumelia was annexed to Bulgaria, and irregular service ensued. In 1908, Bulgaria was proclaimed independent and stopped payment of the annuity. Cyprus's contribution was also reduced by 20% in 1890. This stream of revenue, however, was artificial for the Porte coffers because Cyprus had been under British political and financial control since 1878.

51. Wynne (1951, p. 60, fn. 26).

a French syndicate for an annual rental of £680,000.[52] The net profits of the *régie* were limited and had to be divided according to a sliding scale among the monopolist, the government, and the debt council.[53] The lion's share of the indirect contributions was in the salt monopoly, administered directly by the OPDA, as were the four other revenues: stamps, alcohol, fisheries, and silk.

Between 1881 and 1914, receipts from indirect contributions increased by 75 percent[54]—however, this was largely because of the low levels of collection prior to the OPDA takeover. Modernizing the five industries in which it participated,[55] the OPDA took steps to combat phylloxera, developed an export trade in salt (opening the Indian market), and promoted better methods of sericulture. It also regularized the rule of law in the areas of its jurisdiction and adopted high standards in its own (foreign) management.[56] The OPDA paid salaries when due and combated bribes and retention of collected receipts by local revenue agents.[57] And it took a leading role in attracting fresh capital from Europe to finance railways across the country, allowing the generation of more and faster revenue.[58] Net of operational expenses, revenue of the OPDA increased from £1.8 million in the period from 1882 to 1886, to £2.3 million in the period from 1902 to 1906—enough to meet the debt service target.[59]

In 1889, the OPDA took over the administration of revenues not listed in the Decree of Muharrem. New loans were necessary to suppress another insurrection in Crete. In order to foster credibility, the sultan farmed to the OPDA the collection of hypothecated revenues of previous military and railroad loans.[60] Proceeds from the "delegated taxes" collected by the OPDA quadrupled from 1889 to 1913.

To evaluate the impact of the OPDA on local tax capacity, all these numbers must be contextualized. To this end, I focus on the ability of the OPDA to mobilize revenue through taxation vis-à-vis the state, the incorporation of know-how, bureaucratic modernization, and fiscal policy.

52. The Societé de la Régie Co-intéressée des Tabacs de l'Empire Ottoman was established in 1883 for that purpose.

53. See Birdal (2010, ch. 5) for an in-depth account of the *régie*.

54. Tunçer (2015, figure 8.4)

55. Birdal (2010); Eldem (2005).

56. Wynne (1951).

57. Blaisdell (1929, p. 7).

58. Blaisdell (1929, p. 125).

59. Caillard and Gibb (1911).

60. Tunçer (2015, p. 74).

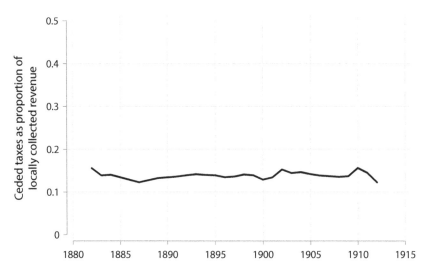

FIGURE 5.2. Revenue from Ceded Taxes vs. Locally Collected Revenue in the Ottoman Empire. Ceded tax revenue drawn from Tunçer (2015) and locally collected revenue drawn from Güran (2003).

Revenue Mobilization

Tax receipts managed by the OPDA increased over time, but did it outperform the local administration? In figure 5.2, I compare the ratio of ceded to nonceded taxes (i.e., collected by the local government) from 1881 to 1913. The ratio remained fairly stable, oscillating between 12.5 and 15.5 percent, and showed no time trend; that is, it did not improve in favor of ceded taxes over time. This result could mean that the local government adopted administrative reform independently or by emulation of the OPDA, boosting nonceded receipts. No such indication exists as will become clear below.

How substantial were revenue gains under FFC overall? In figure 5.3a, I plot total tax revenue before the imposition of the OPDA in 1881 (thick solid line) followed by the three series that came afterward: ceded, nonceded, and delegated taxes. To maintain perspective, figure 5.3b plots the same series along with outstanding debt. Two interesting patterns emerge: First, tax revenue increased from 1843 (earliest year) to 1876, when the country announced default. This increase is consistent with qualitative accounts and reforms occurring after the Tanzimat Decree in 1839; however, those efforts should not be exaggerated. By 1876, tax receipts lagged behind outstanding external debt by one order of magnitude (see figure 5.3b).

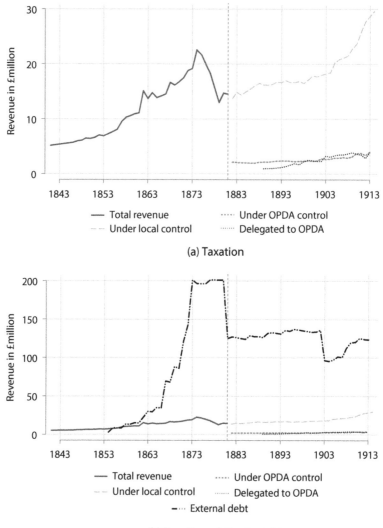

FIGURE 5.3. Tax Revenue and External Debt in the Ottoman Empire. The vertical dotted line indicates the establishment of the OPDA in 1881. Data from Güran (2003). These data represent budgeted revenue. Shaw (1975, table 1) shows that the difference between budgeted and actually collected revenue fell by 13 percentage points.

Second, taxation dropped between 1876 and 1881, coinciding with default, political instability, and war with Russia. Shortly after 1881, when the OPDA was instituted, tax receipts expanded once again. As discussed previously, receipts from ceded and delegated taxes grew over the next decades, but they started from very low levels, hence the large percentage increases in both tax categories. Relative to tax receipts under government control, the share of the OPDA revenue remained rather modest through-out. The difference even widened in the mid-1900s, coinciding with the arrival of the Young Turks, the reestablishment of constitutional order, and an attempt to diminish foreign dependence.

The Young Turks, elites born in Turkey and educated in France, put for-ward a battery of reforms in the administrative apparatus: public services were purged of superfluous or incompetent officials; extravagant expenses were cut; foreign financial advisers were employed; the departments of the government were reorganized, and the first double-entry budget was instituted.[61] "The difficulties [the new regime had] to surmount were enor-mous, but the new broom swept clean."[62]

Some of the reforms put forward by the Young Turks coincided with new wars in Italy and the Balkan States in 1911–1913. These were financed by external loans and new tax proceeds resulting from the ambitious reform program. This might have presented a unique opportunity to capitalize the war effort and recent tax reform and to catch up with European powers; however, fiscal policy was put in place to serve geostrategic ends when Turkey joined World War I efforts in support of Germany. Debt service to French and British bondholders was suspended in 1915. At the same time, the Turkish government floated seven war loans in Berlin and Vienna for a total of £173 million. These loans were never repaid because they were canceled by the Allied powers after the war, punishing Germany.[63] Impor-tantly, external finance of war without repayment unraveled the debt-tax equivalence of public finance once again. The OPDA, as initially con-ceived, was never reestablished after WWI and was officially disbanded in 1922.

Enforcement and Know-How

One could assess foreign financial intervention based on transmission of managerial practices and know-how. For instance, after the amendment of the Decree of Muharrem in 1903, the Turkish government put forward a series of measures to fight smuggling and contraband, two obstacles to ful-filling the mandate of the OPDA.[64] Qualitative accounts suggest that the

61. Feis (1930, p. 316).

62. Blaisdell (1929, p. 179). See Findley (1980, ch. 6) for additional details of bureaucratic reform under the Young Turks. For the political agenda of this group, which included the restoration of the national parliament and executive control, see Yapp (1987, pp. 189–195).

63. Suter (1992, p. 170).

64. Blaisdell (1929, p. 118).

government became less tolerant of smugglers and that the OPDA revenues increased.[65] To incentivize the Turkish government to combat smuggling, the reform provided that three-quarters of the surplus revenues of the OPDA above a fixed annuity of £2 million would go to the government. Although this reform was sweetened with a new haircut, the revised Decree of Muharrem increased the interest rate of the outstanding principal, the lion's share of debt service.[66] All things considered, the net effect of this reform was ambiguous.

The OPDA might have also induced the adoption of double-entry book-keeping in Turkey.[67] This budgeting technology, used widely in Europe and also by the OPDA, was received with admiration by Ottoman officials. Would bookkeeping have been introduced in Turkey had the OPDA not been established? Most likely. The first attempt to introduce this technique took place in 1879, two years prior to the establishment of financial control.[68] Double-entry bookkeeping had also been used by the IOB since its founding in 1863. The OPDA seems neither necessary nor sufficient for the adoption of double-entry bookkeeping in Turkey. In fact, this technique was incorporated into the national budget only after the Young Turks assumed office, 25+ years into FFC.

Bureaucratic Capacity

Did bureaucratic capacity expand under foreign intervention? The sultan did not mirror the internal management of the tax administration under his control. Financial control "did not usher in a period of reform in the financial policy and administration of the Porte."[69] Extravagant expenses, corrupt administrations, and the lack of budgetary control remained at least until the late 1900s. If we look at the resources budgeted for the Treasury (or *Maliye*), this ministry was not better endowed under the tenure of the OPDA than it was before. The major change in the series in table 5.2 followed the arrival of the Young Turks in the early 1900s.

65. Caillard and Gibb (1911).

66. Feis (1930, p. 315).

67. Birdal (2010, p. 177).

68. The Royal Edict of 1879 replaced the Merdiban method (a local system of accounting with more than a thousand years of history) with double-entry bookkeeping (Guvemli and Guvemli, 2007). This account is consistent with Orten (2006), who argues that the method had been incorporated endogenously by Turkish students dispatched to France years earlier in order to acquire first-rate training in accounting techniques—the Young Turks.

69. Wynne (1951, p. 476).

TABLE 5.2. Funding of the Central Treasury in the Ottoman Empire

	Amount in kuruş	% of Public expenses
1846/7	0	0
1861/2	80,744	5.80
1875/6	174,190	6.00
1887/8	103,034	4.50
1905/6	135,033	6.10
1916/7	446,472	11.20

Source: Güran (2003).

FIGURE 5.4. Budget Balance before and after Financial Control in the Ottoman Empire. Negative values indicate deficit in percentage points. The dashed line indicates the onset of foreign financial control. Data drawn from Güran (2003).

Balanced Budget

The OPDA could have stopped the borrowing mania of previous decades, avoided new debt service outlays, and put an end to a history of chronic deficits—by incorporating the "Gladstonian" economic principles professed by European diplomats. Figure 5.4 suggests this did not happen. Unbalanced budgets remained the norm as did the use of external finance as a palliative to poor budget management.[70] Of the 26 loans floated between

70. Owen (1981, p. 201).

1881 and 1914, 21 were officially issued to balance the budget.[71] Fresh loans were possible thanks to and because of the OPDA. By ensuring strict respect for guarantees, it facilitated the quotation of new external credits. Average interest rates after 1881 dropped from an effective 11 percent to barely over 4 percent.[72] After 30 years of the OPDA, cheap credit brought the Porte to where it was in 1876—into high indebtedness.

5.3.5 OTHER EVALUATION CRITERIA

If the OPDA is to be judged for keeping the "sick man of Europe" alive, then it was a success. It probably prevented economic collapse and helped Turkey integrate into global trade networks. If the OPDA is to be interpreted as an example of successful FFC, capable of enhancing the capacity to tax the local economy, accumulated evidence does not support that claim. Real change in the administration came from within: under the command of the sultan, tax revenues increased moderately but steadily. In the early twentieth century, under brief constitutional rule, tax receipts increased rapidly on a par with ambitious administrative reform.

One may argue that foreign financial control allowed the Turkish government to expand its military, another form of state capacity; however, a military without a sound fiscal apparatus cannot travel far. The "military-fiscal state" requires a simultaneous growth of military prowess and fiscal muscle. The former needs the latter, as the European experience proved.[73] The OPDA allowed the Turkish government to keep expanding its military machine while deepening external dependence. Ottomans were "regularly coerced or seduced [under FFC] into buying the latest weapons from the factories of Vickers or Krupp,"[74] requiring fresh loans and new hypothecation.

Finally, the analysis of the Ottoman case raises questions about which is the right counterfactual in historical analysis. In the absence of external finance, would the Ottoman Empire have raised enough taxes to fight against the Russians and build a stronger state apparatus? Or would it have been conquered and looted by Russia and experienced worse outcomes than those under the OPDA? This is impossible to know. The decision to borrow money to fund the war may have avoided Russian control; however,

71. Suvla (1966, pp. 104–106).
72. Blaisdell (1929, pp. 147–153) and Tunçer (2015, ch. 4).
73. Hoffman (2015).
74. Owen (1981, p. 199).

that choice had long-term ramifications along the lines of the country's fiscal capacity. This book sheds light on those lasting consequences.

5.4 Foreign Financial Control in Late-Qing China

Why did the Ottoman Empire end up under foreign control? One reason is easy access to external capital; but another is the sultan's reluctance to assume the costs of tax reform, as attested by the brevity of the First Constitutional Era, 1876–1878. The Ottoman sultans were not the only autocrats pushing their country into a debt trap. Others followed suit, Imperial China included.

The Qing dynasty accumulated large external debt in the last decades of the nineteenth century and succumbed to foreign pressures in 1911, when its most efficient tax administration was put in the hands of foreign powers for 18 long years. I briefly examine FFC in China by emphasizing the Qing's reluctance to engage in tax bargaining with provincial rulers. This case illustrates the coupled (although arguably asymmetric) responsibility for FFC: predatory investment and irresponsible local leadership.

5.4.1 FALLING INTO A DEBT TRAP

The Treaties of Nanking (1842) and Tientsin (1858), following the First and Second Opium Wars, respectively, forced China to open its economy and limit tariffs on European imports. Military humiliation against Western powers plus 14 years of devastating civil war[75] motivated a battery of half-hearted "self-strengthening" administrative and military reforms in the 1860s. Fiscally exhausted, the Qing could not secure enough funds domestically to meet the expenses of modernization programs.[76] Between 1861 and 1911, China floated 78 bonds overseas.[77] Some loans went to the coffers of the central government and others to provinces, although all loans were guaranteed by the empire.

Before the Sino-Japanese War of 1894, external finance was largely voluntary and resulted from a combination of political will and possibility. The

---

75. The Taiping Rebellion, 1850–1864, was a full-fledged civil war, causing 30–50 million casualties.

76. See Rosenthal and Wong (2011, ch. 6) for the military and fiscal decline in the nineteenth century, and Ma and Rubin (2019) and Sng and Moriguchi (2014) for principal-agent problems in imperial rule in China.

77. Goetzmann, Ukhov, and Zhu (2007, appendix I).

government's view about foreign loans is summarized by the statesman and military leader Zuo Zongtang (1812–1885):

> To borrow money by a government for wars is common in the West. Foreign traders are willing to lend money [to us], unlike Chinese merchants who are reluctant [to lend for wars]. Also, the more one borrows from foreigners the lower the interest he pays. This is also very different from the Chinese merchants' practice [who charge more if they lend more].[78]

Accordingly, by 1894, 75 percent of China's loan issue was intended for military purposes.[79] The worst was coming: in 1898, sovereign debt quadrupled when the country was obliged to pay a war indemnity of Hk.Tls.200 million to Japan, 2.5 times its total annual revenue. Only three years later, in 1901, war indemnities to European powers for the Boxer Rebellion added Hk.Tls.450 million to China's external debt. As the financial position of China deteriorated, European creditors required the hypothecation of the main sources of revenue: the *likin*—the internal toll tax and most lucrative tax in the empire—customs, salt monopoly, and railways. In 1911, at the verge of default, foreign bondholders backed up by their national governments took over the Maritime Customs Service (MCS) and turned it into a receivership, establishing FFC over China.

The MCS was the most efficient tax administration in China. Its origins can be traced back to 1854, when three foreigners were appointed to the Shanghai Customs House on an experimental basis.[80] Shanghai was one of the ports opened to Western trade after the First Opium War (1838–1842). The Treaty of Nanking stipulated that Britain would appoint consular officers to facilitate trade (e.g., disband trade monopolies) and to assess customs duties (i.e., assure that high tariff rates were not levied on British products).

In 1853, the Shanghai Customs House was shuttered when supporters of the Taiping Rebellion occupied the city. Rebels were expelled by loyal troops within a year, but the customshouse remained closed. The British consul in Shanghai conceived the idea of reopening the port by allowing the local authorities to manage daily operations while maintaining foreign

78. The original quote is from Zuo Zongtang (1890), and I drew it from Deng (2015, p. 332), who inserted the text in brackets.

79. von Glahn (2016, table 9.9).

80. van de Ven (2014, p. 26).

supervision. This agreement was convenient for the British because they lacked the (military) capacity to control and enforce the maritime trade provisions stipulated in the Treaty of Nanking. The agreement was also convenient for the local authorities, who needed to resume trade for economic and military reasons—tariff revenue was needed to meet civil war expenses.

The 1861 Xinyou coup brought Prince Gong to power. He was the sponsor of the self-strengthening movement, an imperial initiative to reshuffle the military and bureaucratic apparatus to resist European powers.[81] To secure the means for modernization, he recognized and institutionalized the Shanghai experiment and extended it to all the open ports. The now "imperial" Maritime Customs Service was led by an inspector general (IG) appointed by imperial edict but of foreign nationality. The IG and his staff were given monitoring powers, but the actual collection of taxes was left to local (native) authorities. The "IG would always have to bow to Chinese supremacy"—until 1911.[82]

The MCS became one of the most sophisticated administrations in the country. By the same token, it also became increasingly attractive in the eyes of foreign investors, into whose hands the MCS fell after 20 years of trying. It all began with the indemnity loans of the second half of the 1890s—arguably the onset of the "scramble for concessions."[83] In 1894, China was obliged to pay a Hk.Tls.200 million war indemnity to Japan within three years, but annual total revenue was less than half that, Hk.Tls.80 million. To assume reparations, the Chinese government floated three loans in Europe: the 4 percent Franco-Russian loan of 1895, the 5 percent Anglo-German loan of 1896, and the 4.5 percent Anglo-German gold loan of 1898, £16 million each.

The first indemnity loan came with a concession of a link of the Trans-Siberian Railway through Manchuria to the Russo-Chinese Bank, under the influence of the Russian government. This concession carried extraterritorial rights, including exemptions from Chinese taxes and permission to deploy the Russian army to protect the premises if needed. After the Boxer Rebellion, this latter provision was used by Russia to take control over Manchuria.[84] The second indemnity loan, negotiated by the Rothschilds

81. Rosenthal and Wong (2011, p. 212) for a critical review of the initiative.
82. van de Ven (2014, p. 11).
83. Cain and Hopkins (2016, ch. 13) for a dedicated account.
84. Rich (1992, p. 320).

with British and German official support, was collateralized by uncommitted revenue under MCS supervision plus additional securities if customs proved insufficient. The third and last indemnity loan, also issued by a syndicate of Anglo-German investors, was secured by additional customs revenue under MCS supervision,[85] a first charge on the *likin* revenue of four provinces, and sections of the Salt Tax Administration (a state monopoly). The loan contract allowed foreign powers to take over these agencies if China failed to service debt—in other words, extreme conditionality. As if that were not enough, the loan contract extended the British supervision of the MCS to 45 years.

In 1901, China fought in the Boxer Rebellion against an alliance of seven European powers plus Japan. China lost again, and reparations were raised to Hk.Tls.450 million (or £67 million), an inflated figure that nevertheless proved binding.[86] Lacking the ability to pay, China agreed to a new trade treaty that raised import tariffs to 5 percent ad valorem, increasing customs revenue (to be used for debt liquidation) and confirming the loss of tariff autonomy. Because customs proceeds were insufficient, uncommitted salt tax and a miscellany of other revenues were added to the list of pawned assets. The Boxer Rebellion reparations were cumbersome enough to survive until after World War II.

Opposition to these and other concessions, including ports, land, railways, and sections of the postal service, grew strong and lay at the origins of the 1911 revolution.[87] Arguably, social turmoil in the late 1910s was the opportunity that foreign financiers had long awaited. Higher political risk combined with poor financial performance caused by the revolution changed the mandate and composition of the MCS. Instead of supervising compliance with international treaties, the MCS took control over customs revenues and sent them to Shanghai to service debt, from which foreign obligations to European bondholders were paid.[88] The mandate of the MCS was also changed. Whereas foreign loans had been collateralized on customs revenue before 1911, these monies were not necessarily used to service debt. The central government allocated quotations to the administrators of provinces, who decided how to meet them. This

---

85. Notice that by 1898 70% of customs revenue in China was hypothecated (van de Ven, 2014, p. 142).

86. King (2006).

87. Young (1970, ch. 2) for a survey of concessions to British, French, German, Belgian, and Russian investors and governments.

88. van de Ven (2014, p. 162).

changed after 1911 by prioritizing debt service to any other local expense. By switching the priorities of the MCS, the Great Powers had transformed it into a receivership similar to those installed in Egypt and the Ottoman Empire.

To secure foreign control of the institution, local high-ranking officials (or "superintendents") were removed. Conveniently, for European bond-holders, "if in the case of the Ottoman Empire and Egypt, for example, their creditors had to put in place an agency to enforce debt collection, in the Chinese case they did not even have to do that: the Customs Service was already in place."[89] That is, FFC in China did not build local capacity but seized it. The revolutionaries accepted and continued these arrangements because the MCS was, after all, their only way to finance a state in fiscal decline since the 1850s. A new loan was floated by the revolutionary government in 1913: the £25 million reorganization loan, another textbook case of extreme conditionality. The government hypothecated all remaining MCS revenue and allowed the MCS to take control of the *likin*, the Salt Tax Administration (the second largest source of revenue of the central government), and local customs stations near treaty ports. The bond was so popular in European markets that it was four times oversubscribed.

The favorable conditions for investors of the 1911 and 1913 loans cannot be explained without reference to creditor government interference.[90] Not only did the Foreign Office participate in the negotiation of these loans, but the 1913 prospectus explicitly stated that the loan also had the "satisfaction of the Ministers of Great Britain."[91]

When foreign powers took control of the MCS, the Chinese government was deprived of its most efficient tax administration—the opposite of state building. By keeping China on the brink of a financial meltdown, foreign control assured the government's dependence on fresh loans. "The cost of capital was low, but it may not have been such a bargain [for China's interests]."[92] And in van de Ven's words:

> The consequence [of financial control] was that the Service became not the kernel of a modern administration for China, as Hart [the original IG] had wanted, but a debt-collection agency for foreign bondholders.[93]

---

89. van de Ven (2014, p. 135).
90. van de Ven (2014, p. 164).
91. van de Ven (2014, p. 168).
92. Goetzmann, Ukhov, and Zhu (2007, p. 284).
93. van de Ven (2014, p. 134).

5.4.2 THE DOMESTIC POLITICS OF THE SCRAMBLE

Why did China lose financial sovereignty in 1911 (only recovered in 1929)? Cheap capital and diplomatic pressures were key factors, but not the only ones. The scramble also happened because an autocratic dynasty preferred to assume the risks of foreign finance over the political repercussions of taxation.

The modernization of the fiscal system in China required the centralization of the tax system, which—due to the government's military weakness—could be done only by bargaining with local elites, specifically by sharing fiscal powers. The Qing refused to consider this option and, exposed to multiple military pressures, lost the modest fiscal power it still retained.[94] Taking advantage of the government's weakness, local elites took over the four main sources of revenue: the land tax, the *likin*, customs, and the state salt monopoly.[95] Lacking the key to provincial treasuries, the government also lost the monopoly on coercive power.[96] Tax yields seized by provincial authorities were used to grow militias and provide local public goods, consolidating warlords' power.[97] Regional militias facilitated domestic insurrection but also weakened further the country's ability to respond to foreign aggression.[98]

Self-strengthening reforms in the 1860s bore some fruit, but they were largely insufficient. General government revenue increased from 42.5 million silver taels in 1849 to 292 million in 1908; however, a third of this increase is explained by the appreciation of silver, not improvements in tax capacity; more importantly, only 18 to 28 percent of total revenue was actually sent to Beijing.[99] Lacking domestic funds, the Qing relied increasingly on foreign capital to balance the budget. The inclusion of pledges in loan contracts proved crucial to overcome credit rationing and to keep rates at competitive levels,[100] but the hypothecation of assets exposed the country to financial control, which eventually occurred in 1911. At the heart of the problem lay the Qing's reluctance to share fiscal powers with provincial elites.

94. Koyama, Moriguchi, and Sng (2018, p. 182).
95. von Glahn (2016, table 9.7) and Wakeman (1975, p. 232).
96. Wakeman (1975, p. 232).
97. Wakeman (1975, pp. 181–182).
98. Dincecco and Wang (2020).
99. He (2013, p. 159).
100. Goetzmann, Ukhov, and Zhu (2007).

5.4.3 TOO LITTLE REFORM, TOO LATE

At the turn of the century, China was already in a precarious financial position. The Qing desperately needed more provincial contributions, but local elites—military viceroys and provincial governors—were unwilling to relinquish control over tax revenues unless concessions were granted. In 1901 after two recent defeats, first to Japan and then to Western powers (plus Japan), the Qing set in motion a battery of political reforms somewhat reminiscent of a constitutional monarchy.

Provincial legislatures elected under a highly restricted franchise were inaugurated. A handful of representatives of these legislatures—monopolized by provincial elites—were in turn appointed to the also new National Assembly in Beijing. In principle, these reforms were an opportunity to build power-sharing institutions—facilitators of fiscal centralization in other parts of the world.[101] However, provincial elites had expectations for the new chambers different from those of the Qing.[102] The latter saw the new legislatures as an instrument to connect with the populace—an instrument of legitimacy building in times of nationalistic fervor and discontent with international interference and hypothecation of national assets. Provincial elites saw these chambers as an opportunity for the "transfer of considerable local and national power into their own hands."[103] In practice, the National Assembly was given only an advisory role. Excluded from national politics, provincial elites distanced themselves from the Imperial Palace and joined the nationalistic constitutional movement that put an end to dynastic rule.[104]

The Qing's aversion to strike deals with domestic elites was also manifested by its reluctance to issue domestic bonds despite the expansion of local credit markets during this period.[105] The Imperial Bank of China was created in Shanghai in 1897. Among its twelve directors, eight were powerful Chinese bankers and merchants.[106] To limit their power over fiscal policy, the bank was denied the monopoly on issuing paper money.

Hesitancy about resorting to domestic credit could be attributed to the first and only negative experience with currency issue in the

---

101. Dincecco (2011).
102. Wakeman (1975, pp. 234–237).
103. Wakeman (1975, p. 236).
104. Zheng (2018).
105. He (2013, pp. 175–179) and Goetzmann, Ukhov, and Zhu (2007, p. 275).
106. He (2013, p. 175).

1850s;[107] however, this is also an expected behavior if a ruler anticipates domestic creditors' demands for executive constraints and protection of property rights (i.e., honoring debt contracts) in return for domestic loans, a hypothesis that resonates with Debin Ma's account of the financial revolution in Republican China in 1911–1949.[108] Ironically, the Qing's fears were realized. After the revolution, Chinese bankers "attempted at numerous occasions to place constraint on the power of the [new Republican] government with regards to fiscal spending."[109]

5.4.4 STATE UNMAKING IN CHINA

The decay of China during the nineteenth century is best illustrated by its share of world GDP: 30 percent in 1830, 20 percent in 1860, and 6 percent in 1900.[110] Commercial and financial openings played a key role:

> China emerged out of the 1911 Revolution not proudly as Asia's first republic but as a state governed by a man who depended on foreign goodwill and foreign money. The Japanese indemnity had taken China to the scaffold of its financial executioners, the Boxer Indemnity had pushed its head through the noose of the hanging rope, and the 1911 Revolution had opened the trapdoor.[111]

External finance is only part of the story, however. The Qing shared some responsibility for state unmaking in China because it preferred to serve a foreign master rather than the people, or trajectory E instead of A/B in figure 1.3. Reluctance to strike tax deals with provincial leaders and domestic financiers proved self-defeating.[112] Agreements with foreign financiers at the cost of national sovereignty fueled the nationalistic fervor that eventually put an end to Qing rule.[113] Ironically, the new leadership after the 1911 Revolution collateralized additional assets to avoid credit rationing (e.g., the 1913 reorganization loan). By then, however, China had already fallen prey to foreign investors.

---

107. Goetzmann, Ukhov, and Zhu (2007); He (2013).
108. Ma (2016). See also Goetzmann, Ukhov, and Zhu (2007, p. 280).
109. Ma (2016, p. 16).
110. van de Ven (2014, p. 130).
111. van de Ven (2014, pp. 169–170).
112. Refer to Ma and Rubin (2019) for a deep historical account of absolutist rule in China.
113. Wakeman (1975); Zheng (2018).

Whether power-sharing institutions would have consolidated fiscal centralization and militarization and avoided the scramble in full or in part is hard to say; however, the Qing's preference for external finance sheds light on the significance of the political costs for a sitting ruler derived from sharing powers with domestic elites in return for tax compliance. This case speaks also to sitting rulers' myopia: the short-term low costs of external finance turned fatal in the long run. Foreign loans shrank the tax base of the country and eroded regime popularity, leading to the demise of the Qing dynasty.

5.5 Conclusion

Figure 1.3 depicts various paths to state building and state decay. If countries finance war (or other major fiscal shocks) externally, interrupt debt service, but eventually repay the loan, then the debt-tax equivalence of public finance holds. From this point of view, FFC may facilitate state building by compelling debtor countries to reshuffle the tax administration and amass new sources of revenue to service debt, expanding their fiscal capacity on a permanent basis. This is arguably the mandate of FFC in modern-day interventions led by multilateral organizations like the IMF and the World Bank.[114]

Things worked differently in the Bond Era. The main if not only goal of financial control was to repay private bondholders based overseas. Reform of local bureaucracies would be considered only if it maximized the profit of foreign private investors. Unsurprisingly, the literature overwhelmingly shows that FFC performed poorly in terms of building tax capacity in the Bond Era. Even the OPDA, which undoubtedly grew the Turkish economy, did not outperform the local administration in mobilizing revenue through taxation.

The mandate of FFC in the Bond Era is important to understand why external finance might exert negative consequences on state building in the long run. If FFC were meant to extract (or loot) local resources to service debt—not to enact fiscal improvement—states would have regained access to international capital markets without having strengthened their capacity to raise taxes. That itself would have challenged the equivalence

---

114. See Kentikelenis, Stubbs, and King (2016) for a critical assessment of modern-day conditionality.

between debt and war for the purposes of state building. If, in addition, states returned to credit markets having only a portion of their tax base to work with, then new budget deficits were to be expected, fresh loans needed, and tougher conditionality accepted. In order to understand the magnitude of the problem, the second part of the book investigates short- and long-term effects of external finance on fiscal capacity, and how it also influenced political and bureaucratic reform.

Although external finance often preempted state building in the Bond Era, the responsibility cannot be attached to foreign investors alone. The reluctance of autocratic leaders to strike tax bargains with domestic elites is noteworthy and helps us explain why significant advances in state building require unequivocal commitment to power-sharing institutions. I resume this discussion in chapter 9, where I review paths to positive state building as opposed to debt traps and state decay.

The Consequences of Global Finance for State Building

I characterized the rise of global finance, advanced an original hypothesis for the secular reduction of the bond spread, and investigated the effects of international financial control in part I. Evidence indicates that the global periphery had access to international capital at favorable terms relative to early-modern Europe and the developing world today. In part II, I examine the consequences of early access to external capital for short- and long-term fiscal capacity building.

War yields the biggest fiscal shock for any treasury, hence my focus on the connection between war finance and state making. In chapter 6, I revisit the occurrence of war in the developing world before 1914. In light of its frequency, intensity, and duration, I argue that war outside Europe was more consequential than often believed. I also show that military expenses of sovereign and nonsovereign countries were externally financed. Building on this evidence, I examine in chapter 7 the effect of waging war with and without access to international capital markets for short- and long-term fiscal capacity in more than 100 countries. I find that availability of external finance weakened incentives to build fiscal capacity, as shown by lower contemporaneous and long-term direct tax ratios as a percentage of total tax revenue and GDP.

Why are the effects of war finance long-lasting? I address this question in chapters 8 and 9. Chapter 8 advances statistical evidence of the activation of the political and bureaucratic mechanisms of transmission in conditions of capital exclusion. In chapter 9, I examine state building and external finance in Argentina, Chile, Ethiopia, Japan, and Siam to elaborate further on the political dilemmas of public finance and the lasting consequences of early fiscal decisions.

Overall, part II suggests that early access to cheap credit markets pushed many borrowers into debt traps characterized by weak state capacity and political immobilism. Counterintuitively, developing nations might have benefited from a less dynamic international credit market in the early stages of state formation.

6

War Finance

War is the paramount example of a fiscal shock. To cover military expenses, rulers may put forward fiscal innovations that outlast wartime, growing state capacity in the long run. This chapter shows that interstate wars were common in the nineteenth century in the Global South and that they shared key characteristics with wars in early-modern Europe. Once the prevalence of war is established, I show that governments regularly floated loans overseas to cope with this fiscal shock. The evidence calls for a reinterpretation of the *haute finance hypothesis,* under which international bankers were reluctant to fund war because of its destabilizing macroeconomic consequences. In the final part of this chapter, I reflect upon the consequences of external war finance for long-term state capacity.

6.1 War or No War?

Before the expansion of the welfare state in the twentieth century, war was the main driver of fiscal innovation.[1] The strong association between war and state making originates in the "military revolution," occurring approximately in the second half of the sixteenth century, when new military technologies raised the cost of war to unprecedented levels.[2] Monarchs

1. See Lindert (2004) for the expansion of welfare spending after 1914, and Mares and Queralt (2015, 2020) and Beramendi, Dincecco, and Rogers (2019) for nonbellicose drivers of fiscal capacity before 1914.
2. Hoffman (2015); Rogers (1995).

were then compelled to tap into new sources of wealth, standardize measures and collection techniques, and create professional tax bureaucracies.[3] The financial innovations and new bureaucracies made for war were seldom dismantled, creating a persistent or ratchet effect on taxation.[4] States made war, and war made states.[5]

The so-called bellicist hypothesis of state formation draws heavily from the history of state building in Europe; however, evidence outside the European context is mixed. A positive relationship between warfare and state building is found by Cárdenas, Schenoni, and Thies in Latin America,[6] by Stubbs in Asia,[7] and by Thies in Africa.[8] Others claim that the connection between warfare and state building outside Western Europe is conditional on initial factors, including the level of urbanization[9] and social cohesion.[10] A majority, however, conclude that the bellicist hypothesis gains no traction outside Western Europe. Centeno and Herbst are two prominent advocates of the latter position.[11]

In his 1990 piece, Herbst focuses on war in Africa in the second half of the twentieth century, the postcolonial world. He (rightly) claims that "African states have seldom fought interstate wars" after gaining independence, hence the absence of strong states.[12] Herbst's assessment of military conflict before and during the Scramble for Africa (1881–1914) is different: interstate war among native African states or agents of European aggressors were indeed frequent; however, war was often financed with revenue from the slave trade.[13] This phenomenon, interestingly, resonates with the main thesis of this book: alternatives to taxation break the connection between war and state making. In addition, the slave trade exerts negative effects on long-term social trust,[14] a key input for tax compliance.[15]

---

3. Ardant (1975); Brewer (1988); Ertman (1997); Dincecco (2011); Hintze (1975); Mann (1984); O'Brien (2001).

4. Peacock and Wiseman (1961); Rasler and Thompson (1985).

5. Tilly (1990).

6. Cárdenas (2010); Schenoni (2021); Thies (2005).

7. Stubbs (1999).

8. Thies (2007).

9. Karaman and Pamuk (2013).

10. Kurtz (2013); Soifer (2015); Taylor and Botea (2008).

11. Centeno (1997, 2002); Herbst (1990, 2000). Comprehensive surveys of the bellicist hypothesis by Sørensen (2001) and Goenaga, Sabaté Domingo, and Teorell (2018) are illustrative of the mixed results.

12. Herbst (1990, p. 123).

13. Herbst (2000, pp. 42–43).

14. Nunn and Wantchekon (2011).

15. Besley (2020).

Offering an enlightening account of state building in Latin America in the nineteenth and twentieth centuries, Miguel Centeno claims that warfare on this continent was short and not capital intensive, limiting its contribution to state and nation building.[16] Centeno draws this conclusion by comparing war in the nineteenth century to war in the twentieth[17]—a problematic comparison, however, because it includes the two world wars, which "severely skew our sense of what war is."[18] Historically, interstate war was shorter and seldom involved mass mobilization.

I suggest running a different and arguably fairer comparison between war in the nineteenth century in Latin America (and other regions) and war in Europe in early-modern times, when territorial states were still building core capabilities. The analysis that follows suggests that the Global South experienced levels of interstate war in the Bond Era comparable to European counterparts in the formative centuries of state formation—the fifteenth to the seventeenth.

6.1.1   WAR INTENSITY IN THE PERIPHERY

In order to draw an estimate of war intensity outside Western Europe, I rely on a war compendium compiled by Brecke, in which he coded every violent conflict between a central government and an armed party resulting in 32 or more battlefield deaths from 1400 to 2000.[19] Conveniently, Brecke mapped military conflict into 12 different regions. For presentational purposes, I collapse these into five groups: Western Europe, where the bellicist hypothesis receives virtually unanimous support,[20] as well as Eastern Europe (including Eurasia), the Americas, Africa, and Asia.

Brecke's data include 3,682 military conflicts, 82 percent of which occurred before 1914. All types of conflicts are considered in that dataset: from relatively minor intrastate skirmishes to large interstate wars. The bellicist hypothesis suggests, however, that state making should follow significant resource mobilization. War makes states when rulers are compelled to enact institutional transformation to wage costly war. To size the intensity of war, I focus on war casualties, considering a war large if it falls within

16. Centeno (1997, 2002). See Kurtz (2013), López-Alves (2000), and Soifer (2015) for related arguments.
17. Centeno (2002, ch. 2).
18. Fazal and Poast (2019, p. 7).
19. Brecke (1999).
20. See Abramson (2017) for an important exception.

TABLE 6.1. Large Military Conflicts by Region since 1400

Century	Western Europe	Eastern Europe	Americas	Africa	Asia
15th	2	2	0	0	2
16th	8	14	1	1	6
17th	12	12	0	0	4
18th	12	13	3	3	10
19th	16	16	11	15	29
20th	3	20	11	47	40

Source: Author's calculations based on Brecke (1999).
Note: A military conflict is considered to be large if it falls within the top quartile of the historical distribution of war fatalities, which starts at 20,000 casualties.

the top quartile of the historical distribution of casualties. This group includes wars resulting in 20,000 casualties or more.

Table 6.1 reports the frequency of large wars across continents. The breakdown is consistent with the accepted understanding of military conflict in early-modern times—namely, that it was concentrated in Europe. Furthermore, some wars before the nineteenth century included unprecedented mass-scale war mobilization, including the Thirty Years' War (1618–1648), the War of Spanish Succession (1701–1714), and the Seven Years' War (1756–1763), all of which changed the scope of the European state for good. Outside the European context, only Asia experienced similar war before 1800. The nineteenth century represents a break in the series. After 1800, all regions in the world experienced major wars on a regular basis and did so at rates similar to their European counterparts in the formative centuries of state making.

Unfortunately, Brecke's data do not distinguish between interstate and intrastate conflict. This distinction is important because the bellicist hypothesis builds on the positive effects of war against external threats, namely, interstate wars. Fighting against a foreign enemy helps overcome domestic barriers to the monopoly of coercive power and fiscal centralization. By contrast, the effect of civil war on state building is disputed.[21] Because civil war might undo local institutions, decentralize coercive power, and disintegrate the fiscal apparatus, I assess the incidence of the bellicist hypothesis outside Western Europe by focusing on interstate war.

21. See the special issue of the *Journal of Peace Research*, edited by Sobek (2010), for a discussion of civil war and state capacity.

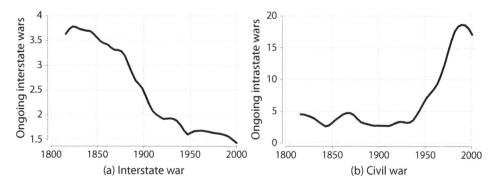

FIGURE 6.1. War outside Western Europe from 1816 to 2001. These plots show the total number of military conflicts in the world on a yearly basis. Author's calculations based on Wimmer and Min (2009).

To that end, I distinguish what proportion of war in table 6.1 is interstate from what is intrastate by relying on Wimmer and Min's war compendium,[22] who revise and augment three standard datasets in war research—Clodfelter's, Richardson's, and Sarkees and Wayman's, also known as Correlates of War (COW).[23]

Wimmer and Min list the location of and participants in war around the world from 1816 to 2001 for wars with more than 1,000 battle deaths. This dataset projects the location of conflict into current geographic units, and it lists war participants regardless of having sovereign status and international recognition by the time they went to war. It offers, in sum, an exhaustive list of interstate and civil war around the globe since the early nineteenth century.

Using these data, I plot the average yearly incidence of interstate and civil war from 1816 to 2001 outside Western Europe in figure 6.1. The frequency of both types of warfare was relatively even until the turn of the nineteenth century (notice the change in scale). For instance, in 1890 approximately three interstate as well as three civil wars were ongoing somewhere outside of Europe. Gradually, interstate war became infrequent and turned rare in the twenty-first century. In contrast, civil war never lost impulse in the developing world. Coinciding with the beginning of decolonization, civil war grew more frequent, reaching a historical maximum in the late 1990s. Based on casualties and frequency, if interstate war is meant

22. Wimmer and Min (2009).
23. Clodfelter (2002); Richardson (1960); Sarkees and Wayman (2010).

to make states in the periphery, the nineteenth century should be the focus of attention.

Another critique of the nature of war in the nineteenth century speaks to its duration: wars were short, the argument goes, and did not require sustained resource mobilization to fund new infrastructure and administration.[24] Based on Wimmer and Min's (2009) data, the mean and median duration of interstate war in 1816 and 1913 was 6.6 and 4 years, respectively. These values are significantly larger than Tilly's calculation of the mean duration of war in Europe from 1400 to 1900, always under 2 years.[25] War efforts outside Europe were also more technological than is often understood. Jonathan Grant compiled statistics of cruiser, battleship, armored vessel, and ironclad exports delivered by European and North American firms by region between 1863 and 1914. Out of the 83 units exported during this period, 31, 37, and 15 were delivered to Asia, South America, and Eastern Europe, respectively. Torpedo boats and gunboats were also exported to these regions. Out of 371 orders, 121 went to South Asia, 86 to South America, and 164 to Eastern Europe.[26] These and other military exports (e.g., rifles, guns, ammunition) were overwhelmingly financed with European capital.

6.1.2 WAR HISTORIOGRAPHIES

The previous section suggests that interstate warfare in the periphery in the nineteenth century was more prevalent and capital intensive than generally understood if judged by casualties, frequency, duration, and technology. Still, some of these numbers may be statistical artifacts if they confound war efforts from imperial campaigns led by European powers, particularly in colonial Africa and Asia. To address this question, one can turn only to war historiographies.

Multiple accounts of Latin America and Asia suggest that war and military modernization were substantial in these regions during the nineteenth century. Since independence, Latin American countries tried to emulate the armies of European countries by purchasing military equipment from European powers.[27] Consistent with this generalization, the world's second

---

24. Centeno (2002); Sørensen (2001).
25. Tilly (1990, table 3.1).
26. Grant (2007, pp. 147–148).
27. Dawson (1990); Grant (2007); Marichal (1989).

encounter between armored ships took place in 1879 between Chilean and Peruvian vessels, which were, in fact, purchased from Europe.[28]

Until the turn of the nineteenth century, Latin American governments had few functions other than building a national army and monopolizing coercive use of power.[29] Even developmental states like Argentina were using vast amounts of the national budget for military purposes. As late as 1895–1899, Argentina was spending 34 percent of its ordinary budget on the army and the navy. These funds were used to raise a standing force of 105,000 and to acquire new artillery and vessels from German manufacturers.[30] Although external loans did not officially finance much of the military expenses in the last decades of the nineteenth century,[31] the massive armies that Argentina and other Latin American countries assembled at the time would have been impossible to afford without relying on external finance to pay for nonmilitary expenses: that is, infrastructure and debt obligations. The fungibility of external funds is indeed fundamental to understand why focusing only on explicitly military loans is not a productive enterprise to evaluate the consequences of external finance for war and state making in the Bond Era.

The new military equipment acquired by Latin American governments was not reserved for military parades. They put it to work, waging roughly the same number of wars as European states in the nineteenth century, only longer and deadlier.[32] Roberto Scheina's detailed surveys of Latin American wars during this time leave little doubt of how frequent and fatal military conflict was in that corner of the world.[33] "Looking at nineteenth-century South America, then, one sees patterns of peace and war, intervention, territorial predation, alliances, arms-racing, and power-balancing quite similar to those found *in eighteenth-century Europe*"[34]—a fairer comparison than to the two world wars.

War in Asia in the nineteenth century was also prevalent, and it involved war against neighboring countries and European powers. Butcher and Griffiths quantify the occurrence of interstate and intrastate war in this and other peripheral regions between 1816 and 1895. They show that South

28. Sater (2007, p. 21).
29. Rouquié (1989, ch. 3).
30. Resende-Santos (2007, pp. 196–200).
31. Marichal (1989, table 3.1).
32. Schenoni (2021, p. 408).
33. Scheina (2003a, b).
34. Holsti (1996, p. 152); emphasis added.

and Southeast Asia had higher rates of interstate war incidence and onset than Western Europe during the same period.[35] Some states resisted European aggression (e.g., Siam[36]); others succumbed but not without putting up a fight (e.g., Burma[37]). To respond to external threats, armies and navies were modernized across the region.[38] External debt issued in Persia, China, and Japan was used to hire European military instructors, build new arsenals, and acquire military equipment from British, German, and French armorers and shipyards.[39] Some of those loans carried negative consequences for state capacity building, as the late-Qing China example in chapter 5 shows. Meiji Japan, on the other hand, suggests that external finance was not necessarily detrimental. I return to this case in chapter 9, where I argue that succesful state building in Japan was grounded on a preexisting credit market, a rarity in the developing world.

Compared to Latin America and Asia, war historiographies for Africa and the colonial world are scarce. Most accounts of colonial war focus on the colonizers' experience.[40] Offering an exhaustive account on this matter is impossible, but next I present an overview of war in Africa before and after the Scramble for Africa, as well as in key Asian colonies: India (British), Indochina (French), and Indonesia (Dutch). These accounts suggest that war was prevalent in Africa and Asia throughout the nineteenth century and that military efforts were financed with a combination of local resources (not necessarily modern taxation), external debt, and imperial subsidies—hence the modest effect on state building. Readers familiar with war in these parts of the world may skip to section 6.2, where I elaborate on war loans specifically.

War in Africa

Reid and Vandervort offer illuminating surveys of warfare in the nineteenth century, ones that challenge conventional wisdom. They show that African states were immersed in a military revolution before the arrival of the Europeans.[41] Ideological-religious war (e.g., the Ethiopians

---

35. Butcher and Griffiths (2015).

36. Ingram (1955).

37. Bruce (1973)

38. Black (2009).

39. Cronin (2008); Feis (1930); Ralston (1990).

40. A survey of colonial wars in Africa and Asia can be found in edited volumes by Wesseling (1978) and Moor and Wesseling (1989).

41. Reid (2012); Vandervort (1998). See Bates (2014) for a concise account.

fought in the name of Christianity) was exceptional and limited in time and space. War was waged first and foremost to gain control over global trade routes.[42] American and European rifles flooded African markets: an estimated 16 million guns were acquired by African native armies in the course of the nineteenth century.[43] The old muzzleloader was gradually replaced by the faster and lighter breechloaders, the rifle used by European colonizers.[44]

Before the Scramble for Africa, war had transformed the African continent. New military technologies were incorporated, including the professionalization of the military corps, the use of camouflage and siege tactics, and in some cases (e.g., Ethiopia and Tukolor) the manufacture of firearms. Local economies were transformed for the purpose of war. Specialization was required to finance the purchase of new military equipment and to secure enough agricultural produce to sustain the military state. The army became an elevator of social status. Militarized societies gave rise to new collective identities or the reinforcement of existing ones.[45]

Regional interstate war was common in the first half of the nineteenth century. Because of greater contact with Europeans, armies in the North modernized the most. In Egypt, Muhammad Ali (r. 1805–1849) imported manufacturing technologies to produce weapons locally. Increased defense expenses required simultaneous economic reform. The fiscal-military state put forward by Ali allowed him to raise a powerful army of 200,000 men.[46] Taking advantage of military superiority, Ali forcibly took over Syria, the Sudan, and Palestine.[47]

In western sub-Saharan Africa, the Yoruba, the Dahomey, and the Ashanti were immersed in an imperial race that required sustained war mobilization.[48] The Yoruba invested in fortified urbanization and imports of European weaponry: first matchlocks and flintlocks and after 1870 breechloaders as well. The Ashanti army was made up entirely of infantry, and its troops were equipped with standard European trade muskets.[49]

42. Reid (2012, p. 112).

43. Reid (2012, p. 108).

44. For details on the arms trade, see Grant (2007).

45. Reid (2012, p. 142).

46. See Ralston (1990, ch. 4) for details on military modernization under Ali and his successors.

47. Reid (2012, p. 130).

48. The Yoruba were based in modern-day Nigeria, Benin, and Togo; the Dahomey in modern-day Benin; and the Ashanti in modern-day Ghana.

49. Vandervort (1998).

The Tukolor and the Samori invested in local gunsmiths, who were able to repair and modify imported firearms.[50] Tukolor elite troops were also supported by artillery—although their weapons were seized in early skirmishes with the French.[51] The Samori acquired firearms from British traders, but eventually they learned how to manufacture them locally.[52] In the East, Ethiopia surpassed all other African states in terms of social complexity and military capacity, developing its own military industry while adopting Western military techniques. Unlike in Egypt, the new arsenal was paid for mostly with domestic resources, which proved crucial to minimize exposure to foreign interference. I return to this case in chapter 9.

European presence in sub-Saharan Africa before 1880 was limited to the coastline. Before the Suez Canal was inaugurated (1869), African ports were crucial to securing trade routes to Asia. European interests in the hinterland accelerated in the 1880s.[53] Despite the advances of African militaries, native armies could not compete with the structure, organization, and tactics of European powers, let alone with their state-of-the-art weaponry (e.g., the Maxim gun). The Ashanti and the Zulu initially resisted European conquest, eventually succumbing just as every other native state had.[54] The technology differential was too great for any sustained military engagement. Local armies, if active, retreated to the mountains and forests and engaged in guerrilla warfare, a type of combat that deviates from the type of sustained war mobilization that Hintze or Tilly associate with state building.

Following the Berlin Conference of 1884, a new opportunity to build capacity was presented under colonial rule. Because the cost of deploying permanent European armies in Africa was prohibitive, the bulk of colonial conquest of the hinterland was executed by African soldiers under European command.[55] African regiments emulating the European model were created by poaching from local armies. The British set rule in modern-day Uganda by recruiting Ganda soldiers and making them fight against their old regional rival, the Bunyoro.[56] Imperial African regiments were formed

---

50. The Tukolor were based in modern-day Senegal, Mali, and Mauritania; and the Samori were spread into modern-day Guinea, Sierra Leone, Mali, Ivory Coast, and Burkina Faso.

51. Reid (2012, p. 127).

52. Black (2009, ch. 9).

53. Herbst (2000).

54. Vandervort (1998). The Zulu were based in modern-day KwaZulu-Natal in South Africa.

55. Robinson (1978).

56. Reid (2012, p. 139).

in Gambia, Sierra Leone, and the Gold Coast.[57] Following suit by recruiting Bambara soldiers to conquer Southern Sahara, the French raised a locally financed army in French Equatorial Africa to expand colonial rule into the hinterland and put together the *Tirailleurs Senegalais* in modern-day Senegal to defeat the Muslim Tukolor Empire.[58] Eventually, these regiments were integrated into the imperial defense system and used to fight domestic and foreign enemies.[59]

Encyclopedic accounts by Reid and Vandervort suggest striking similarities between the interstate competition in sub-Saharan Africa in the nineteenth century and that experienced in Western Europe in early-modern times. If Africa similarly experienced a military revolution, why did war not translate into more capable states? Reid and Bates argue that European colonization in the 1880s put a stop to endogenous state building. The Scramble for Africa interrupted interstate competition, a key (although brutal) way to forge authority and build legitimacy and eventually strong states.

In addition to colonial interference, I draw attention to how war was financed before and after the scramble. Before colonial conquest, native warfare was largely funded by slave (and ivory) exports. Despite being a banned practice in Europe, illicit slave trade persisted in West Africa and grew stronger in East and Central Africa over the course of the century. Raids and the sale of slaves for weapons was a common practice among native African states.[60] The Yoruba financed the imports of European weapons with slave exports;[61] so did the Dahomey state, the Sokoto, and the Tukolor caliphates (in the African savanna), as well as the sultanate of Zanzibar and the kingdom of Mirambo (modern-day Tanzania) in the East.[62] Slave soldiers played an important role in local armies and on plantations in peacetime. For the purpose of state building, the use of slaves to generate revenue and populate the army does not necessarily translate into more capable states. For one, slave raids are likely to generate

---

57. Reid (2012, p. 148).

58. Reid (2012, p. 140) and Black (2009).

59. The *Tirailleurs Senegalais* regiment was deployed in Western Europe during WWI, a sign of their military competence.

60. Herbst (2000).

61. Reid (2012, p. 111).

62. Reid (2012, pp. 111–115). The Ashanti gradually moved out of the slave trade. This may have been the only major sub-Saharan state not raising significant revenue from slave exports.

lasting negative social and economic consequences.[63] In addition, the use of slave soldiers might have enabled rulers to dodge negotiations over taxation with economic and regional elites, impeding the articulation of power-sharing institutions.[64] After the scramble, regional war continued; but it was disproportionally financed with external funds, mostly imperial subsidies, thereby the modest effect on state building. At the end of this chapter, I illustrate the negative consequences of colonial war for local tax mobilization with a specific example from South Africa.

War in British India

Militarism on the Indian subcontinent has a long tradition. By 1600, several Indian states (the Delhi sultanate, the Rajput states, the Deccan sultanates, and the Vijayanagara Empire) had acquired military prowess forged through sustained interstate competition.[65] The next long century was dominated by the Mughal Empire, which put together fiscal-military machinery comparable to the European model.[66] The empire fragmented in the eighteenth century, but its constituent parts kept growing their military capabilities. In 1795, the Dutch East India Company relinquished all their colonies to the British to prevent occupation by the French, a mutual enemy. By the early nineteenth century, the British were the only European power on the subcontinent. Resistance and military disputes between the British and indigenous states remained the norm until the completion of annexation in the late 1850s.[67]

Precolonial fiscal militarism was inherited and reinforced under British rule.[68] Although the bulk of the officer corps was European, the army was staffed with local soldiers.[69] The strength and size of the Indian army posed a constant threat to British dominion, especially following the Indian Mutiny, or Indian Rebellion of 1857, after which the British engineered a meticulous recruitment system to raise barriers to collective action and avoid further rebellion.[70] Likewise, the British never again supplied the

---

63. Nunn and Wantchekon (2011).

64. Blaydes and Chaney (2013) for the effect of slave soldiers on political institutions in the Muslim world before 1500 CE.

65. Roy (2013, ch. 2).

66. de la Garza (2016); Richards (1995).

67. Lee (2017); Iyer (2010).

68. Dincecco, Fenske, Menon, and Mukherjee (2019); Stein (1985).

69. Wilkinson (2015, p. 39).

70. Wilkinson (2015, pp. 38–44).

Indian army with the latest technology.[71] War making in India, however, remained the rule rather than the exception. Unlike the vast majority of colonies, India met the principle of self-sufficiency and paid for most of its military expenses. Despite being a net contributor to the empire, it was granted virtually no fiscal autonomy, remaining "legally at the mercy of whatever policies its British governors and the authorities in Whitehall might devise."[72]

The Indian army had three major purposes: keeping domestic order, fighting frontier wars, and participating around the world as part of the imperial army. Indian troops fought three proxy wars with Burma and two with Afghanistan. The first Anglo-Burmese war in the 1820s and the second Anglo-Afghan war in the late 1870s were particularly expensive. The former cost £5 million (equivalent to £370 million in 2015), the latter £25 million (£2 billion in 2015)—80 percent of it financed locally.[73] Indian troops also played a key role in imperial defense, deployed overseas on a regular basis: the Abyssinian campaign (1868), the Boxer Rebellion (1899–1901), East and Central Africa (1897–1898), the East African and Somaliland campaigns (1902–1904), Egypt (1882–1885), Persia (1856–1857), the Second Boer (1899–1902), and Tibet (1903–1904).[74] Most of the expenses associated with war overseas was funded by Indian taxpayers, and the subcontinent remained financially self-sufficient and militarily active under colonial rule.[75]

War in French Indochina and Dutch Indonesia

Following the Franco-Spanish expeditions of 1858–1862, the French began the conquest of modern-day Vietnam, moving from south to north. The French built upon the military efforts of Emperor Minh Mạng, who tried during his rule (1821–1841) to build a modern army, mirroring Western technologies, uniforms, and discipline;[76] but his efforts fell short matched against the European military might.

The colonization of Indochina commenced in early 1862, when the French took over the three eastern provinces of Cochin China. The annexation of the northern territories required raising a local army, so native ranks

71. Black (2009, ch. 9).
72. Davis and Huttenback (1986, p. 14).
73. War cost estimates drawn from Webster (1998, pp. 142–145).
74. Davis and Huttenback (1986, p. 154) and Robinson (1978, p. 149).
75. O'Brien (1988).
76. Black (2009, ch. 6).

were poached from preexisting regiments, conscription, and volunteers.[77] Native troops, who served alongside French soldiers, were first tested in the Sino-French War (1884), repelling Chinese troops from the northern frontier. The colonial army was crucial to forcibly annexing the northern provinces—Tonkin and Annam—and creating the Indochinese Union in 1887. The majority of military and administrative expenditures during the French occupation were assumed locally,[78] and Cochin China remained a net contributor—one of the few—to French imperial defense until independence.

Following the example of the British and French, the Dutch raised local armies to expand their Asian dominions. The Dutch colonial army in Indonesia, the most important colony, saw a gradual expansion of local soldiers, from 52 percent in 1815 to 61 percent in 1909.[79] These troops were employed in numerous wars in the region, contributing to its gradual militarization; however, the military expenses remained heavily subsidized by the metropole.

Taking Stock

Both the quantitative and qualitative accounts above suggest that interstate war in the nineteenth century was a common phenomenon outside Western Europe. Figure 6.2 offers one final overview of war in this period by plotting the number of war years in modern-day state borders (darker color indicates higher occurrence). This figure clearly shows that no region was safe from military hostilities. By will or force, old and new states, colonies, and dominions waged numerous wars in the long nineteenth century, 1816–1913. Consistent with the Hundred Years' Peace, relatively few wars took place in Western Europe. Beyond the European frontiers, the Hundred Years' Peace appears more like a myth reflecting the Eurocentric bias of the time.

In the context of regional military competition and imperial threat, states outside Western Europe, sovereign or not, put their efforts into strengthening armies and navies by adopting new technologies and organizational structures. The modernized militaries were soon activated, participating in wars that, based on casualties, frequency, and duration, were arguably similar to conventional warfare in the formative centuries of the European states—fifteenth to seventeenth.

77. Taylor and Botea (2008, p. 40).
78. López Jerez (2020, pp. 112–117).
79. Bossenbroek (1995, p. 29).

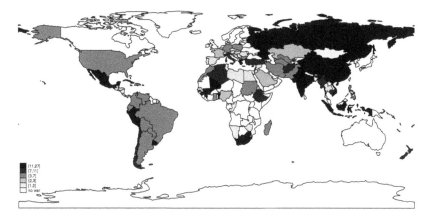

FIGURE 6.2. Geography of Warfare in the Long Nineteenth Century. This figure presents the geography of warfare—namely, the location of war—mapped into state boundaries as of 2000. The figure includes interstate war as well as independence or "nationalist secessionist war," that is, war intended to create a modern nation-state, as determined by Wimmer and Min (2009). Categories in the figure legend denote the total number of war years in any given territory between 1816 and 1913, with 0 and 27 being minimum and maximum, respectively. Darker colors indicate more years of war in a given territory.

If war were really meaningful, why has existing research shown no robust relationship between war and state building in the periphery? I argue that external finance weakened incentives to expand tax capacity, hence disconnecting war efforts from long-term state building. The remainder of this chapter provides evidence that war was indeed financed externally, and in chapters 7–9, I analyze the consequences for state building.

6.2 Haute Finance?

When studying war finance, distinguishing between public and private creditors is necessary. International law banned government loans from neutral countries to belligerent countries; however, no such limit existed for loans from private investors.[80] In light of this crucial distinction, I focus on private lending, which happened to monopolize international lending during the Bond Era.

Although permitted, private financing of war may not have been possible for two other reasons: geopolitical interests and macroeconomic stability. Officially, British and French investors were banned from lending to

80. Borchard (1951, p. 151).

countries fighting their troops or jeopardizing their geopolitical interests. Circumstantial evidence, however, suggests that investors found ways to escape official constraints. Large issuing houses had franchises in the various financial centers of Europe. Whenever a loan conflicted with municipal foreign policy, the float would be pushed to another financial capital in the continent.[81]

Blatant negation of national policy, even by respected houses, also occurred. The Rothschilds contravened the British government embargo on Russia in 1853 and marketed a Russian bond when Russia was fighting the British and their allies in Crimea.[82] Four years earlier, the Barings and the Rothschilds had floated another series of Russian and Austrian loans despite knowing the intent of those funds was to finance a war to suppress the Hungarian revolutionaries sponsored by the British Foreign Office. Similar examples can be found in France. For instance, Japanese bonds were marketed in the Paris Bourse in 1903–1904, when Japan was at war with Russia, a key ally of France. A few years later, French capitalists issued a loan to Turkey to fund the Balkan Wars, causing a new diplomatic incident between France and Russia.[83] In foreign lending, private interest often found its way.

International investors may have been reluctant to lend for military purposes if they expected participants to default after war. Military expenses could lead to fiscal strain, inflation, and currency devaluation, putting service of debt at risk. In anticipation of capital exclusion, states did not wage war, hence the Hundred Years' Peace—Polanyi claimed.[84] The so-called haute finance hypothesis was recently expanded by Kirshner, who emphasizes the negative macroeconomic consequences of war in international capital markets, affecting war participants as well as nonparticipants.[85] Anticipating such negative shocks, international investors would punish warring states with increased difficulty in borrowing abroad.[86] Following this logic, one should see hardly any war financed with foreign capital.

Some facts are inconsistent with a strict interpretation of the haute finance hypothesis. First, Shea and Poast find no systematic relationship

---

81. Jenks (1927, p. 284).
82. Jenks (1927, pp. 285–286).
83. Viner (1929, pp. 437–447).
84. Polanyi (2001).
85. Kirshner (2007).
86. Kirshner (2007, p. 206).

between war and sovereign default.[87] Second, the Hundred Years' Peace did not really hold outside European soil, as I showed earlier in the chapter. Third, a close reading of Polanyi suggests that the investors' opposition to financing war was specific to war between the Great Powers:

> The chief danger, however, which stalked the capitalists of Europe was not technological or financial failure, but war—not a war between small countries (which could be easily isolated) nor war upon a small country by a Great Power (a frequent and often convenient occurrence) but a general war between the Great Powers themselves.[88]

All things considered, the haute finance hypothesis faces several credibility challenges, particularly in relation to war in the Global South. What is more, the lending euphoria in the Bond Era could have been a prime outcome of the globalization of military markets. British, French, and German rifles, cannons, and warships were exported around the world. African armies fought the British and French armies with European rifles,[89] as did Indonesian troops against Dutch colonizers.[90] Latin America, Eastern Europe, the Ottoman Empire, Japan, China, and India were prime purchasers of European armaments. No doubt contraband played an important role,[91] but so did European governments, which brokered loans to third nations as long as they purchased military equipment from national producers.[92] In studying the global arms trade in the Bond Era, Jonathan Grant concludes that the military industry in Europe was indeed a crucial push factor in sovereign lending: "The armament manufacturers led the financial interests, not vice versa."[93]

6.3 War Finance in the Bond Era

The evidence of external finance of war is abundant but fragmented. Centeno, Feis, Marichal, Suzuki, and Thies, among others, have shown that war outside Western Europe was financed with European capital.[94] A

---

87. Shea and Poast (2018).
88. Polanyi (2001, p. 15).
89. Vandervort (1998); Killingray (1989).
90. de Moor (1989, pp. 63–64).
91. Reid (2012).
92. Feis (1930, chs. 5 and 6).
93. Grant (2007, p. 7).
94. Centeno (2002); Feis (1930); Marichal (1989); Suzuki (1994); Thies (2005).

comprehensive war-specific database on war finance (i.e., what percentage of a given war was funded with tax, debt, and other instruments) is, however, missing in the literature; and it is probably impossible to produce, given the scarcity of historical data, changing accounting techniques, and fund fungibility.

The best approximation to this ideal dataset is offered by Cappella Zielinski.[95] Based on rigorous triangulation and case-by-case qualitative accounts, she establishes whether a war participant borrowed overseas to pay for some fraction of the war, namely, the extensive margin. Drawn from a sample of 17 sovereign countries and 19 interstate wars before 1914, Cappella Zielinski's data indicate that 56 percent of country wars in the Bond Era were at least partially financed with external capital.[96] To shed further light on the prevalence of external war finance in the Bond Era, I first identify explicit war loans floated in European markets and then quantify capital inflows during wartime regardless of their denomination.

6.3.1 EXPLICIT WAR LOANS

Flandreau and Flores revisit the haute finance hypothesis by delving into the lending decisions made by prestigious intermediaries or underwriters in London.[97] Their data, drawn from primary sources at the Rothschild Archives, lend support to some aspects of haute finance. They find that prestigious intermediaries were rarely interested in financing war: they had little to win and much reputation to lose in the eyes of small bondholders. Selected underwriters had enough market power to impose conditional lending clauses prohibiting borrowers from diverting funds to war purposes. The 1831 loan to France, for instance, required its finance minister to publicly announce that the French government had no intention to wage a new war.

Whereas prestigious intermediaries did not lend to warring states (with important exceptions, including the Franco-Prussian War, the largest war on European soil), second-tier underwriters did. Flandreau and Flores

---

95. Cappella Zielinski (2016).

96. Countries in the sample are Argentina, Brazil, Chile, China, Denmark, France, Greece, Italy, Japan, Mexico, Morocco, Paraguay, Peru, Russia, Spain, Turkey, the UK, and the US.

97. Flandreau and Flores (2012b).

identify 15 wartime loans between 1845 and 1913, equivalent to 20 percent of the 51 interstate wars considered in their sample.

Following Flandreau and Flores's example, one could search for loans that were explicitly issued for war and military purposes. By *explicitly*, I mean that borrowers were open about the end use of foreign capital. In that spirit, table 6.2 lists more than 40 of these loans drawn from secondary sources. This could be sufficient evidence to prove that war in the nineteenth century was often financed with external capital; however, if the haute finance hypothesis is right or even partially right, some hesitancy should be anticipated among investors about buying bonds earmarked explicitly for war purposes. Governments could be expected to obfuscate their true intentions by floating loans for war that officially served other purposes. Take Greece, for instance. Almost the entire proceeds of the 5 percent Greek loan of 1890 for £3.6 million were diverted from its "expressly assigned purpose"—the railway from Piraeus to Larissa—and spent on more pressing budgetary needs, including the mobilization of the army against Turkey.[98] To account for this or other accounting tricks, next I examine foreign capital inflows regardless of their official (i.e., explicit) purpose.

6.3.2 CAPITAL INFLOWS DURING WARTIME

Examining foreign capital inflows during wartime presents three advantages: First, it allows the study of the intensive margin of war finance, that is, how much capital borrowers were able to mobilize from international sources. Second, governments might issue loans to finance war while camouflaging their intentions to investors—if only because war could be penalized with higher spreads.[99] Consistently, the expression "war loan" is exceptionally rare in the prospectuses circulated among British investors. Third, even if some sovereign loans were statutorily banned for war purposes, local treasuries could still redirect domestic revenue to war and finance contemporaneous nonmilitary spending with external capital. All things considered, focusing on capital inflows can capture any systematic relationship between international emission and war that would otherwise be overlooked.

98. Wynne (1951, pp. 300–302).
99. Mauro, Sussman, and Yafeh (2006).

TABLE 6.2. Explicit War and Military Loans

Year	Entity	Rate	Description	Year	Entity	Rate	Description
1822	Colombia	6%	War loan (Marichal 1989)	1867	Chile	7%	War (Marichal 1989)
1822	Chile	6%	Chilean Navy (Marichal 1989)	1868	Argentina	6%	War expenses (Sicotte and Vizcarra 2009)
1822	Peru	6%	Military expenses (Vizcarra 2009)	1863	Confederate	7%	US Civil War (F&F 2012)
1824	Buenos Aires	6%	Government and military (Marichal 1989)	1870	France	6%	Franco-Russian War (F&F 2012)
1824	Colombia	6%	Government and military (Marichal 1989)	1873	Chile	5%	Railways and military (Marichal 1989)
1824	Mexico	5%	Government and military (Marichal 1989)	1877	Turkey	5%	Russian War (Birdal 2010)
1824	Greece	5%	Independence War (Reinhart and Trebesch 2016)	1882	Argentina	6%	Military (Marichal 1989)
1825	Peru	6%	Military expenses (Vizcarra 2009)	1885	China	7%	Sino-French War (F&F 2012)
1825	Mexico	6%	Government and military (Marichal 1989)	1888	Turkey	5%	Military equipment (Birdal 2010)
1825	Peru	6%	Government and military (Marichal 1989)	1894	China	7%	Sino-French War (F&F 2012)
1825	Greece	5%	Independence War (Reinhart and Trebesch 2016)	1895	China	6%	Sino-French War (F&F 2012)
1852	Brazil	4.5%	Argentina-Brazil-Uruguay War (F&F 2012)	1896	Turkey	5%	Military equipment (Birdal 2010)
1854	Turkey	6%	Crimean War (Birdal 2010)	1898	Sierra Leone		Hut Tax War (Gardner 2017)
1855	Turkey	4%	Crimean War (Birdal 2010)	1904	Japan	6%	Russo-Japanese War (1st loan) (F&F 2012)
1855	France	3.75%	Crimean War (Fenn 1869)	1904	Japan	6%	Russo-Japanese War (2nd loan) (F&F 2012)
1864	Venezuela	6%	War expenses (Sicotte and Vizcarra 2009)	1905	Japan	4.5%	Russo-Japanese War (1st loan) (F&F 2012)
1864	Mexico	6%	Military (Marichal 1989)	1905	Japan	4.5%	Russo-Japanese War (2nd loan) (F&F 2012)
1865	Mexico	6%	Military and refinance	1905	Turkey	4%	Military equipment (Birdal 2010)
1865	Brazil	5%	Triple Alliance War (F&F 2012)	1913	Turkey	5.5%	Military equipment (Birdal 2010)
1865	Chile	6%	Military (Marichal 1989)	1913	Romania	4.5%	2nd Balkan War (F&F 2012)
1865	Chile	6%	Military (Marichal 1989)	1914	Turkey	5%	Libyan and Balkan Wars (Birdal 2010)
1865	Peru	5%	War expenses (Sicotte and Vizcarra 2009)				
1866	Chile	6%	Military (Marichal 1989)				
1866	Argentina	6%	Triple Alliance War (F&F 2012)				

Note: Sources in parentheses. F&F stands for Flandreau and Flores 2012a.

I draw capital emissions from Stone, who lists loans issued in Britain to government and private ventures in 25 countries from 1865 to 1913.[100] I focus on government loans only because I am interested in sovereign borrowing. Stone's data overrepresent Europe and South America, yet selected economies in Africa and Asia are included.[101] For each country in the sample, I establish whether interstate war took place in any given year between 1865 and 1913. War data are drawn from Wimmer and Min's dataset, which expands the universe of interstate warfare by including the war participation of nonsovereign countries.[102]

The resulting dataset includes 1,125 country-years. A bivariate analysis shows that of the 41 interstate wars in the dataset, 17, or 41 percent, were waged while the government received foreign capital flows. These wars are listed in table 6.3. Of the 24 wars remaining, 7 were fought while the government was in default (hence excluded from capital markets); in 2, Great Britain was an opponent—another cause of exclusion; in 11, participants were France and Germany, which could rely on domestic lending. The rest—4 wars in total—could have been financed with German or French credit (recall that Stone's data are limited to British capital) or not financed with foreign capital at all. The general pattern is nevertheless consistent with the theoretical expectation: if external finance is available, warring countries will try to secure foreign capital inflows. Even if loans do not cover all war costs, they alleviate budget constraints and subsidize other expenses.

Next, I reexamine the same data under a multivariate regression format. This technique models capital inflows as a function of war while factoring out time-invariant, country-specific characteristics (e.g., friendly relationship with Great Britain), secular trends in capital markets (i.e., booms and busts in capital markets), and the three pull factors discussed in chapter 4: the gold standard, reputation (proxied by episodes of recent default), and the empire effect.

I allow war loans to occur in preparation for, during, or after war (for instance, to pay for demobilization costs or reparations). I capture all these possibilities by fitting two lags of warfare and two leads alongside current war:

---

100. Stone (1992).

101. The panel is balanced and includes the following countries: Argentina, Australia, Austria, Brazil, Canada, Chile, China, Cuba, Egypt, France, Germany, Greece, India, Italy, Japan, Mexico, New Zealand, Peru, Rhodesia (now Zimbabwe), Russia, South Africa, Spain, Turkey, Uruguay, and the US.

102. Wimmer and Min (2009). Further details on the war data appear earlier in this chapter.

TABLE 6.3. War and External Capital Inflows from 1865 to 1913

Borrower	War years	War name
Interstate war		
Mexico	1865	Franco-Mexican
Peru	1865	Spanish-Chilean
Brazil	1865	War of the Triple Alliance
Brazil	1866	War of the Triple Alliance
Russia	1866	Russia vs. Kokand and Bokhara
Chile	1866	Spanish-Chilean
Argentina	1866	War of the Triple Alliance
Argentina	1868	War of the Triple Alliance
Argentina	1869	War of the Triple Alliance
Argentina	1870	War of the Triple Alliance
Brazil	1870	War of the Triple Alliance
France	1870	Franco-Prussian
Germany	1870	Franco-Russian
France	1871	Franco-Prussian
Germany	1871	Franco-Prussian
France	1873	Franco-Tonkin
France	1875	Franco-Tonkin
China	1876	Franco-Tonkin
China	1877	Franco-Tonkin
China	1878	Franco-Tonkin
Turkey	1877	Russo-Turkish
Turkey	1878	Russo-Turkish
France	1881	Franco-Tonkin
France	1881	Franco-Tunisian
France	1882	Franco-Tonkin
France	1882	Franco-Tunisian
France	1882	Franco-Indochinese
China	1885	Franco-Tonkin
China	1885	Sino-French
France	1886	Mandingo War
China	1894	Sino-Japanese
China	1895	Sino-Japanese
United States of America	1898	Spanish-American
South Africa	1899	Boer War
South Africa	1901	Boer War
South Africa	1902	Boer War
Japan	1904	Russo-Japanese
Japan	1905	Russo-Japanese
Secessionist war		
Spain	1870	Spanish-Cuban
Spain	1871	Spanish-Cuban
Spain	1872	Spain vs. Carlists
Spain	1873	Spain vs. Carlists
Turkey	1875	Ottoman Empire vs. Christian Bosnians
Turkey	1877	Ottoman Empire vs. Christian Bosnians
South Africa	1880	Boer War
South Africa	1881	Boer War

TABLE 6.3. Continued.

Borrower	War years	War name
Greece	1888	Ottoman Empire vs. Cretans
Greece	1889	Ottoman Empire vs. Cretans
Turkey	1889	Ottoman Empire vs. Cretans
United States of America	1899	Philippine-American

Note: This table lists interstate and secessionist wars waged while belligerents received external loans. Calculation is based on Stone (1992) and Wimmer and Min (2009). The sample contains 25 countries and covers the period from 1865 to 1913. Further details appear in the text.

$$\text{Government Loans}_{i,t} = \beta_0 + \beta_1 \text{War}_{i,t-2} + \beta_2 \text{War}_{i,t-1} + \beta_3 \text{War}_{i,t}$$
$$+ \beta_4 \text{War}_{i,t+1} + \beta_5 \text{War}_{i,t+2} + \beta_6 \text{Gold Standard}_{it}$$
$$+ \beta_7 \text{Default} < 10\text{Years}_{it} + \beta_8 \text{Colonial Status}_{it}$$
$$+ \beta_9 \text{Government Loans}_{i,t-1} + \eta_i + \gamma_t + \epsilon_{i,t} \quad (6.1)$$

where i, t stand for country i in year t, respectively. The distribution of government loans is highly skewed, with 62 percent of country-year observations having a value of 0. A logarithmic transformation does not normalize the distribution of the outcome variable while attenuating any financial shock derived from war. Hence, I work with the original variable. To capture any latent propensity to obtaining loans and going to war, I fit a first lag of the outcome variable plus country fixed effects. I also add a battery of year fixed effects to account for common shocks in international market liquidity.

Figure 6.3 plots the estimates for $\beta_1 - \beta_5$ with 95 percent confidence intervals (I do not report the remaining covariates in expression 6.1). The height of the bars denotes deviations in loan inflows from the sample average when war takes place, all other controls being constant. Figure 6.3 suggests a systematic association between warfare and external government funds. In particular, capital flows precede hostilities by one year, arguably in preparation for future hostilities. The effect is substantial: capital inflows increase by £0.9 million right before war, almost a 100 percent increase relative to the yearly sample mean, £1.03 million. Interestingly, too, none of the lags and leads are negative, a pattern seemingly inconsistent with the haute finance hypothesis, according to which a significant reduction in capital flows should be expected before and after war.

Next, I consider a second type of conflict: independence or "nationalist secessionist" war, in which one of the contenders plans to create a new,

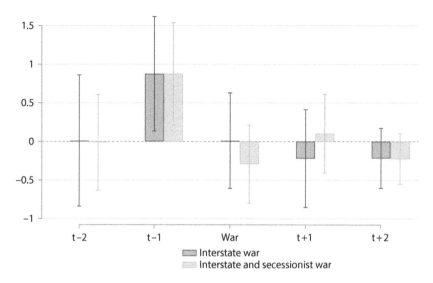

FIGURE 6.3. Marginal Effect of War on External Capital Inflows. Both models include a first lag of the dependent variable, a battery of country and year fixed effects, gold standard, default within last 10 years, and time-varying colonial status. 95% CI. Errors are clustered at country level.

separate nation-state.[103] Both the central government and secessionist territories might receive loans to fund war expenses, as did Greece in 1824 and 1825 before becoming a sovereign country.[104] Wimmer and Min's data list 12 secessionist wars between 1865 and 1913 in the 25 countries considered. Of these 12 conflicts, 5 of them were waged while external funds flowed into the coffers of the war participants. These wars are listed at the bottom of table 6.3. Results for the regression model are also plotted in figure 6.3 (light gray). They confirm average effects while improving the efficiency of the estimates.

The statistical analysis reveals that a substantial number of the sampled interstate and secessionist wars, 41 percent and 42 percent, respectively, were waged while receiving international flows from London. By expanding the time and country coverage and focusing on the intensive margin of capital inflows, these results offer a more precise account of the frequency and size of foreign finance of war in the nineteenth century. In fact, these values represent just a lower-bound approximation of external war finance because the data refer to British capital exports only. Belligerents might well have floated loans in Paris, Berlin, or Vienna in substitution for or addition

103. Wimmer and Min's 2009 coding of secessionist war depends on intentions, not outcome.
104. Reinhart and Trebesch (2016, p. 12).

to those issued in London. Results do not necessarily raise questions about the haute finance hypothesis on European soil (although important exceptions apply) but cast profound doubts on its applicability outside the old continent.

6.4 War Finance in the Colonial World

The quantitative analysis samples sovereign states and British offshoots, but how did dependent colonies finance war? Although similar statistical data do not exist for these countries, qualitative evidence suggests that war by European colonies was largely subsidized by the metropole, hence the modest effect on fiscal capacity.

Colonial war was often waged along the imperial border. Some of these wars were small by twentieth-century standards: the Ashanti War of 1873–1874 cost £1 million, as did the Zulu War of 1879; the Ninth Frontier War of 1877–1879 in Southern Africa cost £2 million, and the Gun War two years later £4.3 million.[105] At the time, however, these wars were not considered small and consumed more resources than the metropoles were willing to admit.[106]

British and French colonies and dominions were required to pay for their security (army and police) and administrative expenses;[107] however, financing military expenses was often a cause of disagreement between the metropole and the colony. Colonial authorities did not feel compelled to fund imperial wars because they believed them to be alien and imposed.[108] In the British Empire, the initial expenses of war were covered by an imperial fund created by the British treasury—a government-to-government loan. The colonies resorted to this fund and later negotiated the terms under which the loans were repaid; however, "the British treasury usually enjoyed but small success in recouping its monetary advances."[109]

Officially, colonies could not issue war loans, but exceptions occurred: for instance, a £2 million loan at zero interest rate was granted to India

---

105. War costs drawn from Davis and Huttenback (1986) and Ranger (1969).

106. Davis and Huttenback (1986).

107. Frankema and van Waijenburg (2014); Gardner (2012).

108. This problem was sizable with self-governing colonies. As early as 1862, the British Parliament issued the *1862 Colonial Military Expenditure Report*, which accepted British responsibility for military expenses arising from "imperial" policy. The same report made internal order the "main responsibility" of colonies (Gordon, 1965, p. 22).

109. Davis and Huttenback (1986, p. 149).

to finance part of the Second Afghan War of 1878–1880.[110] Sierra Leone and Gold Coast, British colonies, also financed frontier wars with zero interest rate loans floated in London. At other times, colonies received advances from Crown agents to balance budget shortages. Once the hostilities were over, the agents recovered the money with the proceeds of new issues.[111] Metropolitan subsidies or grants-in-aid were also common. For instance, the equipment of the Egyptian and Sudanese soldiers in the imperial campaigns led by Herbert Kitchener were heavily subsidized by British taxpayers.[112] So were the military efforts of the Cape in the Second Boer War, a case I return to below.

With multiple options to finance war externally, colonial officials exerted little effort in mobilizing domestic resources for war. The disproportional burden of military expenses is manifested when examining per capita expenditures: between 1860 and 1912, British taxpayers paid £0.64 per capita in imperial defense; those in self-governing colonies paid £0.12 and in dependent colonies £0.02 (£0.15 if police expenses were included); for reference, developing sovereign nations in the same period spent £0.22 per capita.[113]

Leaving India aside, five colonies (of more than 160) assumed two-thirds of the total colonial contribution to the military maintenance of the British Empire: the Straits (now Singapore), Hong Kong, Ceylon (now Sri Lanka), Mauritius, and Egypt.[114] Not coincidentally, the few colonies that paid for war with domestic resources have relatively strong states today, consistent with the argument of the book. For the vast majority of colonies, however, imperial war was heavily subsidized by Britain. In the opinion of Davis and Huttenback, "of all the subsidies enjoyed by the colonies, none was more lucrative than that for the defense."[115]

Paris faced similar challenges, if not worse. France colonized poorer and less economically integrated territories than the British, hence a thinner tax base. Between 1830 and 1891, France's military expenses in imperial dominions were almost three times larger than total local receipts—

---

110. The total cost of the war was £23.5 million. India paid £18.5 million and Great Britain £5 million (Benians, 1960, pp. 187–188).

111. Gardner (2017, pp. 247–248).

112. Black (2009).

113. Davis and Huttenback (1986, table 5.2).

114. Davis and Huttenback (1986, p. 159).

115. Davis and Huttenback (1986, p. 145).

3.5 billion francs compared to 1.3 billion.[116] Not until 1893 did the French government impose a tax on the colonies to share local expenses, and not until 1900 did they impose the cost of troops on each colony.[117] Still in 1901, colonies paid only 11 percent (of a total of 101 million francs) of local military expenses.

Exceptions also occurred within the French Empire. All early revenue in Gabon was spent on the conquest of the northern territories of Chari (modern-day Central African Republic) and Chad—which together formed the French Equatorial Africa Federation.[118] In Southeast Asia, the pacification of Tonkin and Annam (today, northern and eastern Vietnam, respectively) were paid with substantial contributions from the budget of Cochin China (now South Vietnam);[119] however, these cases were uncommon. Most often, military expenses were subsidized by the French Ministry of War and the Ministry of the Colonies.[120]

In sum, colonies forcefully participated in imperial and colonial wars, but (understandably) mobilized few domestic resources to pay for them. Colonial authorities relied on access to external capital, mostly in the form of soft loans and subsidies. Although the form and mechanisms to secure foreign capital differed,[121] it weakened colonial authorities' incentives to mobilize resources for war in a similar fashion that regular loans did for rulers of sovereign countries. The Second Boer War offers a good illustration of that.

6.5 Colonial War in Southern Africa: A Tale of Two States

The Second Boer War (1899–1902) pitted Britain and two British colonies, Cape of Good Hope and Natal, against the two neighboring Boer Republics, the Transvaal (officially the South African Republic) and the Orange Free State (see map in figure 6.4). The war was won by Britain, and the two republics were incorporated into the empire in 1902. Eight years later,

---

116. Vignon (1893, p. 286) quoted in White (1933, p. 83, fn. 1). For reference, the franc-pound conversion rate in 1880 was 1 franc = 0.04 pound sterling.

117. White (1933, p. 81).

118. Coquery-Vidrovitch (1969, p. 176).

119. López Jerez (2020, pp. 112–117).

120. Cogneau, Dupraz, and Mesplé-Somps (2021, p. 448).

121. Refer to chapter 3 for details.

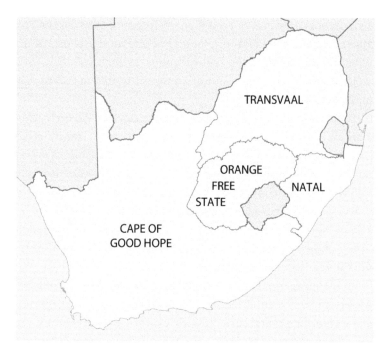

FIGURE 6.4. South African Provinces until 1976. *Source*: Wikipedia, Htonl/CC BY-SA/ Creative Commons.

the four territories formed the Union of South Africa, retaining significant revenue and expenditure powers.

Access to external capital was secured for the four territories before and after the war, but the Transvaal and the Orange Free State were excluded from international credit markets during the war years. I take advantage of that to examine responses to fiscal shocks caused by war in colonial and sovereign countries with and without access to external finance. To simplify the analysis, I focus on the Transvaal and the Cape, the two wealthiest territories on each side of the conflict. The Transvaal had unlimited access to gold, and the Cape to diamonds.

The Second Boer War had multiple causes, chief among them the disagreement around installing a customs union between the Cape and the Transvaal. The latter was landlocked, and it needed to export gold via either Capetown (to the south) or Lourenço Marques (Mozambique) to the east, under Portuguese control. For years, the Transvaal and Cape governments and various British high commissioners negotiated ways to split the Transvaal's customs revenue (collected at port of entry) if the tariff union came to exist. The Transvaal disagreed with all proposals. In 1895, the Cape government tried a different path, orchestrating a conspiracy against the highly popular Transvaal president, Paul Kruger. The so-called Jameson Raid calamitously failed and put the four colonies on a collision course.

Before the war, the two Boer Republics had issued a small amount of debt in London.[122] Most of the external capital, however, came from Germany and the Netherlands, and it was used to build the public railway from the goldfields to the Delagoa Bay.[123] In 1899, the Germans concluded that their interests would be better protected under British rule and sided with the British.[124] Interestingly, the policy switch was a by-product of extreme conditionality. The 1898 British-German agreement brought the two Great Powers together to extract concessions from Portugal in return for fresh loans. Specifically, Portugal would hand off its African possessions if it defaulted on its foreign debt, and Lourenço Marques would be handed over to Germany. As a gesture of goodwill with its circumstantial ally, the Germans agreed not to interfere with British affairs in South Africa, de facto abandoning the Boer Republics to their own fate.[125]

By the time the war broke out, the Transvaal was diplomatically and financially isolated. "Its strength lay, above all, in its self-sufficiency,"[126] and they did not waste time. Kruger put together an army of 50,000 men, a few thousand foreign volunteers, and 5,000 Cape rebels.[127] These men were armed with imported weapons from Germany,[128] which had been flowing in at least since the Jameson Raid.[129] The government reconverted the dynamite monopoly into a wartime industry, producing firearms and bullets and distributing supplies by taking control of the railways.

Given the precarious position of customs revenue and exclusion from capital markets, the government of the Transvaal had to elevate pressure on domestic taxes: it raised the alcohol excise (between 6 and 10 percent per gallon, compared to 4 percent in the Cape),[130] the land tax, and revenue from dynamite, cement, and brick monopolies—key inputs for gold extraction. Most importantly, it passed a new 5 percent tax on the profit of

122. Ferguson and Schularick (2006, p. 296).
123. Gwaindepi and Siebrits (2020, p. 283).
124. Van-Helten (1978, p. 388).
125. Krüger (1969, pp. 343–344).
126. Pakenham (2000, p. 258).
127. Krüger (1969, p. 346).
128. Judd and Surridge (2002).
129. Krüger (1969, p. 342).
130. De Kock (1924, p. 412).

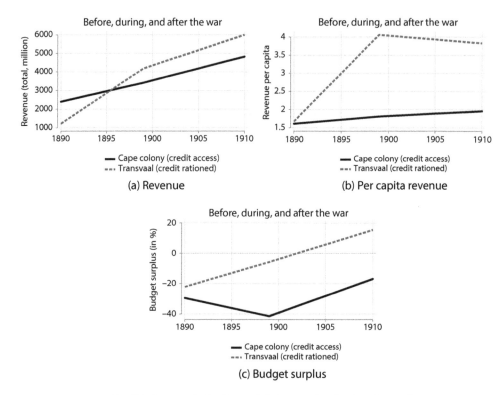

FIGURE 6.5. Fiscal Performance in the Cape and the Transvaal in the Second Boer War. Data are drawn from Gwaindepi and Siebrits (2020).

gold mines, and a 2.5 percent tax on the gross yield of gold from *mynpacht* (leased) areas.[131] The monthly £100,000 raised from the new direct taxes virtually paid the entire cost of the war.[132]

When the war was over, some of these taxes remained in place, including the land tax and the gold mine profit tax, which the new colonial authorities raised to 10 percent.[133] As reflected in figure 6.5, strong domestic mobilization of resources allowed the Transvaal Republic to maintain a balanced budget despite engaging in a war against the most powerful army in the world and losing it. The fiscal effect, measured in nominal and per capita tax burden, persisted for at least 10 years after the war.

131. De Kock (1924, p. 424).
132. Pakenham (2000, p. 258).
133. De Kock (1924, pp. 423–424).

The Cape's fiscal trajectory was remarkably different. The colony traditionally relied on customs revenue to finance colonial expenditures. Trade
taxes represented 51 percent of revenue before the war.[134] Instead of pushing for new taxes, the Cape would finance new expenses with debt. Because
the domestic credit market was underdeveloped, these loans were floated
in London.[135]

Despite being a key instigator of the war, the Cape (or Natal) made no
significant effort to finance the Second Boer War. This had been a regularity for almost every military engagement of the Cape. The occupation
of Rhodesia in 1896 had been heavily subsidized by British taxpayers.[136]
Before that, the Zulu War of 1879, the Ashanti War of 1873, and the Ninth
Frontier War were also financed with British capital.[137]

Per capita tax ratios in the Cape remained virtually flat before, during,
and after the war. At the same time, the Cape's external debt increased from
£24 million before the war, to £31 million during the war, and to £52 million after the war,[138] figures that contrast with the meager £2.5 million in
outstanding external debt of the Transvaal in 1903.[139] Income taxes were
passed in the Cape and Natal only after the war, in 1904 and 1908, respectively; however, they were eliminated in 1910 because they did not raise any
significant money.[140] Most of the £218 million cost of the Second Boer War
was eventually assumed by the British taxpayer. As Robert Lower (later
Lord Sherbrooke), Gladstone's first chancellor of the Exchequer, wrote:
"Instead of taxing them [South African colonies] as our forefathers claimed
to do, we, in the matter of this military expenditure, permit them in a great
degree to tax us."[141]

The paired comparison in South Africa illustrates the different incentives to mobilize tax revenue depending on external capital access and
colonial status. When countries wage war excluded from capital markets,
even retrograde leaders like those in the Transvaal are compelled to undertake tax reform to secure government funds, enabling lasting gains in
fiscal capacity. Such efforts are harder to observe when local authorities,

134. De Kock (1924, p. 411).
135. Gwaindepi and Siebrits (2020, fn. 18).
136. Headlam (1936, p. 538).
137. Davis and Huttenback (1986, pp. 150–151).
138. De Kock (1924, p. 394).
139. British Parliament (1908, p. 295).
140. Lieberman (2003, pp. 111–112).
141. Quoted in Davis and Huttenback (1986, p. 119).

sovereign or colonial, rely on external finance in the form of loans and imperial subsidies.

6.6 Conclusion

Historically, interstate war is the main driver of state building. Based on this premise, this chapter pursued two goals: First, I documented the incidence and magnitude of war around the world over the last two centuries for both sovereign and nonsovereign countries. Descriptive statistics of historical war data suggest that interstate warfare outside Europe was a pervasive phenomenon in the nineteenth century—not so much after 1914. If interstate war is a cause of state building, evidence of such in the nineteenth century, not later, should be apparent.

Chapters 3 and 4 showed that external finance was readily available for countries around the world regardless of their economic fundamentals. Chapter 5 showed that loans to the developing world were often repaid in specie, not tax money, unraveling the long-term equivalence between loans and taxes for public finance. This chapter showed that consolidated and recently created countries and colonies in the Bond Era seized the lending frenzy to pay for war. Now that all ingredients are aligned, I investigate the short- and long-term consequences of the external finance of war for state building in the next three chapters.

7

War, Credit, and Fiscal Capacity

The political economy of public finance advanced in chapter 2 suggests that funding military expenses with taxation should contribute to state building because doing so stimulates self-strengthening reform. By contrast, financing war with foreign capital might not necessarily lead to stronger states if countries default on war debt and surrender national assets and entire revenue lines to foreign bondholders as part of debt readjustment agreements. In this chapter, I investigate the short- and long-term effects of external capital access on fiscal capacity, namely, the ability to raise taxes. I first show that access to external finance during wartime in the Bond Era decreased the likelihood of strengthening fiscal capacity, measured by direct tax ratios. Then I investigate whether early tax efforts (or their absence) had long-term repercussions. I show that war finance in the Bond Era shaped fiscal capacity all the way into the early twenty-first century. Countries that disproportionally financed war externally in the nineteenth century show lower tax capacity circa 2000 than countries that relied on domestic resource mobilization. To come to this conclusion, I address various threats to inference and decompress history by showing intermediate effects. This chapter sheds light on the mixed evidence that often surrounds empirical accounts of the bellicist hypothesis after 1800. The means to finance war are key to understanding the conditions under which war makes states.

7.1 Theoretical Expectations

A key implication of the theoretical discussion in chapter 2 is that fiscal shocks strengthen state capacity when rulers are compelled to undertake tax reform to mobilize domestic resources, a course of action that cannot be taken for granted. The "transaction costs"[1] of enforcing a new tax unilaterally are high: obliging the populace to pay taxes by intimidation and force is expensive and inefficient. To induce "quasi-voluntary compliance" with new taxation, the ruler might grant taxpayers some political say over fiscal policy—namely, power-sharing institutions, which convey information to taxpayers about who owns what (i.e., what the tax base is) and how tax yields are to be spent, limiting the ruler's discretion over government funds (thus the expression *limited government*).

Power-sharing institutions are second-best solutions for rulers who seek to maximize wealth and power. Besides reducing the ruler's discretion over fiscal policy today, in the future political rivals might choose to use the enhanced tax capacity against the best interests of today's ruler if they achieve office. Together, current and future costs of taxation explain rulers' hesitancy to rely on taxation.[2]

Rulers will consider policy alternatives to meet fiscal shocks while not sharing power with taxpayers or having to spend resources in the tax bureaucracy. External finance is one such policy alternative. Foreign capital inflows can be put to work immediately. In case of war, they can be used to purchase new military equipment, mobilize a larger army, or feed the troops; alternatively, foreign loans can subsidize government consumption in other areas, freeing domestic resources to pay for war. Either way, external finance allows rulers to meet an expenditure surge while not having to strengthen fiscal capacity, postponing the (unwelcome) political ramifications of higher taxation.

In the remainder of this chapter, I test several aspects of the political economy of war finance. First, I show that the disproportional use of external finance during wartime did not build tax capacity during the Bond Era—the short term. Then I document its negative consequences for long-term fiscal capacity. Overall, results suggest that the average ruler reshuffled the tax administration and raised new taxes when pressed by circumstances, that is, if excluded from international credit markets. Once

---

1. Levi (1988).

2. Acemoglu (2003) and Besley and Persson (2011) formalize the ruler's fear of future extraction if the opposition takes over and uses enhanced tax capacity against the former ruler.

enhanced, however, fiscal capacity did not revert to prewar years, a phenomenon commonly known as the ratchet or "displacement" effect of war.[3] In chapter 8, I elaborate on the causes of persistence, the so-called mechanisms of transmission.

7.2 War Finance and Short-Run Gains in Fiscal Capacity

To test the first part of the argument—rulers prioritize external finance over taxation to minimize political and administrative costs—I examine the evolution of fiscal capacity as a joint function of war (the paramount fiscal shock before 1914) and access to international capital markets. I expect tax capacity of country i at year t to evolve in the following form:

$$\text{Tax Capacity}_{i,t} = \beta_0 + \beta_1 \text{War}_{i,t-1} + \beta_2 \text{Exclusion from External Finance}_{i,t-1}$$
$$+ \beta_3 \text{War}_{i,t-1} \times \text{Exclusion from External Finance}_{i,t-1}$$
$$+ \beta_4 \text{Tax Capacity}_{i,t-1} + X\Gamma + \eta_i + \gamma_t + \epsilon_{i,t} \qquad (7.1)$$

where X denotes a vector of country-level controls, and η_i and γ_t full batteries of country and year fixed effects, respectively. If rulers seek to minimize the political ramifications of taxation, they will only strengthen fiscal capacity when they run out of options. Building from this premise, I expect tax capacity to increase when countries wage war—the fiscal shock—while excluded from capital markets, therefore $\beta_3 > 0$. By contrast, waging war with access to external capital should relax incentives to increase tax capacity if only to avoid sharing fiscal powers with taxpayers and new administrative expenses, hence $\beta_1 = 0$.

One could use the experience of Spain with war finance as a heuristic. This country participated in three waves of war in the second half of the nineteenth century: In the first wave, Spain waged war in Cochin China (1858–1862), Morocco (1859–1860), Santo Domingo (1863–1865), and Chile (1864–1866). Two years later, it waged war against Cuban rebels (1868–1878)—the second wave—and lastly the Philippines (1896–1898) and Cuba again (1895–1898)—the third wave. Based on the magnitude of military expenses, the first wave of war was the least costly of the three,[4] but it was also the only one in which Spain was excluded from international capital markets. Domestic resources were mobilized: the tax-to-GDP ratio

---

3. Peacock and Wiseman (1961).

4. In temporal order, the three waves of war consumed 35.1, 48.7, and 43.7 percent of the budget, respectively (Comín, 2015).

increased by 1.7 points within seven years, from 7.1 percent to 8.8 percent (a 23 percent increase). Small as it was by modern standards, the tax pressure remained at that level for roughly 25 years, until the early 1890s. The other two military campaigns were financed with a mix of external debt, colonial debt, and inflation tax.[5] Despite being significantly more expensive, the second and third waves of war increased tax ratios by 0.40 and 0.88 points of GDP, respectively, a quarter and a half of the increase in the first wave. The Spaniards, like many other nations at the time, exerted meaningful fiscal effort when they could not rely on borrowed money overseas.

7.2.1 DESIGN AND MEASUREMENT

The period between 1816 and 1913 was one of sustained military conflict (see chapter 6) and coincided with the advent of global finance (see chapter 3), thus my focus on the long nineteenth century. Before 1914, fiscal efforts were largely driven by military need. The boom in welfare spending following World War I makes isolating the effect of war on fiscal capacity thereafter more difficult because the newly created social programs also required higher taxation. In addition, because the financial costs of the two world wars were unprecedented, the most active participants were countries with high fiscal capacity to begin with. Expanding the analysis beyond 1913 would exacerbate problems of selection.

For the dependent variable, I rely on an important dataset on public finance recently assembled by Andersson and Brambor, who put together an unbalanced panel of tax ratios for 31 countries in Europe, Latin America, Oceania, and Japan as early as 1800.[6] To examine advances in tax capacity before 1914, I follow Dincecco and Prado and my earlier work,[7] employing the share of direct taxes as a percentage of total taxation. Direct taxes (income and property taxes) require a sophisticated bureaucratic apparatus to assess wealth and monitor compliance of an atomized tax base.[8] Efforts to increase direct taxation in the nineteenth century signal rulers' resolve to strengthen fiscal capacity.

Table 7.1 lists the effective sample for the empirical analysis, reduced to 23 countries because of limited tax data before 1914. The other two key

5. Comín (2012).
6. Andersson and Brambor (2019).
7. Dincecco and Prado (2012); Queralt (2015).
8. Daunton (2001); Tilly (1990).

TABLE 7.1. Sample Coverage of Direct Tax Ratios Prior to 1914

Argentina	1895	1913	Mexico	1867	1895
Australia	1910	1913	Netherlands	1816	1913
Austria	1816	1913	New Zealand	1879	1913
Belgium	1830	1912	Norway	1851	1913
Chile	1817	1913	Peru	1899	1913
Denmark	1820	1913	Portugal	1833	1913
Ecuador	1830	1913	Spain	1845	1913
Finland	1882	1913	Sweden	1850	1913
France	1816	1913	Switzerland	1875	1913
Germany	1906	1913	United Kingdom	1816	1913
Italy	1862	1913	Uruguay	1903	1913
Japan	1868	1913			

Source: Andersson and Brambor (2019).
Note: First and last observation per country (N = 23).

covariates are war and access to international finance. War data are drawn from Wimmer and Min for reasons provided in chapter 6: their data are representative of the universe of warfare waged by sovereign and nonsovereign countries in the nineteenth century.[9] For each year, I compute the total number of interstate and independence (or secessionist) wars fought by any given country, or the intensive margin of war. For robustness purposes, I also consider the Correlates of War dataset, but the number of wars decreases because it lists only interstate wars waged by internationally recognized states, that is, those with diplomatic relations with both the French and the British.

To determine access to international capital, I resort to episodes of external default as early as 1800 coded by Reinhart and Rogoff, who define sovereign default as the failure of a government to meet a principal or interest payment on the due date (or within the specified grace period).[10] Consistent with the Wimmer and Min war data, Reinhart and Rogoff define states based on international borders as of the early 2000s. The median duration of default episodes in the period under consideration is six years.[11] Critically, while in default, countries are excluded from the international lending market. I expect war waged during episodes of default to stimulate improvements in wealth assessment, tax enforcement, and institution building.

9. Wimmer and Min (2009).
10. Reinhart and Rogoff (2009).
11. Reinhart and Rogoff (2009, p. 81).

Tax capacity is a slow-moving variable. To account for serial correlation of the outcome variable, I include its first lag as an additional control. To adjust for time-invariant unobserved characteristics between countries, I add a battery of country fixed effects. Any secular trend that affects, for instance, access to credit and tax capacity is accounted for with a full battery of year fixed effects. To minimize selection bias, I control for the cumulative number of wars and external defaults, accounting for differences in military and financial trajectories that could affect the likelihood of being at war at any particular time (i.e., the more war a country has waged in the past, the more likely that country is to wage war in the future[12]) and of being in default (i.e., past default might increase the chances of future exclusion[13]).

The point estimates for β_1 and β_3 in expression 7.1 are plotted in figure 7.1. This first set of results suggests that the effect of war on tax capacity hinges on external capital access. When a country is in default, hence excluded from international capital markets, war exerts a positive effect on direct tax ratios. The effect is the opposite and half its size when a country has access to external capital. The magnitude of the estimates is substantial given that it speaks to immediate fiscal effects: for each additional war year excluded from external capital, the direct tax ratio increases by 0.7 percentage points, all else held constant. Based on these estimates, fighting an entire war (four years on average) while in default would increase direct tax ratios by 2.8 percentage points, an 11-point increase relative to the sample average. Against expectation, waging war with access to capital does not have a null effect but, in fact, decreases tax capacity. For reasons of popularity, rulers might be willing to relax the tax pressure while at war but at the same time secure sovereign loans to meet military expenses. If so, bringing tax ratios back to prewar levels after hostilities cease might require additional efforts, increasing the chances of default.[14]

7.2.2 GLOBAL CREDIT CRUNCHES

Although intuitive, using a country-specific measure of external default to establish external capital access is problematic. Countries that wage war in default might differ from those that postpone war until foreign capital is available in ways that also affect long-term fiscal capacity. In this

12. Gennaioli and Voth (2015).
13. Tomz (2007).
14. The interested reader can refer to table 7.4 for results in regression format.

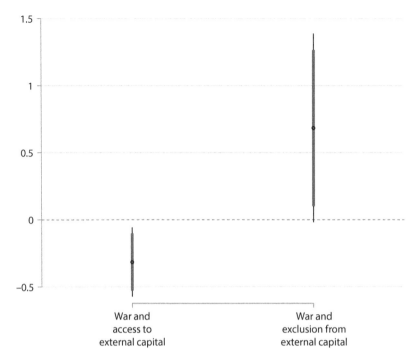

FIGURE 7.1. Effect of War on Direct Taxation as a Function of Default Episodes. The outcome variable is the annual share of direct taxes to total tax revenue between 1816 and 1913. Regression estimates for expression 7.1 using external default episodes to measure external capital access. Covariates (unreported) include a first lag of the outcome variable, cumulative war and default episodes, and country and year fixed effects. Sample size (N) = 1,225. Errors clustered at country levels with 90% and 95% CI.

section, I address endogeneity in capital access by exploiting global credit crunches. In the period under observation, European countries experienced economic and banking crises that rapidly reverberated in sovereign debt markets.[15] I take advantage of unanticipated global credit crunches initiated in Europe, also known as "sudden stops,"[16] to identify periods in which countries were precluded from financing war externally irrespective of their (un)observed characteristics. In the words of Reinhart and Rogoff,

> banking crises in global financial centers (and the credit crunches that accompany them) produce a "sudden stop" of lending to countries at the periphery.... Essentially, capital flows from the "north" dry up

15. Eichengreen (1990); Neal (2015).
16. Calvo (1988).

TABLE 7.2. Banking Crises and Stock Market Crashes in London, 1816–1913

Banking crises		Stock market crises
1825	1849	1865
1837	1850	1866
1838	1857	1867
1839	1866	1910
1840	1873	1911
1847	1890	1912
1848		1913

Note: Dates drawn from Reinhart and Rogoff (2009). 1873 banking panic added by author.

in a manner *unrelated* to the underlying economic fundamentals in emerging markets.[17]

Building on this intuition, I examine whether incentives to finance war with tax money grew stronger in periods in which international capital dried up for reasons exogenous to the borrower's characteristics. To identify the onset and duration of global credit crunches, I draw on banking and stock market crises in Britain, the world's banker, before 1914 (table 7.2). Crashes in London rapidly spread to Paris, Berlin, and New York. Contagion took different routes, including arbitrage in commodities and securities and movement of money in various forms (specie, bank deposits, bills of exchange), cooperation among monetary authorities, and pure psychology.[18] One way or another, financial crashes in London dried up international lending *on a global scale*.[19]

Important for exogeneity purposes, the causes of the British financial collapses in the nineteenth century are domestic—certainly the case for the major crises of 1825, 1847, 1857, and 1866 but less true for the 1890 panic, in which a large financial imbalance in Argentina halted British lending.[20] More importantly, British panics did not respond to defaults by borrowers, which would cast doubt on the exogeneity of these shocks. Most of the countries that defaulted in the nineteenth century were in the periphery.

17. Reinhart and Rogoff (2009, p. 74); emphasis added.
18. Kindleberger (1996, p. 109).
19. Bordo (2006).
20. For the domestic origins of the 1825, 1847, 1866, and 1890 crises, see Neal (1998), Dornbusch and Frenkel (1982), Mahate (1994), and Kindleberger (1996), respectively.

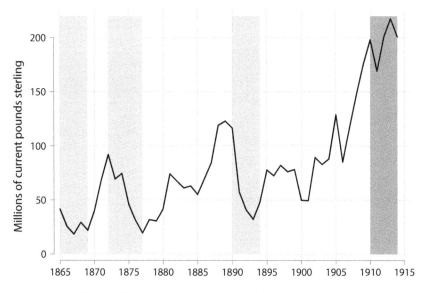

FIGURE 7.2. British Capital Exports from 1865 to 1914. In light gray: Banking panics of 1865, 1873, and 1890. In dark gray: The stock crisis of 1907. *Sources*: Reinhart and Rogoff (2009); Stone (1992).

Although the defaulted quantities were significant relative to their home economies, from a global perspective they were merely a "sideshow"[21] for the British economy. All things considered, the periods of sudden stops can be safely treated as exogenous to every country except Great Britain and 1890 Argentina.

For the purposes of illustration, figure 7.2 shows the evolution of British capital exports since the earliest date, while indicating the years of banking panics and stock crashes as dated by Reinhart and Rogoff.[22] Figure 7.2 reflects the boom-and-bust cycles preceding and following a banking crisis, as exemplified by those occurring in 1873 and 1890. Prior to each bust, lending was ferocious, but once the debt bubble burst, international capital flows temporarily dried up across the board. Precisely, during periods of sudden stop, I expect rulers to have stronger incentives to finance military campaigns by means other than external borrowing; namely, taxes.[23]

21. Eichengreen (1991, p. 151).

22. Reinhart and Rogoff (2009).

23. In light of figure 7.2, banking crises might be more damaging than stock market crashes (e.g., 1907). In appendix I in Queralt (2019), I show that results hold when stock market crashes are disregarded.

TABLE 7.3. Frequency and Duration of War as a Function of Endogenous and Exogenous Credit Access in the Short-Run Test Sample

	Endogenous measure		Exogenous measure	
	Not in default	In default	Credit flows	Credit stops
Frequency	94%	6%	43%	57%
Duration in years	3.06	1.89	2.01	2.42
	(0.21)	(0.35)	(0.18)	(0.17)
Duration difference	1.17**		−0.41	

Note: The total number of war years is 162. Credit stops refer to periods of sudden stop. Standard error in parentheses. *** $p < 0.01$, ** $p < 0.05$, * $p < 0.1$.

Sudden stops in the nineteenth century lasted four years on average.[24] Accordingly, I establish four-year windows following the onset of each sudden stop and assume that within these windows countries had no access to external loans. If sudden stops are predictable, countries may go to war before their onset, casting doubt on the exogeneity of this historical accident. To assess the unanticipated nature of sudden stops, table 7.3 shows the frequency and duration of war when the endogenous measure of capital access is considered—being in default or not—and when the exogenous measure is used instead. The first two columns show that few war years took place while participants were in default, confirming concerns about endogenity in using this intuitive measure. By contrast, the breakdown for the exogenous measure is fairly balanced: 57 percent of war years coincide with periods in which the international lending market is down. This distribution speaks favorably to the unpredictability of global credit crunches.

Now I consider the decision to *end* war, a second threat to inference. A weak state that finances war externally may be more prone to surrender during sudden stops. If that is the case, weak states would eventually experience a higher proportion of war years when credit flows and a lower proportion of war years during sudden stops. This would bias the estimation results toward finding a negative effect of war for years when credit flows. If this pattern were systematic, on average shorter wars during periods of sudden stops should be observed. However, table 7.3 suggests that the duration of war in and outside sudden stops is fairly balanced: 2.42 years in periods of sudden stops compared to 2.01 years when credit

24. Catão (2006).

flows, the difference not being statistically significant. These numbers contrast with the breakdown for the endogenous measure: wars in times of default are shorter than those in which participants have access to capital. If war is judged by its frequency and duration, table 7.3 suggests a comparison of apples to apples when tackling war waged during periods in which international lending flows and war waged during sudden stops of credit.

Results with Global Credit Crunches

Next, I reestimate expression 7.1, substituting the endogenous measure of external capital access (i.e., default episodes) for the exogenous measure (i.e., sudden stops). To maximize exogeneity, I drop Great Britain (the world's banker), as well as France and Germany, which by 1880—the average year in the effective sample—had already assumed an important role in international financial networks. I plot the point estimates of β_1 and β_3 in figure 7.3 and report results in regression format in table 7.4.

The first model, reported in column 1 of the table, uses four-year windows to approximate the average duration of a credit crunch. Results confirm the opposite effect of war on fiscal capacity with reliance upon an exogenous measure of capital access. When countries wage war with access to external capital, the effect of war on fiscal capacity is negative. By contrast, waging war excluded from external credit increases short-run fiscal capacity. Based on the new set of estimates, an additional war year excluded from capital access increases tax ratios by 7.6 percentage points relative to the sample mean.

For robustness purposes, models 2 and 3 set global credit crunch windows to three and five years, respectively. Because shorter and larger windows add noise to the exclusion measure, coefficients in models 2 and 3 attenuate relative to those in model 1. In model 4, I include a control of per capita GDP drawn from Bolt, Inklaar, de Jong, and van Zanden,[25] arguably a relevant control: direct taxation requires high levels of monetization, which correlates with income levels. Likewise, wealthier countries are expected to access international capital at better terms and build stronger armies, increasing the likelihood of going to war. The downside of this control is that GDP relies heavily on linear interpolation and reduces the sample size. As expected, this control attenuates the point estimates $\hat{\beta}_1$ and

---

25. Bolt, Inklaar, de Jong, and van Zanden (2018).

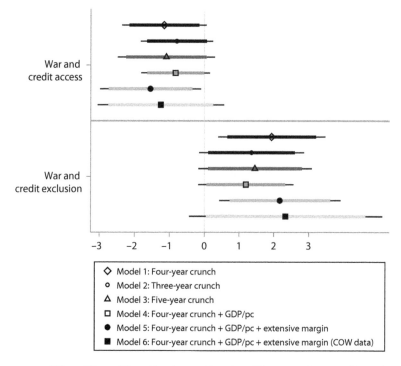

FIGURE 7.3. Effect of War on Direct Taxation as a Function of Exogenous Access to External Capital. The outcome variable is the annual share of direct taxes to total tax revenue between 1816 and 1913. Regression estimates for Expression 7.1 using global credit crunches as an exogenous shock for external capital access. Great Britain, France, and Germany are dropped from the sample to maximize exogeneity. All models include the following covariates: first lag of the outcome variable, cumulative war and default episodes, and country and year fixed effects. Additional controls are included as indicated in the figure legend. Errors clustered at country levels with 90% and 95% CI.

$\hat{\beta}_3$ relative to model 1; however, the substantive interpretation remains the same.

The relationship between the number of wars in which a country is involved in any given year and the intensity of war might be inversely correlated—a country can wage only so many major wars at once. Model 5 maintains the income control while replacing the intensive measure of warfare used so far by its extensive version, measured by an indicator variable equal to 1 when a country is waging war in any given year regardless of the number of wars in which it is involved. Results across specifications are virtually identical: waging war with access to external finance decreases short-run taxation, whereas fighting war excluded from capital increases it.

TABLE 7.4. Effects of War and External Capital Access on Short-Term Fiscal Capacity

	Figure 7.1	Figure 7.3					
		(1)	(2)	(3)	(4)	(5)	(6)
$\hat{\beta}_1$: War	−0.316**	−1.146*	−0.787	−1.085	−0.825*	−1.540**	−1.244
	(0.124)	(0.576)	(0.493)	(0.663)	(0.469)	(0.689)	(0.866)
$\hat{\beta}_2$: External capital exclusion	−0.309	−11.336***	−11.252***	−11.228***	−11.816***	−11.985***	−11.022***
	(0.389)	(1.483)	(1.453)	(1.470)	(1.675)	(1.720)	(1.253)
$\hat{\beta}_3$: War × external capital exclusion	0.684*	1.936**	1.356*	1.455*	1.195*	2.174**	2.336*
	(0.339)	(0.736)	(0.721)	(0.779)	(0.656)	(0.832)	(1.326)
External capital measure[a]	Default	Crisis	Crisis	Crisis	Crisis	Crisis	Crisis
War margin[b]	Intensive	Intensive	Intensive	Intensive	Extensive	Extensive	Extensive
Global financial centers[c]	Included	Excluded	Excluded	Excluded	Excluded	Excluded	Excluded
Credit crunch window	–	4-year	3-year	5-year	4-year	4-year	4-year
Lagged outcome variable	Yes	Yes	Yes	Yes	Yes	Yes	Yes
Cumulative default years	Yes	Yes	Yes	Yes	Yes	Yes	Yes
Cumulative wars	Yes	Yes	Yes	Yes	Yes	Yes	Yes
Year FE	Yes	Yes	Yes	Yes	Yes	Yes	Yes
Country FE	Yes	Yes	Yes	Yes	Yes	Yes	Yes
Observations	1,225	1,024	1,024	1,024	1,001	1,001	1,001
R-squared	0.831	0.812	0.811	0.811	0.820	0.820	0.822
Countries	23	20	20	20	20	20	20

Note: This table reports results in figures 7.1 and 7.3 in regression format. Fiscal capacity is measured by the share of direct taxes to total tax revenue. Robust standard errors clustered at the country level in parentheses. Intercept not reported. *** $p < 0.01$, ** $p < 0.05$, * $p < 0.1$.

[a] External capital access is measured by country-specific default episodes (endogenous measure) or a global financial crisis (exogenous measure).

[b] War is measured at the intensive margin (total wars per year) or extensive margin (war or no war in any given year).

[c] Great Britain, France, and Germany, the three global financial centers, are excluded in models in figure 7.3 to maximize exogeneity of the financial shock in the last decades of the nineteenth century.

Models 1–5 rely on Wimmer and Min's war data.[26] Model 6 reruns the same specification as in column 5 while using war data from the Correlates of War (COW) project,[27] a broadly used dataset in the historical study of warfare. As I explained in chapter 6, the COW dataset includes fewer interstate wars than Wimmer and Min's because it lists only wars waged by internationally recognized countries—namely, those having diplomatic relations with Britain and France. Likewise, the main COW dataset lists only interstate wars, excluding wars of independence.[28] The merits of COW clearly outnumber its limitations and it is worth confirming results once COW war data are used. Results for that test are reported in model 6. The point estimates are virtually identical to those in model 5. The confidence intervals are slightly larger because of statistical power issues derived from having fewer wars listed in COW relative to Wimmer and Min.

Altogether, figure 7.3 suggests that waging war during the period from 1816 to 1913 yielded heterogeneous consequences on short-term taxation depending on whether or not a country had access to external capital. War waged while excluded from capital markets increased tax pressure, whereas war waged while having access to capital did not and sometimes decreased it (statistical significance is borderline with 90 percent confidence intervals). Together, figures 7.1 and 7.3 shed light on the mixed results that scholars have found for the relationship between war and state making in the era of international finance. The globalization of capital arguably distorted the rulers' incentives to mobilize domestic resources when they were most needed.

7.3 War Finance and Long-Run Gains in Fiscal Capacity

Financing war with external funds might not damage state capacity in the long run. If the debt-tax equivalence of public finance holds, rulers will assume responsibility for war debt and enhance taxation to service debt after military conflict, thus contributing to state making. Generalized debt relief and the exchange of war debt for nontax revenue in case of default may, however, preempt self-strengthening reform—as I argued in chapter 5—unraveling the equivalence of taxes and loans for the purpose of state

26. Wimmer and Min (2009).

27. Sarkees and Wayman (2010).

28. The auxiliary COW datasets list wars of independence but do not map them into current state borders.

building. In light of the (at best) uncertain effects of external finance on capacity building, I expect long-term fiscal capacity to be stronger among countries that disproportionally relied on taxation to finance war relative to foreign loans, holding everything else constant.

7.3.1 DESIGN

To test for the long-term effects of war finance on fiscal capacity, longitudinal conflict-specific data regarding the manner in which war was financed in the past (i.e., tax and loan shares) can be exploited and used to model tax capacity in the long run. As I mentioned in chapter 6, the ideal dataset on war finance does not exist beyond a select number of cases, most of them in Western Europe. To move the analysis beyond advanced economies, I propose comparing the frequency with which war was waged with and without access to external capital in the Bond Era, and using that information to model tax capacity circa 2000. Drawing from the political economy of war in chapter 2 plus results in the first part of this chapter, I assume that if external capital were available, rulers would disproportionally resort to it to fund war.

For each country and war in the nineteenth century, I establish whether war was waged while having access to international credit markets. To establish access, I rely on episodes of default (endogenous but intuitive) and international financial crunches (unanticipated common shocks). With that information in hand, I regress tax ratios today on the number of years at war in the long nineteenth century with and without access to external finance while controlling for a battery of confounders, including war duration, casualties, and war outcome. Formally,

Tax Capacity$_{i,2000}$

$$= \alpha + \beta_1 (\text{\#Years at War between 1816 and 1913} \mid \text{No Credit Access})$$

$$+ \beta_2 (\text{\#Years at War between 1816 and 1913} \mid \text{Credit Access})$$

$$+ X_i \delta + \gamma + \rho + \epsilon_i \tag{7.2}$$

where the baseline category is fighting no war in the nineteenth century. I expect war making to strengthen rulers' incentives to invest in fiscal capacity whenever the country cannot finance externally, contributing to long-term fiscal capacity, $\beta_1 > 0$. The effect of war financed externally is ambiguous: countries may exert a fiscal effort after war to service debt and thus expand tax capacity (path C in figure 1.3), yet other countries may suspend debt service. Default settlements may include debt-equity swaps and foreign international control, which potentially shrink the tax base of the borrowing government (path E in figure 1.3). Less stringent adjustments of external debt might involve debt relief and extension of maturities, which relax the need to build capacity. Together, I expect a null (if not negative) effect of war making the more countries wage war while having access to external credit, $\beta_2 \leqslant 0$.

Two clarifications are in order: First, the expectation $\beta_2 \leqslant 0$ works against the debt-tax equivalence of war finance for the purpose of state building. Note that if the equivalence holds, borrowing and taxes should be indistinguishable for long-term state capacity, implying $\beta_1 \approx \beta_2 > 0$, all else being constant. Second, in the absence of external credit, rulers might resort to printing money, seeking domestic loans, trading slaves, or engaging in financial repression to finance the means of war.[29] If any, these alternatives introduce a downward bias on β_1 because they relax the incentives to enhance taxation in times when external credit dries up.

To measure fiscal capacity today, I rely on the personal income tax (PIT) as a percentage of GDP. Implementing a PIT requires a sophisticated bureaucratic apparatus capable of assessing a highly atomized tax base, enforcing compliance, and sanctioning evaders. In light of its administrative challenges, this tax is considered to be the endpoint of fiscal capacity building.[30] For the same reason, it sets a compelling benchmark to establish how far each country has gone in building tax capacity since 1914. To minimize the influence of anomalous observations (for instance, following a temporal economic shock), I work with *average* PIT-to-GDP ratios between 1995 and 2005.[31]

Note an important change in the data structure with respect to the first part of the chapter. In the short-run models, I exploited longitudinal cross-sectional data; here the variation is purely cross-sectional. The sample is no longer restricted by nineteenth-century tax data, which is relatively scarce; as a result, the long-term models include over four times the number of countries, covering a wider spectrum of developed and developing nations,

---

29. Cappella Zielinski (2016).

30. Besley and Persson (2011); Tilly (1990).

31. Note that the denominator in this ratio is GDP, not total taxation. GDP is a better choice because it conveys the extractive capacity relative to the tax base. PIT-to-GDP ratios are unavailable in the historical data. For data sources and the use of value-added taxes (or VATs) as a proxy of tax capacity today, refer to appendix M in Queralt (2019).

sovereign and dependent. Dependent countries, I argue in chapter 6, resorted to a mix of international loans and subsidies from the metropole to finance local and imperial war, conditions under which I expect few gains in long-term state building. War data again are drawn from Wimmer and Min.

Because the data are cross-sectional, instead of country fixed effects, I consider a series of potential confounders, X, affecting fiscal capacity today, as well as war participation or credit access or both in the nineteenth century. First, I add an indicator to identify Great Powers.[32] These countries had strong capacity and access to finance and were likely to wage war. Second, I consider a measure of initial wealth because wealthier countries are more likely to go to war and have stronger fiscal capacity in the first place.[33] In the absence of systematic GDP data for developing countries in the early nineteenth century, I include a measure of population density as of 1820, a standard proxy of economic prosperity before the Industrial Revolution.[34] Third, I include two geographic characteristics that could affect both sides of expression 7.2. The first one, sea access, is defined as the percentage of the land surface area of each country that is within 100 kilometers of the nearest ice-free coast. I expect sea access to correlate with trade activity, hence the geostrategic value of the country as well as its integration in international capital markets.[35] The second geographic control is the percentage of territory that is desert. I expect deserts to inhibit industrial growth and preempt monetization, but desert territory might also work as a natural barrier to foreign invasion, thus reducing the frequency of war.[36] Finally, I control for an important source of nontax revenue that could shape incentives to go to war (or suffer attack): being an oil producer.[37] Arguably, this variable gains relevance for the later years of the period under consideration.

Finally, all models below include a battery of region fixed effects, γ, that account for continent-specific characteristics in the frequency of war, access to credit, and statehood timing; and a battery of colonial origins indicators, ρ, because I expect opportunities of the colonies to go to war,

---

32. Great Powers were Austria-Hungary (treated as two different states), France, Germany, Italy, Russia, and Great Britain.

33. Gennaioli and Voth (2015).

34. Tilly (1990).

35. Salvucci (2006) for the strong ties between commerce and finance.

36. Data for sea access and desert territory are drawn from Nunn and Puga (2012).

37. Oil production data are drawn from Wimmer and Min (2009).

the tax structure that they build up, and the terms of external credit to be conditioned by the metropole.[38]

7.3.2 NAIVE ESTIMATES

The first set of results are plotted in figure 7.4. To establish a meaningful benchmark, I first plot the estimate for the unconditional version of the bellicist hypothesis—namely, more war, more state—for all the states sampled in Reinhart and Rogoff for which I can gather full information (63 out of 68).[39] The specification for the unconditional model is as follows:

$$\text{Fiscal Capacity}_{i,2000} = \alpha + \beta(\#\text{Years at War between 1816 and 1913})$$
$$+ X_i \delta + \gamma + \rho + \epsilon_i$$

including the same covariates, X, and region and colony fixed effects, γ and ρ, respectively, as above. The coefficient for number of years at war between 1816 and 1913, represented by a circle in the top portion of figure 7.4, is positive but not significant at 90 percent, consistent with the mixed findings mentioned in the literature review on the bellicist hypothesis in chapters 1 and 6.

Model 1's unconditional estimate in figure 7.4 should be compared to the six that follow, which distinguish the effect of war fought in default from that of war fought with access to international credit markets, β_1 and β_2, respectively, in expression 7.2. The first pair of point estimates (model 2, represented by squares) set a baseline. The signs of the coefficients are consistent with expectations: $\hat{\beta}_1$ is positive and statistically different from zero; $\hat{\beta}_2$ is centered around zero. Substantively, the benchmark specification means that a one-standard-deviation increase in the number of years at war while in default expands the PIT-GDP ratio today by 0.41 points. This is equivalent to a 15 percent increase with respect to the mean PIT.

---

38. Accominotti, Flandreau, and Rezzik (2011); Ferguson and Schularick (2006).

39. Reinhart and Rogoff (2009). Breakdown of countries in my analysis by region: Africa: Egypt, Ivory Coast, Kenya, Morocco, Nigeria, South Africa, Tunisia, Zambia, Zimbabwe; Asia: China, India, Indonesia, Japan, Malaysia, Myanmar, Philippines, South Korea, Sri Lanka, Thailand, Turkey; Europe: Austria, Belgium, Denmark, Finland, France, Germany, Greece, Hungary, Iceland, Ireland, Italy, Netherlands, Norway, Poland, Portugal, Romania, Russia, Spain, Sweden, Switzerland, United Kingdom; South America: Argentina, Bolivia, Brazil, Chile, Colombia, Costa Rica, Dominican Republic, Ecuador, El Salvador, Guatemala, Honduras, Mexico, Nicaragua, Panama, Peru, Uruguay, Venezuela; North America: Canada, United States; Oceania: Australia, New Zealand.

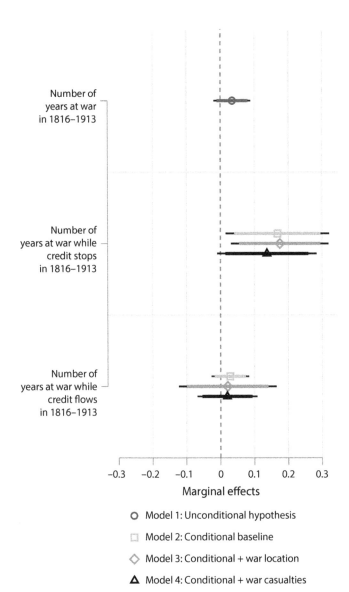

FIGURE 7.4. Long-Run Fiscal Capacity as a Function of War and Endogenous Credit Access. This figure plots marginal effects of war and credit access on personal income tax as a percentage of GDP circa 2000. N = 63. OLS, 90% and 95% CI. Credit access and exclusion are given by episodes of default. All four models include the following covariates: region and colonial origins fixed effects, total years in default, population density as of 1820, being an oil producer, sea access, desert territory, and a Great Powers indicator. Estimates in models 3 and 4 are drawn from models that include baseline controls plus war location and war casualties, respectively.

The estimate of β_2, by contrast, suggests that wars waged with access to international markets exert no lasting effect on fiscal capacity.

War causes destruction, but damage may vary depending on the location of military engagement. The tax base can be badly hurt when military conflict takes place within national boundaries, thus inhibiting investment in fiscal capacity. The location of war is thus likely to be a confounding variable. To address this logic, in model 3 I rerun the benchmark model while adding a control for the location of the conflict.[40] The new estimates for β_1 and β_2 (represented by diamonds) remain virtually identical to those in the benchmark model.

Not all wars are created equal. Bloodier and longer wars might overcome resistance to taxation while maximizing rulers' incentives to invest in fiscal capacity. To address this possibility, in model 4 I add a control for the intensity of warfare, measured by the total number of battle deaths between 1816 and 1913.[41] The inclusion of a measure of war casualties does not substantively affect the point estimates of the coefficients of interest, β_1 and β_2, now represented by triangles.

This first analysis yields results consistent with theoretical expectations: if countries wage war while excluded from international credit markets, the incentives to invest in tax capacity are strong and long-term state capacity follows. By contrast, when states have access to foreign capital, war (on average) does not translate into state making.

7.3.3 THREATS TO INFERENCE

Although intuitive, the analysis above is arguably plagued by endogeneity concerns. Being in default is not exogenous nor is the decision to wage war or which war to fight. Next, I address stepwise both sets of issues.

Global Credit Crunches and Long-Term Capacity

As discussed in section 7.2.2, one can replace country-specific default episodes for global credit crunches and use them as exogenous shocks in external capital access. These sudden stops of credit originated in the

---

40. War location is the sum of the years at war fought abroad minus the years at war fought at home from 1816 to 1913. This variable is positive when a country fights more wars abroad than at home, negative when military disputes at home are more frequent than abroad, and zero when countries never go to war. Data for war location are drawn from Wimmer and Min (2009).

41. Data for war casualties from 1816 to 1913 are drawn from Dincecco and Prado (2012).

TABLE 7.5. Frequency and Duration of War as a Function of Exogenous Credit Access in the Long-Run Test Sample

	Interstate war		Interstate and secessionist war	
	Credit flows	Credit stops	Credit flows	Credit stops
Frequency	47.74%	52.25%	50.89%	49.11%
Duration in years	2.32	2.25	2.23	2.29
	(1.87)	(1.51)	(1.73)	(1.58)
War-year-country	465		615	
Countries	107		107	

Note: Credit stops refer to periods of sudden stop. Standard deviation in parentheses. Countries in sample by regional breakdown are as follows: Africa: Burundi, Chad, Congo, Democratic Republic of the Congo, Egypt, Ethiopia, Guinea, Ivory Coast, Kenya, Lesotho, Madagascar, Mali, Morocco, Namibia, Nigeria, Rwanda, Senegal, South Africa, Swaziland, Tunisia, Zambia, Zimbabwe; Asia: Bangladesh, Bhutan, Cambodia, China, Cyprus, India, Indonesia, Iran, Israel, Japan, Lebanon, Malaysia, Mongolia, Myanmar, Nepal, Pakistan, Philippines, South Korea, Sri Lanka, Thailand, Turkey, Vietnam, Yemen; Europe: Albania, Armenia, Austria, Azerbaijan, Belarus, Belgium, Bosnia and Herzegovina, Bulgaria, Croatia, Czech Republic, Denmark, Estonia, Finland, France, Georgia, Germany, Greece, Hungary, Iceland, Ireland, Italy, Kazakhstan, Latvia, Lithuania, Macedonia, Moldova, Netherlands, Norway, Poland, Portugal, Romania, Russia, Slovakia, Slovenia, Spain, Sweden, Switzerland, Tajikistan, Ukraine, United Kingdom; Latin America: Argentina, Bolivia, Brazil, Chile, Colombia, Costa Rica, Dominican Republic, Ecuador, El Salvador, Guatemala, Honduras, Mexico, Nicaragua, Panama, Paraguay, Peru, Uruguay, Venezuela; North America: Canada, United States; Oceania: Australia, New Zealand.

financial capitals of the world, went unannounced, and lasted, on average, four years. Conveniently, by relying on global credit crunches, I create a measure of external capital access that is also unconstrained from country-level default data availability in Reinhart and Rogoff,[42] effectively expanding the sample size to 100+ countries in the world. For each of them, I count the number of years at war inside and outside periods of global capital freeze.

Table 7.5 illustrates the *exogenous* character of these shocks: half of total war years in the sample were waged during global credit crunches, and the average duration of wars was balanced across periods. The balanced distributions grant credibility to the unanticipated nature of sudden stops.[43]

In figure 7.5, I plot the point estimates $\hat{\beta}_1$ and $\hat{\beta}_2$ in expression 7.2 net of the influence of other controls, together with the scatterplot between

42. Reinhart and Rogoff (2009).

43. See text explanation of table 7.3 for the importance of balance in terms of duration. Refer to appendix W in Queralt (2019) for evidence of war not being waged in anticipation of sudden stops.

tax capacity today and the distribution of the number of years at war with and without access to external capital, respectively. Figure 7.5a suggests that the more war was waged without access to capital markets in the nineteenth century, the higher the PIT as a percentage of GDP today, holding everything else constant. Conversely, that relationship turns negative when focusing on the number of years at war waged while having access to external credit, figure 7.5b. Before drawing further conclusions, I address the second threat of endogeneity: selection into war.

The Decision to Go to War

Countries that wage war when international credit is tight (even for exogenous reasons) might be more capable than those that wait for lending to resume. To account for differences in initial state capacity, I consider two covariates: Bockstette, Chanda, and Putterman's state antiquity index[44] and *census capacity*. If older states exist because they won wars in the past, the *state antiquity index* should reflect cumulative military and administrative capacity.[45] Census technology, initially adopted to establish the tax base and conscription potential within a given territory, should likewise reflect the administrative capacity of the state. To control for *initial* administrative capacity, I create the indicator variable "modern census by 1820," which equals 1 if country i has conducted a modern census by 1820.[46]

Initial controls are recommended to account for intrinsic characteristics that make a country more likely to go to war, access external credit, and build a tax administration. They are, so to speak, a good substitute for the absence of country fixed effects; however, following the onset of a sudden stop, a ruler can still choose whether to wage war or what kind of war to fight. I address this form of selection bias by considering only wars that are initiated while the market is still lending and eventually dries up as a result of a financial crisis. These wars are initiated without the expectation of a sudden stop. Thus, the decision to go to war or what type of war to fight is disconnected from external credit access.[47]

44. Bockstette, Chanda, and Putterman (2002).

45. Note that in the short-run models, this property is measured by the cumulative number of wars in the nineteenth century.

46. To create this variable, I manually coded the date of the first modern census ever implemented in all 107 countries in the sample. This information is retrieved from Goyer and Draaijer (1992a, b, c).

47. The 222 country-year wars taking place during sudden stops fall to 72 once I consider only wars that are ongoing by the onset of a sudden stop.

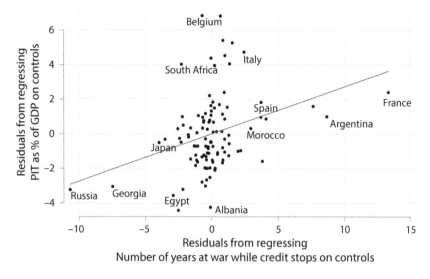

(a) War while credit stops

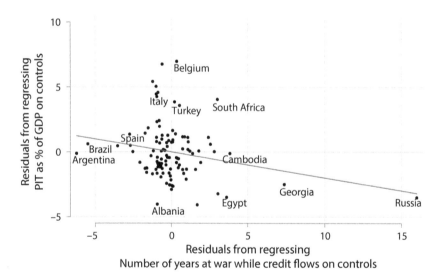

(b) War while credit flows

FIGURE 7.5. Long-Run Fiscal Capacity as a Function of War and Exogenous Credit Access. Estimates reflect partial correlations of a full model of personal income tax as a percentage of GDP circa 2000 as a function of the number of years at war with and without access to external finance (established by international credit crunches) between 1816 and 1913 with the following controls: population density as of 1820, oil producer, sea access, desert territory, colonial origins fixed effects, and region fixed effects. N = 106 (Great Britain is excluded). Only a few country names are shown to avoid cluttering. Refer to appendix E in Queralt (2019) for models that drop Russia, Georgia, and France, potential influential outliers. Results hold.

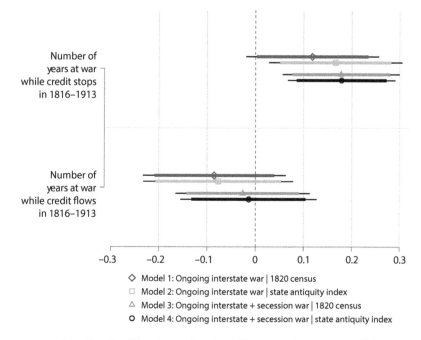

Number of
years at war
while credit stops
in 1816–1913

Number of
years at war
while credit flows
in 1816–1913

−0.3   −0.2   −0.1   0   0.1   0.2   0.3

◇ Model 1: Ongoing interstate war | 1820 census
□ Model 2: Ongoing interstate war | state antiquity index
△ Model 3: Ongoing interstate + secession war | 1820 census
○ Model 4: Ongoing interstate + secession war | state antiquity index

FIGURE 7.6. Long-Run Fiscal Capacity as a Function of Exogenous Credit Access and Ongoing War Plus Initial State Capacity Controls. This figure plots marginal effects of war and credit access on personal income tax as a percentage of GDP circa 2000. N = 106. I run separate analyses for interstate war and interstate plus secessionist war. Access to international credit markets is exogenized by global credit crunches. Also, only "ongoing wars" are considered: namely, only wars initiated while the market is still lending and eventually dries up as a result of a financial crisis. Great Britain is excluded to maximize exogeneity. All models control for region and colonial origins fixed effects, population density as of 1820, being an oil producer, sea access, desert territory, and Great Powers status. In addition, I control for initial state conditions, including the use of a modern census by 1820 and the state antiquity index of Bockstette, Chanda and Putterman (2002).

Models 1 and 2 in figure 7.6 show point estimates for β_1 and β_2 in expression 7.2 when access to credit is exogenized by sudden stops, and selection into war is addressed by including controls for initial capacity (census, diamonds; state antiquity, squares) and subsetting for ongoing wars.[48] Based on the new estimates, a one-standard-deviation increase in the number of ongoing wars increases long-term average PIT by 12.5 percent, a sizable long-term effect. By contrast, $\hat{\beta}_2$ is no longer negative (as it appeared to be before selection into war was considered in figure 7.5(b) but zero, which is still inconsistent with the unconditional interpretation of the bellicist

48. The interested reader may refer to table 6 in Queralt (2019) for separate analyses.

hypothesis—more war, more state—and the debt-tax equivalence of war finance for the purpose of state building, by which loans should behave as deferred taxes.

To conclude this section, I also consider secession (or independence) wars. Leaders in secessionist territories might engage in calculations similar to those of sovereign rulers. For instance, in the 1820s Greek rebels negotiated external loans to finance the war of independence against Turkey. Default followed soon after, and independence loans were a matter of dispute for decades to come.[49] Models 3 and 4 in figure 7.6 show results once the ongoing war criterion is implemented to both interstate and secessionist war.[50] The point estimates are substantively identical, suggesting that secessionist wars have long-term effects on tax capacity similar to those of interstate war by sovereign nations.

Effects on the Periphery

The distinct effect of war on state building and on long-term tax capacity is robust to sample changes and additional controls, including military alliances or exclusion from war in which the British or its colonies participated. I refer the reader to Queralt (2019) for a full battery of robustness checks. Here I focus attention on the sample composition. So far, I have considered Great Powers and other wealthy countries (US and the Netherlands) in the sample. These were all militarily powerful states capable of substituting external for internal credit in times of crisis and deeply embedded in international capital networks.

Coping with financial shocks may be qualitatively different for developing nations, which are arguably more exposed to exogenous changes in global credit liquidity. Based on this premise, in table 7.6, I reestimate β_1 and β_2 after dropping from the sample all Great Powers plus all the foundational members of the OECD—namely, current advanced economies. For consistency, these models incorporate the various strategies to tackle endogeneity in credit access and war participation I elaborated above. The point estimates for developing nations in table 7.6 are of the same magnitude as those for the entire sample (figure 7.6), but they are more efficiently estimated. If anything, the periphery-specific analysis suggests that developing nations had more to gain from not having easy access to international

49. Reinhart and Trebesch (2015).

50. Substantially fewer secessionist wars than interstate wars appear in Wimmer and Min. Hence, I pool them together instead of analyzing them separately.

TABLE 7.6. Models of Personal Income Tax as Percentage of GDP circa 2000 in the Global Periphery as a Function of War and Exogenous Credit Access in the Long Nineteenth Century

	(1)	(2)	(3)
# Years at war while credit stops 1816–1913	0.116**	0.108**	0.117**
	(0.056)	(0.054)	(0.058)
# Years at war while credit flows 1816–1913	0.048	0.057	0.056
	(0.109)	(0.108)	(0.120)
Baseline controls	Yes	Yes	Yes
Census 1820 control	No	Yes	No
State antiquity control	No	No	Yes
Region FE	Yes	Yes	Yes
Colonial origins FE	Yes	Yes	Yes
Observations	96	96	93
R-squared	0.538	0.553	0.580

Note: Great Powers and foundational OECD countries are excluded from this analysis. Only "ongoing wars" are considered. Credit access exogenized by credit crunches. Baseline controls include population density, oil producer, sea access, and desert territory. Intercept not reported. Robust standard errors in parentheses. *** $p < 0.01$, ** $p < 0.05$, * $p < 0.1$.

credit markets at early stages of state building. Arguably, too much capital access too soon distorted incentives to build capacity in the developing world.

War Noninitiators in COW

An alternative route to tackle selection into war is to study the effect of war making and credit access for states that did not choose to go to war but were dragged into it. The identification assumption for this test is that states did not strike first in anticipation of a likely attack.

To implement this test, I rely on the Correlates of War (COW) dataset, which identifies the initiator of each military conflict.[51] Although COW reduces the representativeness of the universe of war and war participants—as discussed above—it guarantees that countries are sovereign, hence in full command of their military and fiscal policy.[52] Conveniently, COW also facilitates information to control for war outcomes. This is substantively compelling because military outcomes potentially affect the

51. Sarkees and Wayman (2010).

52. The sample of interstate wars now comprises 37 conflicts and 172 war years in total; 78 were fought when credit flowed, and 96 when credit had suddenly stopped. Average war duration was 1.57 (SD = 1.04) and 1.76 (SD = 1.23) years, respectively.

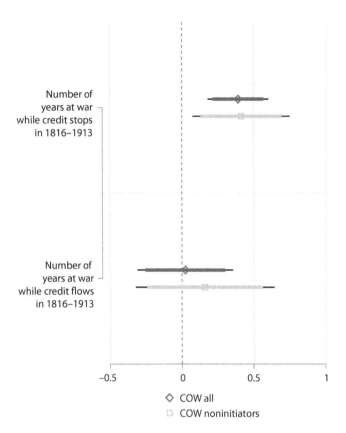

FIGURE 7.7. Long-Run Fiscal Capacity as a Function of Exogenous Credit Access and Correlates of War Data, Subsetting for Noninitiators and Controlling for War Outcomes. This figure plots marginal effects of war and credit market access on personal income tax as a percentage of GDP circa 2000. $N = 106$ (Great Britain is excluded). War data are drawn from COW. One of the models uses the entire sample and the other focuses on war noninitiators as defined by COW. Access to credit markets is exogenized by global credit crunches. All models control for region and colonial origins fixed effects, population density as of 1820, oil producer status, sea access, desert territory, net victory, and Great Powers status. The models include one of the two initial state capacity measures: census capacity by 1820.

incentives to invest in fiscal capacity; for example, winners might extract from losers, reducing the need to build capacity to pay for war.

Figure 7.7 reports the coefficients for the full COW sample and for the noninitiator subsample. Both models control for the history of military victories and losses in the period from 1816 to 1913.[53] Results are similar across subsamples: waging war with access to external finance exerts

53. This is measured by *net victory*, which indicates the number of wars won between 1816 and 1913 by country i net of wars lost during the same period.

null effects regardless of whether a country initiates war or is dragged into it. By contrast, going to war, voluntarily or forcibly, without access to external finance leads to long-term tax capacity. Based on these estimates, a one-standard-deviation increase in the number of years at war waged without access to credit increases average PIT ratios today by 25.7 percent, a stronger effect than I found in figure 7.6, likely because COW data overrepresents wealthier states.

Combined, results in table 7.6 and figures 7.4, 7.6, and 7.7 suggest that foreign loans potentially unraveled the connection between war and state making, shedding light on the reasons that war did not make stronger states in the last two hundred years in large parts of the developing world.

7.4 Addressing History Compression

So far I showed evidence of short- and long-term effects of war finance on taxation. What happened in between? I address concerns of "history compression"[54] by evaluating war effects at intermediate points in time. Specifically, I show persistence of the effects of war from 1816 to 1913 on tax ratios between 1945 and 1995, the post—World War II era. Given data constraints, I approximate fiscal capacity with the share of total tax revenue *not* accrued from trade taxes. This share measures the effort to raise revenue through sophisticated taxes (e.g., income tax, value-added tax) instead of tariffs, a tax handle that low-capacity countries often use.[55]

To conduct this test, first I compute decennial averages of nontrade taxes as a percentage of total taxation from 1945 to 1995; then I regress those ratios on the number of years at war with and without access to external loans in the nineteenth century plus controls, or expression 7.2, for each decade in the second half of the twentieth century. Data for nontrade tax revenue are limited. To minimize unobserved heterogeneity across units while maximizing degrees of freedom, I include a former colonial status indicator, which collapses the three previous dummy variables (British, Iberian, and Other Colonies) into one; and a Great Powers indicator, which adjusts for the systematic difference in European core powers. In addition, I include a control for initial wealth (population density in 1820), as well as controls for oil production and sea access. Because the sample size is small, particularly in the earlier decades, I report 90 percent confidence intervals. Results are reported in figure 7.8.

54. Austin (2008).
55. Cagé and Gadenne (2018); Queralt (2015); Soifer (2015).

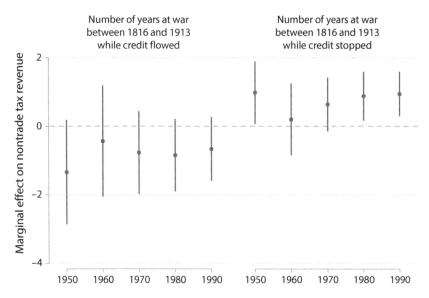

FIGURE 7.8. Effect of Past Warfare and Exogenous Credit Access on Fiscal Capacity from 1945 to 1995. These figures plot the marginal effects of the number of years at interstate war with and without access to external credit between 1816 and 1913 on nontrade tax revenue from 1945 to 1995 (decennial averages centered at the first year of the decade). OLS, 90% CI. Data on nontrade tax revenue are drawn from Cagé and Gadenne (2018). Sample sizes are 34 (1946–1955), 37 (1956–1965), 55 (1966–1975), 71 (1976–1985), 84 (1986–1995). Great Britain is excluded. Controls are former colonial status indicator, Great Powers indicator, population density in 1820, oil producer, and sea access.

The estimates for the 1945–1995 decennial tax ratios are generally consistent with previous findings: the plot on the left in figure 7.8 suggests that waging war in the nineteenth century with access to external credit is not associated with post-WWII fiscal capacity, whereas waging war without access to international finance is (right plot). Approximately, an additional year at war in the nineteenth century without external finance increases post-WWII nontrade tax revenue by 1 percent, all else held constant. More importantly, figure 7.8 suggests that the different types of war finance can have lasting effects because they push countries onto different paths of state building, consistent with figure 1.3.

7.5 Conclusion

This chapter is data intensive because it seeks to establish short-, medium-, and long-term effects of war and external finance on fiscal capacity. Despite usual limitations of historical data, results suggest that incentives to expand tax capacity strengthen when external capital is unavailable, and that those efforts are capitalized on in the medium and long run. The findings also draw attention to the potentially negative consequences of financing war externally at a time when international bondholders were allowed to impose severe conditions on loan contracts, growing the share of debt service in the national budget at best and enabling asset seizure and foreign control at worst. Now that the short- and long-run relationship among war, international credit, and state making are documented, I devote chapter 8 to elaborating on the mechanisms of persistence, namely, the reasons that past war finance exerts lasting effects. In chapter 9, I reexamine the effects of war on fiscal capacity and their transmission with a series of case studies.

8

Mechanisms of Persistence

In chapter 7, I showed that war exerts opposite and lasting effects on fiscal capacity depending on access to international capital. Why do these effects persist? I advance two "channels" or mechanisms of transmission, which serve as the reasons that past war finance shapes fiscal capacity today. The first mechanism builds on the political repercussions of domestic resource mobilization. When rulers are excluded from external capital markets, incentives to strike deals with domestic taxpayers are stronger. Tax bargaining is more likely to materialize in power-sharing institutions in smaller and densely populated polities, where taxpayers face low coordination costs. Once in place, power-sharing institutions make taxation self-sustaining, carrying the fiscal effects of war into the future. The second mechanism of transmission puts emphasis on bureaucratic innovation and potentially applies to sovereign and nonsovereign countries alike. In other words, the bureaucracies created to fund war oppose disinvestment in fiscal capacity, securing their survival in the long run. Drawing from historical data on political and bureaucratic reform, I find empirical evidence consistent with both mechanisms.

8.1 The Ratchet Effect of War

The ratchet or "displacement" effect of war involves a regularity in public finance by which tax revenue gains during wartime do not return to prewar levels afterward—hence growing the size of government over time.[1] The existence of a ratchet effect, however, is not immediately obvious. Rulers could raise tax rates during wartime and bring tax pressure down to prewar times once hostilities are over. Were this the case, one should expect no lasting impact of war on long-term state capacity.

Peacock and Wiseman suggest that the ratchet effect of war exists because it grows people's tolerance of a high tax burden and because new obligations appear after war, including the provision of war pensions and nonmilitary expenses, for example, public employment for demobilized soldiers.[2] Consistently, Scheve and Stasavage find that mass warfare can change perceptions of social fairness, making nonelites more demanding of redistribution via taxation and elites more welcoming to such demands.[3] The rise of income tax progressivity coinciding with mass mobilization in World War I and its persistence afterward speak of a permanent change in preferences for taxation and social spending in advanced economies.

Mass warfare—namely, the mobilization of at least 2 percent of the adult male population—was rare before 1914 as were demands for a welfare state, particularly outside Western Europe.[4] To shed light on the causes of the ratchet effect of war in the nineteenth century, I contemplate two alternative and mutually complementary mechanisms: one is political, the other bureaucratic, and both derive from the political economy of external finance advanced in chapter 2.

8.2 The Political Channel of Persistence

The political economy of war finance discussed in chapter 2 suggests that rulers may grant political rights to taxpayers to overcome credibility issues in tax policy and to minimize transaction costs in tax collection. Because both the ruler and the ruled benefit from power-sharing institutions, the new tax becomes self-enforcing, maintaining the fiscal effect of war in the long run.

Before I offer further specifics, three important clarifications are in order: First, war finance is not the only path to political reform. Political

---

1. Peacock and Wiseman (1961). See Rasler and Thompson (1985) for evidence of this pattern in major Western economies.

2. Peacock and Wiseman (1961, pp. 26–27).

3. Scheve and Stasavage (2010, 2012, 2016).

4. Lindert (2004).

ideas,[5] economic development,[6] and political fragmentation[7] are also key drivers of power-sharing institutions. Second, these institutions, which are not equivalent to democracy, refer to institutional configurations designed to address credibility problems on the ruler's end—in our case, spending policy.[8] A representative parliament is one (advanced) manifestation of power-sharing institutions, but not the only one—as will become clearer below.[9] Third, fiscal capacity can be created in the absence of political reform. Great empires experienced sustained investment in capacity while not adopting power-sharing institutions. For instance, during the Warring States era in ancient China, the Qin dynasty (356–221 BCE) conducted self-strengthening reforms without adopting any recognizable form of power-sharing institutions.[10] Likewise, the Umayyad caliphate initiated bureaucratic and military reform in the eighth century, spanning over three centuries while articulating no known form of executive constraint.[11] The Chakri dynasty in Siam is a specific Bond Era example of ambitious bureaucratic reform that carried no political consequences, at least not in the short run. I return to it in chapter 9. Keeping these important considerations in mind, I next elaborate how tax-based war finance might lead to political reform and a ratchet effect of war, holding everything else constant.

8.2.1   WAR AND THE FISCAL CONTRACT

The connection between war finance and political reform has a long tradition in the literature of state formation.[12] From ancient times to the Roman Empire, war expenses strained the state's coffers and became the top preoccupation of sitting chiefs, emperors, and monarchs.[13] Far from

---

5. Pitkin (1967); Manin (1997).

6. Abramson and Boix (2019); Lipset (1959); Jha (2015).

7. Stasavage (2016).

8. Schultz and Weingast (1998).

9. Refer to Boix and Svolik (2013), Gandhi (2008), Gandhi and Przeworski (2007), Meng (2020), and Svolik (2012) for comprehensive accounts of power-sharing institutions in modern autocracies.

10. Hui (2004).

11. Kennedy (2015, pp. 398–401). At its height, the caliphate spread from the Iberian Peninsula and the Maghreb in the west to modern-day Pakistan in the east and the Arabian Peninsula in the south.

12. A cursory review of recent work includes Abramson and Boix (2019), Boix (2015), Boucoyannis (2015), Cox (2016), Dincecco (2011), Ferejohn and Rosenbluth (2016), Scheve and Stasavage (2012), Stasavage (2011), and Van Zanden, Buringh, and Bosker (2012).

13. Boix (2015); Diamond (1997); Scott (2017); Tan (2015).

declining, war expenses grew larger in the last millennium. In the high and late Middle Ages, monarchs regularly summoned estates to raise funds to wage war.[14] Beginning in the sixteenth century, the introduction of new war technologies—the longbow, the pike, and gunpowder—multiplied the financial needs of the Crown;[15] however, elites feared that rulers would wage the wrong war—one that pursued only personal aggrandizement—or that they would spend tax yields foolishly.[16]

To credibly commit to avoid wasting subjects' money, European rulers relinquished power over spending decisions to big taxpayers and government lenders—often the same individuals.[17] Some power-sharing arrangements took the form of representative assemblies with extensive powers over fiscal policy. "The power of the purse" was conferred upon Parliament as early as 1572 in the Netherlands and 1688 in England with astonishing fiscal outcomes.[18] This modern form of political representation extended to the rest of Western Europe in the nineteenth century.[19]

Power-sharing institutions other than representative assemblies were adopted in parts of continental Europe before 1800.[20] The paramount of absolutism, Louis XIV (r. 1661–1715), was compelled to share fiscal powers with tax farmers in order to secure funds for ongoing wars.[21] J. B. Colbert, his finance minister, promoted the creation of the Company of General Farms, which allowed an oligopoly of tax farmers, by then also government bankers, to keep the king's fiscal policy in check.[22] Because tax farmers secured tax revenue and public credit for the king, they were able to exclude him from obtaining fresh funds in case of default. There rested their capacity to constrain the French monarch's power.[23] For his part, by assuming

14. Marongiu (1968); Stasavage (2011).

15. Rogers (1995).

16. Hoffman and Rosenthal (2000).

17. Bates and Lien (1985); Levi (1988); North and Weingast (1989); Stasavage (2011).

18. 'tHart (1999) and Tracy (1985) for the Netherlands; Dickson (1967), Cox (2016), and O'Brien and Hunt (1993) for England.

19. Dincecco (2009, 2011).

20. See Downing (1993) and Van Zanden, Buringh, and Bosker (2012) for the dissolution or loss of powers of national assemblies in Europe coinciding with the military revolution.

21. Balla and Johnson (2009); Mousnier (1974). See also Spruyt (1994, p. 106) for the origins of tax bargaining between the king and the town burghers in late medieval times, and Le Bris and Tallec (2019) for the fiscal constraints that provincial assemblies imposed on the king in the absolutist era.

22. Tax farmers collected indirect taxes. Under Louis XIV, tax farm revenue accounted for virtually half the ordinary revenues of the Crown (Balla and Johnson, 2009, p. 815).

23. Schultz and Weingast (1998, p. 34).

the "significant political costs"[24] of default, the king laid the foundations of cheaper, long-term sovereign debt.[25]

Louis XIV's fiscal innovation exemplifies the notion of power-sharing institutions that might be put in place as a result of war.[26] Tax bargaining between rulers and tax subjects does not have to result in a legislative assembly in which large groups of society are represented. Power-sharing institutions involve any institutional system designed to overcome the incumbent's credibility issues in spending policy.[27]

8.2.2   THE FISCAL CONTRACT AND SUSTAINED TAXATION

The importance of power-sharing institutions for long-term taxation cannot be overstated. Executive constraints on fiscal policy grant credibility to promised returns for taxes and transform taxation into a self-sustaining nonzero-sum game: revenue is secured by the ruler, whom taxpayers hold fiscally accountable, facilitating sustained investment in tax capacity. Deviations from this equilibrium activate a sanctioning mechanism, by which the ruler is denied tax receipts (i.e., taxpayers withdraw tax payments) or excluded from domestic loans.

Besley and Persson formalize the opportunities of sustained cooperation in tax policy in "common-interest states."[28] These states are characterized by political institutions that impose checks and balances on the executive and constrain the policies of incumbent governments.[29] When such institutions are in place, taxation becomes a win-win game: the ruler secures a constant stream of funds to produce public goods while taxpayers are given guarantees that contributions will be spent responsibly. Because gain is mutual, power-sharing institutions are conducive to sustained investment in fiscal capacity.

24. Potter (2000, p. 622).

25. Hoffman, Postel-Vinay, and Rosenthal (2000). Constrained by the same institutions that Louis XIV—his great-great-grandfather—put in place a hundred years earlier, Louis XVI was forced to call the estates general in 1779, which eventually led to fundamental fiscal and political reforms (Balla and Johnson, 2009, p. 825).

26. Another example of limited government in a so-called absolutist regime can be found in Austria in the second half of the eighteenth century (Godsey, 2018).

27. Schultz and Weingast (1998). See Boix and Svolik (2013) for the foundations of limited authoritarian government.

28. Besley and Persson (2011, chs. 2 and 3).

29. A common-interest state can also be achieved if the opposition is represented in the policymaking process.

More recently, Acemoglu and Robinson speak of "the Red Queen effect" to characterize a similar self-enforcing equilibrium between elites, who want to maximize state capacity, and nonelites, who seek to maximize individual liberties.[30] Power-sharing institutions (e.g., constitutional checks and balances) are institutionalized mechanisms that balance the state's and society's powers and enable mutually beneficial solutions for the state and society—the ruler and taxpayers, respectively.

Stasavage argues that, once in place, power-sharing institutions are self-reinforcing because collective action problems are more easily overcome a second time; that is, taxpayers learn to coordinate their actions to hold the ruler accountable.[31] Levi has also theorized about the benefits of addressing credibility issues with power-sharing institutions.[32] Once the ruler's promises turn credible, the costs of enforcement of taxation decrease, expanding the capacity to tax and fund public goods. In light of the social benefits of higher fiscal pressure, taxpayers are willing to comply "quasi-voluntarily"[33] with taxation. Consistently, Dincecco shows that limited government in Europe increased total tax revenue in the long term.[34] This evidence draws from an original and precious dataset on tax revenue and institutional reform for 11 European countries as early as 1650. Within-country variation allows Dincecco to assess the marginal change in tax collection derived from the adoption of limited government while keeping time-invariant country characteristics constant (e.g., geography and cultural traits).[35]

8.2.3 THE FISCAL CONTRACT AND EXTERNAL FINANCE

To understand the conditions under which the political mechanism of war finance is set in motion, an examination of the ruler's incentives to assume the political ramifications of taxation is necessary. Incentives to strike deals with taxpayers—namely, abiding by a fiscal contract—can be expected to be endogenous to the set of alternatives to taxation. European monarchs might not have shared fiscal powers with taxpayers had they had access to

30. Acemoglu and Robinson (2019).

31. Stasavage (2011, 2020).

32. Levi (1988).

33. Levi (1988, p. 52).

34. Dincecco (2009, 2011).

35. The effect of limited government is maximal when the country has achieved fiscal centralization.

cheap external finance.[36] Philip II of Spain (r. 1556–1598), who can be used as a reasonable counterfactual, had access to external finance from Genoese bankers, thanks to the silver that poured in from the Americas and was used as collateral. Despite the many wars waged, Philip II and his successors did not implement significant self-strengthening reform. After the defeat of the armada in 1588, the Castilian parliament, known as the Cortes, was summoned by the king and briefly gained a voice in fiscal policy in return for new tax concessions; however, this arrangement was unsustainable. Cities were too dispersed to effectively overcome collective action problems in monitoring the Crown.[37] In addition, the greatest downside of silver

> was that it weakened the bargaining position of the Cortes vis-à-vis the Crown. Because of silver revenues, Castile's rulers could spend freely using borrowed funds and effectively present the Cortes with the bill.[38]

In other words, imperial rule and war were mainly funded by silver from the Americas, allowing the Spanish kings to escape the political cost of taxation: limited government. After 1663, the Cortes was summoned only on ceremonial occasions, and fiscal fragmentation became an endemic problem. Spain entered a long period of economic and political decay.[39]

Far from surprising, the behavior of Philip II and his successors is consistent with the political economy of external finance elaborated in chapter 2: A ruler will share fiscal powers with taxpayers only as a last resource; namely, when other sources of revenue are unavailable or fall short, key among them external finance. Genoese bankers were long gone in the nineteenth century, but emerging economies had access to British capital (and later French, German, and American too). Cheap money siphoned in from Europe helped rulers in large parts of the developing world finance war and public infrastructure while saving them the political costs of taxation. Economic historian Leland H. Jenks summarized this logic as follows:

> There was endless preparation for war. And there was war itself—an expensive pastime—inspired by the general excitation and apologized for by the fashion of nationality. All these things were progress. They all meant profit for the fortunate contractors [the underwriters]. They meant money for which the taxpayers must not be burdened.

36. Refer to chapter 3 for the globalization of external finance in the nineteenth century.
37. Stasavage (2011, pp. 147–150).
38. Drelichman and Voth (2014, p. 267).
39. Elliott (1963); Grafe (2011).

They meant continuous appeals to the money market. Between the universal desire for progress and the equally universal desire for lower taxes there was a discongruity which could be bridged only by public borrowing.[40]

The idea that foreign credit allows incumbents to dodge political accountability is not new. Because taxation "constitutes the largest intervention of government[s] in their subjects' private li[ves],"[41] tax hikes are expected to make taxpayers (elites or the general public or both) more attentive to the way government spends tax receipts. This is even more compelling in wartime, when the lives and assets of taxpayers may be at stake. To minimize political contestation, rulers may finance war in other ways, including confiscation or inflation, alternatives that might secure funds but can also create new grievances: government confiscation of factories or tithes can easily escalate into open conflict with elites or masses or both. Printing money may solve the liquidity shortage but can rapidly derail the economy.[42] In order to avoid political and economic problems, rulers may turn to a less invasive war-financing mechanism: borrowing.

Along these lines, Patrick Shea claims that democracies are more likely to win war when external credit is cheap, not simply because it allows for more military spending but also because it mitigates the societal and political pressures attached to higher taxation. "Rulers who do not have to depend on their citizens for tax revenue or other economic resources have a freer hand in enacting policy."[43] Kreps offers a fascinating historical account of how American leaders deflect public opposition to war by turning to credit markets instead of imposing more visible and onerous war taxes. Borrowing allows rulers to "diffuse and defer" the cost of war compared to the "direct and immediate impact of taxation";[44] that is, borrowing loosens public constraints today and shifts the responsibility of servicing debt to future leaders. Ironically, this strategy seems to do the trick: using experimental surveys in the United States and the United Kingdom, Flores-Macías and Kreps show that public support for war declines by 10 percent

40. Jenks (1927, p. 264).

41. Tilly (2009, p. xiii).

42. For the negative consequences of inflation tax at wartime, see Sprague (1917); for the manner in which the perceived benefits of inflation tax can change in light of experience, see Fujihira (2000).

43. Shea (2013, p. 773).

44. Kreps (2018, p. 9).

as soon as respondents learn that war expenses will result in a new war tax (relative to a baseline condition in which war is funded with ordinary receipts and debt).[45]

Results in Kreps's single-authored work and jointly with Flores-Macías are illuminating because they draw from stable regimes with institutions that anticipate the long-term consequences of today's actions. Most emerging economies in the nineteenth century lacked institutional stability that could infuse fiscal policy with a long-term perspective. Market-based constraints were no stronger. The modest size and high vulnerability of native financial institutions to fluctuations in international markets[46] limited the ability of local bankers to monopolize public debt issue, and hence their capacity to discipline government.[47]

In sum, for roughly a century external capital remained a key source of government funding in the Global South, offering as many opportunities as perverse incentives to unconstrained rulers. Foreign creditors' enthusiasm to lend beyond the reasonable in expectation of high margins did not help. From the viewpoint of a sitting ruler, high indebtedness and draconian clauses in case of default were a problem for the future and likely somebody else's.

8.2.4 AN EMPIRICAL EXAMINATION OF THE POLITICAL CHANNEL

The foregoing discussion suggests that the likelihood of any given ruler setting in motion the political mechanism of transmission—namely, agreeing to power-sharing institutions—is inversely proportional to having access to external capital. In other words, rulers will agree to assume the political costs of taxation only if they run out of options.

To evaluate this proposition empirically, I examine whether a history of war and credit exclusion in the long nineteenth century increased the likelihood of having limited government on the eve of World War I. If power-sharing institutions transform taxation into a nonzero-sum game

---

45. Flores-Macías and Kreps (2017).

46. In 1873 alone, 20 banks in Latin America (22% of the total) went bankrupt because of the global financial crisis.

47. Marichal and Barragán (2017) for strengths and weaknesses of early public banking in Latin America, and Calomiris and Haber (2014) for a political economy theory of financial underdevelopment. Accounts reflective of financial underdevelopment in Asia and Africa before 1914 can be found in the edited volume by Austin and Sugihara (1993).

benefiting both the ruler and taxpayers, limited government in the long run may be predicted based on past forms of war finance. Following this logic, I also evaluate the strength of power-sharing institutions circa 2000 as a function of war and credit exclusion in the nineteenth century. The empirical design replicates expression 7.2 while substituting the original outcome variable, a measure of state capacity, for one of power-sharing institutions: executive constraints. This variable, drawn from the Polity IV Project,[48] encapsulates an immediate consequence of relinquishing fiscal power to taxpayers.

One important result in the political economy of external finance in chapter 2 is that the political cost of funding government with taxes depends on the initial level of power-sharing institutions. The marginal cost of one additional tax dollar is greater for an autocrat than for an elected president. Empirically, this calls for a control for *initial* political institutions. Data on executive constraints for the early nineteenth century are limited and over-represent countries internationally recognized by the 1820s. In order to maximize the number of cases, I compute the average level of executive constraints between 1800 and 1830. This variable ranges from 0 (minimal constraint) to 7 (maximal constraint).[49]

Figure 8.1a plots the marginal effect of waging interstate war with and without access to international capital from 1816 to 1913 on average executive constraints by 1913, holding everything else constant. Figure 8.1b plots these estimates for the 2000s. These models indicate that a one-standard-deviation increase in the number of years at war while credit is tight in the nineteenth century increases average executive constraints by 16 percent in 1913 and 4.5 percent in the 2000s. By contrast, war waged with access to external credit is not associated with political change in the short or long term. If any, that relationship is negative.

Although modest, these results suggest that political reform is more likely when incumbents cannot escape the political costs of domestic taxation, that is, when they are at war but lack external finance. But does taxation always lead to advances in power-sharing institutions? In chapter 2, I pointed out two scope conditions that students of democracy find important for the rise and persistence of representative institutions: geographic scale and capital mobility. In large polities, taxpayers find it difficult

---

48. Marshall and Jaggers (2000).

49. Refer to appendix L in Queralt (2019) for alternative variables and time ranges to measure initial political conditions.

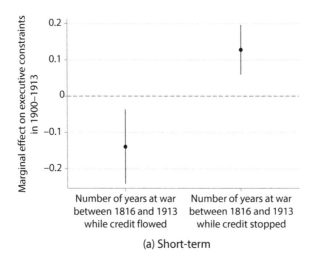

(a) Short-term

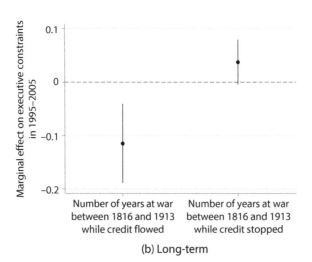

(b) Long-term

FIGURE 8.1. Effect of War Finance on Executive Constraints in the Short (1900–1913) and Long Run (1995–2005). This figure plots marginal effects of the number of years at war from 1816 to 1913 when international capital flowed and stopped on short- and long-term executive constraints. Short-run executive constraints take the average value of executive constraints in Marshall and Jaggers (2000) between 1900 and 1913. Long-term executive constraints take the average value from 1995 to 2005. Capital access (or lack thereof) is measured by global shocks in capital flows or "sudden stops" (more in chapter 7). Interstate war data are drawn from Wimmer and Min (2009). Models control for population density in 1820, oil production, sea access, colonial past, and initial executive constraints (average from 1800 to 1830). The latter control restricts the sample to N = 30, 90% CI reported. Countries in the sample are Argentina, Austria, Belgium, Bolivia, Brazil, Chile, China, Denmark, Ecuador, France, Greece, Iran, Japan, Mexico, Morocco, Nepal, Netherlands, Norway, Paraguay, Peru, Portugal, Russia, Spain, Sweden, Thailand, Turkey, United States, Uruguay, and Venezuela. Great Britain is excluded to maximize exogeneity of capital access.

to coordinate and monitor the executive, particularly so when the means of transportation and communication are antiquated.[50] The ability of taxpayers to escape taxation is also important to understand when power-sharing institutions are set in motion. Rulers are compelled to grant power-sharing institutions when they seek to tax owners of mobile capital, such as traders and financiers, and less so when taxpayers derive income from fixed capital, such as land.[51]

I reexamine the association between war finance and executive constraints through the prism of these scope conditions. I interact the number of years at war waged without access to external capital with measures of geographic scale and capital mobility. I expect collective action problems of taxpayers to be milder in smaller-scale polities, and their bargaining power vis-à-vis the ruler to be stronger in urbanized and monetized societies, which I approximate by levels of population density in 1820. I expect the interaction term between the number of years at war while credit stops in 1816–1913 and the proxies of geographic scale and capital mobility to be negative and positive, respectively.[52]

In column 1 of table 8.1, we see that the effect of tax-funded war on executive constraints attenuates as the geographic scale of a country increases.[53] In column 2, I report results with region fixed effects to account for unobserved heterogeneity between continents. Results hold, although attenuated. Figure 8.2a shows a visualization of this interaction. Under capital exclusion, the marginal effect of war on executive constraints is positive as long as the size of the polity is below ln(Area) = 3, the size of the United Kingdom. In larger polities, the effect of war on executive constraints is zero. In columns 3 and 4, I evaluate the effect of war and capital exclusion for different levels of urbanization in 1820, the proxy of capital mobility.[54] There we observe that the effect of tax-funded war

50. Stasavage (2011).

51. Bates and Lien (1985); Boix (2003).

52. These models have the same covariates as those in table 8.1. However, I do not include a control for initial executive constraints because it is potentially endogenous to the conditioning variables: geographic scale and capital mobility. Because the sample expands from N = 30 to N = 49 once I drop the control for initial executive constraints, I recover the region fixed effects to minimize unobserved heterogeneity.

53. Here I opted for a log transformation of the country size variable, but results are the same if a linear effect is assumed.

54. I stick to the original variable in this analysis, hence consistent with every other test. Results hold if I log-transform population density, as I do with country area.

TABLE 8.1. Scope Conditions for the Activation of the Political Mechanism of Persistence

	(1)	(2)	(3)	(4)
# Years at war while credit stops 1816–1913 × ln(Area)	−0.101*** (0.036)	−0.064* (0.036)		
# Years at war while credit stops 1816–1913 × population density			0.460*** (0.169)	0.284* (0.159)
# Years at war while credit stops 1816–1913	0.451*** (0.156)	0.325** (0.138)	−0.189* (0.102)	−0.099 (0.109)
ln(Area)	0.713* (0.417)	0.512 (0.434)	0.791** (0.314)	0.600* (0.327)
Population density			2.559* (1.397)	3.430*** (1.217)
# Years at war while credit flows 1816–1913	−0.064 (0.081)	−0.025 (0.091)	−0.115 (0.088)	−0.035 (0.075)
Controls	Yes	Yes	Yes	Yes
Region FE	No	Yes	No	Yes
Observations	49	49	49	49
R-squared	0.284	0.529	0.358	0.612

Note: The outcome variable is the average value of executive constraints between 1900 and 1913 in Marshall and Jaggers (2000). Capital access (or lack thereof) is measured by global shocks in capital flows or "sudden stops" (more in chapter 7). Interstate war data, urban density by 1820, and land area are drawn from Wimmer and Min (2009), World Mapper (www.worldmapper.org), and Nunn and Puga (2012), respectively. Models control for oil production, sea access, and colonial past. Countries in the sample: Argentina, Australia, Austria, Belgium, Bhutan, Bolivia, Brazil, Bulgaria, Canada, Chile, China, Colombia, Costa Rica, Denmark, Dominican Republic, Ecuador, El Salvador, Ethiopia, France, Germany, Greece, Guatemala, Honduras, Hungary, Iran, Italy, Japan, Mexico, Morocco, Nepal, Netherlands, New Zealand, Nicaragua, Norway, Panama, Paraguay, Peru, Portugal, Romania, Russia, South Africa, Spain, Sweden, Switzerland, Thailand, Turkey, United States, Uruguay, and Venezuela. Intercept not reported. Great Britain is excluded to maximize exogeneity of capital access. *** $p < 0.01$, ** $p < 0.05$, * $p < 0.1$.

on executive constraints strengthens as population density increases. The relationship turns statistically different from zero at Population Density = 0.68, corresponding to the value of Italy in 1820.

Results in table 8.1 and figure 8.2 suggest that the political mechanism of transmission of war finance activates under limited conditions: small geographic scale and high initial wealth. When these conditions are met, mobilization of domestic resources for war finance puts in motion political bargaining between rulers and taxpayers, transforming taxation into a nonzero-sum game and carrying the fiscal effects of war into the long run. Not coincidentally, small scale and relative wealth were conditions generally met in the formative period of state building in Europe.

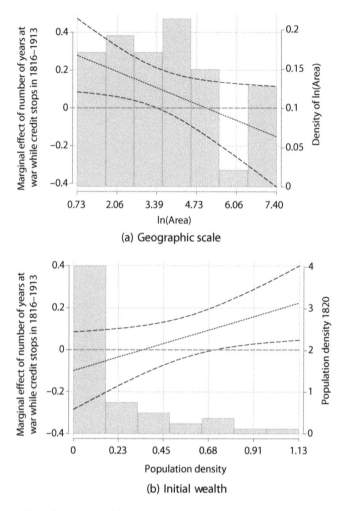

FIGURE 8.2. War and Activation of the Political Mechanism. These figures plot marginal effects of the number of years at war from 1816 to 1913 when international capital stopped on executive constraints in 1900–1913 as a function of geographic scale and initial wealth. Estimates drawn from saturated models in columns 2 and 4 in table 8.1. Due to small sample size, I report confidence intervals at 90%. Model specification and sources shown in table 8.1.

8.3 The Bureaucratic Channel of Persistence

Countries that did not meet the scope conditions for the activation of the political mechanism—large and low-populated economies—or that were deprived of self-government by a foreign power[55] might have capitalized

---

55. Tax bargaining and power-sharing institutions occurred exceptionally outside white settler colonies. For instance, in Ghana local chiefs organized into a local legislative assembly as early

on tax-financed warfare by articulating a stronger administrative apparatus. That was the state building path chosen by some European economies before the nineteenth century (e.g., Prussia[56]) and by China during the Warring States period, 475–221 BCE.[57] Next, I study the transmission of war effects through this alternative bureaucratic channel.

8.3.1 YES, MINISTER

The modern Weberian tax administration was created for and by war.[58] Tax bureaucracies were necessary to assess wealth and collect taxes as well as to resist the natural aversion to having one's sources of income monitored.[59] Once created, bureaucracies entrenched, grew larger, and became states within states.[60] In Charles Tilly's words,

> The organizations that were necessary to amass revenue [for war] developed interest, rights, perquisites, needs, and demands requiring attention on their own. . . . Bureaucracies developed their own interests and power bases throughout Europe.[61]

More generally, institutions originally built to finance the means of war can give rise to a body of bureaucrats that organically develops a vested interest in safeguarding institutional survival.[62] Based on this logic, we can expect tax bureaucrats to oppose disinvestment in administrative capacity, carrying the fiscal effects of past warfare into the future.[63]

---

as 1852 to negotiate the terms of direct taxation (the poll tax) with British authorities (Aboagye and Hillbom, 2020; Prichard, 2015). The legislative assembly never met again after 1852, but it was replaced by other forms of local representation, including the Aborigines' Society, a group of native elites (barristers, teachers, merchants, chiefs), which effectively gained veto power over fiscal policy (Wight, 1947, pp. 25–26). Other examples of fiscal contracts under colonial rule can be found in Bräutigam (2008) and Makgala (2004), but these cases were hardly the norm.

56. Downing (1993); Ertman (1997).

57. Hui (2004).

58. See Brewer (1988) for Europe and Young (1994) for an application to colonial Africa.

59. Daunton (2001).

60. Fischer and Lundgreen (1975); Schumpeter (1991); Weber (1978).

61. Tilly (1990, p. 115).

62. Niskanen (1994, ch. 4).

63. See Porter (1994, ch. 7) for the growth of federal bureaucracy and (nonmilitary) agencies in the US following each major war waged by the US since independence. See Carpenter (2001) and Skowronek (1982) for earlier achievements in bureaucratic autonomy in the US, and Silberman (1993) for a comparative study of bureaucratic growth and development in advanced economies.

The bureaucratic channel potentially operates in sovereign *and* colonial states. As I discussed in chapter 6, colonies were responsible for financing administrative, infrastructural, and defense expenses. To secure funds, colonies relied on a variety of methods, including tariffs, excises, and poll taxes.[64] Although defense expense was heavily subsidized, colonies were expected to contribute to imperial war.

European colonialism in the nineteenth century relied on direct and indirect rule, and generally a mix of both.[65] Direct rule implanted bureaucratically centralized states with a substantial presence of European administrators. Indirect (or customary) rule relied on precolonial leaders (or chiefs) to maintain political and legal power, requiring low investment in colonial administration. Indirect rule has been generally associated with worse economic and political outcomes;[66] however, recent work by political scientist Kate Baldwin and others offers a more benign assessment of chieftaincy for public goods provision and state development in the modern day.[67]

Although the direct-indirect division is heuristically convenient, many scholars argue that both forms of rule were often combined within the same colony. Capital cities were predominantly under direct rule, and the hinterland relied on different degrees of indirect rule depending on the strength of preexisting institutions and geographic conditions. Mamdani employs the expression "bifurcated state" to characterize the unequal presence of colonial rule within African countries,[68] and Boone and Ricart-Huguet show rich qualitative and quantitative evidence of it, respectively.[69]

Thandika Mkandawire claims that domestic resource mobilization during colonial times "left an institutional and infrastructural residue that still plays a major role in the determination of tax policies and the capacity to collect tax."[70] Dan Berger offers an illustration by exploiting a rare geographic discontinuity in northern Nigeria: his cleanly identified empirical

---

64. Refer to edited volume by Frankema and Booth (2019) and Gardner (2012) for an overview.

65. See Lange, Mahoney, and vom Hau (2006) for an excellent summary of colonial rule, including for ideal types: settler, direct, indirect, and hybrid rule colonialism.

66. Acemoglu, Reed, and Robinson (2014); Crowder (1964); Mamdani (1996); Lange (2009). See Iyer (2010) for a competing view.

67. Baldwin (2015); Baldwin and Holzinger (2019); Logan (2009); Von Trotha (1996); van der Windt, Humphreys, Medina, Timmons, and Voors (2019).

68. Mamdani (1996, p. 18). See also Berman (1984).

69. Boone (2003); Ricart-Huguet (2021).

70. Mkandawire (2010, p. 1648).

analysis finds evidence of the long-run persistence of colonial tax efforts as late as the 2000s.[71]

Evidence of the bureaucratic persistence of colonial tax institutions is also found in Latin America[72] and Asia,[73] and is the subject of a recent collective monograph edited by Ewout Frankema and Anne Booth.[74] Building on this evidence and keeping in mind that colonial rule was heterogeneous between and within colonies, and that military expenses were largely subsidized by the metropole, I expect the incentives of colonial administrators to mobilize local tax revenue to strengthen *if only at the margins* in times of war and low liquidity in international capital markets, relative to times of war and high liquidity.

8.3.2 AN EMPIRICAL EXAMINATION OF THE BUREAUCRATIC CHANNEL

Drawing from historical data for both sovereign countries and colonies, next I investigate whether a history of war and exclusion from external finance in the nineteenth century fostered bureaucratic advances by 1913 and whether early reform persisted until the current day. In the absence of systematic data on the size or composition of the tax bureaucracy in the early twentieth century, I measure bureaucratic capacity on the eve of WWI with two reasonable proxies: census capacity (a measure introduced in chapter 7) and primary school enrollment.

Censuses have been conducted since antiquity for tax and conscription purposes.[75] Modern censuses, which cover the entire territory and population regardless of gender, race, or legal status, were first implemented in the second half of the eighteenth century (Sweden conducted the earliest modern census in 1751). Censuses were key instruments in tax capacity building in the Global South too. For instance, they allowed for an extractive head or capitation tax, which was "the mortar with which, block by block, the colonial state [in Africa] was built."[76] The implementation of modern censuses was challenging because it required a systematized

---

71. Berger (2009). Hassan (2020) offers a case-specific account of administrative continuity in Kenya. See Berman and Tettey (2001) and Lange (2004) for comparative findings.

72. Lange, Mahoney, and vom Hau (2006).

73. Booth (2007); Cheung (2005); Slater (2010).

74. Frankema and Booth (2019).

75. Scott (2017).

76. Young (1994, p. 127).

collection of information by an army of trained or professional surveyors who had to travel the entire territory while standardizing data collection.[77] These population surveys represented a major administrative and logistical achievement for the state.[78]

Along with census technology, I rely on primary school enrollment as an alternative measure of bureaucratic capacity in the early twentieth century. Public systems of education were meant to homogenize civil values,[79] if only because a sense of belonging—national identification—made the population willing to fight war and pay tax.[80] The nationalization of public education was a major administrative endeavor, requiring a solid bureaucratic structure to secure local funds, recruit instructors, standardize curricula, and enforce attendance. Modern states were built around a national system of public education.[81]

Public education was also an important feature of state building in the colonial world, particularly for the French. Huillery finds persistence in education investments in French West Africa: higher ratios of teachers to students in the early twentieth century predict higher school attendance by 1995.[82] Similarly, Wantchekon, Klašnja, and Novta show positive effects of early colonial schooling on living standards in Benin today.[83] The British externalized education provision to Christian missions but subsidized school infrastructure on a regular basis.[84]

Building on the empirical design of chapter 7, I model the two proposed proxies of bureaucratic strength by 1913 on the number of years at war with and without access to external capital (refer to expression 7.2 for details). Column 1 in table 8.2 reports a linear probability model in which having a modern census by 1913 is regressed on war making and exogenous credit access between 1816 and 1913 plus controls. With 90 percent confidence, the probability of having adopted a modern census by 1913 increases by 3 percentage points for each additional year of war waged without access to external credit. Column 2 runs the same specification, replacing census

77. D'Arcy and Nistotskaya (2018); Lee and Zhang (2017).

78. Brambor, Goenaga, Lindvall, and Teorell (2020).

79. Bandiera, Mohnen, Rasul, and Viarengo (2019); Paglayan (2021); Ramirez and Boli (1987); Weber (1976).

80. Alesina, Reich, and Riboni (2017); Levi (1997).

81. Ansell and Lindvall (2020); Weber (1976); Soifer (2015).

82. Huillery (2009).

83. Wantchekon, Klašnja, and Novta (2015).

84. Frankema (2012).

TABLE 8.2. Effect of Past Warfare and External Capital Access on State Capacity on the Eve of World War I

	(1) Census by 1913	(2) Primary education by 1913	(3) Census delay (all)	(4) Census delay (colonies)
# Years at war while credit stops 1816–1913	0.030* (0.018)	0.935* (0.508)	−3.024*** (0.827)	−3.465** (1.591)
# Years at war while credit flows 1816–1913	−0.012 (0.016)	−0.135 (0.577)	2.233** (0.970)	−1.598 (3.897)
Region FE	Yes	Yes	Yes	Yes
Colonial origins FE	Yes	Yes	Yes	Yes
Observations	98	76	103	56
R-squared	0.362	0.863	0.565	0.649

Note: Primary education enrollment is drawn from Lee and Lee (2016). Information of census capacity is coded by author from Goyer and Draaijer (1992a, b, c). External capital access is exogenized by global credit crunches. Column 1 fits a linear probability model. Columns 2–4 are OLS. Controls include population density by 1820, sea access, desert territory, and state antiquity index (columns 3 and 4). Column 4 model includes only countries with colonial past (N = 56). Intercept not reported. Great Britain is excluded to maximize exogeneity of capital access. Robust standard errors in parentheses. *** $p < 0.01$, ** $p < 0.05$, * $p < 0.1$.

technology for primary school enrollment by 1913. The latter increased by approximately 1 percentage point for each additional year that a country was at war while excluded from credit markets between 1816 and 1913. By contrast, waging war with access to international capital markets had no effect on either proxy of bureaucratic strength.

In column 3, I take advantage of the escalated dates of census adoption by assessing whether capital exclusion accelerated adoption (regardless of whether it took place before or after 1913). In that column, higher values of the dependent variable imply delay in census adoption.[85] The estimates indicate that fighting wars under market exclusion between 1816 and 1913 accelerated census adoption at the rate of three years per additional war year. Fighting wars with access to credit delayed adoption at the rate of two years per war year. Finally, in column 4, I repeat the analysis only for states under colonial rule in the nineteenth century. Results are roughly equivalent: waging war while being part of an empire in periods of tight capital markets accelerated census adoption (hence the negative sign in the first entry in column 4). By contrast, when capital was abundant, war did not

---

85. To account for differences in initial state capacity, I include a control for the state antiquity index. Refer to chapter 7 for further details.

spur improvements in legibility in the colonies (that estimate is negative but not statistically different from zero).

Results in table 8.2 suggest that war finance in the nineteenth century shaped the bureaucratic breadth of states on the eve of WWI. Sovereign and colonial authorities were seemingly compelled to mobilize local resources at times when they could not count on external funding. Now, if bureaucracies are meant to stay—namely, if the bureaucratic channel holds—similar results may be found in the longer run. To examine this possibility, I focus on the size and endowment of tax administrations circa 2000. One may argue that large bureaucracies signal extended patronage practices, not state capacity. Ertman and Geddes show that this was the case in parts of early-modern Europe and twentieth-century Latin America, respectively.[86] In figure 8.3a, I evaluate this possibility with contemporary data. Specifically, I plot the size of the tax administration circa 2005, measured by the number of tax officials per thousand capita, against total tax revenue. These two variables correlate at 0.68. Arguably, deviations from the mean might be suggestive of some patronage, but on average more staffed tax bureaucracies seem to point to more fiscal capacity.

Next, I assess the extent to which tax administrations today are shaped by war finance in the long nineteenth century. For consistency with previous tests, I fit expression 7.2, replacing the personal income tax variable with tax staff per thousand capita circa 2005. In figure 8.3b, I plot the marginal effects of the coefficients of interest. Based on this model, the effect of a one-standard-deviation increase of the number of war years under exclusion is equivalent to a jump from the twenty-fifth to the seventy-fifth percentile of the tax staff distribution. By contrast, waging war with access to international capital does not contribute to long-term bureaucratic capacity.

Figure 8.3b might raise concerns of history compression. To address this point, I work with data collected by Tait and Heller for a few selected countries regarding the structure of tax administration in the late 1970s and early 1980s.[87] These data include the size of the finance and planning administration per hundred capita, which I interpret as the extensive margin of the effect of war. In the absence of budget data, I approximate the intensive margin of war finance on bureaucratic development—namely, how many

---

86. Ertman (1997); Geddes (1994).
87. Tait and Heller (1983).

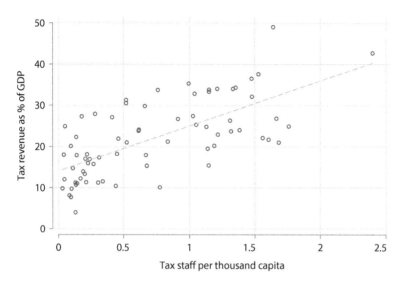

(a) Tax as % of GDP circa 2005 vs. tax staff per thousand capita circa 2005

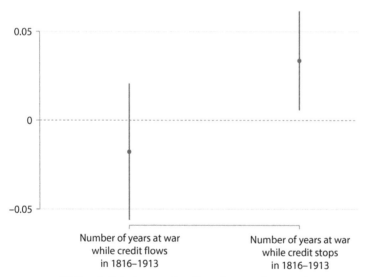

(b) Tax staff today as a function of war and external capital access in the long nineteenth century

FIGURE 8.3. Current and Historical Correlates of Tax Administration and War Finance. Tax staff per thousand capita and total taxation to GDP are drawn from USAID (2012). The regression model in (b) includes the following controls: Region FE, colonial origins FE, population density in 1820, oil production, sea access, desert territory, Great Powers indicator, and state antiquity index. Great Britain is excluded to maximize exogeneity of capital access. N = 78, 90% CI.

resources are put into the tax administration—by the wage premium of the finance administration employees relative to other branches of central government.

Despite the very small sample size, figure 8.4 suggests that nineteenth-century war waged without access to external finance is associated with larger and better-funded finance administrations in the 1970s, whereas war waged with access to external finance is not. In particular, a one-standard-deviation increase in the number of years at war when credit is tight in the nineteenth century raises the average size and the wage premium of the finance administration in the late 1970s by 49 percent and 22 percent, respectively.[88]

Together, figures 8.3 and 8.4 suggest that nineteenth-century war exerted a differential and persistent effect on bureaucratic capacity depending on external capital access. In the absence of foreign loans, rulers were compelled to articulate state strengthening institutions to collect funds for war. Once created, these new bureaucracies were to stay and expand over time. The case of Siam in the next chapter offers a good example.

8.3.3 CAPACITY OR WILLINGNESS

Results in figures 8.3 and 8.4 are helpful in assessing a common concern with empirical measures of state building, namely, the debate between willingness and capacity. Performance measures like income tax ratios may confound the effect of institutions with that of preferences. Countries with a long history of warfare may forge a strong sense of national identity,[89] key to creating reciprocity norms, including taxation compliance.[90] Results above suggest that high tax ratios are not just the result of intrinsic preferences but of stronger bureaucratic capacity. Countries that funded war in the past (partially) with taxes articulated larger bureaucracies and filled them with public servants, who, subject to strict controls and relatively sheltered from the spurious fleeting interests of passing incumbents, carried the fiscal effect of past warfare into the present day. That is the bureaucratic mechanism of persistence.

---

88. The prediction for administration size is unusually high because both this variable and the key predictor are highly skewed.

89. Alesina, Reich, and Riboni (2017).

90. Besley (2020); Levi (1997).

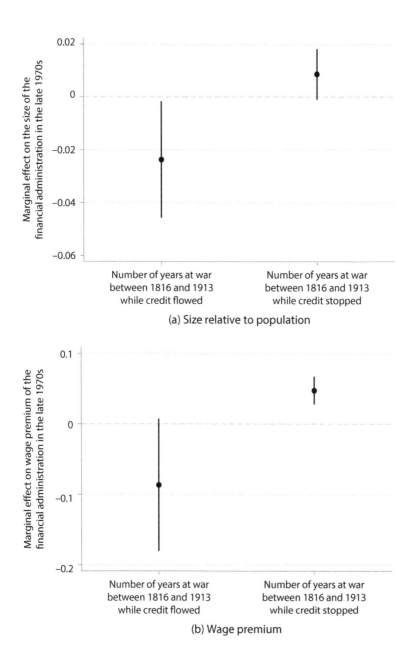

(a) Size relative to population

(b) Wage premium

FIGURE 8.4. Effect of War Finance on the Size and Wage Premium of the Finance Administration in the Late 1970s and Early 1980s. These figures plot 90% CI. Sample size is limited by Tait and Heller's (1983) data and covariate availability. For the tax size administration sample, full data are available for 23 out of the 35 countries in Tait and Heller (1983): Argentina, Belgium, Congo, Cyprus, Ecuador, El Salvador, Germany, Guatemala, Iceland, Ireland, Japan, Netherlands, New Zealand, Panama, Senegal, South Africa, South Korea, Sri Lanka, Swaziland, Sweden, United States, Zambia, and Zimbabwe. For the wage premium sample, full data are available for 15 out of the 26 countries in Tait and Heller (1983): Argentina, Cyprus, Ecuador, El Salvador, Iceland, Japan, New Zealand, Panama, South Africa, South Korea, Sri Lanka, Swaziland, United States, Zambia, and Zimbabwe. Great Britain is excluded to maximize exogeneity of capital access. Controls include population density as of 1820, oil producer, desert territory, and Great Powers and former colony indicators.

8.4 Conclusion

Building from the political economy of external finance in chapter 2, I articulate two explanations for the ratchet effect of war finance from the nineteenth century onward. The first explanation builds from the history of limited government in Western Europe. Political reform resulting from war finance can transform taxation into a nonzero-sum game: rulers secure funds for war, whereas taxpayers hold them accountable for spending decisions. Mutual gain makes the fiscal contract self-enforcing, carrying the effects of warfare into the future. Similar forms of tax bargaining between rulers and taxpayers, I argue, were set in motion in the Bond Era, coinciding with periods of low international liquidity and war; that is, when rulers were compelled to mobilize resources *domestically*. Now, taxation did not always lead to advances in executive constraints. Scope conditions for the taxation-representation connection in Europe seem to apply to the larger world: smaller and more densely populated states in the Bond Era were more likely to couple domestic resource mobilization during wartime with (stronger) representative institutions. The next chapter offers one such example: Chile.

Second, I claim that efforts to raise taxation for war to substitute for external capital can trigger persistent improvements in the tax administration in sovereign and nonsovereign countries. Once bureaucratic reforms are set in motion, the new administrators are likely to safeguard organizational survival by pressing for larger and better endowed structures, channeling the effects of past warfare into the future. I tested the political and bureaucratic mechanisms with available historical quantitative data, often less complete and accurate than one would wish. To reinforce the plausibility of the argument, next I reexamine both mechanisms of transmission with case studies for Argentina, Chile, Ethiopia, Japan, and Siam. Together, the quantitative and qualitative analyses seek to provide coherent and compelling observable evidence of the theoretical argument of the book.

9

State Building Trajectories

Figure 1.3 traced five ideal trajectories of state building, A–E. There I argued that most European countries in early-modern times followed paths A and B, involving domestic resource mobilization in the form of taxes and domestic credit.[1] Most developing nations in the Bond Era, by contrast, followed paths C–E, characterized by substantial external finance. In chapter 5, I focused on the thin line that separates paths C–E, and why developing nations often dropped from C (under which debt is repaid with tax money and state capacity is strengthened) to E (under which debt service is suspended and followed by foreign control).

Opportunities to escape path E may be present, however, when external finance is tight and public funds are in high demand. Under those conditions, rulers' incentives to mobilize domestic resources in the form of taxation grow stronger.[2] Those tax efforts, I claim, are likely to persist because tax administrations generate an interest in organizational survival—the bureaucratic mechanism of transmission—and because new taxes can open the door to power-sharing institutions—the political mechanism.[3]

In this chapter, I expand on the two mechanisms of transmission by examining five historical cases: Japan, Argentina, Siam, Ethiopia, and Chile. In selecting cases, I draw from a group of non-European *sovereign*

1. Refer to chapter 8 for discussion.
2. Refer to chapter 7 for quantitative evidence.
3. Refer to chapter 8 for quantitative evidence.

nations because that condition is required to study the political mechanism, denied outside white-settler colonies. The discussion is organized in three parts: First, I focus on Meiji Japan (1868–1912), which I briefly compare to Argentina, a shadow case. Japan financed war overseas and built a strong state, challenging the theoretical expectation in chapter 2. I argue that this country was able to escape a debt trap because it had a preexisting domestic credit market—a rarity in the global periphery. Domestic resource mobilization along path C activated the bureaucratic and political mechanisms of transmission. I compare Japan to Argentina, one of the wealthiest economies of the world in the early twentieth century. Argentina could not follow the steps of Japan, I argue, because it lacked domestic financiers, hence safeguards against external dependence. Foreign debt grew onerous and Argentina fell behind. The Japan-Argentina dyad shows the challenges of staying away from path E when domestic credit markets are tight.

The second part of the chapter brings us to Siam (renamed Thailand in 1939). Siamese kings in the nineteenth century renounced external finance because they feared the consequences of default. Relentless fiscal centralization and military modernization initiated in the late nineteenth century gave way to a military-bureaucratic regime. Lacking a mass of domestic merchants that could withdraw tax payments unless fiscal powers were shared, state building in Siam walked path A but did not activate the political mechanism of transmission. There lies, I argue, the limited gains in fiscal and state capacity after 1932, when state bureaucrats assumed political power. The case of Siam is briefly compared to Ethiopia, the only African country that remained independent in the nineteenth century. Like Siamese leaders, the Ethiopian emperor avoided foreign finance because of the strings attached. Ethiopia also was poor and lacked a mass of merchants that could lend the emperor money and discipline him in exchange. Early efforts of state building improved bureaucratic capacity along path A but carried no political concession to taxpayers. Relative to Siam, the resolution to rely on domestic resources to fund government ceased too early. Increased dependence on foreign loans and international aid under Haile Selassie (r. 1916–1974) pushed Ethiopia into path E and the fragile state it is today.

In the third and last part of the chapter, I examine state building in Chile, where war under capital exclusion put the bureaucratic and political mechanisms of state building in motion. When tax capacity increased, unease with strong presidential power grew among local merchants, concentrated in two large cities and well coordinated. After a violent dispute in 1891, constitutional reform strengthened parliamentary oversight of budgeting powers, enabling sustained investment in state capacity over the next decades. This case suggests that incentives to push forward major financial innovation along path A may happen when the treasury runs out of options—and yet may carry lasting positive consequences.

9.1 Japan

If there is one success case of state building and external finance, that is Japan. By 1850, this country had lived in autarky for two and a half centuries. Within a generation, Japan was integrated in the global economy and had become the regional military power. Modern weaponry was imported and financed with European private capital. Japan scrupulously met its foreign obligations, proving that external finance is not incompatible with state building. As it turns out, local conditions were exceptional. No other country outside Western Europe and the United States could count on a strong local capital market. That changed it all.

9.1.1 MILITARY AND ECONOMIC MODERNIZATION

In the Tokugawa era (1603–1867), Japan was organized into a collection of semiautonomous feudal domains, and the central government, or shogunate, had no fiscal powers nor monopoly of coercion. This suddenly changed in 1854 when a military envoy of the United States, Commodore Matthew C. Perry, forced the opening of trade ports and tariff limits on imports. The opening (first to the US, soon after to European powers) caused political turmoil within the Japanese leadership, divided about the appropriate response to the Western threat. In 1868, a coup orchestrated by court nobles and domain officials ended the Tokugawa regime. Political centralization under the figure of the Meiji emperor became the top priority of the new regime—a goal largely met: "[Japan] began the Meiji period as one of the modern world's most fractured polities, [but] emerged within a generation as one of its most centralized states."[4] The new regime was markedly oligarchic,[5] and the first years were characterized by frequent insurrections, even civil war.[6] However, and despite the frequent power

4. Jansen (2000, pp. 334–335).
5. Ramseyer and Rosenbluth (1998).
6. Vlastos (1989, p. 368) computes 343 peasant protests just between 1868 and 1872.

struggles within the elite, the national government pushed forward an agenda of military and economic modernization.

China, the almighty regional power,[7] had been humiliated by European powers in the two Opium Wars. The negative consequences of foreign aggression in China resonated in Meiji leaders' minds,[8] solidifying support for military modernization. Within decades, Japan put together a powerful military force supported by a system of mass conscription (adopted as early as 1873) and modern armament. Military officials were hired in Europe to teach modern strategy, and state-of-the-art military equipment was imported from England and Germany. Between 1897 and 1902, for instance, all (six) of the battleships of the new Imperial Japanese Navy were built in Britain.[9] Railroad networks, a second modernization goal, grew in parallel to military investment; however, railroads were disproportionally financed with local capital. By 1902, 73 percent of the rail network was owned by local conglomerates.[10] Partial nationalization took place between 1906 and 1907. Subsequent expansion was evenly divided between public and private initiatives.

To fund military and economic modernization, the government put forward an ambitious plan of monetary and fiscal centralization. The Bank of Japan (inaugurated in 1882) and the new convertible currency (adopted in 1885) allowed for tighter control of capital and commercial flows with the West.[11] Fiscal centralization began as early as 1871, when the new imperial government abolished the autonomy of 260 estates and domains, assumed their outstanding debt, and declared political and fiscal sovereignty over all the territory.[12]

Agrarian reform was the first consequence of centralization. Following a nationwide land survey, property rights were granted to small farmers in 1872.[13] Ownership came with increased taxation, causing mass opposition. The government reduced the rates in response—the start of a gradual decline of land tax in the national budget. Whereas in the early 1870s land tax yields represented over 90 percent of total tax revenue, by 1914 they accounted for less than 20 percent.[14] The Ministry of Finance,

7. Kang (2020).

8. Refer to chapter 5 for details on Chinese-Western relations.

9. Suzuki (1994, p. 178).

10. Tang (2014, p. 868).

11. Sylla (2002) for the development of domestic capital markets in Japan.

12. Nakabayashi (2012, p. 388).

13. Vlastos (1989, p. 373).

14. Nakabayashi (2012, p. 389).

"a major bastion of Westernizing officials,"[15] replaced land taxes with modern tax types. Excise taxes on sake became a major source of revenue, particularly after the war with China (at a time new foreign loans were quoted). Initially, the collection of the excise was delegated to local officials, but in 1880 it was assumed by the Ministry of Finance, replicating the successful beer excise administration in Britain.[16] By 1914, the liquor tax represented 28 percent of total tax revenue (up from 10 percent in 1880).[17] The income tax was adopted in 1887. Initially collected by private financial institutions, the National Tax Agency took over in 1896 after inaugurating regional tax offices.[18] Although the early proceeds of the income tax were small, this tax raised more than 11 percent of total revenue by 1914.[19]

The central bureaucratic apparatus was also modernized following the example of Western countries. In 1873, the state administration was purged of *kuge*—old-regime, high-status samurai—and meritocratic criteria for public service were introduced along the lines of the French public service.[20] By 1900, access to the administration required specific training and passing a certification exam, and bureaucrats were insulated from the clout of ministerial officers and local notables thanks to a system of tenure promotion and public pensions.[21] "Within the span of [a] generation an administrative structure [emerged] that has continued to be the basis for civil service up until the present."[22]

Fiscal reform was fruitful. By 1868, the share of taxes as a percentage of GDP was as low as 0.05 percent (not a typo).[23] Taxes represented only 10 percent of total revenue of the central government, the remaining coming from government enterprises, state monopolies, stamps, currency emissions, and borrowing. On the eve of the Great War, the tax ratio had risen to 8.1 percent of GDP, and taxes represented 51.2 percent of all government revenue. From 1886 onward, all budgets were in surplus.

---

15. He (2013, p. 88).

16. He (2013, p. 111). Brewer (1988) and Nye (2007) for the excise system in Britain.

17. Nakabayashi (2012, p. 402).

18. Onji and Tang (2017, p. 446).

19. Nakabayashi (2012, p. 402).

20. Silberman (1993, pp. 159–168).

21. Silberman (1993, ch. 7). Ramseyer and Rosenbluth (1998, ch. 5) for a more skeptical and possibly more balanced assessment of bureaucratic independence in the Meiji period.

22. Silberman (1993, p. 166).

23. Tax and debt figures in this paragraph are drawn from the Bank of Japan historical compendium published in 1966.

9.1.2 EXTERNAL FINANCE

The spectacular growth in fiscal capacity did not suffice to fund modernization. Economic reform (industry, telecommunications, and railroads) was mainly financed with tax revenue and domestic bonds. Foreign direct investment in those sectors was kept to a minimum (unlike in China or Argentina, discussed below). By contrast, external public finance played a key role in military modernization. Seventy-five percent of total loan issue (net of conversion loans) was used to pay for military outlays.[24] In other words, European capital flowed into Japan in the form of sovereign loans, mostly to fund military expenses.

Access to foreign funds came with a risk. Meiji leaders "recognized that defaults led to a loss of fiscal sovereignty to foreign powers,"[25] and were "anxious about the risk of being colonized by Western powers."[26] The example of Egypt, which had fallen prey to foreign powers after default, was "constantly held up"[27] in policy discussions. Aversion to external finance relaxed during the war with Russia (1904–5) because military expenses could not be financed without major loan proceeds. Between 1904 and 1905, Japan raised £107 million in Europe.[28]

Loans were initially floated in London, but Paris and Berlin joined after the turn of the century. The first £1 million loan was issued in April 1870, carrying a 9 percent effective interest rate (about 200 percent higher than consol yields at the time).[29] Over time, loans grew bigger and the rates more competitive, remaining under 5 percent after 1897. The adoption of the gold standard in 1897 and victory over Russia in 1905 strengthened the creditworthiness of Japan in European financial capitals.[30] That was also reflected in the bond maturity, between 13 and 25 years prior to 1894 and about 60 years thereafter.[31]

Japan met its foreign obligations scrupulously. What explains the pristine fiscal behavior of Japan? Geographic scale and domestic credit, namely, conditions that helped war make states in Western Europe.

---

24. Suzuki (1994, p. 181).
25. Nakabayashi (2012, p. 392).
26. Nakabayashi (2012, p. 378). See also Vlastos (1989, p. 373).
27. Jansen (2000, p. 373). See chapter 4 for details of foreign financial control in Egypt.
28. Sussman and Yafeh (2000, p. 446).
29. Sussman and Yafeh (2000, p. 450).
30. Sussman and Yafeh (2000).
31. Sussman and Yafeh (2000, p. 446).

Geographic Scale

In comparing the divergent paths of China and Japan, Koyama, Moriguchi, and Sng point to the smaller size of Japan as a facilitator of military and fiscal centralization.[32] The relatively small scale increased the efficiency gains of common defense relative to a decentralized structure (the status quo) and reduced collective action costs of building and enforcing the new fiscal apparatus.[33] Despite disagreement on the speed and method of reform and frequent intraelite disputes, Meiji leaders agreed on the benefits of pooling military and fiscal resources to secure sovereignty.[34]

Political and fiscal centralization was not exempt from renegotiations, trial and error, and tensions within the elite and the general populace. Tax increases and mass conscription by the central government soon led to popular demand for an elected national assembly.[35] The promulgation of a Prussian-style constitution in 1889 was arguably a "tactical concession" to the rising urban class, excluded from the circles of power.[36] Franchise for the new Diet remained restricted to big taxpayers, and liberal rights (e.g., freedom of expression) required the consent of the Imperial Diet.[37] These were, however, standard provisions in other advanced economies at the time.[38]

The Meiji constitution was far more consequential for the balance of power between competing elite factions, which rapidly coalesced into two large parties, Liberal and Conservative.[39] Under the new constitution, the Diet was endowed with taxation and expenditure powers (other than military outlays) and the executive had to gain the legislature's approval to pass the annual budget.[40] This power-sharing mechanism set the stage

32. Koyama, Moriguchi, and Sng (2018).

33. By 1850 (i.e., before the railroad), a trip between the two largest cities, Edo (Tokyo) and Osaka, took only four days, and no one in Japan lived farther than 120 km (75 miles) from the sea (Sng and Moriguchi, 2014, p. 445).

34. Koyama, Moriguchi, and Sng (2018, p. 192). This point is sustained by Jansen (2000, p. 333).

35. Initially, demands for elections were channeled by disenchanted Meiji leaders, who capitalized on social discontent with high taxation among local notables (the old-regime elite) and small farmers (Vlastos, 1989, pp. 402–425).

36. Vlastos (1989, p. 426).

37. Jansen (2000, p. 418).

38. For instance, male franchise in Europe also discriminated in favor of big taxpayers (Mares and Queralt, 2015, 2020).

39. Ramseyer and Rosenbluth (1998, ch. 3).

40. Nakabayashi (2012, p. 391).

for compromise. For instance, after the war with China, a tax increase was negotiated with the Liberal opposition after expansion in infrastructure spending (of the latter's liking) had been agreed upon. The "power of the purse" turned out to be a key source of power of the Diet vis-à-vis conservative and militarist executives appointed by the emperor.[41]

Fiscal reform and political stability in a context of external menace was a delicate equilibrium to keep, and the relatively small scale of the country combined with good roads and maritime transportation facilitated elite coordination and rapid suffocation of local insurrections.[42] Not coincidentally, small scale was also a key factor in explaining the rise and persistence of power-sharing institutions in Western Europe.[43]

Domestic Credit Markets

Public credit was not new in Japan. The financial institutions in the Meiji period were largely inherited from the Tokugawa shogunate. What is more, the armed overthrow of the old regime in 1868 was financed with loans from big local merchants, or *zaibatsu*.[44] From the beginning, these centenary conglomerates (e.g., Mitsui, Kōnoike, and Yamaguchi) were embedded in the financial structure of the new regime. In the first decades of the restoration, they assumed responsibility for tax collection outside the capital, a role they kept until the National Tax Agency was ready to do the job.[45] The *zaibatsu* also helped build up public banking. The Mitsui group, for instance, funded (along with Ono) the first national bank in 1873, which was granted a monopoly on banknote issue. Three years later Mitsui established the largest private bank in the country.[46] Not surprisingly, big merchants were close to political power and sponsored the careers of top politicians.[47]

Even though Japan borrowed overseas, domestic loans took a prominent role in public finance. Until war with Russia, external finance represented less than 20 percent of long-term government debt. After war with Russia broke out in 1904, external loans gained weight in total public debt,

---

41. Jansen (2000, p. 418).
42. See Vlastos (1989) for three waves of localized insurrection.
43. Stasavage (2011).
44. Asakura (1967, p. 277); He (2013, p. 86).
45. Asakura (1967); He (2013, ch. 3).
46. Asakura (1967).
47. Jansen (2000, p. 373).

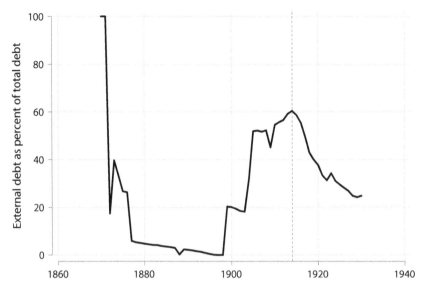

FIGURE 9.1. Foreign Public Debt as Percentage of Total Public Debt in Japan. Data drawn from the Bank of Japan (1966, p.158). From 1868 to 1870, data for domestic bonds are missing, hence the high ratio.

as reflected in figure 9.1. In 1914, that ratio reached its maximum, 60 percent, and declined afterward.[48] The great importance of domestic credit in funding the early decades of the Meiji period played a key role in securing fiscal discipline. Suspending debt service (internal or external) would have reduced government funds substantially, stressed domestic credit markets, and cost political support of the new regime. In Japan, financial oligarchs played a role similar to that of cabal tax farmers in seventeenth-century France:[49] that is, keeping the feet of the sovereign close to the ground in matters of fiscal policy.

Local finance was also important for its role in compensating the losers of the Meiji Restoration: the samurai and local notables in the Tokugawa era. In 1871, following the elimination of the feudal states and the samurai monopoly of military and administrative positions—a "hereditary caste system"[50]—these two groups were compensated with a stipend in rice and government bonds.[51] Initially, the ex-samurai and their families (comprising two million people in total) were generously compensated with

48. Bank of Japan (1966, p. 158).
49. Johnson and Koyama (2014).
50. Jha (2012, p. 15).
51. Nakabayashi (2012, p. 388).

a pension, but that policy dragged the national budget down—it consumed 30 percent of ordinary expenses in 1873.[52] The stipends were commuted for government bonds in 1876.[53] The government created a special bank to guide the ex-samurai in their investments, and the wealthier members put their money in the new financial institutions of the country.[54] As a result, Japan saw a dramatic expansion of private banks, from 7 to 150 branches within two years.[55]

In sum, domestic bonds were strategically granted to develop a vested interest in economic growth and political stability among the losers of the Meiji reform.[56] What was good for the country's finances was good for the ex-samurai.[57] By the same token, avoiding suspension of debt service was of utmost importance to please the social and political foundations of the new regime. Much as had happened in Great Britain and the Netherlands,[58] capital markets in Japan aligned the interests of winners and losers of reform and infused support for financial probity and continued investment in tax capacity.

9.1.3 APPRAISAL AND A SHADOW CASE: ARGENTINA

Japan had the right conditions to connect foreign threats to state building. It was relatively small and had levels of capital accumulation that enabled *domestic* public credit, government accountability, and investment in tax capacity to honor debt. Did other countries follow a similar state building trajectory? Argentina is a good candidate. On the eve of World War I, this Latin American republic was a sovereign and wealthy economy often compared to British offshoots.[59] Yet Argentina's prosperity turned out to be a giant with feet of clay. Its economic vigor faded away as foreign debt piled up. Why did it end that way?

Following independence from Spain in the 1810s, Argentina experienced a series of regional interstate and civil wars requiring vast

---

52. He (2013, p. 97).

53. Vlastos (1989, p. 392).

54. Jansen (2000, p. 365).

55. Jha (2012, p. 16).

56. Jha (2012).

57. Arguably, the *kizoku*—the noble but less numerous ex-samurai—disproportionally benefited from this policy, leaving the ordinary ex-samurai behind.

58. Sylla (2002).

59. See, for instance, Taylor (1992) or Schwartz (1989).

mobilization of domestic and external resources.[60] Pacification in the 1860s gave way to (limited) political centralization, the adoption of a liberal constitution, and state building.[61] Broadly speaking, Argentina walked path A of state building for decades after independence. Thereafter and gradually, Argentina became a pole of attraction of foreign capital. But the boom came only in the 1880s: within 10 years, British investment in Argentina grew from £25 million to £150 million, the latter being a lower-bound estimate.

The British investment during the 1880's expanded at a rate astonishing by standards of that age and greater than during any subsequent decade. The year 1889 was, indeed, an *annus mirabilis* when Argentina absorbed between 40 and 50 per cent of all British funds invested outside the United Kingdom.[62]

Despite the potential benefits of public investment,[63] external debt service became unmanageable, consuming 50 percent of export revenue—a critical measure of debt sustainability, according to Flandreau and Zumer.[64] Default followed in 1890, causing the Baring Crisis, a major crisis in financial history. In 1900, after a long cycle of debt restructuring was completed, outstanding debt had increased tenfold relative to 1880.[65] Debt service had risen to a point that Argentina became a net capital exporter by the end of the decade.[66] The new capital inflows were not for productive purposes either. Every new loan between 1890 and 1914 was to wash out old debts, including the liquidation of the railway guarantees to British investors.[67]

60. Halperin Donghi (1982); López-Alves (2000, ch. 4); Oszlak (2004, ch. 2); Rock (2000).

61. Cox and Saiegh (2018); della Paolera and Taylor (2001, ch. 1); Saiegh (2013).

62. Ferns (1960, p. 397).

63. Marichal (1989, p. 80) shows that the share of military spending in external finance declined over time in favor of infrastructure spending.

64. Flandreau and Zumer (2004). Ford (1956, p. 141) offers larger estimates of debt service, as high as 60% of export revenue.

65. Cortés-Conde (1995, p. 163). Half of this quantity resulted from provincial and municipal debt, assumed by the central state in exchange for fiscal centralization.

66. Marichal (1989, p. 163); Ford (1956, p. 149).

67. The control of British firms of the rail network in Argentina took two steps: In 1890, the government sold major public lines to British firms to obtain liquidity to service external debt. In 1896, a £10 million loan was floated in London to liquidate the 5% and 7% railway guarantees (or subsidies) held by a dozen British railway companies operating in the country. Those loans had been raised during the years of bonanza, and the guarantees were consuming a significant portion of the revenue. The £10 million was transferred directly to the coffers of these companies. Although the sale of national networks in 1890 and the railway guarantees raised political opposition, the national state moved ahead because it was part of the larger debt restructuring negotiations (Marichal, 1989, pp. 163–165). The revision of the railway code of 1907 produced a

Economic austerity in the 1890s was followed by a period of sustained growth, the Belle Epoque, 1900–1914. These years were characterized by an export boom that sanitized the national budget. Despite improvements, fiscal deficits remained the norm (unlike Japan),[68] debt service consumed at least twice the resources in Argentina as in Japan (figure 9.2a), and the ratio of total public debt to revenue remained twice the size of Japan's (figure 9.2b).

The origins of debt were also starkly different: whereas external debt in 1914 in Japan represented an all-time-high 60 percent of total public debt (see figure 9.1), that level was still a fraction of Argentina's 86 percent.[69] The lack of domestic credit markets in Argentina—an old problem[70]—pushed the government back to external markets (New York, specifically) right after WWI.[71] Total debt nearly doubled between 1920 and 1930, increasing from 850 million to 1,600 million pesos. More than 60 percent of debt contracted in that decade was still used for nonproductive purposes: refinancing old debt, armaments, and unbudgeted expenses.[72]

External debt is arguably not the only cause of Argentina's economic decline, but it played a key role.[73] The fiscal imbalance generated by overborrowing in the 1880s was never fully addressed. Access to external capital (even if only to wash out old debt) kept tax reform to a minimum.[74]

---

new set of favorable conditions for further expansion of the private (hence British) network (Cain and Hopkins, 2016, p. 270). The virtual monopoly over railroads (plus new gains in the banking and insurance sectors thanks to weak conditions of local competitors) put British investors at the forefront of the export boom in the 1900–1914 years, hence first in line to accrue profit.

68. Author's calculation based on Ferguson and Schularick's (2006) data.

69. Peters (1934, p. 143).

70. Saylor (2014, p. 94).

71. There are at least two reasons for the small size of domestic holders of government bonds in Argentina: One points to the demographic composition of the country (Taylor, 1992), another to the weak incentives of landowners or *estancieros* and local banks to invest in government securities given the high rates of return of land acquisition and industrial production (Peters, 1934, p. 34).

72. Peters (1934, p. 104).

73. Key explanations include the inability to control inflation (della Paolera and Taylor, 2001) and the denomination of debt in foreign currency—the "original sin" (Eichengreen and Hausmann, 2005). Illuminating surveys can be found in della Paolera and Taylor's (2003) edited volume *A New Economic History of Argentina*, and Glaeser, Di Tella, and Llach's (2018) special issue of *Latin American Economic Review*.

74. Oszlak (2004, pp. 230–250); Schwartz (1989, ch. 6). Kurtz (2013) points to the early incorporation of the middle class into politics (a phenomenon Oszlak relates to discontent from austerity policy in the 1890s) as the main cause of languid elite support of tax reform in Argentina.

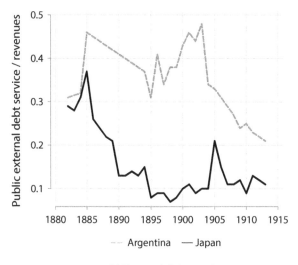

(a) External debt service

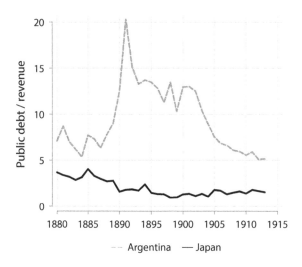

(b) Public debt to revenue

FIGURE 9.2. Public Debt in Japan and Argentina before 1914. Data drawn from Ferguson and Schularick (2006).

Argentina's underinvestment in tax capacity is no surprise in light of the political economy of public finance elaborated in chapter 2. Japan's commitment to fiscal discipline is. Preexisting debt markets surely played a key role in keeping Japan off a foreign debt trap during critical stages of state building. Chance might have played a role too. By 1914, external service was rapidly accelerating in Japan. To avoid debt service suspension, the Ministry of Finance had to be bailed out by the Bank of Japan and Yokohama Specie Bank.[75] Increased exports stimulated by war demand and subsequent tightening of international credit helped Japan refocus on domestic resource mobilization. "Japan was lucky"[76] that the international credit bubble burst before it was too late.

9.2 Siam

In the early 1870s, Siam was not a territorial state proper. Bangkok maintained tributary relations with the periphery, a common power structure in Asia known as a mandala state. The country had no standing military or common currency. And yet by 1914 Siam had become a centralized entity, raised a national army, and participated in international trade. The rapid overhaul of the country was a response to external threats and primarily involved investment in bureaucratic capacity. These changes were purposively undertaken without resorting to external capital, considered by local elites as a form of subjugation to Western powers.[77] Consistent with the bureaucratic channel of persistence, areas of Siam that were centralized early had a stronger bureaucratic apparatus as early as 1917 and as late as 2000.[78]

The emphasis on building a strong but unaccountable Leviathan came with strings attached. The very same civil servants that the Chakri dynasty had recruited and nurtured for 60 years terminated the absolutist era in 1932, replacing it with a bureaucratic regime. Following the 1932 revolution—and arguably until the present day—different factions within the bureaucratic apparatus have vied for power, welcomed external finance, and limited opportunities of political participation to the populace.

9.2.1 FOREIGN THREATS AND STATE BUILDING

Although Siam never lost national sovereignty, the risk of colonial occupation intensified in the middle of the nineteenth century. The British had defeated the Chinese in the First Opium War (1839–1842), and Burma—Siam's regional rival—followed suit in 1852. The French occupied

---

75. Suzuki (1994, p. 183).
76. Suzuki (1994, p. 184).
77. Swam (2009, p. 3).
78. Paik and Vechbanyongratana (2019).

Cochin China in 1861 and pressed Siam from bordering Cambodia. Despite multidirectional threats, Siamese rulers were able to play British and French colonial ambitions against each other and secure for itself buffer state status between both powers.[79]

The foreign menace compelled the Chakri dynasty to put forward a battery of administrative, fiscal, and military reforms. The task was daunting because the playing field was not level. To preempt foreign intervention, King Mongkut (r. 1851–1868) signed the 1855 Bowring Treaty with the British. The treaty was meant to open the Siamese economy to foreign competitors. Among the many clauses, it capped tariffs at 3 percent, hence precluding the ability to use trade taxes as a source of revenue. The treaty also banned any modification of the land tax rate and internal tolls as well as the creation of new taxes.[80] Revenue, badly needed to build a new army, could grow only from better enforcement of existing taxes on land, state monopolies, and forced labor, or *corvée*. And that is what happened.

King Mongkut initiated a battery of reforms, but his son and successor, King Chulalongkorn (r. 1868–1906), was responsible for the giant leap forward in fiscal capacity. He reformed the entire government and bureaucratic structure as a means of fiscally centralizing the state. New ministries were created, the king's personal finances were separated from the general revenues, auditing techniques were incorporated, and annual budgets were first drafted and published.[81] Between 1868 and 1915, tax revenue increased almost tenfold, from 8 to 74 million baht.[82] Fiscal discipline became a matter of national security. The king was wary that economic distress would encourage international powers to take over the country, as they had done with China.[83] Between 1850 and 1922, Siam enjoyed a fiscal surplus every single year. Fiscal discipline implied that productive investment (e.g, roads, ports) was executed piecemeal. No risks were taken.

Domestic loans were not an option to fund government—a local credit market would not exist until after the Great War.[84] Between 1905 and 1925, Siam floated five loans overseas for a total of £13.6 million, 44 percent of which was used to reinforce credit instead of domestic investment

79. Tej (1968, p. 79).
80. Ingram (1955, p. 177).
81. Ingram (1955, p. 177).
82. Ingram (1955, pp. 176, 185).
83. See chapter 5 for details.
84. The first record of domestic sovereign loans dates from 1933 (Wilson, 1983, p. 251).

activity.[85] These loans turned out to be extremely political, with British, French, and German representatives competing for access, which reinforced the kings' fears of external finance. Low reliance on foreign credit slowed down economic progress, but for that very reason it compelled the Siamese kings to undertake ambitious, self-strengthening reforms that increased state capacity in the short and long run.

9.2.2 CENTRALIZATION AND BUREAUCRATIC GROWTH

Tributary governance in Siam had never required central government presence outside Bangkok, but that changed in the mid-nineteenth century. Kings Mongkut and Chulalongkorn understood that national sovereignty required securing the outer frontiers, and to that end they replaced local political and administrative elites on the frontier with loyal delegates and career bureaucrats.

Administrative reform was initiated in 1873 with the creation of the central government Revenue Office, to which regional tax farmers directed local revenue. The Audit Office, inaugurated in 1874, was intended to keep tax collection under the tight supervision of the central government and limit embezzlement and corrupt practices by regional tax farmers and elites.[86] Shortly thereafter, central government commissioners were deployed in the provinces to directly supervise the collection from tax farms. In 1875, the government founded the Survey Division, which created the first complete map of Siam by 1897, enabling the government to set up telegraph lines linking it to areas under external pressure.[87] To radiate state power further, in 1887 a new Department of Education was inaugurated, enabling the expansion of public education, and new military and survey schools were opened to recruit military and civil officials.

Fiscal and bureaucratic reform extended the king's grip over the territory against the will of regional leaders. To overcome resistance, King Chulalongkorn raised a private professional army of 15,000 troops and 3,000 marines, financed with the monies collected by the new Revenue Office.[88] Despite significant progress, the war with France in 1893 was a warning call for the king. The country remained powerless against European military

85. Ingram (1955, p. 182).
86. Tej (1968, pp. 88–89).
87. Tej (1968, p. 117).
88. Tej (1968, pp. 92–94).

might. Fiscal and political centralization accelerated thereafter,[89] and to that end the cabinet was reorganized into 12 specialized ministries, including the powerful Ministries of Finance[90] and the Interior,[91] which shared responsibilities for tax collection.

The Ministry of the Interior assumed the production of the first modern census, conducted at the provincial level in 1903 and at the national level in 1910.[92] Censuses were not new in Siam. They had been crucial for the *corvée*, conscription, and taxation.[93] However, the new modern techniques applied in the 1910 census perfected the ability of the central government to "see like a state."[94] To supply the new bureaucracies with qualified officials, new professional public service schools were inaugurated in 1899.[95]

Bureaucratic reform put forward in the long nineteenth century had lasting effects—some good, some bad. On the positive side of the balance, advances in the infrastructural power of the state increased short- and long-run economic output and human capital: exploiting historical geographic variation, Paik and Vechbanyongratana show that provinces that were centralized early on were those exposed to higher external threats. They find that centralization was manifested in higher density of the rail line and larger presence of public schools and teachers by 1917. Those differences remained in the year 2000.[96] In other words, early bureaucratic reform had persistent positive effects on state capacity. The strong emphasis on a strong but unaccountable administration, however, led to the demise of the absolutist regime as well as the democratic era that briefly followed it.

9.2.3 A SHORT DEMOCRATIC SPRING

By renouncing external finance, Siamese rulers were compelled to put forward a battery of bureaucratic innovations to secure government funds with domestic resources, but no political change followed. Quite the contrary, King Chulalongkorn's policies were meant to consolidate central

---

89. Riggs (1966, p. 139).
90. Brown (1992).
91. Tej (1968).
92. Tej (1968, p. 215).
93. Tej (1968, p. 17).
94. Scott (1998).
95. Tej (1968, p. 240).
96. Paik and Vechbanyongratana (2019).

power over a constellation of tributary states. What Chulalongkorn did not anticipate is that his successors would lose control over the bureaucracy that he and his father had put in place.[97] A coalition of new urban classes and career officials unsatisfied with nepotism led a revolution in 1932 that ended with the abdication of King Prajadhipok (r. 1925–1935), the promulgation of a constitution, and national elections.[98]

Demands for limited government were not new in Siam. In 1885, Western-educated elite members petitioned the king for a constitutional monarchy emulating the British model. Coups to replace the monarchy with a constitutional government were aborted in 1912 and 1917.[99] Unlike during previous coup attempts, the financial position of the country in the early 1930s was in dire straits. Global demand and trade tax revenue plunged following the crash of 1929.[100] To finance the deficit, King Prajadhipok considered floating a loan overseas, but the terms were unbearable.[101] Effectively excluded from credit markets, the king proposed the implementation of a general income and property tax. The new tax followed a public petition in the *Bangkok Times*, the leading journal in Siam, which recommended heavier taxes on the wealthy and more government spending to palliate economic distress.[102] The princes in the Supreme Council—a consultation body that the king had created in 1926—flatly rejected the income tax by arguing that it would hit their fortunes hardest. Pressed from above and below, the king opted for a compromise: the income tax was adopted, but key sources of wealth remained exempt to minimize opposition from the rich. To balance the budget, government spending was cut by reducing salaries of civil servants and slashing the military budget. Effectively, the income tax shifted the tax burden onto the urban middle class and penalized civil servants.[103]

97. Riggs (1966, p. 131).

98. Batson (1984).

99. Handley (2006, pp. 35–37).

100. Handley (2006, p. 42).

101. Britain, which had abandoned the gold standard after the crash to keep the economy afloat, was off the table. Despite lacking US dollars in their foreign reserves—overwhelmingly denominated in pounds sterling—Siamese delegates approached American financiers. Liquidity in the US was tight too, and requirements draconian, including control over customs revenue and the northern and northeastern rail lines. This would have "give[n] foreign interests a degree of economic control which Thai governments for a century had skillfully maneuvered to avoid" (Batson, 1984, p. 195).

102. Batson (1984, p. 188).

103. Handley (2006, p. 37).

Public criticism to fiscal policy grew stronger. The *Bangkok Times* denounced the passing of an "unfair tax" for the middle class and raised issues of "taxation without representation."[104] The king sought to appease popular opposition by passing a constitution that allowed for some "degree of representative government without unleashing forces of radical change."[105] It was too late. The king was deposed soon after by a diverse coalition comprising nonroyal military officers, civilian bureaucrats, and urban dwellers, whose only common goal was to "strip the throne of its powers and creat[e] a constitutional government."[106]

9.2.4 A LONG BUREAUCRATIC WINTER

The limited opportunities to participate in politics recognized by the 1932 constitution placed political power in the hands of state bureaucrats—the very same officials that the monarchy had nurtured for over 50 years.[107] The working class was excluded from the circles of power, and there was no room for career politicians either. In the decades that followed, civil and military officials held a virtual monopoly on positions in the cabinet and a majority in the national parliament.[108]

Career officials were divided into two rival groups: those in favor of a constitutional government and those in favor of military rule.[109] Relentless competition for power within the state apparatus was manifested in rapid government turnover: from 1932 to 2006, Siam (Thailand after 1939) went through 20 constitutional texts, 36 prime ministers, and endless coups and autocoups (some successful, others not). The common denominator of all administrations was their appreciation for self-indulgency. The Ministries of the Interior and Defense alone consumed on average 34.5 percent of the national budget.[110]

As years passed, Thailand became a paramount example of an inefficient but persistent state, as defined by Acemoglu, Ticchi, and Vindigni (namely, a coalition between bureaucrats, state, employees, and plutocrats,

104. Batson (1984, p. 221).

105. Batson (1984, p. vi).

106. Handley (2006, p. 44).

107. Riggs (1966) for a long and compelling elaboration.

108. See Wilson (1966, p. 155), Riggs (1966, p. 316), and Thak (2007) for longitudinal statistical evidence of overrepresentation of civil and military officials in the executive and legislature.

109. Baker and Phongpaichit (2014, p. 120).

110. Average for 1953–1973 computed by the author based on data in Thak (2007, p. 227).

united against democracy and wealth redistribution).[111] Consistently, little attention was paid to the working class and farmers in the countryside. And despite sustained economic growth, no major investment in infrastructure or improvements in fiscal capacity occurred after World War II.[112]

To minimize social contestation, tax pressure remained low. Tax revenue as a percentage of GDP grew from 4.9 percent to 12.3 percent from 1950 to 1978,[113] but remained considerably low by regional and international standards.[114] Tax receipts grew momentarily before the financial crisis of 1997, but returned to preboom times soon after, stabilizing at around 15 percent of GDP.[115]

To fund the government, postrevolutionary administrations welcomed foreign capital, hence deviating from their absolutist predecessors. Loans and aid from the United States flowed in the 1950s.[116] The International Bank for Reconstruction and Development and the Commonwealth countries and Japan (the Colombo Plan) chipped in with developmental programs.[117] International aid proved largely inefficient because the programs prioritized foreign military interests over local needs.[118] Besides, aid money in the hands of Thai officials often ended up in blatant corruption: "The generals focused on dividing up the spoils of the massive dollar inflows and the resulting increase in government budgets and business profits."[119]

Along with international aid, external public debt grew after WWII. As a percentage of GDP, foreign debt quintupled between 1970 and the late 1980s.[120] Strong dependence on foreign capital in the public and private

---

111. Acemoglu, Ticchi, and Vindigni (2011). For the collusion between bureaucrats and big businessmen in Thailand, refer to Baker and Phongpaichit (2014, ch. 9).

112. Doner (2009) and Slater (2010, pp. 241–250), respectively.

113. Author's calculation based on Wilson (1983).

114. Sachs and Williamson (1985, p. 544) show that tax revenue as a percentage of GDP in Thailand in 1982 was 13.9 points, whereas East Asian and Latin American averages were 20.6 and 22.2 points, respectively.

115. IMF Government Finance Statistics Yearbooks, WB, and OECD, https://data.world bank.org/indicator/GC.TAX.TOTL.GD.ZS?locations=TH (retrieved May 11, 2021).

116. Baker and Phongpaichit (2014, ch. 6). Note that US administrations used Thailand as a bastion against communism in the region.

117. See Wilson (1983, pp. 255–268) for disaggregated international aid data to Thailand.

118. Thak (2007, pp. 167–177).

119. Baker and Phongpaichit (2014, p. 169).

120. Outstanding public or public-guaranteed external debt was 4.57% in 1970 and 27.53% in 1987. World Bank, International Debt Statistics, https://data.worldbank.org/indicator/DT .DOD.DPPG.CD (retrieved May 11, 2021).

sectors led to two financial crises, one in the 1980s and another in the 1990s. Massive unemployment and poverty followed.[121] Afterward, spending austerity, low taxation, and political instability remained the norm.

9.2.5 APPRAISAL AND A SHADOW CASE: ETHIOPIA

After seven decades of sustained bureaucratic strengthening, the Chakri dynasty had built one of the strongest Leviathans in all of Southeast Asia.[122] The Crown's early success, however, contained the seeds of its own demise. In the "bureaucratic polity"[123] that followed absolutism, political effort was put on seizing and keeping power. Fiscal orthodoxy and external dependence were relaxed, preempting major advances in state capacity.

Siam illustrates the dilemmas and limits of building a strong bureaucratic state without a proper system of checks and balances. Coercion can secure tax compliance up to a point; however, compliance with higher rates is hardly implementable without securing consent—and for that, political change is required. In the nineteenth century, Siam lacked a mercantile class capable of extracting concessions from the king in return for tax compliance. Long distance, rugged terrain, and poor means of communication did not allow peripheral leaders to coordinate and negotiate terms of fiscal centralization. Absolutism followed.

The case of Siam shares important characteristics with the only African country that escaped European colonization in the nineteenth century: Ethiopia. This country was big (about 1.7 times the size of France), poor, and ethnically diverse. Threats of foreign invasion propelled state building efforts involving virtually no external finance.[124] And bureaucratic strengthening received most of the attention. Unlike Siam, Ethiopian rulers succumbed too soon to the temptation of external finance, pushing their country into a debt trap and state weakness that persist today.

Although Ethiopia had a centenary tradition of statehood, the modernization of the state apparatus accelerated in the last decades of the nineteenth century primarily because of war considerations. State reform was implemented by Emperor Menilek II (r. 1889–1913), who had accessed the throne after two decades of civil war. Seeking to build a modern

---

121. In 1997 alone, over two million jobs were destroyed and GDP growth plummeted by 11 percentage points.

122. Slater (2010, p. 241).

123. Riggs (1966).

124. Tibebu (1995, ch. 2).

nation-state, he created a national currency, revamped the taxation system, introduced Western-style property inheritance law, established a cabinet system of government, opened modern schools and hospitals, and adopted the telegraph and telephone, among others reforms.[125] The military also received Menilek II's attention: modern weaponry (rifles, cannons, ammunition) were imported from France, Italy, and Russia and paid for partly in cash and partly in specie: ivory, gold, and civet.[126] To make reforms self-sustaining, Menilek II ruled key parts of the empire only indirectly, allowing local rulers to retain power in return for taxes and tributes.[127]

The Horn of Africa was a key geostrategic position for trade routes with Asia and within Africa. Italy, the main European power in East Africa as of the Berlin Conference (1884–1885), sought to gain the sympathy of the new Ethiopian emperor. In 1889, the two countries signed the Treaty of Wuchale, and as a sign of goodwill, the Italians offered a loan to Menilek of 4 million lire ($800,000), half of it to acquire military equipment.[128] The loan carried extreme conditionality: it was secured by the customs revenue from the city of Harar, which would pass into the hands of Italy should Menilek default on external debt.[129]

A disagreement about the key stipulations of the treaty—Had Ethiopia become an Italian protectorate upon its signature?—convinced Menelik II to terminate the relationship with the Italians. By 1893, he had returned the loan to safeguard independence.[130] Further disagreements led to the First Italian-Ethiopian War of 1895–1896. The Italians mobilized 20,000 troops, half of them African. Menelik II mobilized over 100,0000 men, including 80,000 riflemen, 8,600 cavalry, 32 artillery and machine gun batteries, plus 20,000 hangers-on armed only with spears, lances, and swords.[131] To finance the increased expenses of war, a new tax on wealth and land was levied on farmers.[132]

Ethiopia won the war against the Italians and confirmed its independence for years to come. To avoid tripping over the same stone twice,

125. Mennasemay (2005); Pankhurst (1968).
126. Pankhurst (1968, pp. 591–602).
127. Marcus (1969, pp. 451–453).
128. Vestal (2005, p. 24).
129. Zewde Gabre-Selassie (2005, p. 107).
130. Marcus (1969, p. 433).
131. Marcus (1969, p. 435).
132. Pankhurst (1968, p. 537).

Menelik II closed the country to external capital.[133] By 1914, Ethiopia was not a modern Weberian state, but the fiscal efforts made during Menelik II's tenure were fundamental to fund economic modernization, continue the arms imports from Europe, and initiate a second phase of bureaucratic modernization after his passing.[134]

Why did Ethiopia become one of the world's poorest countries? Some responsibility lay in external finance in the second half of the twentieth century. After WWII, Haile Selassie (regent 1916–1930; emperor 1930–1974) made economic modernization a priority. Because military expenses consumed most domestic funds, he turned to international markets to finance developmental programs.[135] Haile Selassie soon realized that he could secure military aid from the West by exploiting the geostrategic value that Ethiopia had acquired in the Cold War era.[136] In 1959, for instance, he threatened to accept $100 million from the Soviet Union unless the US did not commit to a new military outlay. Between 1950 and 1970, Ethiopia received $200 million from the US and $121 million more from the World Bank.[137] By 1970, almost two-thirds of total US military aid to Africa was allocated to Ethiopia.[138]

In addition to military aid, Haile Selassie negotiated bilateral and multilateral loans from official creditors.[139] Loans were often offered on concessional terms (i.e., with conditions more favorable than those offered by the market) as part of official developmental aid (ODA). Between 1960 and 1974, ODA loan issue alone grew by 250 percent in constant prices.[140] External funds became important for the emperor and enabled a period of "personal rule," which gradually eroded "governmental efficiency."[141]

While external capital poured in, tax reform came to a halt—much like in Siam. Some half-hearted efforts were made under Haile Selassie.[142] The

---

133. There was one important exception: French and British investors financed a railway that connected Addis Ababa (the capital) to the port of Djibouti, de facto opening Ethiopia to international markets (Ram, 1981).

134. Keller (1991); Pankhurst (1968).

135. Keller (1991, pp. 95–102).

136. Marcus (2002, ch. 11).

137. Hess (1970).

138. Broich (2017, p. 18).

139. Lemi (2007).

140. OECD, Query Wizard for International Development Statistics, https://stats.oecd .org/qwids (last retrieved May 13, 2021).

141. Marcus (2002, p. 166); Kissi (2000); Zewde (2001, ch. 5).

142. Keller (1991, pp. 113–118).

land tax was reformed in 1944, but it did not end with the informal control of landed elites over collection, and receipts declined over time; corporate taxation was sliced to attract foreign direct investment;[143] and the new income tax passed in 1966 was systematically eluded by the urban elites. Tax reform failed because Haile Selassie sought to increase the tax pressure while retaining full power over fiscal policy.[144]

A Marxist revolutionary junta deposed Haile Selassie in 1974. When the new government approached the USSR for support, the latter flooded the country with fresh military aid, including heavy subsidies to wage war against Somalia in 1977–78.[145] When the West resumed aid programs in the 1980s, fresh cash was often diverted for clientelistic purposes or captured by regional insurgents.[146] To balance the central government budget, the junta issued new external loans: by 1988, debt service consumed $530 million a year, a tenfold increase relative to 1974.[147] In the meantime, the military share of the budget had grown from 18 percent in 1974 to 50 percent in 1988.[148]

The military regime collapsed in 1991, and a (highly imperfect) parliamentary regime was inaugurated. External debt generously surpassed 100 percent of GDP for most of the 1990s, and aid kept coming at faster rates than ever.[149] Since 2000, Ethiopia has been part of the group of highly indebted poor countries (HIPCs) and receives regular assistance from the IMF and the World Bank.[150] Despite recent progress in tax collection, Ethiopia relies on loans and international aid to finance its budget deficit, remains at the head of sub-Saharan African economies in terms of per capita ODA, and is experiencing a rapid acceleration of public external debt relative to GDP, revenue, and exports.[151]

All in all, Thai and Ethiopian rulers in the twentieth century did not share the diplomatic finesse and time horizons of their predecessors.

---

143. Degefe (1992).

144. Complementary efforts to radiate state presence were also abandoned. For instance, public spending in education was reduced in the countryside and concentrated in the capital (Mengisteab, 2002, p. 181).

145. Broich (2017, pp. 33–34).

146. Marcus (2002, p. 209).

147. Marcus (2002, p. 213).

148. Mengisteab (2002, p. 182).

149. Lemi (2007).

150. See Mengisteab (2002) for a critical assessment of state building efforts in the first decade of the democratic regime that followed.

151. Coutts and Laskaridis (2019); Manyazewal (2019).

Accelerating after WWII, Thai and Ethiopian rulers succumbed to the temptation to float external loans and actively searched for international aid. In both states, external finance reduced the impetus to keep building states. When that happened, both countries were at different stages of state building, allowing Thailand to use external funds to grease its strong bureaucratic apparatus and avoid the foreign debt trap and state failure experienced in Ethiopia.

9.3 Chile

The cases I have focused on so far either followed one trajectory of state building from the nineteenth century onward (i.e., Japan) or switched gears along the path favoring external funds (i.e., Argentina, Ethiopia, Thailand). Two questions follow: One, do countries hold any (unobserved) characteristic (e.g., cultural trait, colonial legacy) that makes them more likely to choose and remain on any given path? Two, can states jump into a positive state building trajectory halfway through the game? To address these questions, I examine longitudinal variation in fiscal capacity in Chile, a sovereign country that committed to state building only in the last decades of the nineteenth century, when leaders were compelled by circumstances to mobilize domestic resources for war.

Chile was a relatively small country with mercantile elites concentrated in two major cities, Santiago and Valparaíso, 70 miles apart and connected by telegraph (1851), railroad (1863), and telephone (1880). These favorable conditions enabled economic elites to coordinate, extract, and enforce power-sharing institutions at the time of domestic resource mobilization. Borrowing from empirical strategy in chapter 7, I show here that major tax reform in Chile took place when the government ran out of options. Wartime fiscal efforts activated both the bureaucratic and political mechanisms of transmission, growing state capacity in the long run.

9.3.1 CHILE AT WAR

Chile gained independence from Spain in 1826 after 16 years of war.[152] Chile was never of paramount importance for the Spanish Crown, which was more invested in Peru because of its natural resources.[153] Upon

---

152. Marichal (1989, p. 33).
153. See Dell (2010) and Guardado (2018) for a detailed account of Spanish rule in Peru.

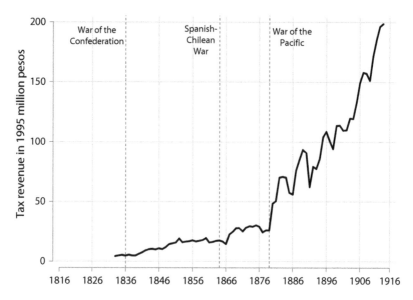

FIGURE 9.3. Tax Revenue in Chile in the Long Nineteenth Century. Data drawn from Wagner, Jofré, and Lüders (2000).

independence, Chile inherited a rather limited state administration with low capacity to raise taxes. Still in 1826, Chile suspended debt service on the only loan it had issued in foreign markets and aimed at funding military expenses.

The War of the Confederation (1836–1839) was the first interstate war waged by Chile as a fully sovereign state. The relationship between Peru and Chile had deteriorated since their split from Spain. Peru failed to repay a loan from Chile to fight Spain, and both countries engaged in a tariff war in the early 1830s. In 1836, Peru and Bolivia formed the Bolivian-Peruvian Confederation. Chile read the move as a direct challenge to its desired hegemony in the South Pacific. That year the confederation also sponsored a failed expedition led by an exiled Chilean general aimed at ousting the Chilean president. This was the onset of a three-year war.[154]

The War of the Confederation had moderate fiscal effects for Chile, as shown in figure 9.3. Based on my calculations, the war cost was ₱ 3 million, equivalent to 25 percent of the ordinary annual receipts. War expenses were financed with taxes and domestic credit, the latter playing only a minor

154. For further contextualization of this war, including Argentina's participation, see Collier (2003, ch. 3).

role.[155] Tax receipts were raised from customs (over 60 percent of total revenue), excises, and mining receipts. The war coincided with the tenure of Renjifo and Tocornal, two orthodox finance ministers who reshuffled the tax system twice to balance the budget. In 1837, the four ministries (interior, justice, finance, and war) were restructured and given specific functions as part of an integral plan of financial reform,[156] and in 1839, customs duties were marginally raised to cover additional war expenses.[157]

The budget, balanced during wartime with only a fifth of a percentage point deviation over the GDP in 1839, remained stabilized or in surplus during the next 15 years; and tax revenue increased by 50 percent, although from a very low base. The main impact of the War of the Confederation was arguably political. Bringing much political stability in the decades that followed, the war unified conservative families and forged a national spirit among elites and nonelites alike.[158] Centeno summarizes the effect of the War of the Confederation in these words: "If any war 'made' Chilean exceptionalism, it was this one, as it provided a rare legitimacy while also establishing a stable civil-military relationship."[159]

In 1842, a healthy financial position allowed the Chilean government to settle the debt that had been in default since 1826. In the early 1850s, significant tax reform took place with the adoption of *la contribución territorial*, a new land tax that required the assessment of property holdings by the state.[160] Revenue stemming from these taxes was, however, largely insufficient to meet the expenses of the next interstate war fought by Chile in the nineteenth century: the Chincha Islands War, also known as the Spanish-Chilean War. The archipelago, located about 20 miles off the southern coast, held Peru's largest deposit of guano, a highly effective soil fertilizer in high demand in Europe and considered "more precious than gold."[161]

---

155. Three-fourths of war expenses were covered with tax revenue; the remaining with domestic public debt. Credit markets were tight in Chile. In August 1836, the executive tried to float ₱400,000 at 4% to expand the navy (Barros Arana, 1880, p. 38). This quotation failed and the target was reduced in September to half that quantity. Only ₱105,000 was contracted in the end, one-fourth the original target. Additional sources were liberated by a 10% domestic debt relief and by inducing taxpayers in arrears to repay in full in return for a reduction in the interest rate (Cruchaga, 1878, p. 50).

156. Humud (1969, p. 86).

157. Pastén (2017).

158. Collier (2003, p. 24).

159. Centeno (2002, p. 57).

160. Soifer (2015, p. 163).

161. Hollett (2008). See Vizcarra (2009) for European demand of guano.

The Chincha Islands War (1864–1866) was initiated by Spain as part of a new, aggressive offensive in imperial foreign policy led by Queen Isabella II. The pretext was the death in Peru of some Spanish agricultural workers after marching for improvements in working conditions. A Spanish naval squadron occupied the Chincha Islands in retaliation. From that position of force, Spain negotiated concessions from the Peruvian government. Following pro-Peruvian comments in the Chilean press, the Spanish bombarded the coastal city of Valparaíso.[162] When Chile rapidly organized an international coalition with Bolivia and Ecuador to fight Spain, the allied forces contained Spain's ambitions to regain colonial influence in the region. The Spanish navy soon realized that they could not win the war despite having more than twice the cannons of Chile and Peru combined. The cost of war for Chile was ₱ 32 million, twice annual ordinary receipts. In order to fund war expenses, Chile floated three loans in London.

After the war, Chile was able to honor external debt from ordinary receipts. No major tax reform followed.[163] In the early 1870s, the global recession caused a marked reduction in customs receipts. In order to balance the budget, the Chilean government floated three new external loans between 1870 and 1875. Debt service then became onerous, consuming roughly a third of tax revenue.[164] Chile was on the brink of default in July 1878, and rumors extended to London that Chile would suspend the sinking fund payments. Despite an initial denial, the Chilean government announced the suspension of amortization in April 1879, days after a new war with Bolivia and Peru had begun.

Excluded from external capital, Chile waged the third, final, and largest interstate war of the nineteenth century: the War of the Pacific (1879–1883), which was essentially about the control of nitrate fields in the desert of Atacama.[165] This territory, one of the driest in the world, has perfect conditions for the natural production of *salitre*, a nitrogen-based fertilizer used in agriculture and munitions production in Europe. The Atacama Desert, which incorporated the fields of Antofagasta and Toco, was located in Bolivian national territory; however, most of the extractive companies in the region and 90 percent of the population were Chilean.[166] In 1879, the Bolivian government increased unilaterally the export duties of

162. Farcau (2000, p. 17).
163. Saylor (2014, p. 64).
164. Sicotte, Vizcarra, and Wandschneider (2010, p. 300).
165. Ortega (1984).
166. Faundez (2007, p. 49).

salitre, which contravened an agreement signed in 1874 not to raise taxes on any Chilean corporation mining in Atacama for a period of 25 years.[167] This incident triggered war with Bolivia as well as Peru because these two countries had signed a military agreement of mutual defense against Chile in 1873.

The war lasted four years. The first two years involved traditional army-to-army combat; the last two involved guerilla warfare in Peru and Bolivia, resulting in most of the Chilean casualties. Eventually, Chile prevailed and annexed the Bolivian province of Atacama plus the Peruvian province of Tarapacá—the jewel in the crown of the *salitre* mining industry.

War mobilization was significant for the three countries involved: 2 percent of Chilean male adults were called to arms; more than 1 percent of Peruvian male adults and more than 2 percent of adult male Bolivians were drafted.[168] Belligerents put into action the new rifles, artillery, guns, and ironclads purchased for the fleet after the Chincha Islands War. The total cost of the war for Chile was ₱75 million,[169] twice the cost of the war against Spain 15 years earlier. Lacking external funding, the Chilean government sought to float domestic bonds, but this operation failed. The domestic banking sector was still recovering from the 1870s crisis—all but one of the national banks were insolvent—and denied the government capital.[170] Credit constrained, the government decided to abandon convertibility and reluctantly issued paper money, doing so three times during wartime, commencing in April 1879. In total, Chile issued ₱28 million in paper money, which paid for one-third of war expenses.[171] The remainder was paid with tax money.

Prewar tax receipts fell short. Pressed by growing military expenses, the Ministry of Finance pushed for the tax reform that had failed the year before: "In May of 1879, in desperation, Congress passed the *mobiliaria*, the income tax it had rejected the previous year."[172] The *mobiliaria* was a tax on capital gains, certain types of securities, and all income exceeding ₱300. Essentially, it was a tax on the rich—hence a tax on sitting deputies. Despite high levels of evasion in its first year of implementation, the income tax (together with the inheritance tax adopted one year earlier) became by 1883

167. Sater (2007, p. 18).
168. Sater (2007, pp. 21–22).
169. Subercaseaux (1922, p. 96).
170. Sater (1985, p. 142).
171. Subercaseaux (1922, pp. 94–98).
172. Collier and Sater (1996, p. 147).

the third most lucrative tax, following only customs and state monopoly revenues.[173]

Following Chile's seizure of the two nitrate fields in Atacama—Antofagasta and Toco—plus Tarapacá, the export tax rate quadrupled uniformly across the country, hitting new and old firms in the Chilean territory, including the Antofagasta Nitrate and Railway Company, the largest conglomerate in the recently annexed territory. The new rate was set at an unprecedented 12 percent of the company's profit. The nitrate tax legislation passed despite the strong political ties of this company: 11 of its shareholders were deputies or senators, including two members of the cabinet.[174] In that regard, Sater writes:

> The passage of the nitrate export tax surprised many. Powerful forces had done everything, including trying to buy votes in the Chamber of Deputies, to stop the nitrate levy [of 1880] from becoming law. Even the normally blase *Chilian Times* appeared stunned: "Large sums of money and the influence of many of the most important men in the country have failed to prevent the bill from passing a very large majority. Nearly all the papers in the country had been bought in vaine: influence, generally so potent in this country, could do nothing."[175]

Annexing Atacama and Tarapacá, Chile became the world monopolist of *salitre*. Propelled by the new levies on nitrates, export receipts became the first source of revenue.[176] In four years, exports doubled and revenues increased by approximately 500 percent.[177]

9.3.2 CHILE AND THE POLITICAL ECONOMY OF EXTERNAL FINANCE

In the previous section, I suggested that war finance was conditioned on the availability of foreign capital. This section revisits the discussion, emphasizing the political economy of public external finance advanced in chapter 2. In light of the argument articulated there, rulers should be inclined to finance war with external loans instead of taxes, everything else being constant. Higher tax pressure might spur demands of (further) political rights

173. Sater (1976, p. 328).
174. O'Brien (1980, p. 20).
175. Sater (1985, p. 140).
176. Mamalakis (1976, table 6.1).
177. Sater (1985, p. 140).

FIGURE 9.4. War Financing in Chile as a Function of External Capital Access. External public debt and tax revenue data drawn from Braun et al. (2000). War data from Wimmer and Min (2009).

for taxpayers, namely, the ability to decide on spending or new levies or both. In addition, an increase in the tax burden during war might damage the economy when resources are most needed. In light of political and economic costs, I expect rulers to consider taxation only as a last resort, that is, when they are precluded from more politically neutral options like external borrowing.

War finance in Chile in the nineteenth century is consistent with this logic. Figure 9.4 plots the share of tax revenue and public foreign debt as a percentage of GDP from 1833 (earliest year) to 1913. The years during which Chile was at war are shaded. I differentiate wars fought while

Chile was in default (light gray)—thus excluded from the international markets—from wars fought while Chile had access to the international credit market (darker gray).

One lesson to draw from the previous section is that war is financed in multiple ways; however, consistent with the argument advanced in chapter 2, the debt-tax mix is less favorable to taxes when rulers have access to the international credit market. Take the two larger wars—the Chincha Islands War (1864–1866) and the Pacific War (1879–1883). In 1865, Chile was allowed to borrow from international lenders, and so it did. Between November 1865 and February 1867, the Chilean government floated four war loans in London totaling ₱ 47.6 million, which grew outstanding external debt by over 300 percent with respect to prewar years.[178] In stark contrast, tax revenue remained virtually flat during this period, both in real terms (figure 9.3) and as a share of GDP (figure 9.4).

Things were different in 1879. This time the country was excluded from international capital markets. The government's delegate in London tried to convince investors to float a new loan to finance war costs. All efforts were in vain: London denied credit to the Chilean government because suspended service had not yet been settled.[179] Chile had to mobilize resources at home. Leaving monetary policy aside, total tax revenue increased by over 75 percent within three years. Importantly, the incidence of the new taxes fell mainly on the wealthy—namely, the members of Parliament and the elites they represented.

Kurtz argues that taxation and state capacity expanded in nineteenth-century Chile because elites were fairly cohesive.[180] Vergara and Barros show that the socioeconomic conditions of the deputies of the three main parties in Chile (Conservatives, Liberals, and Radicals) were indeed indistinguishable among political families.[181] Cohesion, a constant, cannot explain the change in behavior observed after 1879. Something else changed: warfare *plus exclusion* from international capital reshaped incentives to increase taxation among Chilean elites. Previous attempts to pass that legislation had failed because members of Congress found adoption insufficiently pressing.[182] Decisive capacity building moved forward only when the availability of alternative forms of war financing was absent.

178. Interest at yield was between 6.6 (min) and 8.2 percent (max).
179. O'Brien (1979, p. 105).
180. Kurtz (2013, pp. 81–93).
181. Vergara and Barros (1972).
182. Sater (1976, pp. 324–326).

The growth of tax revenue in Chile was not merely a by-product of winning the war and seizing new sources of revenue. The war initiated fundamental political and bureaucratic reform—stronger executive constraints and administrative growth and modernization—which transformed the Chilean state well beyond the nitrate boom following the War of the Pacific.[183] Next, I elaborate on the political and bureaucratic mechanisms activated by this war.

9.3.3 TAX CAPACITY AND PRESIDENTIAL ABUSE

In 1886, a new president took office, the first one after the War of the Pacific, the Liberal José Manuel Balmaceda, well regarded on both sides of the aisle. Balmaceda put forward an ambitious program to modernize the economy—investing nitrate revenue in public works, the military, and education—so that when nitrate receipts declined, the country could easily specialize in a new competitive industry.[184] To coordinate his ambitious plan, Balmaceda inaugurated a new Ministry of Industry and Public Works, the apex of an overhaul of the ministerial organization, which emphasized specialization and meritocratic recruitment.[185] Within five years, the Ministry of Industry and Public Works doubled public investment in railroads, telegraph, and bridges. The public administration was also expanded: new hospitals, prisons, and government offices were opened.[186] Primary school enrollment grew from 79,000 pupils in 1886 to 150,000 in 1890.[187]

183. How did the War of the Pacific affect tax capacity in Peru and Bolivia, also in default? The impact for Peru was devastating; however, this country had lost control of its main sources of revenue to foreign bondholders years before the war. Both guano and railways were in the hands of European investors as part of loan contracts and default settlements signed in 1869 and 1870–1872 (details in chapter 2), hence their limited ability to respond to Chile's aggression. In Bolivia, war increased tax receipts relative to prewar years (Peres-Cajías, 2014; Sicotte, Vizcarra, and Wandschneider, 2008), arguably because the baseline was low to begin with. Importantly, the War of the Pacific put in motion a series of political and state building reforms in Bolivia, which crystallized in the next decades (Klein, 2011, p. 143). On the eve of WWI, central government revenue as a percentage of GDP in Bolivia had more than doubled relative to 1883, and the budget was regularly balanced (Peres-Cajías, 2014). For specific accounts of the fiscal effects of the War of the Pacific in Peru and Bolivia, see Sabaté Domingo and Peres-Cajías (2020) and Sicotte, Vizcarra, and Wandschneider (2008, 2010).

184. Blakemore (1974).

185. Barría Traverso (2008).

186. In 1880, inhabitants numbered 838 per public employee. In 1900, that number decreased to 244, a change that illustrates massive administrative growth (Barría Traverso, 2015, table 2).

187. See Cariola Sutter and Sunkel (1982) for a comprehensive survey of public investment.

Before Balmaceda assumed office, national defense and debt service consumed most of the budget. Under his administration, the state became actively involved in promoting economic growth by investing in infrastructure and human capital;[188] however, not everyone agreed with Balmaceda's program. Conservatives preferred using nitrate receipts to retire the inconvertible paper money issued during the war, adhering once again to the gold standard. A preoccupation with the expansion of state administration grew, putting into the hands of the president the means to intensify patronage tactics to deliver electoral majorities on election day. Last but not least, the expansion of education was also perceived as a threat to the oligarchic class, whose members lacked the skills required to steer the modern economy.[189]

Along with economic considerations, a preoccupation with the abuses of presidential power also grew. Balmaceda had assumed office promising to end the "interference" of the president in congressional elections. This was an old problem. The constitution of 1833 granted extensive powers to the executive, key among them the ability to manipulate congressional elections to build support coalitions in the legislative branch and weaken parliamentary oversight of his actions.[190] The web of patronage knitted by the president made Congress a secondary institution without much capacity to hold the executive accountable. The purpose of the constitutional amendments of the 1870s was to limit this form of "authoritarian presidentialism."[191]

Beginning in 1871, the presidential term was limited to one nonconsecutive mandate. In 1874, direct elections were established for the Senate and emergency powers were restricted. "Such changes were a blow, but not by any means a body-blow to presidential power."[192] Election interference persisted—also under Balmaceda.

Soon after assuming office, Balmaceda walked away from his electoral pledge and manufactured a Liberal victory in the 1888 congressional

---

188. Vergara and Barros (1972).

189. Blakemore (1974).

190. Electoral interference by the president involved manipulation of voter registration (*calificaciones*) and intimidation by the national guard on election day, among other tactics. The president also replaced some public administrators with would-be congressmen as a means of buying their loyalty. All presidents use these informal powers to build support coalitions in Congress (Collier and Sater, 1996, pp. 55–58).

191. Heise González (1974, p. 133).

192. Collier and Sater (1996, p. 122).

election. He consolidated his power by removing all opposition members from the cabinet, contravening an unwritten rule in Chilean politics. Both decisions antagonized Conservatives as well as key deputies in his own party. Balmaceda's actions in the congressional elections of 1888 were the first of many decisions aimed at weakening parliamentary oversight of executive powers.

Balmaceda created new administrative departments without due congressional approval and also antagonized nitrate producers, both British and Chilean, by entertaining the idea of nationalizing the industry. Production restrictions put in place by the nitrate oligopoly conflicted with the revenue needs of Balmaceda's investment program. Key to understanding how events unfolded, some of the nitrate owners he alienated were sitting in Parliament[193] while foreign owners had strong connections with key members of Balmaceda's Liberal party.[194]

Grievances persisted when Balmaceda handpicked Enrique Safuentes to be his successor and placed him in his cabinet, blatantly contravening the original electoral platform. Only a few months later, Balmaceda put a loyal supporter of Safuentes in charge of the Ministry of Industry and Public Works, hence in command of the patronage machine. In late 1889, Balmaceda shut down Congress when one of his controversial decisions—the cancellation by presidential decree of the Nitrate Railways Company—was deemed unconstitutional by sitting deputies.

With Congress back in session in 1890, Balmaceda tried to pass a constitutional reform that would have dissolved two counterbalancing institutions in the Republic—the Consejo de Estado and the Comisión Conservadora—and established direct elections of the president with an extended mandate of six years. The reform was dismissed by Congress, but that did not stop Balmaceda in his quest for stronger presidential powers. In late 1890, Balmaceda shut down Congress a second time when his budget was denied. In retaliation, a significant group of congressmen and senators declared him unfit for office. On January 1, 1891, Balmaceda moved ahead without the approval of Congress (no longer in session) and extended the previous year's budget, a decision that exceeded presidential powers. The country was ready for civil war: Congress fled north and received the support of the navy, the pride of the Chilean military. The president remained in Santiago, guarded by the national army. After a seven-month civil war

193. Vergara and Barros (1972, appendix tables).
194. Blakemore (1974, p. 170).

and 10,000 casualties, the *congresionistas* prevailed. Having sought refuge in the Argentinean embassy, Balmaceda committed suicide.

9.3.4 CONSTRAINING THE EXECUTIVE

The road to civil war in Chile may resonate with the history of limited government in Western Europe. The accumulation of tax powers in the presidency in a context of weak executive constraints precipitated a political crisis. Tax revenue doubled during the 10 years following the last war with Peru and Bolivia. The state had assumed key functions in economic development and education ever since. By putting forward a massive program of public investment in education, military, and railroads, Balmaceda created new captive constituencies that could be mobilized to his advantage. Weak checks and balances left Congress exposed to a heightened era of executive election meddling. Staging a coup, Chilean elites sought to weaken presidential powers and made Congress the center of fiscal policy.[195]

The 1891 civil war was not a conflict—as earlier historians like Edwards and Ramírez Necochea put it[196]—between a president chasing the general interest and a Congress advancing the interests of an old, oligarchic regime captured by foreign capitalists.[197] This was a political crisis between two branches of government—executive and legislative—about the division of powers. Constitutionally, Congress had budgeting powers, but election interference allowed the president to build supportive majorities that excused him from accountability to congressional oversight. This became a major problem when the budget of the republic doubled and the state acquired an unprecedented role in steering the national economy.

"[Balmaceda's] relation to the parliament was much like that of Charles I,"[198] the English monarch whose actions led to the English Civil War and eventually the Glorious Revolution. Congress accused Balmaceda of usurping its prerogatives, ruling by decree, and intervening in the electoral

---

195. Vergara and Barros (1972, pp. 87–90).

196. Edwards (1945); Ramírez Necochea (1969).

197. Balmaceda opposed monopolies, not foreign ownership; for instance, he coalesced with British investors to dismantle the Nitrate Railways Company but not with the proletariat. He sent the army to repress miners rioting in the north and in Santiago for better labor conditions. See Heise González (1974) for an extensive critique of the antioligarchic interpretation of Balmaceda's policy.

198. Reinsch (1909, p. 513).

process.[199] The civil war put an end to presidential abuse. Once he was overthrown, the oligarchs strengthened the legislature by gaining effective veto power over fiscal policy. Importantly, this was a period of limited government, not modern democracy. Franchise remained restricted, and Congress neglected the needs of a growing urban working class—the so-called social question.[200] The new political equilibrium was one in which power between the executive and the legislative branches was truly shared.

9.3.5 CONTINUED BUREAUCRATIC GROWTH

A new era known as the Parliamentary Regime (1891–1925) began after Balmaceda was deposed, and Congress and political parties became the center of political activity.[201] Congressional control over the executive was strengthened with small constitutional amendments: no public official could sit in Congress, and election monitoring was transferred to municipalities.[202] Both measures took away from the presidency the levers that had allowed it to interfere in national elections for roughly 60 years.[203]

Some argue that the weak presidencies and higher political turnover of the Parliamentary Regime stopped the economic and administrative growth initiated under Balmaceda,[204] but Bowman and Wallerstein challenge that notion with hard data.[205] After only three years of decline, from 1891 to 1893, public expenditure resumed both nominally and on a per capita basis and kept expanding until WWI. School enrollment continued to grow but at a slightly lower rate than under Balmaceda. Most of the investment was concentrated in public works, which benefited both the land- and mining-based elite.

In order to ascertain first hand whether the investment program included bureaucratic capacity, I coded the size of the tax administration from 1845 to 1915 as reported in the national budgets.[206] Figure 9.5 plots the total number of staff working for the Minister of Finance. Three

199. Eaton (2004, p. 90).

200. Kurtz (2013, p. 89). This tension is captured by the Polity IV dataset. Although the overall democracy index decreased two points from 5 to 3 from 1890 to 1891, the executive constraints score increased from 5 to 7 and remained there after WWI (Marshall and Jaggers, 2000).

201. Faundez (2007, p. 59).

202. Collier and Sater (1996, p. 188).

203. Eaton (2004).

204. Edwards (1945); Ramírez Necochea (1969).

205. Bowman and Wallerstein (1982).

206. I retrieved this information for budgets of fiscal years ending in 0 and 5.

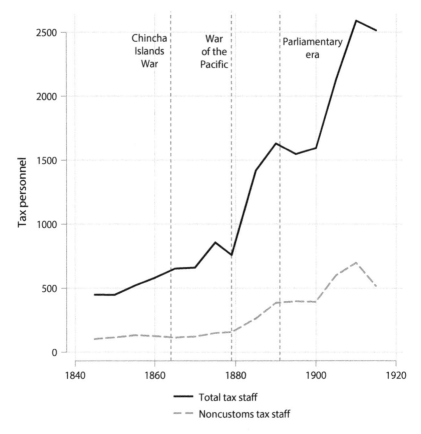

FIGURE 9.5. Tax Personnel in Chile from 1845 to 1915. Data coded from national budgets between 1845 and 1915.

patterns emerge: First, the Chincha War was inconsequential in terms of expanding the tax administration. This is consistent with figures 9.3 and 9.4, where no increase in tax receipts is shown during or after wartime. Second, and in stark contrast, the War of the Pacific was highly consequential for the tax administration. The personnel working for this administration grew by 83 percent between 1879 and 1885. The annexation of nitrate fields in Peru and Bolivia occurred alongside the expansion of customs services involving collecting export duties at every *oficina* (extraction site) and international port. Crucially, the increase in customs officials was accompanied by an increase in tax officials in other branches of the tax administration, including excise collection.[207] Third, bureaucratic growth

207. My estimates are slightly more conservative than those in Sabaté Domingo and Peres-Cajías (2020), who nevertheless show the same general pattern: 82% of the 684 employees in the

continued after Balmaceda's tenure. In the early years of the Parliamentary Regime, the growth of the tax administration stopped (never declined) momentarily because the executive sought to use nitrate revenue to forge a stable monetary policy. Various attempts to burn unconvertible paper money failed, however, and within three years massive public investment resumed. So did the tax apparatus, with the adoption of new taxes to manage: alcohol (1902), insurance companies (1906), tobacco, playing cards, and inheritance (1910), and banks (1912).[208]

Under the overarching power-sharing agenda, the Parliamentary Regime put forward a program of political and fiscal decentralization. In 1893, the income, inheritance, and capital taxes adopted during the War of the Pacific were transferred to municipalities. Decentralization under the Parliamentary Regime is often criticized by historians because it put in the hands of local elites the organization of elections, causing vote buying and clientelism.[209] On the fiscal front, however, performance of municipalities was remarkably good: total revenue of municipalities (in constant prices) almost tripled between 1902 and 1925 (earliest and latest data), and the decentralized direct taxes became the major source of local government funds, accounting for 39 percent of municipal revenue.[210]

To keep municipalities in check, the central government kept veto power over the adoption and change of any existing tax rate at the municipal level.[211] Present in 200 municipalities, more than 8,300 central government agents (also known as "tax police") were granted powers to monitor the collection of municipal taxes—including a veto over any policy that could damage the national interest.[212] State legibility was secured as well, thanks to records of economic activities, wealth, and occupation of city residents kept by the central government agents.[213]

All in all, state building in Chile took off during the War of the Pacific and kept expanding under the Parliamentary Regime despite the nitrate bonanza and decentralization. As manifested in figure 9.6, the share of internal taxes (national and municipal) relative to total tax revenue grew

Ministry of Finance in 1870 worked in customs, compared to 74% of the 1,599 employees in 1900 (Sabaté Domingo and Peres-Cajías, 2020, table 6).

208. Bowman and Wallerstein (1982, p. 451).

209. See for instance, Gleisner (1988, p. 109).

210. Rojas Böttner (2019, pp. 90, 94). See Edwards (1917) for compelling evidence that municipalities remained underfunded for the many tasks they were expected to execute—but that is another debate.

211. Soifer (2015, p. 174).

212. See Rojas Böttner (2019, table 12) for longitudinal data of tax police officers.

213. Soifer (2015, p. 163).

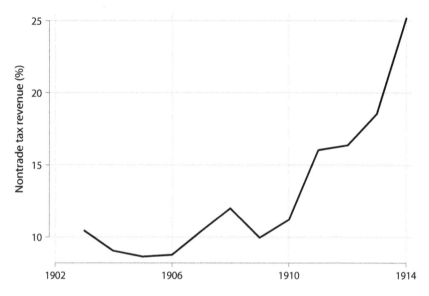

FIGURE 9.6. Share of Nontrade Tax to Total Tax Revenue in Chile. Nontrade tax revenue combines internal taxation and municipal taxation. Total revenue accounts for trade and nontrade tax revenue. *Source*: Soifer (2015, table 5.8).

over time, indicating continued efforts to expand the tax base beyond nitrate exports. On the eve of WWI, Chile had stronger executive contraints and a more capable state, namely, a strong bureaucratic apparatus capable of taxing and administering public goods and services benefiting the merchant elite, from infrastructure to education.

9.4 Conclusion

The trajectories discussed in this chapter suggest that opportunities of state building are shaped by initial conditions (e.g., is there a mass of merchants who can negotiate the terms of taxation?), the rulers' time horizons, access to external funds—and a grain of luck too. Take the case of Japan: it benefited enormously from external finance, but, unlike any other case in this chapter and arguably the world, it also relied on domestic capital to fund daily government expenses. Lower dependence reduced exposure to financial pressures and solidified political consensus for state building. And yet, Japan's foreign debt rapidly escalated before WWI. Ironically, the Great War might have saved Japan from following the same path as Argentina.

Chile, the other success case, only committed to state building when its leaders were compelled to finance war domestically in the late 1870s. This case suggests that entrenched and geographically concentrated economic elites do not automatically demand power-sharing institutions. Advances in executive constraints happen when elites perceive that the Leviathan is growing too strong and endangering their economic position.

Lastly, the case of Siam speaks to the limits of building states without search for consent, a topic recently debated in Acemoglu and Robinson as well as Stasavage.[214] Coercion can be a stable, revenue-generating policy, but it secures tax compliance only up to a point. Power-sharing institutions not only transform taxation into a nonzero-sum game; they also reduce "transaction costs" of tax collection,[215] making stronger and more efficient states.

214. Acemoglu and Robinson (2019); Stasavage (2020).
215. Levi (1988).

10

Conclusion

In this final chapter, I first reexamine the reasons that public credit made states in Western Europe but seldom outside it. As should now be evident, the answer to this question builds on the argument and findings presented throughout the book: European states benefited from foreign capital scarcity. Second, I elaborate on the implications of this book for three debates in the literature on development: loan conditionality, foreign intervention, and the resource curse. Third, I propose two ways to extend the analysis of external finance on state building—one focusing on postcolonial institutions, the other on civil conflict. I conclude the chapter with some thoughts on the joint examination of debt and tax instruments in the study of state building.

10.1 Why Did Public Debt Make States in Europe?

International financial markets in early-modern Europe were small and expensive.[1] Lacking an outside option, European monarchs were compelled to turn inward to cope with growing war expenses, the main budget obligation at the time. As early as the thirteenth century, Italian and German city-states had borrowed long term from local elites, usually urban merchants, who also decided on the taxes that funded the debt.[2] Territorial

1. Homer and Sylla (2005); Prestwich (1979).
2. Epstein (2000, p. 26).

states followed suit: as of the second half of the sixteenth century, Elizabeth I (r. 1558–1603) stopped issuing short-term loans in Antwerp at rates between 12 and 14 percent and switched to London merchants, who charged 2 points less than their Flemish counterparts.[3] That switch laid the foundations of public credit in England.

Almost simultaneously in France, Henry IV (r. 1598–1610) began to borrow from Parisian merchants, marginalizing increasingly expensive Italian lenders.[4] Far from exceptional, domestic debt expanded under absolutist kings. The Company of General Farms, an oligopoly of tax farmers created by J. B. Colbert, became the primary lender of the French Crown.[5] Credibly excluding the ruler from new quotations in case of default, French kings gained access to increasingly competitive long-term loans.[6]

Public credit in the Low Countries developed by imposition from Madrid. Charles V (r. 1519–1556) had made the Dutch provincial assemblies responsible for collection and repayment of the long-term debt of the empire. Local merchants were heavily represented in the provincial estates and secured tax revenue to refund the same government bonds that they had previously acquired.[7] The Low Countries kept this system in place after independence (declared in 1581, recognized by Spain in 1648). Strict control by taxpayers over spending decisions brought Dutch credit to unprecedented levels and consolidated the Low Countries as the financial capital of Europe until the turn of the eighteenth century.

Over centuries, city-states, Britain, France, and the Low Countries created robust systems of domestic public credit. The local nature of sovereign debt is crucial to understanding its consequences for state building and political reform. The reason lies in the consequences of defaulting and how those consequences structured the incentives of monarchs to expand tax capacity and—even unintentionally—initiate political reform. Default on domestic debt carried severe repercussions for a sitting ruler: loss of access to credit and asset seizure in the best case, and overthrow in the worst-case scenario.[8] National and regional parliaments and tax farm oligopolies eased merchants' coordination to monitor the monarch's actions and deny

---

3. Outhwaite (1966, 1971).

4. Stasavage (2011).

5. Johnson and Koyama (2014).

6. Hoffman, Postel-Vinay, and Rosenthal (2000).

7. Tracy (1985).

8. Saylor and Wheeler (2017).

fresh loans unless standing obligations were met.[9] Seizing loan collateral was credible because it was often directly managed by the same merchants who lent to the Crown.[10] Ultimately, the monarch's tenure in office hinged on the support of big taxpayers and Crown lenders, who were willing to withdraw political support if the monarch breached the fiscal contract, replacing him or her by a new one of their liking.[11]

Because the political cost of domestic default was both sizable and credible, European monarchs implemented fiscal innovations to meet debt obligations. Over time, new and more efficient taxes were passed, fiscal centralization and the professionalization of the tax administration were adopted, and treasuries and central banks were inaugurated for the purpose of government funding and public debt repayment. From an analytical point of view, the political cost of domestic default for a sitting monarch sustained the long-term equivalence between debt and taxes for the purpose of state building. That is, loans in early-modern Europe acted as deferred taxes, and for that reason war and military budgets made the state.[12]

10.2 Why Did Public Debt Not Make States in the Global South?

In general, domestic capital markets in the periphery in the nineteenth century were tight or nonexistent; however—and here lies the key difference—recently created countries and those forced to join the Western international system had access to vast sources of capital in European financial centers, first London and later France and Germany as well. The first round of sovereign loans in the 1820s quickly ended in default. Debt readjustment negotiations were lengthy because bondholders had not perfected sanctioning mechanisms. In the second half of the nineteenth century, imperial competition among the Great Powers accelerated. Foreign bondholders seized geopolitical rivalry to impose harsher clauses in sovereign bonds, extracting new concessions and enabling temporary confiscation of state monopolies or revenue sources in case of default. I refer to this practice as *extreme conditionality*.

---

9. Johnson and Koyama (2014); Stasavage (2011).

10. Tracy (1985, p. 58).

11. Schultz and Weingast (1998, p. 23).

12. Refer to chapter 8 for a counterfactual in early-modern Europe: Genoese loans to Philip II of Spain.

Whether intentionally or compelled by geostrategic considerations, creditors' governments became involved in private financial markets. They exerted diplomatic pressure, brokered fresh loans, and participated in default settlements. Military involvement or gunboat diplomacy was rare, something to be expected if all actors behaved consistent with their beliefs—the definition of rationality. A sign that asset and revenue confiscation in case of default turned credible was that pledges in loan contracts in London reduced the premium levied on borrowing countries in the decades of high imperialism.

Foreign financial intervention and debt-equity swaps were unpopular and should have disciplined leaders to float only necessary loans and spend them wisely. The fiscal exigencies of war, blatant corruption, and local political instability in many emerging economies probably led to downplaying the political costs of a hypothetical default. From an incumbent's viewpoint, default sanctions were a problem of the future, very likely someone else's; well negotiated (e.g., if accompanied by substantial debt relief), pledging might have been perceived as the lesser of two evils compared to the immediate costs of taxation, particularly sharing fiscal policy powers with taxpayers.

Thus, extreme conditionality did not preempt rulers from floating new loans. All types of state monopolies and sources of revenue were pawned. Unsurprisingly, the precarious fiscal position of recently formed countries brought many to suspend debt service. Default settlements would execute previously agreed terms—debt-equity swaps and receiverships—or impose them as part of the debt readjustment negotiations. One way or another, foreign bondholders took control of state monopolies and sources of revenue while injecting fresh sovereign loans to reactivate the economy. The tax base available to the local government thinned and outstanding debt grew. A new budget crisis often followed, requiring fresh debt, more concessions, and further hypothecation. This cycle pushed many countries into debt traps, creating lasting fiscal disequilibria.

From an analytical point of view, the exchange of external debt obligations for nontax revenue (and debt relief in the best-case scenario) precluded the long-term equivalence between debt and taxes for the purpose of state building. War and major expenses would be financed with foreign debt and repaid in specie, not tax money, preempting advances in local fiscal capacity—the central pillar of the modern state. Counterintuitively, countries in the Global South may have benefited from less dynamic international lending markets because that would have strengthened the incentives to raise taxes to finance government, stimulate domestic borrowing, and conduct the political reform associated with long-term fiscal capacity—which Europeans had been pushed to do only centuries before, when international credit markets were virtually nonexistent.

Consistent with this argument, the empirical exercises and qualitative evidence in chapters 7–9 suggest that rulers who were excluded from international capital markets during wartime—that is, when government funds were badly needed—were compelled to reshuffle the tax administration and assume the political cost of taxation, namely, power-sharing institutions. Those early reforms potentially put in motion the political and bureaucratic mechanisms of transmission advanced in this book, carrying the effects of war finance into the long run. All in all, the erratic behavior of international capital markets in the first globalization of capital offered opportunities for both change and continuity in fiscal capacity building.

10.3 State Building beyond War Finance

The *domestic* nature of public credit is one key reason for political compromise and fiscal innovation in Europe, but not the only one. State building is a multifaceted process with multiple causes, and students of state making should at least consider the roles of economic enlightenment, institutional emulation, and political competition. Joel Mokyr's scholarship shows that a "market for ideas"[13] was a fundamental driver of economic prosperity and cultural pluralism in Western Europe. Economic enlightenment transformed the economies and the relationships of individuals with their environment. The search for innovation-friendly policy created political institutions that solidified one of the three pillars of capable states: property rights protection, also known as legal capacity.[14] Innovation-driven economic growth expanded commerce and monetized the economy, growing the bargaining power of holders of mobile assets (traders and financiers) vis-à-vis monarchs, facilitating political compromise and investment in capable states.

13. Mokyr (2017, p. 170).

14. Mokyr (2017, pp. 183–185) for the origins of property rights protection of science and innovations; Jones (1981) and North (1981) for the paramount importance of property rights protection for economic growth; and Besley and Persson (2011) for the central role of legal capacity in state building.

"Institutional learning"[15] is a second important reason for the proliferation of capable states. In Europe, the Hanseatic League and Italian city-states gradually and voluntarily adopted efficient institutions from territorial states. They standardized coinage, reduced the number of weights and measures, and created legal certitude by strengthening internal hierarchy. Lowering transaction and information costs, these smaller polities survived the expansion of territorial states until the mid-nineteenth century.[16] Meiji Japan is the paramount example of state building by emulation in the Bond Era.

Finally, investment in state capacities can occur for purely political reasons. Tax policy creates opportunities of cooperation and competition between different elites, who might agree to tax reform for mutual benefit or to penalize political rivals. Once in place, the sponsors of fiscal innovation may lose control of it or be ousted from power, offering opportunities to new political players to expand the scope of taxation and state capacities in the long run. My work with Isabela Mares on the origins of the income tax in Western Europe offers one such example. Initially adopted in the mid-nineteenth century to exclude the working class from the political arena, the income tax became after WWI the most progressive tax instrument ever seen.[17]

Economic enlightenment, institutional learning, and political competition are proven non-bellicose paths to state building, giving hope and arguments to students and practitioners of state building today.[18] Our understanding of the causes of state capacity benefit from studying its multiple causes—bellicose and not—and from unpacking their microfoundations and potential complementarities. The goal of this book is to place external public finance on a par with existing explanations of state building (and its stagnation) in recent world history.

10.4 Implications for Today

Whereas the core of the argument focuses on how the first globalization of finance pushed countries into different state building trajectories, the

---

15. Spruyt (1994, p. 179).

16. Abramson (2017).

17. Mares and Queralt (2015, 2020).

18. See Mokyr (1991, pp. 184–185) for the orthogonality between economic innovation and war before the Industrial Revolution.

findings speak to a variety of other modern-day issues, including debates on loan conditionality, foreign intervention, and the oil curse.

10.4.1 LOAN CONDITIONALITY

I advanced the notion of extreme conditionality, that is, the hypothecation of national assets as a requirement to access foreign credit, to shed light on the secular decline of interest rates in the nineteenth century. Extreme conditionality and its implementation—supersanctions—have not been practiced since WWII (perhaps with the exception of Chinese loans[19]) for at least three reasons. First, asset seizure via debt-equity swaps and receiverships was feasible only because bondholders' governments were involved in imperial competition. These severe political sanctions represented strong breaches to national sovereignty—ironically implemented in the era of "absolute" judicial sovereign immunity—that could not have been executed without diplomatic pressure from creditor governments.

Second, the key players in international finance have changed and with them the mandate of foreign financial intervention. Private lending to foreign governments declined after WWI and was replaced by official lending, virtually nonexistent before 1914.[20] Although private funds gained some momentum in the last decades of the twentieth century, private-only loans today represent less than 11 percent of all sovereign debt.[21] Financial crises are also managed differently. To balance the budget, borrowers do not have to grant concessions or extraterritoriality rights to foreign investors. Since WWII, the IMF has acted as the lender of last resort, specializing in ordered debt restructuring. Despite orthodoxy and limitations of IMF conditionality—the source of inspiration for vibrant research[22]—this institution never sought to make profit out of intervention,

---

19. Some authors argue that the goals of China's aid and loans do not differ from bilateral and multilateral overseas lending from the West (Brautigam, 2020; Dreher and Fuchs, 2015); however, conclusions are generally drawn from partial datasets. Horn, Reinhart, and Trebesch (2020) show that official statistics between 1949 and 2017 are missing 50 percent of China's lending to developing countries. Gelpern, Horn, Morris, Parks, and Trebesch's (2021) closer look at 100 debt contracts reveals collateral arrangements, such as lender-controlled revenue accounts, reminiscent of the Bond Era. The debate about "debt-trap diplomacy" remains open.

20. Stallings (1972, p. 15).

21. Bunte (2019, p. 7).

22. Copelovitch (2010); Stallings and Kaufman (1989); Vreeland (2007).

unlike receiverships in the Bond Era. IMF conditionality is meant to bring fiscal stability to the borrowing country even if it is at the price of one-size-fits-all neoliberal policy. In recent years, the IMF has recognized the importance of building local capacity, and it includes it as part of new bailout programs.[23] Back to figure 1.3, international bailouts today push distressed countries into path D of state building, leaving no room for extreme conditionality.

Third, as of the 1970s, the notion of "absolute" sovereign immunity was relaxed in American and British courts.[24] This legal change allowed private bondholders to bring to court sovereign debtors who had defaulted on their external debt. The institutionalization of dispute resolution in international lending made coercive strategies like debt-equity swaps and privately run receiverships unnecessary.[25]

Extreme conditionality and supersanctions in the nineteenth century are important today for another reason: these practices unraveled the long-term equivalence of debt and taxes for state building. The confiscation of state monopolies and revenue sources by foreign investors allowed debtor countries to settle on their debt and regain access to international credit markets without first having made significant efforts to improve their capacity to tax. Loans did not act as deferred taxation. What is worse, by putting parts of their already thin tax base in the hands of foreign investors, debtor countries remained highly exposed to new fiscal setbacks, requiring fresh loans and further hypothecation. Debt traps, characterized by high indebtedness, strong dependence on foreign capital markets, a thin tax base, and a weak tax apparatus, often followed.

Importantly, unlike Hobson's one-sided imperialist view of international finance, my research suggests that the responsibility for debt traps and long-run underdevelopment was shared between aggressive foreign investors and irresponsible domestic rulers who preferred to assume the risk of foreign intervention over tax reform and power sharing with taxpayers. Foreign lenders were certainly no angels, but neither were domestic leaders.

---

23. Berg et al. (2009).

24. Verdier and Voeten (2015). See Weidemaier and Gulati (2018) for a critical interpretation.

25. Schumacher, Trebesch, and Enderlein (2021) suggest that specialized distressed debt funds, or "vulture investors," recently pushed for seizing assets, but located in the creditor country (e.g., bank accounts).

10.4.2 FOREIGN INTERVENTION

Although tangentially, the findings of this book speak to the challenges of foreign financial control aimed at state building. In the Bond Era, foreign financial control differed from modern applications in many ways: it was guided by private interests and profit-maximizing considerations, not capacity building. Neither version of foreign control, however, seems to have met the goals they once pursued. The lack of legitimacy of international interventions may amplify when foreign agents seek private gain—be it in the realm of tax collection in the Bond Era or security provision today (e.g., Blackwater, later Academi, in Iraq and Afghanistan after 2003). Foreign-led state building is an extremely challenging task, and profit maximization may not be the right approach to overcome legitimacy obstacles.

10.4.3 THE "EASY MONEY" CURSE

The perverse consequences of external finance for the ruler's incentives to build capacity resonate with those associated with foreign aid and oil. Unearned income is said to have two negative effects: First, it precludes accountability mechanisms associated with taxation.[26] The ruler does not need to grant political rights to citizens to induce tax compliance because government is funded with nontax revenue from oil royalties and aid flows. Morrison and Ross show ample evidence of the negative effects of oil revenue for democracy,[27] and Ahmed and Smith, among others, find equivalent results for foreign aid.[28] Second, abundant nontax revenue is meant to weaken state capacity because it makes investment in the tax administration expendable.[29]

The two effects of easy money—accountability and bureaucratic weakening—are consistent with those elaborated in this book for external public finance. Access to credit overseas offers endless opportunities to developing nations, from tax smoothing[30] to overcoming growth barriers.[31] No policy, however, comes without trade-offs. Broner and Ventura warn about unintended macroeconomic effects of external public finance,

26. Paler (2013).
27. Morrison (2009); Ross (2004, 2012).
28. Ahmed (2012); Smith (2008).
29. Bates (2001, ch. 4); Bräutigam and Knack (2004); Moore (1998).
30. Barro (1979); Lucas and Stokey (1983).
31. Rajan and Zingales (1998); Summers (2000).

including crowding out domestic credit markets.[32] This book contributes to the debate by pointing out unintended political consequences: easy money in the form of sovereign loans can distort rulers' incentives to strike deals with taxpayers and preempt long-term bureaucratic reform.

The foreign aid community has come to recognize the perverse incentives of unearned income in local governance and has strengthened the monitoring of the use of funds.[33] Similar efforts might be necessary in the design of official lending to the developing world. In other words, conditionality might complement current technical conditions designed at building capacity (e.g., the adoption of value-added taxes) with *political* provisions (e.g., transparency standards and public dissemination of information) aimed at activating tax bargaining between rulers and taxpayers. By fostering political accountability locally, foreign intervention may overcome common legitimacy obstacles to state building.

10.5 What's Next?

I envision two paths to continue the study of external public finance in the realm of state building and political reform: one focuses on the relationship between colonial public finance and long-term political institutions; the other, on the connection between civil war finance and state building.

10.5.1 COLONIAL FINANCE AND POLITICAL OUTCOMES

European colonies had access to the international credit market, and they were also responsible for their own expenses. Imperial war was heavily subsidized by the metropole, but everything else was financed locally. Although colonies were obliged to meet the revenue imperative, they were not allowed to articulate political institutions conducive to quasi-voluntary compliance, specifically representative parliaments. Acemoglu and Robinson as well as Stasavage warn us about the wedge between strong bureaucracies and weak societies. "Despotic Leviathans" emerge when the society lacks the capacity to control the state.[34] Checks and balances are needed to prevent elites from exploiting the state apparatus for their own benefit.

---

32. Broner and Ventura (2016).

33. Dietrich and Winters (2021) for a recent survey and Cruz and Schneider (2017) for an application.

34. Acemoglu and Robinson (2019).

That is, the Leviathan is to be "shackled" so that both elites and nonelites can benefit from advances in state capacity. Stasavage shows that "the early democracy" was created to substitute for strong bureaucracies. In the absence of a coercive capacity, leaders could not rule alone, and decision making was necessarily collective. As the state strengthened and rulers gained the capacity to assess wealth and enforce tax compliance, the search for consent became expendable. Today, "modern democracy" and strong bureaucracies coexist only in some parts of the world, and "sequencing" is important to understand why. Democratic rule is harder to achieve when bureaucratic capacity has grown too strong.[35]

The insights of Acemoglu and Robinson and Stasavage call for a dedicated examination of the long-term effects of public finance on democratic consolidation in the postcolonial world. The consequences for political reform derived from early access to external finance for colonies might have differed from that of emerging sovereign nations. The latter, I have argued, potentially benefited from capital exclusion because rulers were forced to strengthen power-sharing institutions on a par with bureaucratic capacity. In other words, in sovereign countries, war and major fiscal shocks in times of capital exclusion activated both the bureaucratic and political mechanisms of transmission. Under the same circumstances, colonies were expected to strengthen bureaucratic capacity to mobilize government funds while keeping political institutions despotic (details in chapter 8). By implication, colonies that were disproportionally compelled to mobilize domestic resources to fund local government might have initiated the postcolonial era with relatively stronger bureaucracies and weaker political institutions, impeding the consolidation of democratic politics. The specificity of colonial finance calls for a dedicated examination of the obstacles to political reform in the former colonial world with a special focus on sequencing.

10.5.2   CIVIL WAR FINANCE AND STATE BUILDING

Another important area of research leads us to figure 6.1b, which shows a sharp increase in civil conflict after the end of the Cold War. With the exception of DiGiuseppe, Barry, and Frank, one finds little evidence and understanding of the external finance of civil war and its implications for

---

35. Stasavage (2020).

local capacity and political reform.[36] The evidence in this book suggests that the effect of the external finance of independence war, arguably a very specific type of civil conflict, is virtually indistinguishable from that of interstate war for the purpose of state building. Whether this result is generalizable to every type of civil war remains open. Doubtless, this is an important avenue of further research that would make a significant contribution to the understanding of state building and political order in the developing world today.

10.6 Final Remarks

Public debt, internal and external, is on the rise in both the developed and developing world, with no sign of change in the near future. In this book, I sought to broaden our understanding of state building by studying the interaction between taxes and loans—namely, domestic and external sources of government funding. Whereas existing research in political science and economics focuses on one policy tool while keeping the other constant, I argue in favor of their joint consideration as a means to improve understanding of the political dilemmas of public finance for rulers and taxpayers and the consequences for short- and long-run state building. I hope this approach will be followed in the coming years by scholars and practitioners interested in international finance, political change, and state building throughout history and today.

36. DiGiuseppe, Barry, and Frank (2012).

BIBLIOGRAPHY

Aboagye, Prince Young, and Ellen Hillbom. 2020. "Tax Bargaining, Fiscal Contracts, and Fiscal Capacity in Ghana: A Long-Term Perspective." *African Affairs* 119(475):177–202.

Abramson, Scott, and Carles Boix. 2019. "Endogenous Parliaments: The Domestic and International Roots of Long-Term Economic Growth and Executive Constraints in Europe." *International Organization* 73:793–837.

Abramson, Scott F. 2017. "The Economic Origins of the Territorial State." *International Organization* 71(1):97–130.

Accominotti, Olivier, Marc Flandreau, and Riad Rezzik. 2011. "The Spread of Empire: Clio and the Measurement of Colonial Borrowing Costs." *Economic History Review* 64(2): 385–407.

Acemoglu, Daron. 2003. "Why Not a Political Coase Theorem? Social Conflict, Commitment, and Politics." *Journal of Comparative Economics* 31(4):620–652.

Acemoglu, Daron, Tristan Reed, and James A. Robinson. 2014. "Chiefs: Economic Development and Elite Control of Civil Society in Sierra Leone." *Journal of Political Economy* 122(2): 319–368.

Acemoglu, Daron, and James A. Robinson. 2012. *Why Nations Fail: The Origins of Power, Prosperity, and Poverty*. New York: Crown Business.

Acemoglu, Daron, and James A. Robinson. 2019. *The Narrow Corridor: States, Societies, and the Fate of Liberty*. New York: Penguin Press.

Acemoglu, Daron, Davide Ticchi, and Andrea Vindigni. 2011. "Emergence and Persistence of Inefficient States." *Journal of the European Economic Association* 9(2):177–208.

Ahmed, Faisal Z. 2012. "The Perils of Unearned Foreign Income: Aid, Remittances, and Government Survival." *American Political Science Review* 106(1):146–165.

Ahmed, Faisal Z., Laura Alfaro, and Noel Maurer. 2010. "Lawsuits and Empire: On the Enforcement of Sovereign Debt in Latin America." *Law and Contemporary Problems* 73(4):39–46.

Aidt, Toke S., and Peter S. Jensen. 2009. "The Taxman Tools Up: An Event History Study of the Introduction of the Personal Income Tax." *Journal of Public Economics* 93(1–2):160–175.

Alesina, Alberto, Reza Baqir, and William Easterly. 1999. "Public Goods and Ethnic Divisions." *Quarterly Journal of Economics* 114(4):1243–1284.

Alesina, Alberto, Bryony Reich, and Alessandro Riboni. 2017. "Nation-Building, Nationalism and Wars." Technical report 23435, NBER working paper.

Alesina, Alberto, and Enrico Spolaore. 1997. "On the Number and Size of Nations." *Quarterly Journal of Economics* 112(4):1027–1056.

Andersson, Per F., and Thomas Brambor. 2019. "Financing the State: Government Tax Revenue from 1800 to 2012." Version 2.0 dataset. Lund University.

Ansell, Ben W., and Johannes Lindvall. 2020. *Inward Conquest: The Political Origins of Modern Public Services*. New York: Cambridge University Press.

Ardant, Gabriel. 1975. "Financial Policy and Economic Infrastructure of Modern States and Nations." In *The Formation of National States in Western Europe*, ed. Charles Tilly, pp. 164–242. Princeton, NJ: Princeton University Press.

Asakura, Kōkichi. 1967. "The Characteristics of Finance in the Meiji Period (the Period of Take-Off)." *Developing Economies* 5(2):274–299.

Austin, Gareth. 2008. "The 'Reversal of Fortune' Thesis and the Compression of History: Perspectives from African and Comparative Economic History." *Journal of International Development* 20(8):996–1027.

Austin, Gareth, and Kaoru Sugihara. 1993. "Local Suppliers of Credit in the Third World, 1750–1960: Introduction." In *Local Suppliers of Credit in the Third World, 1750–1960*, ed. Gareth Austin and Kaoru Sugihara, pp. 1–26. Chippenham, UK: St. Martin's Press.

Ayer, Jules. 1905. *A Century of Finance, 1804 to 1904: The London House of Rothschild*. London: Neely.

Baker, Chris, and Pasuk Phongpaichit. 2014. *A History of Thailand*. New York: Cambridge University Press.

Baldwin, Kate. 2015. *The Paradox of Traditional Chiefs in Democratic Africa*. New York: Cambridge University Press.

Baldwin, Kate, and Katharina Holzinger. 2019. "Traditional Political Institutions and Democracy: Reassessing Their Compatibility and Accountability." *Comparative Political Studies* 52(12):1747–1774.

Baldwin, Kate, and John D. Huber. 2010. "Economic versus Cultural Differences: Forms of Ethnic Diversity and Public Goods Provision." *American Political Science Review* 104(4):644–662.

Balla, Eliana, and Noel D. Johnson. 2009. "Fiscal Crisis and Institutional Change in the Ottoman Empire and France." *Journal of Economic History* 69(3):809–845.

Ballard-Rosa, Cameron, Layna Mosley, and Rachel L. Wellhausen. 2021. "Contingent Advantage? Sovereign Borrowing, Democratic Institutions, and Global Capital Cycles." *British Journal of Political Science* 51(1):353–373.

Bandiera, Oriana, Myra Mohnen, Imran Rasul, and Martina Viarengo. 2019. "Nation-Building through Compulsory Schooling during the Age of Mass Migration." *Economic Journal* 129:62–109.

Banko, Catalina. 1995. "Los Comerciantes Extranjeros de La Guaira Frente a las Reformas Económicas de José Tadeo Monagas (1848–1850)." *Estudios de Historia Social y Económica de América* 12:591–598.

Bank of Japan. 1966. *Hundred Year Statistics of the Japanese Economy*. Tokyo: Bank of Japan.

Barría Traverso, Diego. 2008. "Continuista o Rupturista, Radical o Sencillísima: La Reorganización de Ministerios de 1887 y su Discusión Político-Administrativa." *Historia* 41(1):5–42.

Barría Traverso, Diego. 2015. "Empleados Públicos y Clase Media, Chile 1880–1920: Un Análisis Exploratorio a partir de Cifras Oficiales." *Revista de Historia y Geografía* 32:77–100.

Barro, Robert J. 1979. "On the Determination of the Public Debt." *Journal of Political Economy* 87(5):940–971.

Barros Arana, Diego. 1880. *Historia de la Guerra del Pacífico*. Santiago: Libreria Central de Servat I.

Bates, Robert H. 2001. *Prosperity and Violence: The Political Economy of Development*. New York: Norton.

Bates, Robert H. 2014. "The Imperial Peace." In *Africa's Development in Historical Perspective*, ed. Emmanuel Akyeampong, Robert H. Bates, Nathan Nunn, and James A. Robinson, pp. 424–446. New York: Cambridge University Press.

Bates, Robert H., and Da-Hsiang D. Lien. 1985. "A Note on Taxation, Development, and Representative Government." *Politics & Society* 14(1):53–70.

Batson, Benjamin A. 1984. *The End of the Absolute Monarchy in Siam.* New York: Oxford University Press.

Bazant, Jan. 1995. *Historia de la Deuda Exterior de México (1823–1946).* Mexico City: El Colegio de México.

Beblawi, Hazem. 1987. "The Rentier State in the Arab World." *Arab Studies Quarterly* 9(4):383–398.

Benians, E. A. 1960. "Finance Trade and Communications." In *Cambridge History of the British Empire*, ed. E. A. Benians, James Butler, and C. E. Carrington, pp. 181–229. Vol. 3. New York: Cambridge University Press.

Beramendi, Pablo, Mark Dincecco, and Melissa Rogers. 2019. "Intra-Elite Competition and Long-Run Fiscal Development." *Journal of Politics* 81(1):49–65.

Berg, Andrew, Norbert Funke, Alejandro Hajdenberg, Victor Lledo, Rolando Ossowski, Martin Schindler, Antonio Spilimbergo, Shamsuddin Tareq, and Irene Yackovlev. 2009. "Fiscal Policy in Sub-Saharan Africa in Response to the Impact of the Global Crisis." IMF staff position notes 2009/10, International Monetary Fund. https://ideas.repec.org/p/imf/imfspn/2009-010.html.

Berger, Daniel. 2009. "Taxes, Institutions and Local Governance: Evidence from a Natural Experiment in Colonial Nigeria." Technical report, New York University. https://leitner.yale.edu/sites/default/files/files/resources/PMF-papers/NigeriaPaper.pdf.

Berman, Bruce. 1984. "Structure and Process in the Bureaucratic States of Colonial Africa." *Development and Change* 15(2):161–202.

Berman, Bruce J., and Wisdom Tettey. 2001. "African States, Bureaucratic Culture and Computer Fixes." *Public Administration and Development* 21:1–13.

Besley, Timothy. 2020. "State Capacity, Reciprocity, and the Social Contract." *Econometrica* 88(4):1307–1335.

Besley, Timothy, and Torsten Persson. 2009. "The Origins of State Capacity: Property Rights, Taxation and Politics." *American Economic Review* 99(4):1218–1244.

Besley, Timothy, and Torsten Persson. 2011. *Pillars of Prosperity: The Political Economics of Development Clusters.* Princeton, NJ: Princeton University Press.

Bignon, Vincent, Rui Esteves, and Alfonso Herranz-Loncán. 2015. "Big Push or Big Grab? Railways, Government Activism, and Export Growth in Latin America, 1865–1913." *Economic History Review* 68(4):1277–1305.

Birdal, Murat. 2010. *The Political Economy of Ottoman Public Debt: Insolvency and European Financial Control in the Late Nineteenth Century.* London: Tauris Academic Studies.

Black, Jeremy. 2009. *War in the Nineteenth Century: 1800–1914.* Malden, MA: Polity.

Blaisdell, Donald C. 1929. *European Financial Control in the Ottoman Empire: A Study of the Establishment, Activities, and Significance of the Administration of the Ottoman Public Debt.* New York: Columbia University Press.

Blakemore, Harold. 1974. *British Nitrates and Chilean Politics, 1886–1896: Balmaceda and North.* London: Athlone Press.

Blattman, Christopher, Jason Hwang, and Jeffrey G. Williamson. 2007. "Winners and Losers in the Commodity Lottery: The Impact of Terms of Trade Growth and Volatility in the Periphery 1870–1939." *Journal of Development Economics* 82(1):156–179.

Blaydes, Lisa, and Eric Chaney. 2013. "The Feudal Revolution and Europe's Rise: Political Divergence of the Christian West and the Muslim World before 1500 CE." *American Political Science Review* 107(1):16–34.

Bockstette, Valerie, Areendam Chanda, and Louis Putterman. 2002. "States and Markets: The Advantage of an Early Start." *Journal of Economic Growth* 7(4):347–369.

Bogart, Dan. 2009. "Nationalizations and the Development of Transport Systems: Cross-Country Evidence from Railroad Networks, 1860–1912." *Journal of Economic History* 69(1): 202–237.

Boix, Carles. 2003. *Democracy and Redistribution*. New York: Cambridge University Press.

Boix, Carles. 2015. *Political Order and Inequality: Their Foundations and Their Consequences for Human Welfare*. New York: Cambridge University Press.

Boix, Carles, and Milan W. Svolik. 2013. "The Foundations of Limited Authoritarian Government: Institutions, Commitment, and Power-Sharing in Dictatorships." *Journal of Politics* 75(2):300–316.

Bolt, Jutta, Robert Inklaar, Herman de Jong, and Jan Luiten van Zanden. 2018. "Rebasing 'Maddison': New Income Comparisons and the Shape of Long-Run Economic Development." GGDC Research Memorandum 174.

Bonilla, Heraclio. 1972. "El Impacto de los Ferrocarriles, Algunas Proposiciones." *Historia y Cultura* 6:93–120.

Boone, Catherine. 2003. *Political Topographies of the African State: Territorial Authority and Institutional Choice*. New York: Cambridge University Press.

Booth, Anne E. 2007. *Colonial Legacies: Economic and Social Development in East and Southeast Asia*. Honolulu: University of Hawai'i Press.

Borchard, Edwin. 1951. *State Insolvency and Foreign Bondholders*. Washington, DC: Beard Books.

Bordo, Michael D. 2006. "Sudden Stops, Financial Crises, and Original Sin in Emerging Countries: Déjà vu?" NBER working paper 12393.

Bordo, Michael D., Michael Edelstein, and Hugh Rockoff. 1999. "Was Adherence to the Gold Standard a 'Good Housekeeping Seal of Approval' during the Interwar Period?" NBER working paper 7186.

Bordo, Michael D., Barry Eichengreen, and Jongwoo Kim. 1998. "Was There Really an Earlier Period of International Financial Integration Comparable to Today?" NBER working paper 6738.

Bordo, Michael D., and Finn E. Kydland. 1995. "The Gold Standard as a Rule: An Essay in Exploration." *Explorations in Economic History* 32(4):423–464.

Bordo, Michael D., and Hugh Rockoff. 1996. "The Gold Standard as a 'Good Housekeeping Seal of Approval.'" *Journal of Economic History* 56(2):389–428.

Borensztein, Eduardo, Olivier D. Jeanne, Paolo Mauro, Jeronimo Zettelmeyer, and Marcos D. Chamon. 2004. "Sovereign Debt Structure for Crisis Prevention." Technical report, International Montery Fund, occasional paper 237.

Borensztein, Eduardo, and Ugo Panizza. 2010. "Do Sovereign Defaults Hurt Exporters?" *Open Economies Review* 21(3):393–41.

Bormann, Nils-Christian, Lars-Erik Cederman, Scott Gates, Benjamin A. T. Graham, Simon Hug, Kaare W. Strøm, and Julian Wucherpfennig. 2019. "Power Sharing: Institutions, Behavior, and Peace." *American Journal of Political Science* 63(1):84–100.

Bossenbroek, Martin. 1995. "The Living Tools of Empire: The Recruitment of European Soldiers for the Dutch Colonial Army, 1814–1909." *Journal of Imperial and Commonwealth History* 23(1):26–53.

Boucoyannis, Deborah. 2015. "No Taxation of Elites, No Representation: State Capacity and the Origins of Representation." *Politics & Society* 43(3):303–332.

Bowman, John R., and Michael Wallerstein. 1982. "The Fall of Balmaceda and Public Finance in Chile: New Data for an Old Debate." *Journal of Interamerican Studies and World Affairs* 24(4):421–460.

Brambor, Thomas, Agustín Goenaga, Johannes Lindvall, and Jan Teorell. 2020. "The Lay of the Land: Information Capacity and the Modern State." *Comparative Political Studies* 53(2):175–213.

Braun, Juan, Matías Braun, Ignacio Briones, José Díaz, Rolf Lüders, and Gert Wagner. 2000. "Economía Chilena 1810–1995. Cuentas." *Instituto de Economía de la Universidad Católica de Chile, Documento de Trabajo* 187.

Bräutigam, Deborah. 2008. "Contingent Capacity: Export Taxation and State Building in Mauritius." In *Taxation and State-Building in Developing Countries*, ed. Deborah Bräutigam, Odd-Helge Fjeldstad, and Mick Moore, pp. 135–159. New York: Cambridge University Press.

Bräutigam, Deborah. 2020. "A Critical Look at Chinese 'Debt-Trap Diplomacy': The Rise of a Meme." *Area Development and Policy* 5(1):1–14.

Bräutigam, Deborah A., Odd-Helge Fjeldstad, and Mick Moore, eds. 2008. *Taxation and State-Building in Developing Countries: Capacity and Consent.* New York: Cambridge University Press.

Bräutigam, Deborah A., and Stephen Knack. 2004. "Foreign Aid, Institutions, and Governance in Sub-Saharan Africa." *Economic Development and Cultural Change* 52(2):255–285.

Brecke, Peter. 1999. "Violent Conflict 1400 A.D. to the Present in Different Regions of the World." Paper presented at 1999 meeting of Peace Science Society. Dataset curated by Centre for Global Economic History. www.cgeh.nl/data#conflict.

Brewer, John. 1988. *The Sinews of Power: War, Money and the English State: 1688–1783.* Cambridge, MA: Harvard University Press.

British Parliament. 1908. *Statistical Tables Relating to British Colonies, Possessions and Protectorates, Part XXXI.* London: Darling & Son.

Broadberry, Stephen, Bruce Campbell, Alexander Klein, Mark Overton, and Bas van Leeuwen. 2012. "British Economic Growth, 1270–1870: An Output-Based Approach." Technical report, School of Economics working paper, University of Kent.

Broich, Tobias. 2017. "U.S. and Soviet Foreign Aid during the Cold War: A Case Study of Ethiopia." MERIT working paper 2017-010, United Nations University—Maastricht Economic and Social Research Institute on Innovation and Technology.

Broner, Fernando, and Jaume Ventura. 2016. "Rethinking the Effects of Financial Globalization." *Quarterly Journal of Economics* 131(3):1497–1542.

Brown, Ian. 1992. *The Creation of the Modern Ministry of Finance in Siam, 1885–1910.* Hampshire, UK: Macmillan.

Brown, Patrick J. 1998. *Bond Markets: Structures and Yield Calculations.* Cambridge, UK: Gilmour Drummon Publishing.

Bruce, George L. 1973. *The Burma Wars, 1824–1886.* London: Hart-Davis MacGibbon.

Bueno de Mesquita, Bruce, and Alastair Smith. 2009. "A Political Economy of Aid." *International Organization* 63(2):309–340.

Bueno de Mesquita, Bruce, and Alastair Smith. 2013. "Aid: Blame It All on 'Easy Money.'" *Journal of Conflict Resolution* 57(3):524–537.

Bulow, Jeremy, and Kenneth Rogoff. 1989. "A Constant Recontracting Model of Sovereign Debt." *Journal of Political Economy* 97(1):155–178.

Bunte, Jonas B. 2019. *Raise the Debt: How Developing Countries Choose Their Creditors.* New York: Oxford University Press.

Butcher, Charles, and Ryan Griffiths. 2015. "Alternative International Systems? System Structure and Violent Conflict in Nineteenth-Century West Africa, Southeast Asia, and South Asia." *Review of International Studies* 41:715–737.

Cagé, Julia, and Lucie Gadenne. 2018. "Tax Revenues and the Fiscal Cost of Trade Liberalization, 1792–2006." *Explorations in Economic History* 70:1–24.

Caillard, Vincent, and Elias Gibb. 1911. "Turkey." *1911 Encyclopedia Britannica.*

Cain, P. J., and A. G. Hopkins. 2016. *British Imperialism: 1688–2015.* 3rd ed. New York: Routledge.

Calomiris, Charles, and Stephen Haber. 2014. *Fragile by Design: The Political Origins of Banking Crises and Scarce Credit.* Princeton, NJ: Princeton University Press.

Calvo, Guillermo A. 1988. "Servicing the Public Debt: The Role of Expectations." *American Economic Review* 78(4):647–661.

Cameron, Rondo. 1966. *France and the Economic Development of Europe, 1800–1914: Conquest of Peace and Seeds of War.* Chicago: Rand McNally.

Cantoni, Davide, Yuyu Chen, David Y. Yang, Noam Yuchtman, and Y. Jane Zhang. 2017. "Curriculum and Ideology." *Journal of Political Economy* 125(2):338–392.

Cappella Zielinski, Rosella. 2016. *How States Pay for War.* Ithaca, NY: Cornell University Press.

Cárdenas, Mauricio. 2010. "State Capacity in Latin America." *Economía* 10(2):1–45.

Cariola Sutter, Carmen, and Osvaldo Sunkel. 1982. *Un Siglo de Historia Económica de Chile: 1830–1930: Dos Ensayos y una Bibliografía.* Madrid: Ediciones Cultura Hispánica.

Carl, George Edmund. 1980. *First among Equals: Great Britain and Venezuela, 1810–1910.* Ann Arbor, MI: University Microfilms International.

Caron, François. 1983. "France." In *Railways and the Economic Development of Western Europe, 1830–1914,* ed. Patrick K. O'Brien, pp. 28–48. New York: St. Martin's Press.

Carosso, Vincent P. 1987. *The Morgans: Private International Bankers 1854–1913.* Cambridge, MA: Harvard University Press.

Carpenter, Daniel P. 2001. *The Forging of Bureaucratic Autonomy: Reputations, Networks, and Policy Innovation in Executive Agencies, 1862–1928.* Princeton, NJ: Princeton University Press.

Cassis, Youssef. 1994. *City Bankers, 1890–1914.* New York: Cambridge University Press.

Catão, Luís. 2006. "Sudden Stops and Currency Drops: A Historical Look." IMF working paper 06/133.

Centeno, Miguel Angel. 1997. "Blood and Debt: War and Taxation in Nineteenth-Century Latin America." *American Journal of Sociology* 102(6):1565–1605.

Centeno, Miguel Angel. 2002. *Blood and Debt: War and the Nation-State in Latin America.* University Park: Pennsylvania State University Press.

Cermeño, Alexandra, Kerstin Enflo, and Johannes Lindvall. 2018. "Railways and Reform: How Trains Strengthened the Nation State." Technical report, STANCE Series working paper. https://portal.research.lu.se/portal/en/publications/railways-and-reform-how-trains-strengthened-the-nation-state(781d6bc0-162c-4072-8fe8-2fbbc624dfab).html.

Chabot, Benjamin, and Veronica Santarosa. 2017. "Don't Cry for Argentina (or Other Sovereign Borrowers): Lessons from a Previous Era of Sovereign Debt Contract Enforcement." *Capital Markets Law Journal* 12(1):9–37.

Chaves, Isaias, Stanley L. Engerman, and James A. Robinson. 2014. "Reinventing the Wheel: The Economic Benefits of Wheeled Transportation in Early Colonial British West Africa." In *Africa's Development in Historical Perspective,* ed. Emmanuel Akyeampong, Robert H. Bates, Nathan Nunn, and James A. Robinson, pp. 321–365. New York: Cambridge University Press.

Cheung, Anthony B. L. 2005. "The Politics of Administrative Reforms in Asia: Paradigms and Legacies, Paths and Diversities." *Governance* 18(2):257–282.

Clemens, Michael A., and Jeffrey G. Williamson. 2004. "Why Did the Tariff-Growth Correlation Change after 1950?" *Journal of Economic Growth* 9(1):5–46.

Clodfelter, Michael. 2002. *Warfare and Armed Conflicts: A Statistical Reference to Casualty and Other Figures, 1500–2000.* Jefferson, NC: McFarland.

Coatsworth, John H. 1979. "Indispensable Railroads in a Backward Economy: The Case of Mexico." *Journal of Economic History* 39(4):939–960.

Coatsworth, John H. 1981. *Growth against Development: The Economic Impact of Railroads in Porfirian Mexico*. DeKalb: Northern Illinois University Press.

Coatsworth, John H. 2005. "Structures, Endowments, and Institutions in the Economic History of Latin America." *Latin American Research Review* 40(3):126–144.

Cogneau, Denis, Yannick Dupraz, and Sandrine Mesplé-Somps. 2021. "Fiscal Capacity and Dualism in Colonial States: The French Empire 1830–1962." *Journal of Economic History* 81(2):441–480.

Cohen, Benjamin J. 1986. *In Whose Interest? International Banking and American Foreign Policy*. New Haven, CT: Yale University Press.

Collier, Paul. 2006. "Is Aid Oil? An Analysis of Whether Africa Can Absorb More Aid." *World Development* 34(9):1482–1497.

Collier, Paul, and Nicholas Sambanis. 2005. *Understanding Civil War: Evidence and Analysis, Volume 1. Africa*. Washington, DC: World Bank.

Collier, Simon. 2003. *Chile: The Making of a Republic, 1830–1865*. New York: Cambridge University Press.

Collier, Simon, and William Sater. 1996. *A History of Chile*. New York: Cambridge University Press.

Comín, Francisco. 2012. "Default, Rescheduling and Inflation: Public Debt Crises in Spain during the 19th and 20th Centuries." *Revista de Historia Económica/Journal of Iberian and Latin American Economic History* 30(3):353–390.

Comín, Francisco. 2015. "Los Presupuestos de las Fuerzas Armadas." In *Historia Militar de España. Vol. 4, Tomo 1: Edad Contemporánea, Siglo XIX*, ed. Miguel Artola Gallego, pp. 221–257. Madrid: Ediciones del Laberinto, Ministerio de Defensa.

Copelovitch, Mark S. 2010. *The International Monetary Fund in the Global Economy*. New York: Cambridge University Press.

Coquery-Vidrovitch, Catherine. 1969. "French Colonization in Africa to 1920: Administration and Economic Development." In *Colonialism in Africa*, ed. L. H. Gann and Peter Duignan, pp. 165–198. Vol. 1. New York: Cambridge University Press.

Cortés-Conde, Roberto. 1995. "La Deuda Pública Externa en Argentina, 1800–1906." In *La Deuda Pública en América Latina en Perspectiva Histórica*, ed. Reinhard Liehr, pp. 155–170. Madrid: Iberoamericana.

Cottrell, P. L. 1976. *British Overseas Investment in the Nineteenth Century*. London: Macmillan.

Coutts, Ken, and Christina Laskaridis. 2019. "Financial Balances and the Development of the Ethiopian Economy." In *The Oxford Handbook of the Ethiopian Economy*, ed. Fantu Cheru, Christopher Cramer, and Arkebe Oqubay, pp. 213–229. New York: Oxford University Press.

Cox, Gary W. 2016. *Marketing Sovereign Promises: Monopoly Brokerage and the Growth of the English State*. New York: Cambridge University Press.

Cox, Gary W., and Mark Dincecco. 2021. "The Budgetary Origins of Fiscal-Military Prowess." *Journal of Politics* 83(3):851–866.

Cox, Gary W., and Sebastian M. Saiegh. 2018. "Executive Constraint and Sovereign Debt: Quasi-Experimental Evidence from Argentina during the Baring Crisis." *Comparative Political Studies* 51(11):1504–1525.

Cromer, Evelyn Baring. 1908. *Modern Egypt*. Vol. II. London: Macmillan.

Cronin, Stephanie. 2008. "Importing Modernity: European Military Missions to Qajar Iran." *Comparative Studies in Society and History* 50(1):197–226.

Crowder, Michael. 1964. "Indirect Rule: French and British Style." *Africa: Journal of the International African Institute* 34(3):197–205.

Cruces, Juan J., and Christoph Trebesch. 2013. "Sovereign Defaults: The Price of Haircuts." *American Economic Journal: Macroeconomics* 5(3):85–117.

Cruchaga, Miguel. 1878. *Estudio sobre la Organización Económica y la Hacienda Pública de Chile*. Santiago: Los Tiempos.

Cruz, Cesi, and Christina J. Schneider. 2017. "Foreign Aid and Undeserved Credit Claiming." *American Journal of Political Science* 61(2):396–408.

Curto-Grau, Marta, Alfonso Herranz-Loncán, and Albert Solé-Ollé. 2012. "Pork-Barrel Politics in Semi-Democracies: The Spanish 'Parliamentary Roads,' 1880–1914." *Journal of Economic History* 72(3):771–796.

Dal Bó, Ernesto, Pablo Hernández-Lagos, and Sebastián Mazzuca. 2015. "The Paradox of Civilization: Preinstitutional Sources of Security and Prosperity." NBER working paper 21829.

D'Arcy, Michelle, and Marina Nistotskaya. 2018. "The Early Modern Origins of Contemporary European Tax Outcomes." *European Journal of Political Research* 57(1):47–67.

Daunton, Martin. 2001. *Trusting Leviathan: The Politics of Taxation in Britain, 1799–1914*. New York: Cambridge University Press.

Daunton, M. J. 2002. "Financial Elites and British Society, 1880–1950." In *Finance and Financiers in European History 1880–1960*, ed. Youssef Cassis, pp. 121–146. New York: Cambridge University Press.

Davis, Lance E., and Robert A. Huttenback. 1986. *Mammon and the Pursuit of Empire: The Economics of British Imperialism*. New York: Cambridge University Press.

Davison, Roderic. 1963. *Reform in the Ottoman Empire, 1856–1876*. Princeton, NJ: Princeton University Press.

Dawson, Frank Griffith. 1990. *The First Latin American Debt Crisis: The City of London and the 1822–25 Loan Bubble*. New Haven, CT: Yale University Press.

Degefe, Befekadu. 1992. *Growth and Foreign Debt: The Ethiopian Experience 1964–86*. Nairobi: African Economic Research Consortium.

De Kock, M. H. 1924. *Economic History of South Africa*. Cape Town: Juta.

de la Cuesta, Brandon, Lucy Martin, Helen V. Milner, and Daniel L. Nielson. 2021. "Foreign Aid, Oil Revenues, and Political Accountability: Evidence from Six Experiments in Ghana and Uganda." *Review of International Organizations* 16:521–548.

de la Garza, Andrew. 2016. *The Mughal Empire: Babur, Akbar and the Indian Military Revolution, 1500–1605*. New York: Routledge.

Dell, Melissa. 2010. "The Persistent Effects of Peru's Mining Mita." *Econometrica* 78(6):1863–1903.

della Paolera, Gerardo, and Alan M. Taylor. 2001. *Straining at the Anchor: The Argentine Currency Board and the Search for Macroeconomic Stability, 1880–1935*. Chicago: University of Chicago Press.

della Paolera, Gerardo, and Alan M. Taylor. 2003. *A New Economic History of Argentina*. New York: Cambridge University Press.

de Moor, J. A. 1989. "Warmakers in the Archipelago: Dutch Expeditions in Nineteenth Century Indonesia." In *Imperialism and War: Essays on Colonial Wars in Asia and Africa*, ed. J. A. de Moor and H. L. Wesseling, pp. 50–71. Leiden, Netherlands: Leiden University Press.

Deng, Kent Gang. 2015. "Imperial China under the Song and Late Qing." In *Fiscal Regimes and the Political Economy of Premodern States*, ed. Andrew Monson and Walter Scheidel, pp. 308–342. New York: Cambridge University Press.

De Santis, Roberto A. 2012. "The Euro Area Sovereign Debt Crisis: Safe Haven, Credit Rating Agencies and the Spread of the Fever from Greece, Ireland and Portugal." Technical report, ECB working paper 1419. https://www.ecb.europa.eu/pub/pdf/scpwps/ecbwp1419.pdf.

Devereux, Robert. 1963. *The First Ottoman Constitutional Reform: A Study of the Midhat Constitution and Parliament*. Baltimore: Johns Hopkins University Press.

Diamond, Douglas W., and Raghuram G. Rajan. 2001. "Banks, Short-Term Debt and Financial Crises: Theory, Policy Implications and Applications." *Carnegie-Rochester Conference Series on Public Policy* 54(1):37–71.

Diamond, Jared. 1997. *Guns, Germs, and Steel: The Fates of Human Societies*. New York: W. W. Norton.

Dickson, P.G.M. 1967. *The Financial Revolution in England: A Study in the Development of Public Credit*. London: Macmillan.

Dietrich, Simone, and Matthew S. Winters. 2021. "Foreign Aid and Quality of Government." In *The Oxford Handbook of the Quality of Government*, ed. Andreas Bågenholm, Monika Bauhr, Marcia Grimes, and Bo Rothstein, pp. 449–471. Oxford, UK: Oxford University Press.

DiGiuseppe, Matthew R., Colin. M. Barry, and Richard W. Frank. 2012. "Good for the Money: International Finance, State Capacity, and Internal Armed Conflict." *Journal of Peace Research* 49(3):391–405.

Dincecco, Mark. 2009. "Fiscal Centralization, Limited Government, and Public Revenues in Europe, 1650–1913." *Journal of Economic History* 69(1):48–103.

Dincecco, Mark. 2011. *Political Transformations and Public Finances: Europe, 1650–1913*. New York: Cambridge University Press.

Dincecco, Mark, James Fenske, Anil Menon, and Shivaki Mukherjee. 2019. "Pre-Colonial Warfare and Long-Run Development in India." Technical report, Centre for Competitive Advantage in the Global Economy (CAGE) working paper 426/2019.

Dincecco, Mark, and Mauricio Prado. 2012. "Warfare, Fiscal Capacity, and Performance." *Journal of Economic Growth* 17(3):171–203.

Dincecco, Mark, and Yuhua Wang. 2020. "Internal Conflict and State Development: Evidence from Imperial China." Technical report, University of Michigan. https://sites.google.com/umich.edu/dincecco/work-in-progress.

Donaldson, Dave. 2018. "Railroads of the Raj: Estimating the Impact of Transportation Infrastructure." *American Economic Review* 108(4–5):899–934.

Doner, Richard F. 2009. *The Politics of Uneven Development: Thailand's Economic Growth in Comparative Perspective*. New York: Cambridge University Press.

Dornbusch, Rudiger, and Jacob A. Frenkel. 1982. "The Gold Standard and the Bank of England in the Crisis of 1847." NBER working paper 1039.

Downing, Brian M. 1993. *The Military Revolution and Political Change: Origins of Democracy and Autocracy in Early Modern Europe*. Princeton, NJ: Princeton University Press.

Drago, Luis M. 1907. "State Loans in Their Relation to International Policy." *American Journal of International Law* 1(3):692–726.

Dreher, Axel, and Andreas Fuchs. 2015. "Rogue Aid? An Empirical Analysis of China's Aid Allocation." *Canadian Journal of Economics/Revue Canadienne d'Économique* 48(3):988–1023.

Drelichman, Mauricio, and Hans-Joachim Voth. 2014. *Lending to the Borrower from Hell: Debt, Taxes, and Default in the Age of Philip II*. Princeton, NJ: Princeton University Press.

Easterly, William. 2006. *The White Man's Burden: Why the West's Efforts to Aid the Rest Have Done So Much Ill and So Little Good*. New York: Penguin Books.

Easterly, William, and Ross Levine. 1997. "Africa's Growth Tragedy: Policies and Ethnic Divisions." *Quarterly Journal of Economics* 112(4):1203–1250.

Eaton, Jonathan, and Mark Gersovitz. 1981. "Debt with Potential Repudiation: Theoretical and Empirical Analysis." *Review of Economic Studies* 48(2):289–309.

Eaton, Kent. 2004. *Politics Beyond the Capital: The Design of Subnational Institutions in South America*. New York: Cambridge University Press.

Edelstein, Michael. 1982. *Overseas Investment*. New York: Columbia University Press.

Edwards, Alberto. 1917. "Datos y Observaciones sobre las Finanzas Municipales de Chile." *Revista Chilena* (1):81–86.

Edwards, Alberto. 1945. *La Fronda Aristocrática en Chile*. Santiago: Editorial del Pacífico.

Eichengreen, Barry. 1987. "Til Debt Do Us Part: The U.S. Capital Market and Foreign Lending, 1920–1955." NBER working paper 2394.

Eichengreen, Barry. 1990. "Trends and Cycles in Foreign Lending." NBER working paper 3411.

Eichengreen, Barry. 1991. "Historical Research on International Lending and Debt." *Journal of Economic Perspectives* 5(2):149–169.

Eichengreen, Barry, Asmaa El-Ganainy, Rui Esteves, and Kris James Mitchener. 2019. "Public Debt through the Ages." NBER working paper 25494.

Eichengreen, Barry, and Ricardo Hausmann, eds. 2005. *Other People's Money: Debt Denomination and Financial Instability in Emerging Market Economies*. Chicago: University of Chicago Press.

Eichengreen, Barry, and Richard Portes. 1986. "Debt and Default in the 1930s: Causes and Consequences." *European Economic Review* 30(3):599–640.

Eichengreen, Barry, and Richard Portes. 1989. "Dealing With Debt: The 1930s and the 1980s." NBER working paper 2867.

Eldem, Edhem. 2005. "Ottoman Financial Integration with Europe: Foreign Loans, the Ottoman Bank and the Ottoman Public Debt." *European Review* 13(3):431–445.

Elliott, John H. 1963. *Imperial Spain 1469–1716*. London: E. Arnold.

Engerman, Stanley L., and Kenneth L. Sokoloff. 2002. "Factor Endowments, Inequality, and Paths of Development among New World Economics." NBER working paper 9259.

Epstein, S. R. 2000. *Freedom and Growth: The Rise of States and Markets in Europe, 1300–1750*. New York: Routledge.

Ertman, Thomas. 1997. *Birth of the Leviathan*. Cambridge, UK: Cambridge University Press.

Esteves, Rui. 2007. "Quis custodiet quem? Sovereign Debt and Bondholders' Protection before 1914." Economics Series working paper 323, University of Oxford, Department of Economics.

Esteves, Rui. 2008. "Between Imperialism and Capitalism: European Capital Exports before 1914." Working paper 8022, Economic History Society.

Esteves, Rui Pedro. 2011. "The *Belle Epoque* of International Finance: French Capital Exports, 1880–1914." Technical report, Economics Series working paper 534, University of Oxford, Department of Economics.

Farcau, Bruce W. 2000. *The Ten Cents War: Chile, Peru, and Bolivia in the War of the Pacific, 1879–1884*. Westport, CT: Praeger.

Farley, J. Lewis. 1872. *Modern Turkey*. London: Hurst and Blackett Publishers.

Faundez, Julio. 2007. *Democratization, Development, and Legality: Chile, 1831–1973*. New York: Palgrave Macmillan.

Fazal, Tanisha M., and Paul Poast. 2019. "War Is Not Over: What the Optimists Get Wrong about Conflict." *Foreign Affairs* 98(6):74–83.

Feis, Herbert. 1930. *Europe, the World's Banker 1870–1914*. New Haven, CT: Yale University Press.

Fenn, Charles. 1838. *Fenn's Compendium of the English and Foreign Funds, Debts and Revenues . . .* Edited by Charles Fenn. 2nd ed. London: E. Wilson.

Fenn, Charles. 1855. *Fenn's Compendium of the English and Foreign Funds, Debts and Revenues . . .* Edited by Henry Ayres. 5th ed. London: E. Wilson.

Fenn, Charles. 1869. *Fenn's Compendium of the English and Foreign Funds, Debts and Revenues . . .* Edited by Robert Lucas Nash. 10th ed. London: E. Wilson.

Fenn, Charles. 1883. *Fenn's Compendium of the English and Foreign Funds, Debts and Revenues . . .* Edited by Robert Lucas Nash. 13th ed. London: E. Wilson.

Fenn, Charles. 1898. *Fenn's Compendium of the English and Foreign Funds, Debts and Revenues . . .* Edited by S. F. Van Oss. 16th ed. London: E. Wilson.

Ferejohn, John, and Frances McCall Rosenbluth. 2016. *Forged through Fire: War, Peace, and the Democratic Bargain.* New York: Liveright.

Ferguson, Niall, 2004. *Empire: How Britain Made the Modern World.* London: Penguin Books.

Ferguson, Niall, and Moritz Schularick. 2006. "The Empire Effect: The Determinants of Country Risk in the First Age of Globalization, 1880–1913." *Journal of Economic History* 66(2):283–312.

Ferguson, Niall, and Moritz Schularick. 2012. "The 'Thin Film of Gold': Monetary Rules and Policy Credibility." *European Review of Economic History* 16(4):384–407.

Ferns, H. S. 1960. *Britain and Argentina in the Nineteenth Century.* Oxford, UK: Clarendon Press.

Findley, Carter Vaughn. 1980. *Bureaucratic Reform in the Ottoman Empire: The Sublime Porte, 1789–1922.* Princeton, NJ: Princeton University Press.

Finnemore, Martha. 2003. *The Purpose of Intervention: Changing Beliefs about the Use of Force.* Ithaca, NY: Cornell University Press.

Fischer, Wolfram, and Peter Lundgreen. 1975. "The Recruitment and Training of Administrative and Technical Personnel." In *The Formation of Nation States in Western Europe*, ed. Charles Tilly, pp. 456–561. Princeton, NJ: Princeton University Press.

Fishlow, Albert. 1965. *American Railroads and the Transformation of the Antebellum Economy.* Cambridge, MA: Harvard University Press.

Fishlow, Albert. 1985. "Lessons from the Past: Capital Markets during the 19th Century and the Interwar Period." *International Organization* 39(3):383–439.

Flandreau, Marc. 2006. "Home Biases, Nineteenth Century Style." *Journal of the European Economic Association* 4(2/3):634–643.

Flandreau, Marc. 2013. "Sovereign States, Bondholders Committees, and the London Stock Exchange in the Nineteenth Century (1827–68): New Facts and Old Fictions." *Oxford Review of Economic Policy* 29(4):668–696.

Flandreau, Marc. 2016. *Anthropologists in the Stock Exchange: A Financial History of Victorian Science.* Chicago: University of Chicago Press.

Flandreau, Marc. 2020. "Vulture Diplomacy: Distressed Sovereign Debt, Creditor Coalitions and the London Stock Exchange in the 19th Century." Technical report, University of Pennsylvania.

Flandreau, Marc, and Juan H. Flores. 2009. "Bonds and Brands: Foundations of Sovereign Debt Markets, 1820–1830." *Journal of Economic History* 69(3):646–684.

Flandreau, Marc, and Juan H. Flores. 2012a. "Bondholders versus Bond-Sellers? Investment Banks and Conditionality Lending in the London Market for Foreign Government Debt, 1815–1913." *European Review of Economic History* 16(4):356–383.

Flandreau, Marc, and Juan H. Flores. 2012b. "The Peaceful Conspiracy: Bond Markets and International Relations during the Pax Britannica." *International Organization* 66:211–241.

Flandreau, Marc, Juan H. Flores, Norbert Gaillard, and Sebastián Nieto-Parra. 2009. "The End of Gatekeeping: Underwriters and the Quality of Sovereign Bond Markets, 1815–2007." NBER working paper 15128.

Flandreau, Marc, and Frédéric Zumer. 2004. *The Making of Global Finance: 1880–1913.* Paris: OECD.

Flores-Macías, Gustavo A., and Sarah E. Kreps. 2017. "Borrowing Support for War: The Effect of War Finance on Public Attitudes toward Conflict." *Journal of Conflict Resolution* 61(5):997–1020.

Fogel, Robert William. 1963. "Railroads and American Economic Growth: Essays in Econometric History." PhD thesis, Johns Hopkins University.

Ford, A. G. 1956. "Argentina and the Baring Crisis of 1890." *Oxford Economic Papers* 8(2):127–150.

Fortna, Virginia Page. 2004. "Does Peacekeeping Keep Peace? International Intervention and the Duration of Peace after Civil Wars." *International Studies Quarterly* 48(2):269–292.

Frankema, Ewout. 2011. "Colonial Taxation and Government Spending in British Africa, 1880–1940: Maximizing Revenue or Minimizing Effort?" *Explorations in Economic History* 48(1):136–149.

Frankema, Ewout, and Anne Booth. 2019. *Fiscal Capacity and the Colonial State in Asia and Africa, c. 1850–1960.* New York: Cambridge University Press.

Frankema, Ewout H. P. 2012. "The Origins of Formal Education in Sub-Saharan Africa: Was British Rule More Benign?" *European Review of Economic History* 16(4):335–355.

Frankema, Ewout, and Marlous van Waijenburg. 2014. "Metropolitan Blueprints of Colonial Taxation? Lessons from Fiscal Capacity Building in British and French Africa, c. 1880–1940." *Journal of African History* 55(3):371–400.

Fremdling, Rainer. 1983. "Germany." In *Railways and the Economic Development of Western Europe, 1830–1914,* ed. Patrick Karl O'Brien, pp. 121–147. New York: St. Martin's Press.

Frieden, Jeffry A. 1991a. *Debt, Development, & Democracy: Modern Political Economy and Latin America, 1965–1985.* Princeton, NJ: Princeton University Press.

Frieden, Jeffry A. 1991b. "Invested Interests: The Politics of National Economic Policies in a World of Global Finance." *International Organization* 45(4):425–451.

Frieden, Jeffry A. 1994. "International Investment and Colonial Control: A New Interpretation." *International Organization* 48(4):559–593.

Fujihira, Shinju. 2000. "Conscripting Money: Total War and Fiscal Revolution in the Twentieth Century." PhD thesis, Princeton University, Political Science Department.

Fund for Peace. 2020. *Fragile States Index: Annual Report 2020.* Technical report, Fund for Peace. www.fragilestatesindex.org.

Gabre-Selassie, Zewde. 2005. "Continuity and Discontinuity in Menelik's Foreign Policy." In *The Battle of Adwa: Reflections on Ethiopia's Victory against European Colonialism,* ed. Paulos Milkias and Getachew Metaferia, pp. 89–132. New York: Algora Publishing.

Gallagher, John, and Ronald Robinson. 1953. "The Imperialism of Free Trade." *Economic History Review* 6(1):1–15.

Gandhi, Jennifer. 2008. *Political Institutions under Dictatorship.* New York: Cambridge University Press.

Gandhi, Jennifer, and Adam Przeworski. 2007. "Authoritarian Institutions and the Survival of Autocrats." *Comparative Political Studies* 40(11):1279–1301.

Gardner, Leigh. 2017. "Colonialism or Supersanctions: Sovereignty and Debt in West Africa, 1871–1914." *European Review of Economic History* 21(2):236–257.

Gardner, Leigh A. 2012. *Taxing Colonial Africa.* Oxford, UK: Oxford University Press.

Geddes, Barbara. 1994. *Politician's Dilemma: Building State Capacity in Latin America.* Berkeley: University of California Press.

Gelpern, Anna, Sebastian Horn, Scott Morris, Brad Parks, and Christoph Trebesch. 2021. "How China Lends: A Rare Look into 100 Debt Contracts with Foreign Governments." Technical report, Peterson Institute for International Economics, Kiel Institute for the World Economy, Center for Global Development, and AidData at William & Mary.

Gelvin, James L. 2005. *The Modern Middle East: A History.* Oxford, UK: Oxford University Press.

Gennaioli, Nicola, and Hans-Joachim Voth. 2015. "State Capacity and Military Conflict." *Review of Economic Studies* 82(4):1409–1448.

Gent, Stephen E. 2007. "Strange Bedfellows: The Strategic Dynamics of Major Power Military Interventions." *Journal of Politics* 69(4):1089–1102.

Glaeser, Edward L., Rafael Di Tella, and Lucas Llach. 2018. "Introduction to Argentine Exceptionalism." *Latin American Economic Review* 27(1):1–22.

Gleisner, Hagen. 1988. *Centralismo en Latinoamérica y Descentralización en Chile: Un Camino hacia el Desarrollo y la Plena Democracia*. Talcahuano, Chile: Pontificia Universidad Católica de Chile.

Gnjatović, Dragana. 2009. "Foreign Long Term Government Loans of Serbia 1862–1914." SEEMHN paper 11, National Bank of Serbia. https://ideas.repec.org/p/nsb/seemhn/11.html.

Godsey, William D. 2018. *The Sinews of Habsburg Power: Lower Austria in a Fiscal-Military State 1650–1820*. Oxford, UK: Oxford University Press.

Goenaga, Agustín, Oriol Sabaté Domingo, and Jan Teorell. 2018. "War and State Capacity in the Long Nineteenth Century." Working paper 6, Lund University, Department of Political Science.

Goetzmann, William N., Andrey D. Ukhov, and Ning Zhu. 2007. "China and the World Financial Markets 1870–1939: Modern Lessons from Historical Globalization." *Economic History Review* 60(2):267–312.

Gordon, Donald C. 1965. *The Dominion Partnership in Imperial Defense, 1870–1914*. Baltimore: Johns Hopkins University Press.

Goyer, Doreen S., and Gera E. Draaijer. 1992a. *The Handbook of National Population Censuses: Africa and Asia*. Westport, CT: Greenwood Press.

Goyer, Doreen S., and Gera E. Draaijer. 1992b. *The Handbook of National Population Censuses: Europe*. Westport, CT: Greenwood Press.

Goyer, Doreen S., and Gera E. Draaijer. 1992c. *The Handbook of National Population Censuses: Latin America and the Caribbean, North America, and Oceania*. Westport, CT: Greenwood Press.

Grafe, Regina. 2011. *Distant Tyranny: Markets, Power, and Backwardness in Spain, 1650–1800*. Princeton, NJ: Princeton University Press.

Grafe, Regina, and Alejandra Irigoin. 2012. "A Stakeholder Empire: The Political Economy of Spanish Imperial Rule in America." *Economic History Review* 65(2):609–651.

Grant, Jonathan A. 2007. *Rulers, Guns, and Money: The Global Arms Trade in the Age of Imperialism*. Cambridge, MA: Harvard University Press.

Green, E.H.H. 1992. "The Influence of the City over British Economic Policy." In *Finance and Financiers in European History 1880–1960*, ed. Youssef Cassis, pp. 193–218. New York: Cambridge University Press.

Greif, Avner, Paul Milgrom, and Barry R. Weingast. 1994. "Coordination, Commitment, and Enforcement: The Case of the Merchant Guild." *Journal of Political Economy* 102(4):745–776.

Guardado, Jenny. 2018. "Office-Selling, Corruption, and Long-Term Development in Peru." *American Political Science Review* 112(4):971–995.

Güran, Tevfik. 2003. *Ottoman Financial Statistics, Budgets, 1841–1918*. Ankara, Turkey: State Institute of Statistics.

Guvemli, Oktay, and Batuhan Guvemli. 2007. "The Birth and Development of the Accounting Method in the Middle East." Technical report, Marmara University.

Gwaindepi, Abel, and Krige Siebrits. 2020. "How Mineral Discoveries Shaped the Fiscal System of South Africa." In *Fiscal Capacity and the Colonial State in Asia and Africa, c. 1850–1960*, ed. Ewout Frankema and Anne Booth, pp. 264–298. New York: Cambridge University Press.

Habyarimana, James, Macartan Humphreys, Daniel N. Posner, and Jeremy M. Weinstein. 2007. "Why Does Ethnic Diversity Undermine Public Goods Provision?" *American Political Science Review* 101(4):709–725.

Halperin Donghi, Tulio. 1982. *Guerra y Finanzas en los Orígenes del Estado Argentino (1791–1850)*. Buenos Aires: Belgrano.

Handley, Paul M. 2006. *The King Never Smiles: A Biography of Thailand's Bhumibol Adulyadej*. New Haven, CT: Yale University Press.

Hansen, Bent. 1983. "Interest Rates and Foreign Capital in Egypt under British Occupation." *Journal of Economic History* 43(4):867–884.

Harwich Vallenilla, Nikita. 1976. "El Modelo Económico del Liberalismo Amarillo: Historia de un Fracaso 1888–1908." In *Política y Economía en Venezuela, 1810–1976*, ed. Miguel Izard, pp. 205–246. Caracas: Fundación John Boulton.

Hassan, Mai. 2020. *Regime Threats and State Solutions: Bureaucratic Loyalty and Embeddedness in Kenya*. New York: Cambridge University Press.

Hawke, G. R. 1970. *Railways and Economic Growth in England and Wales, 1840–70*. New York: Oxford University Press.

He, Wenkai. 2013. *Paths toward the Modern Fiscal State*. Cambridge, MA: Harvard University Press.

Headlam, Cecil. 1936. "The Race for the Interior, 1881–1895." In *Cambridge History of the British Empire*, ed. A. P. Newton and E. A. Benians, pp. 507–538. Vol. VIII. New York: Cambridge University Press.

Heise González, Julio. 1974. *Historia de Chile: El Periodo Parlamentario, 1861–1925*. Santiago: Editorial Andres Bello.

Hensel, Paul R. 2018. ICOW Colonial History Data Set, version 1.1. http://www.paulhensel.org /icowcol.html.

Herbst, Jeffrey. 1990. "War and the State in Africa: Comparative Lessons in Authority and Control." *International Security* 14(4):117–139.

Herbst, Jeffrey. 2000. *States and Power in Africa*. Princeton, NJ: Princeton University Press.

Herranz-Loncán, Alfonso. 2003. "¿Fracasó el Sistema Ferroviario en España? Reflexiones en Torno a la 'Paradoja del Ferrocarril Español.'" *Revista de Historia Industrial* 23:39–64.

Herranz-Loncán, Alfonso. 2006. "Railroad Impact in Backward Economies: Spain, 1850–1913." *Journal of Economic History* 66(4):853–881.

Herranz-Loncán, Alfonso. 2011. "The Role of Railways in Export-Led Growth: The Case of Uruguay, 1870–1913." *Economic History of Developing Regions* 26(2):1–32.

Hess, Robert L. 1970. *Ethiopia: The Modernization of Autocracy*. Ithaca, NY: Cornell University Press.

Hierro, María José, and Didac Queralt. 2021. "The Divide over Independence: Explaining Preferences for Secession in an Advanced Open Economy." *American Journal of Political Science* 65(2):422–442.

Hintze, Otto. 1975. "Military Organization and the Organization of the State." In *The Historical Essays of Otto Hintze*, ed. Felix Gilbert, pp. 178–215. New York: Oxford University Press.

Hobsbawm, Eric. 1987. *The Age of Empire: 1875–1914*. New York: Pantheon Books.

Hobson, C. K. 1914. *The Export of Capital*. London: Constable.

Hobson, J. A. 1902. *Imperialism: A Study*. New York: James Pott.

Hoffman, Philip, Gilles Postel-Vinay, and Jean-Laurent Rosenthal. 2000. *The Political Economy of Credit in Paris, 1660–1870*. Chicago: University of Chicago Press.

Hoffman, Philip T. 1994. "Early Modern France, 1450–1700." In *Fiscal Crises, Liberty, and Representative Government, 1450–1789*, ed. Philip T. Hoffman and Kathryn Norberg, pp. 226–252. Stanford, CA: Stanford University Press.

Hoffman, Philip T. 2015. *Why Did Europe Conquer the World?* Princeton, NJ: Princeton University Press.

Hoffman, Philip T., and Jean-Laurent Rosenthal. 2000. "Divided We Fall: The Political Economy of Warfare and Taxation." Mimeo, California Institute of Technology.

Hollett, David. 2008. *More Precious Than Gold: The Story of the Peruvian Guano Trade*. Madison, NJ: Fairleigh Dickinson University Press.

Hollyer, James R., Peter Rosendorff, and James Raymond Vreeland. 2018. *Information, Democracy and Autocracy: Economic Transparency and Political (In)Stability*. New York: Cambridge University Press.

Holsti, Kalevi J. 1996. *The State, War, and the State of War*. New York: Cambridge University Press.

Homer, Sidney, and Richard Sylla. 2005. *A History of Interest Rates*. 4th ed. Hoboken, NJ: Wiley.

Horn, Sebastian, Carmen Reinhart, and Christoph Trebesch. 2020. "China's Overseas Lending." Technical report 2132, Kiel working paper.

Huenemann, Ralph William. 1984. *The Dragon and the Iron Horse: The Economics of Railroads in China, 1876–1937*. Cambridge, MA: Harvard University Asia Center Publications Program.

Hui, Victoria Tin-bor. 2004. "Toward a Dynamic Theory of International Politics: Insights from Comparing Ancient China and Early Modern Europe." *International Organization* 58(1):175–205.

Huillery, Elise. 2009. "History Matters: The Long-Term Impact of Colonial Public Investments in French West Africa." *American Economic Journal: Applied Economics* 1(2):176–215.

Humud, Carlos. 1969. "El Sector Público Chileno entre 1830 y 1930." PhD thesis, University of Chile.

Hyde, Charles C. 1922. "The Negotiation of External Loans with Foreign Governments." *American Journal of International Law* 16(4):523–541.

Hyde, Susan D. 2007. "The Observer Effect in International Politics: Evidence from a Natural Experiment." *World Politics* 60(1):37–63.

Imlah, Albert H. 1958. *Economic Elements in the Pax Britannica*. New York: Russell & Russell.

Ingham, Geoffrey. 1984. *Capitalism Divided? The City and Industry in British Social Development*. London: Macmillan.

Ingram, James C. 1955. *Economic Change in Thailand since 1850*. Stanford, CA: Stanford University Press.

Irmscher, Tobias H. 2007. "Pledge of State Territory and Property." *Max Planck Encyclopedia of Public International Law*. https://opil.ouplaw.com/view/10.1093/law:epil/9780199231690/law-9780199231690-e1079.

Iyer, Lakshmi. 2010. "Direct versus Indirect Colonial Rule in India: Long-Term Consequences." *Review of Economics and Statistics* 92(4):693–713.

Jansen, Marius B. 2000. *The Making of Modern Japan*. Cambridge, MA: Belknap Press.

Jeanne, Olivier. 2009. "Debt Maturity and the International Financial Architecture." *American Economic Review* 99(5):2135–2148.

Jenks, Leland Hamilton. 1927. *The Migration of British Capital to 1875*. New York: Alfred A. Knopf.

Jha, Saumitra. 2012. "Sharing the Future: Financial Innovation and Innovators in Solving the Political Economy Challenges of Development." In *Institutions and Comparative Economic Development*, ed. Masahiko Aoki, Timur Kuran, and Gerard Roland, pp. 131–151. New York: Palgrave Macmillan.

Jha, Saumitra. 2015. "Financial Asset Holdings and Political Attitudes: Evidence from Revolutionary England." *Quarterly Journal of Economics* 130(3):1485–1545.

Johnson, Noel D. 2015. "Taxes, National Identity, and Nation Building." Working paper 15–33, George Mason University.

Johnson, Noel D., and Mark Koyama. 2014. "Tax Farming and the Origins of State Capacity in England and France." *Explorations in Economic History* 51:1–20.

Jones, Charles A. 1979. "The British Investor and London Press Coverage of Argentine Affairs, 1870–90." Working paper 2, Centre of Latin American Studies. University of Cambridge.

Jones, Daniel M., Stuart A. Bremer, and J. David Singer. 1996. "Militarized Interstate Disputes, 1816–1992: Rationale, Coding Rules, and Empirical Patterns." *Conflict Management and Peace Science* 15(2):163–213.

Jones, Eric L. 1981. *The European Miracle*. New York: Cambridge University Press.

Jordà, Òscar, Moritz Schularick, and Alan M. Taylor. 2016. "Macrofinancial History and the New Business Cycle Facts." In *NBER Macroeconomics Annual 2016, Volume 31*, pp. 213–263. Chicago: University of Chicago Press.

Jorgensen, Erika, and Jeffrey Sachs. 1988. "Default and Renegotiation of Latin American Foreign Bonds in the Interwar Period." NBER working paper 2636.

Judd, Denis, and Keith Surridge. 2002. *The Boer War*. London: John Murray.

Kang, David C. 2020. "International Order in Historical East Asia: Tribute and Hierarchy beyond Sinocentrism and Eurocentrism." *International Organization* 74(1):65–93.

Karaman, Kivanç K., and Şevket Pamuk. 2010. "Ottoman State Finances in European Perspective, 1500–1914." *Journal of Economic History* 70(3):593–629.

Karaman, Kivanç K., and Şevket Pamuk. 2013. "Different Paths to the Modern State in Europe: The Interaction between Warfare, Economic Structure, and Political Regime." *American Political Science Review* 107:603–626.

Kaur, Amarjit. 1980. "The Impact of Railroads on the Malayan Economy, 1874–1941." *Journal of Asian Studies* 39(4):693–710.

Keller, Edmond J. 1991. *Revolutionary Ethiopia: From Empire to People's Republic*. Bloomington: Indiana University Press.

Kelly, Trish. 1998. "Ability and Willingness to Pay in the Age of Pax Britannica, 1890–1914." *Explorations in Economic History* 35(1):31–58.

Kennedy, Hugh. 2015. "The Middle East in Islamic Late Antiquity." In *Fiscal Regimes and the Political Economy of Premodern States*, ed. Andrew Monson and Walter Scheidel, pp. 390–403. New York: Cambridge University Press.

Kentikelenis, Alexander E., Thomas H. Stubbs, and Lawrence P. King. 2016. "IMF Conditionality and Development Policy Space, 1985–2014." *Review of International Political Economy* 23(4):543–582.

Kesner, Richard M. 1977. "Builders of Empire: The Role of the Crown Agents in Imperial Development, 1880–1914." *Journal of Imperial and Commonwealth History* 5(3): 310–330.

Kesner, Richard M. 1981. *Economic Control and Colonial Development: Crown Colony Financial Management in the Age of Joseph Chamberlain*. Westport, CT: Greenwood Press.

Killingray, David. 1989. "Colonial Warfare in West Africa, 1870–1914." In *Imperialism and War: Essays on Colonial Wars in Asia and Africa*, ed. J. A. de Moor and H. L. Wesseling, pp. 146–167. Leiden, Netherlands: Leiden University Press.

Kindleberger, Charles P. 1996. *Manias, Panics, and Crashes: A History of Financial Crises*. New York: John Wiley & Sons.

King, Frank H. H. 2006. "The Boxer Indemnity: 'Nothing but Bad.'" *Modern Asian Studies* 40(3):663–689.

Kirshner, Jonathan. 2007. *Appeasing Bankers: Financial Caution on the Road to War*. Princeton, NJ: Princeton University Press.

Kissi, Edward. 2000. "The Politics of Famine in U.S. Relations with Ethiopia, 1950–1970." *International Journal of African Historical Studies* 33(1):113–131.

Klein, Herbert S. 2011. *A Concise History of Bolivia*. New York: Cambridge University Press.

Kohli, Atul. 2019. *Imperialism and the Developing World: How Britain and the United States Shaped the Global Periphery*. Oxford, UK: Oxford University Press.

Köll, Elisabeth. 2019. *Railroads and the Transformation of China*. Vol. 52. Cambridge, MA: Harvard University Press.

Koyama, Mark, Chiaki Moriguchi, and Tuan-Hwee Sng. 2018. "Geopolitics and Asia's Little Divergence: State Building in China and Japan after 1850." *Journal of Economic Behavior & Organization* 155:178–204.

Krasner, Stephen D. 1999. *Sovereignty: Organized Hypocrisy*. Princeton, NJ: Princeton University Press.

Krasner, Stephen D., and Jeremy M. Weinstein. 2014. "Improving Governance from the Outside In." *Annual Review of Political Science* 17(1):123–145.

Kreps, Sarah E. 2018. *Taxing Wars: The American Way of War Finance and the Decline of Democracy*. New York: Oxford University Press.

Krüger, D. W. 1969. "The British Imperial Factor in South Africa from 1879 to 1910." In *Colonialism in Africa 1870–1960: Volume 1: The History and Politics of Colonialism 1870–1914*, ed. L. H. Gann and Peter Duignam, pp. 325–351. New York: Cambridge University Press.

Kuntz Ficker, Sandra, ed. 2015. *Historia Mínima de la Expansión Ferroviaria en América Latina*. Mexico City: El Colegio de Mexico.

Kurtz, Marcus J. 2013. *Latin American State Building in Comparative Perspective: Social Foundations of Institutional Order*. New York: Cambridge University Press.

Lake, David A. 2016. *The Statebuilder's Dilemma: On the Limits of Foreign Intervention*. Ithaca, NY: Cornell University Press.

Lange, Matthew. 2009. *Lineages of Despotism and Development: British Colonialism and State Power*. Chicago: University of Chicago Press.

Lange, Matthew, James Mahoney, and Matthias vom Hau. 2006. "Colonialism and Development: A Comparative Analysis of Spanish and British Colonies." *American Journal of Sociology* 111(5):1412–1462.

Lange, Matthew K. 2004. "British Colonial Legacies and Political Development." *World Development* 32(6):905–922.

Le Bris, David, and Ronan Tallec. 2019. "Constraints on the Executive: A Reappraisal of the French and English Old Regimes through Parliamentary Activities." Working paper, SSRN. http://dx.doi.org/10.2139/ssrn.3492276.

Lee, Alexander. 2017. "Redistributive Colonialism: The Long Term Legacy of International Conflict in India." *Politics & Society* 45(2):173–224.

Lee, Jong-Wha, and Hanol Lee. 2016. "Human Capital in the Long Run." *Journal of Development Economics* 122:147–169.

Lee, Melissa M., and Nan Zhang. 2017. "Legibility and the Informational Foundations of State Capacity." *Journal of Politics* 79(1):118–132.

Lemi, Adugna. 2007. "Anatomy of Foreign Aid to Ethiopia: 1960–2003." Working paper, SSRN. http://dx.doi.org/10.2139/ssrn.1084936.

Lenin, Vladimir. 1934. *Imperialism: The Highest Stage of Capitalism*. London: Martin Lawrence.

Levandis, John A. 1944. *The Greek Foreign Debt and the Great Powers, 1821–1898*. New York: Columbia University Press.

Levi, Margaret. 1988. *Of Rule and Revenue*. Berkeley: University of California Press.

Levi, Margaret. 1997. *Consent, Dissent, and Patriotism*. New York: Cambridge University Press.

Lewis, Colin M. 1983. "The Financing of Railway Development in Latin America, 1850–1914." *Ibero-amerikanisches Archiv* 9(3/4):255–278.

Lieberman, Evans S. 2003. *Race and Regionalism in the Politics of Taxation in Brazil and South Africa*. New York: Cambridge University Press.

Lindert, Peter H. 2004. *Growing Public: Social Spending and Economic Growth since the Eighteenth Century*. New York: Cambridge University Press.

Lindert, Peter H., and Peter J. Morton. 1989. "How Sovereign Debt Has Worked." In *Developing Country Debt and Economic Performance*, ed. Jeffrey Sachs, pp. 39–106. Vol. 1. Chicago: University of Chicago Press.

Lipset, Seymour Martin. 1959. "Some Social Requisites of Democracy: Economic Development and Political Legitimacy." *American Political Science Review* 53(1):69–105.

Lipson, Charles. 1985. *Standing Guard: Protecting Foreign Capital in the Nineteenth and Twentieth Centuries*. Berkeley: University of California Press.

Logan, Carolyn. 2009. "Selected Chiefs, Elected Councillors and Hybrid Democrats: Popular Perspectives on the Co-existence of Democracy and Traditional Authority." *Journal of Modern African Studies* 47(1):101–128.

López-Alves, Fernando. 2000. *State Formation and Democracy in Latin America 1810–1900*. Durham, NC: Duke University Press.

López Jerez, Montserrat. 2020. "Colonial and Indigenous Institutions in the Fiscal Development of French Indochina." In *Fiscal Capacity and the Colonial State in Asia and Africa, c. 1850–1960*, ed. Ewout Frankema and Anne Booth, pp. 110–136. New York: Cambridge University Press.

Lucas, Robert E., and Nancy L. Stokey. 1983. "Optimal Fiscal and Monetary Policy in an Economy without Capital." *Journal of Monetary Economics* 12(1):55–93.

Ma, Debin. 2016. "The Rise of a Financial Revolution in Republican China in 1900–1937: An Institutional Narrative." Technical report 235/2016, London School of Economics.

Ma, Debin, and Jared Rubin. 2019. "The Paradox of Power: Principal-Agent Problems and Administrative Capacity in Imperial China (and Other Absolutist Regimes)." *Journal of Comparative Economics* 47(2):277–294.

Mahate, Ashraf A. 1994. "Contagion Effects of Three Late Nineteenth-Century British Bank Failures." *Business and Economic History* 12(1):102–115.

Makgala, Christian J. 2004. "Taxation in the Tribal Areas of the Bechuanaland Protectorate, 1899–1957." *Journal of African History* 45(2):279–303.

Mamalakis, Markos. 1976. "The Role of Government in the Resource Transfer and Resource Allocation Processes: The Chilean Nitrate Sector, 1880–1930." In *Government and Development*, ed. Gustav Ranis, pp. 178–209. New Haven, CT: Yale University Press.

Mamdani, Mahmood. 1996. *Citizen and Subject: Contemporary Africa and the Legacy of Late Colonialism*. Princeton, NJ: Princeton University Press.

Manin, Bernard. 1997. *The Principles of Representative Government*. New York: Cambridge University Press.

Mann, Michael. 1984. "The Autonomous Power of the State: Its Origins, Mechanisms and Results." *European Journal of Sociology* 25(2):185–213.

Manyazewal, Mekonnen. 2019. "Financing Ethiopia's Development." In *The Oxford Handbook of the Ethiopian Economy*, ed. Fantu Cheru, Christopher Cramer, and Arkebe Oqubay, pp. 175–190. New York: Oxford University Press.

Marcus, Harold G. 1969. "Imperialism and Expansionism in Ethiopia from 1865 to 1900." In *Colonialism in Africa 1870–1960: Volume 1: The History and Politics of Colonialism 1874–1914*, ed. L. H. Gann and Peter Duignan, pp. 420–461. New York: Cambridge University Press.

Marcus, Harold G. 2002. *A History of Ethiopia*. Berkeley: University of California Press.

Mares, Isabela, and Didac Queralt. 2015. "The Non-democratic Origins of Income Taxation." *Comparative Political Studies* 48(14):1974–2009.

Mares, Isabela, and Didac Queralt. 2020. "Fiscal Innovation in Nondemocratic Regimes: Elites and the Adoption of the Prussian Income Taxes of the 1890s." *Explorations in Economic History* 77:101340.

Marichal, Carlos. 1989. *A Century of Debt Crisis in Latin America*. Princeton, NJ: Princeton University Press.

Marichal, Carlos, and Guillermo Barragán. 2017. "Bancos Nacionales y Consolidación de Estados Nacionales: La Experiencia Latinoamericana, 1870–1890." In *Historia Bancaria y Monetaria de América Latina (Siglos XIX XX): Nuevas Perspectivas*, ed. Carlos Marichal and Thiago Gambi. Santander, Spain: Editorial de la Universidad de Cantabria and Universidade Federal de Alfenas.

Marongiu, Antonio. 1968. *Medieval Parliaments: A Comparative Study*. Translated by S. J. Woolf. London: Eyre & Spottiswoode.

Marshall, Monty G., and Keith Jaggers. 2000. *Polity IV Project: Political Regime Characteristics and Transitions, 1800–2010*. Center for International Development and Conflict Management, University of Maryland.

Maurer, Noel. 2013. *The Empire Trap: The Rise and Fall of U.S. Intervention to Protect American Property Overseas, 1893–2013*. Princeton, NJ: Princeton University Press.

Maurer, Noel, and Leticia Arroyo Abad. 2017. "Can Europe Run Greece? Lessons from U.S. Fiscal Receiverships in Latin America, 1904–31." Working paper, SSRN. https://ssrn.com/abstract=3026330.

Mauro, Paolo, Nathan Sussman, and Yishay Yafeh. 2006. *Emerging Markets and Financial Globalization: Sovereign Bond Spreads in 1870–1913 and Today*. Oxford, UK: Oxford University Press.

Mauro, Paolo, and Yishay Yafeh. 2003. "The Corporation of Foreign Bondholder." Technical report 03/17, IMF working paper.

McDonald, Patrick J. 2011. "Complicating Commitment: Free Resources, Power Shifts, and the Fiscal Politics of Preventive War." *International Studies Quarterly* 55(4):1095–1120.

McGreevey, William Paul. 1971. *An Economic History of Colombia, 1845–1930*. New York: Cambridge University Press.

McLean, David. 1976. "Finance and 'Informal Empire' before the First World War." *Economic History Review* 29(2):291–305.

Meissner, Christopher M. 2005. "A New World Order: Explaining the International Diffusion of the Gold Standard, 1870–1913." *Journal of International Economics* 66(2):385–406.

Melsheimer, Rudolph E., and Samuel Gardner. 1891. *The Law and Customs of the Stock Exchange*. Royal Exchange, London: Effigham Wilson & Co.

Menaldo, Victor. 2016. "The Fiscal Roots of Financial Underdevelopment." *American Journal of Political Science* 60(2):1540–5907.

Meng, Anne. 2020. *Constraining Dictatorship: From Personalized Rule to Institutionalized Regimes*. New York: Cambridge University Press.

Mengisteab, Kidane. 2002. "Ethiopia: State Building or Imperial Revival?" In *The African State: Reconsiderations*, ed. Abdi Ismail Samatar and Ahmed I. Samatar, pp. 177–190. Portsmouth, NH: Heinemann.

Mennasemay, Maimire. 2005. "Ethiopian History and Critical Theory: The Case of Adwa." In *The Battle of Adwa: Reflections on Ethiopia's Historic Victory against European Colonialism*, ed. Paulos Milkias and Getachew Metaferia. New York: Algora Publishing.

Meszaros, Paul Frank. 1973. "The Corporation of Foreign Bondholders and British Diplomacy in Egypt 1876 to 1882: The Efforts of an Interest Group in Policy-Making." PhD thesis, Loyola University.

Meyer, Josefin, Carmen M. Reinhart, and Christoph Trebesch. 2019. "Sovereign Bonds since Waterloo." NBER working paper 25543.

Michalopoulos, Stelios, and Elias Papaioannou. 2018. "Historical Legacies and African Development." NBER working paper 25278.

Michie, Ranald C. 2006. *The Global Securities Market: A History*. New York: Oxford University Press.

Mitchell, Brian. 2005. *International Historical Statistics: Europe, 1750–2005*. London: Macmillan.

Mitchener, Kris James, and Marc Weidenmier. 2005. "Empire, Public Goods, and the Roosevelt Corollary." *Journal of Economic History* 65(3):658–692.

Mitchener, Kris James, and Marc D. Weidenmier. 2009. "Are Hard Pegs Ever Credible in Emerging Markets? Evidence from the Classical Gold Standard." NBER working paper 15401.

Mitchener, Kris James, and Marc D. Weidenmier. 2010. "Supersanctions and Sovereign Debt Repayment." *Journal of International Money and Finance* 29(1):19–36.

Mkandawire, Thandika. 2010. "On Tax Efforts and Colonial Heritage in Africa." *Journal of Development Studies* 46(10):1647–1669.

Mokyr, Joel. 1991. *The Lever of Riches: Technological Creativity and Economic Progress.* New York: Oxford University Press.

Mokyr, Joel. 2017. *A Culture of Growth: The Origins of the Modern Economy.* Princeton, NJ: Princeton University Press.

Moor, J. A., and H. L. Wesseling, eds. 1989. *Imperialism and War: Essays on Colonial Wars in Asia and Africa.* Leiden, Netherlands: Leiden University Press.

Moore, Mick. 1998. "Death without Taxes: Democracy, State Capacity, and Aid Dependence in the Fourth World." In *The Democratic Developmental State: Political and Institutional Design,* ed. Mark Robinson and Gordon White, pp. 84–121. New York: Oxford University Press.

Morrison, Kevin M. 2009. "Oil, Nontax Revenue, and the Redistributional Foundations of Regime Stability." *International Organization* 63:107–138.

Mosley, Layna. 2003. *Global Capital and National Governments.* New York: Cambridge University Press.

Moss, Todd J., Gunilla Pettersson Gelander, and Nicolas van de Walle. 2006. "An Aid-Institutions Paradox? A Review Essay on Aid Dependency and State Building in Sub-Saharan Africa." Center for Global Development, working paper 74.

Mousnier, Roland. 1974. *The Institutions of France under the Absolute Monarchy, 1598–1789: The Organs of State and Society.* Chicago: University of Chicago Press.

Müller-Crepon, Carl, Philipp Hunziker, and Lars-Erik Cederman. 2021. "Roads to Rule, Roads to Rebel: Relational State Capacity and Conflict in Africa." *Journal of Conflict Resolution* 65(2–3):563–590.

Nadal, Jordi. 1975. *El Fracaso de la Revolución Industrial en España, 1814–1913.* Esplugues de Llobregat, Spain: Ariel.

Nakabayashi, Masaki. 2012. "The Rise of a Japanese Fiscal State." In *The Rise of Fiscal States: A Global History, 1500–1914,* ed. Bartolomé Yun-Casalilla and Patrick K. O'Brien, pp. 378–409. New York: Cambridge University Press.

Neal, Larry D. 1990. *The Rise of Financial Capitalism.* New York: Cambridge University Press.

Neal, Larry D. 1998. "The Financial Crisis of 1825 and the Restructuring of the British Financial Systems." *Federal Reserve Bank of St. Louis Review* 80:53–76.

Neal, Larry. 2015. *A Concise History of International Finance: From Babylon to Bernanke.* New York: Cambridge University Press.

Neal, Larry, and Lance Davis. 2006. "The Evolution of the Structure and Performance of the London Stock Exchange in the First Global Financial Market, 1812–1914." *European Review of Economic History* 10(3):279–300.

Niskanen, William A. 1994. *Bureaucracy and Public Economics.* Hants, UK: Edward Elgar.

North, Douglass C. 1981. *Structure and Change in Economic History.* New York: W. W. Norton.

North, Douglass C., and Barry R. Weingast. 1989. "Constitutions and Commitment: The Evolution of Institutions Governing Public Choice in Seventeenth-Century England." *Journal of Economic History* 49(4):803–832.

Nunn, Nathan, and Diego Puga. 2012. "Ruggedness: The Blessing of Bad Geography in Africa." *Review of Economics and Statistics* 94(1):20–36.

Nunn, Nathan, and Leonard Wantchekon. 2011. "The Slave Trade and the Origins of Mistrust in Africa." *American Economic Review* 101(7):3221–3252.

Nye, James. 2015. "Boom, Crisis, Bust: Speculators, Promoters, and City Journalists, 1880–1914." In *The Media and Financial Crises: Comparative and Historical Perspectives*, ed. Steve Schifferes and Richard Roberts, pp. 215–226. London: Routledge Taylor & Francis.

Nye, John V. C. 2007. *War, Wine, and Taxes: The Political Economy of Anglo-French Trade, 1689–1900.* Princeton, NJ: Princeton University Press.

O'Brien, Patrick K. 1988. "The Costs and Benefits of British Imperialism 1846–1914." *Past & Present* 120:163–200.

O'Brien, Patrick K. 2001. "Fiscal Exceptionalism: Great Britain and Its European Rivals from Civil War to Triumph at Trafalgar and Waterloo." Working paper 65, London School of Economics, Department of Economic History.

O'Brien, Patrick K., and Philip A. Hunt. 1993. "The Rise of a Fiscal State in England, 1485–1815." *Historical Research* 66:129–176.

O'Brien, Thomas F. 1979. "Chilean Elites and Foreign Investors: Chilean Nitrate Policy, 1880–82." *Journal of Latin American Studies* 11(1):101–121.

O'Brien, Thomas F. 1980. "The Antofagasta Company: A Case Study of Peripheral Capitalism." *Hispanic American Historical Review* 60(1):1–31.

Obstfeld, Maurice, and Alan M. Taylor. 2004. *Global Capitalism: Integration, Crisis, and Growth.* New York: Cambridge University Press.

OECD. 2017. "Current Account Balance." https://www.oecd-ilibrary.org/content/data/b2f74f3a-en.

Officer, Lawrence. 2008. "Gold Standard." In *EH.net Encyclopedia*, ed. Robert Whaples. http://eh.net/encyclopedia/gold-standard/.

Onji, Kazuki, and John P. Tang. 2017. "Taxes and the Choice of Organizational Form in Late Nineteenth Century Japan." *Journal of Economic History* 77(2):440–472.

Onorato, Massimiliano Gaetano, Kenneth Scheve, and David Stasavage. 2014. "Technology and the Era of the Mass Army." *Journal of Economic History* 74(2):449–481.

Ortega, Luis. 1984. "Nitrates, Chilean Entrepreneurs and the Origins of the War of the Pacific." *Journal of Latin American Studies* 16(2):337–380.

Orten, Remzi. 2006. "Development of Accounting in the First Half of the 20th Century in Turkey." Technical report, Gazi University.

Oszlak, Oscar. 2004. *La Formación del Estado Argentino.* Villa Vallester, Argentina: Ariel.

Outhwaite, R. B. 1966. "The Trials of Foreign Borrowing: The English Crown and the Antwerp Money Market in the Mid-Sixteenth Century." *Economic History Review* 19(2):289–305.

Outhwaite, R. B. 1971. "Royal Borrowing in the Reign of Elizabeth I: The Aftermath of Antwerp." *English Historical Review* 86(339):251–263.

Owen, Roger. 1981. *The Middle East in the World Economy 1800–1914.* New York: I. B. Tauris.

Özmen, Erdal, and Özge Doğanay Yaşar. 2016. "Emerging Market Sovereign Bond Spreads, Credit Ratings and Global Financial Crisis." *Economic Modelling* 59:93–101.

Paglayan, Agustina S. 2021. "The Non-democratic Roots of Mass Education: Evidence from 200 Years." *American Political Science Review* 115(1):179–198.

Paik, Christopher, and Jessica Vechbanyongratana. 2019. "Path to Centralization and Development: Evidence from Siam." *World Politics* 71(2):289–331.

Pakenham, Thomas. 2000. *The Boer War.* London: Abacus.

Paler, Laura. 2013. "Keeping the Public Purse: An Experiment in Windfalls, Taxes, and the Incentives to Restrain Government." *American Political Science Review* 107(4):706–725.

Pamuk, Şevket. 1987. *The Ottoman Empire and European Capitalism, 1820–1913: Trade, Investment and Production.* New York: Cambridge University Press.

Pamuk, Şevket. 2018. *Uneven Centuries: Economic Development of Turkey since 1820*. Princeton, NJ: Princeton University Press.

Panizza, Ugo, Federico Sturzenegger, and Jeromin Zettelmeyer. 2009. "The Economics and Law of Sovereign Debt and Default." *Journal of Economic Literature* 47(3):651–698.

Pankhurst, Richard. 1968. *Economic History of Ethiopia 1800–1935*. Addis Ababa: Haile Sellasie I University Press.

Pastén, Roberto. 2017. "The Political Economy of the Fiscal Deficit of Nineteenth-Century Chile." Technical report, CEPAL review 121.

Peacock, Alan T., and Jack Wiseman. 1961. *The Growth of Public Expenditure in the United Kingdom*. Princeton, NJ: Princeton University Press.

Peres-Cajías, José Alejandro. 2014. "Bolivian Public Finances, 1882–2010: The Challenge to Make Social Spending Sustainable." *Revista de Historia Económica/Journal of Iberian and Latin American Economic History* 32(1):77–117.

Perez, Louis A., and Deborah M. Weissman. 2006. "Public Power and Private Purpose: Odious Debt and the Political Economy of Hegemony." *North Carolina Journal of International Law* 32(4):699–748.

Peters, Harold Edwin. 1934. *The Foreign Debt of the Argentine Republic*. Baltimore: Johns Hopkins University Press.

Peterson, Niels. 2002. "Gentlemanly and Not-So-Gentlemanly Imperialism in China before the First World War." In *Gentlemanly Capitalism, Imperialism and Global History*, ed. Shigeru Akita, pp. 103–122. New York: Palgrave Macmillan.

Pitkin, Hanna F. 1967. *The Concept of Representation*. Berkeley: University of California Press.

Platt, D.C.M. 1968. *Finance, Trade, and Politics in British Foreign Policy: 1815–1914*. Oxford, UK: Clarendon Press.

Poast, Paul. 2015. "Central Banks at War." *International Organization* 69(1):63–95.

Polanyi, Karl. 2001. *The Great Transformation: The Political and Economic Origins of Our Time*. 2nd ed. Boston: Beacon Press.

Polo Muriel, Francisco. 1998. "El Ferrocarril en Colombia, Venezuela y Ecuador (1855–1995): Un Análisis Comparativo." In *Historia de los Ferrocarriles de Iberoamérica (1837–1995)*, ed. Jesús Sanz Fernández, pp. 211–248. Madrid: Ministerio de Fomento.

Porter, Bruce D. 1994. *War and the Rise of the State: The Military Foundations of Modern Politics*. New York: Free Press.

Potter, Mark. 2000. "Good Offices: Intermediation by Corporate Bodies in Early Modern French Public Finance." *Journal of Economic History* 60(3):599–626.

Pratt, Edwin A. 1916. *The Rise of Rail-Power in War and Conquest, 1833–1914*. Philadelphia: JB Lippincott.

Prestwich, Michael. 1979. "Italian Merchants in Late Thirteenth and Early Fourteenth Century England." In *The Dawn of Modern Banking*, ed. Center for Medieval and Renaissance Studies at UCLA, pp. 77–104. New Haven, CT: Yale University Press.

Prichard, Wilson. 2015. *Taxation, Responsiveness, and Accountability in Sub-Saharan Africa: The Dynamics of Tax Bargaining*. New York: Cambridge University Press.

Quataert, Donald. 1977. "Limited Revolution: The Impact of the Anatolian Railway on Turkish Transportation and the Provisioning of Istanbul, 1890–1908." *Business History Review* 51(2):139–160.

Queralt, Didac. 2015. "From Mercantilism to Free Trade: A History of Fiscal Capacity Building." *Quarterly Journal of Political Science* 10(2):221–273.

Queralt, Didac. 2019. "War, International Finance, and Fiscal Capacity in the Long Run." *International Organization* 73(4):713–753.

Rajan, Raghuram, and Luigi Zingales. 1998. "Financial Dependence and Growth." *American Economic Review* 88(3):559–586.

Ralston, David B. 1990. *Importing the European Army: The Introduction of European Military Techniques and Institutions in the Extra-European World, 1600–1914*. Chicago: University of Chicago Press.

Ram, K. V. 1981. "British Government, Finance Capitalists and the French Jibuti-Addis Ababa Railway 1898–1913." *Journal of Imperial and Commonwealth History* 9(2):146–168.

Ramirez, Francisco O., and John Boli. 1987. "The Political Construction of Mass Schooling: European Origins and Worldwide Institutionalization." *Sociology of Education* 60(1): 2–17.

Ramírez, María Teresa. 2001. "Los Ferrocarriles y su Impacto sobre la Economía Colombiana." *Revista de Historia Económica/Journal of Iberian and Latin American Economic History* 19(1):81–122.

Ramírez Necochea, Hernán. 1969. *Balmaceda y la Contrarevolución de 1891*. Santiago: Editorial Universitaria.

Ramseyer, J. Mark, and Frances M. Rosenbluth. 1998. *The Politics of Oligarchy: Institutional Choice in Imperial Japan*. New York: Cambridge University Press.

Ranger, T. O. 1969. "African Reactions to the Imposition of Colonial Rule in East and Central Africa." In *Colonialism in Africa 1870–1960: The History and Politics of Colonialism*, ed. L. H. Gann and Peter Duignan, pp. 293–324. Vol. I. New York: Cambridge University Press.

Rasler, Karen A., and William R. Thompson. 1985. "War Making and State Making: Governmental Expenditures, Tax Revenues, and Global Wars." *American Political Science Review* 79(2):491–507.

Reid, Richard. 2012. *Warfare in African History*. New York: Cambridge University Press.

Reinhart, Carmen M., and Kenneth S. Rogoff. 2009. *This Time Is Different*. Princeton, NJ: Princeton University Press.

Reinhart, Carmen M., Kenneth S. Rogoff, Christoph Trebesch, and Vincent Reinhart. 2018. *Global Crises Data by Country by the Behavioral and Financial Stability Project*. Harvard Business School. https://www.hbs.edu/behavioral-finance-and-financial-stability/data/Pages/global.aspx.

Reinhart, Carmen M., and Christoph Trebesch. 2015. "The Pitfalls of External Dependence: Greece, 1829–2015." NBER working paper 21664.

Reinhart, Carmen M., and Christoph Trebesch. 2016. "Sovereign Debt Relief and Its Aftermath." *Journal of the European Economic Association* 14(1):215–251.

Reinsch, Paul S. 1909. "Parliamentary Government in Chile." *American Political Science Review* 3(4):507–538.

Resende-Santos, João. 2007. *Neorealism, States, and the Modern Mass Army*. New York: Cambridge University Press.

Ricart-Huguet, Joan. 2021. "The Origins of Colonial Investments in Former British and French Africa." *British Journal of Political Science*, 1–22. https://www.cambridge.org/core/journals/british-journal-of-political-science/article/abs/origins-of-colonial-investments-in-former-british-and-french-africa/3C0185F5CD4D8755944E9D741757F9F3.

Rich, Norman. 1992. *Great Power Diplomacy 1814–1914*. Boston: McGraw-Hill.

Richards, John. 1995. *The Mughal Empire*. New York: Cambridge University Press.

Richardson, Lewis Frey. 1960. *Statistics of Deadly Quarrels*. Pittsburgh: Boxwood Press.

Riggs, Fred W. 1966. *Thailand: The Modernization of a Bureaucratic Polity*. Honolulu: East-West Center Press.

Riley, James C. 1980. *International Government Finance and the Amsterdam Capital Market, 1740–1815*. New York: Cambridge University Press.

Rippy, Fred J. 1959. *The Evolution of International Business 1800–1945: Volume 1: British Investment in Latin America, 1822–1949*. New York: Routledge.

Robinson, Ronald. 1978. "European Imperialism and Indigenous Reactions in British West Africa, 1880–1914." In *Expansion and Reaction*, ed. H. L. Wesseling, pp. 141–163. Leiden, Netherlands: Leiden University Press.

Rock, David. 2000. "State-Building and Political Systems in Nineteenth-Century Argentina and Uruguay." *Past & Present* (167):176–202.

Rogers, Clifford J. 1995. *The Military Revolution Debate: Readings on the Military Transformation of Early Modern Europe*. New York: Routledge.

Rogoff, Kenneth. 1999. "International Institutions for Reducing Global Financial Instability." *Journal of Economic Perspectives* 13(4):21–42.

Rojas Böttner, Andrés Sebastián. 2019. "El Fracaso de la Autonomía Municipal y la Consolidación del Centralismo en Chile (1891–1935)." PhD thesis, Autonomous University of Madrid.

Ronald, James H. 1935. "National Organizations for the Protection of Holders of Foreign Bonds." *George Washington Law Review* 3:411–453.

Rosenthal, Jean-Laurent, and R. Bin Wong. 2011. *Before and Beyond Divergence: The Politics of Economic Change in China and Europe*. Cambridge, MA: Harvard University Press.

Ross, Michael L. 2001. *Timber Booms and Institutional Breakdown in Southeast Asia*. New York: Cambridge University Press.

Ross, Michael L. 2004. "Does Taxation Lead to Representation?" *British Journal of Political Science* 34(2):229–249.

Ross, Michael L. 2012. *The Oil Curse: How Petroleum Wealth Shapes the Development of Nations*. Princeton, NJ: Princeton University Press.

Rouquié, Alain. 1989. *The Military and the State in Latin America*. Berkeley: University of California Press.

Roy, Tirthankar. 2013. *An Economic History of Early Modern India*. New York: Routledge.

Sabaté Domingo, Oriol, and José Peres-Cajías. 2020. "Linking War, Natural Resources and Public Revenues: The Case of the War of the Pacific (1879–1883)." Lund University, STANCE working paper, series 1.

Sachs, Jeffrey D., and John Williamson. 1985. "External Debt and Macroeconomic Performance in Latin America and East Asia." *Brookings Papers on Economic Activity* 1985(2): 523–573.

Saiegh, Sebastian. 2013. "Political Institutions and Sovereign Borrowing: Evidence from Nineteenth-Century Argentina." *Public Choice* 156:61–75.

Salvucci, Richard. 2006. "Export-Led Industrialization." In *The Cambridge Economic History of Latin America*, ed. Victor Bulmer-Thomas, John Coatsworth, and Roberto Cortes-Conde, pp. 249–292. Vol. 2. New York: Cambridge University Press.

Sambanis, Nicholas, and Branko Milanovic. 2014. "Explaining Regional Autonomy Differences in Decentralized Countries." *Comparative Political Studies* 47(13):1830–1855.

Sambanis, Nicholas, Stergios Skaperdas, and William C. Wohlforth. 2015. "Nation-Building through War." *American Political Science Review* 109(2):279–296.

Santamaría García, Antonio. 1998. "Los Ferrocarriles de Servicio Público, 1870–1990." *Anuario de Estudios Americanos* 55(2):475–606.

Sanz Fernández, Jesús, ed. 1998. *Historia de los Ferrocarriles de Iberoamérica, 1837–1995*. Madrid: CSIC.

Sarkees, Meredith Reid, and Frank Wayman. 2010. *Resort to War*. Thousand Oaks, CA: CQ Press.

Sater, William F. 1976. "Economic Nationalism and Tax Reform in Late Nineteenth Century Chile." *The Americas* 33(2):311–335.

Sater, William F. 1985. *Chile and the War of the Pacific*. Lincoln: University of Nebraska Press.

Sater, William F. 2007. *Andean Tragedy: Fighting the War of the Pacific, 1879–1884*. Lincoln: University of Nebraska Press.

Saylor, Ryan. 2014. *State Building in Boom Times: Commodities and Coalitions in Latin America and Africa*. New York: Oxford University Press.

Saylor, Ryan, and Nicholas C. Wheeler. 2017. "Paying for War and Building States: The Coalitional Politics of Debt Servicing and Tax Institutions." *World Politics* 69(2):366–408.

Scalabrini Ortíz, Raúl. 1972. *Historia de los Ferrocarriles Argentinos*. Buenos Aires: Plus Ultra.

Scheina, Robert L. 2003a. *Latin America's Wars Volume I: The Age of the Caudillo, 1791–1899*. Washington, DC: Potomac Books.

Scheina, Robert L. 2003b. *Latin America's Wars Volume II: The Age of the Professional Soldier, 1900–2001*. Washington, DC: Potomac Books.

Schenoni, Luis L. 2021. "Bringing War Back In: Victory and State Formation in Latin America." *American Journal of Political Science* 65(2):405–421.

Scheve, Kenneth, and David Stasavage. 2010. "The Conscription of Wealth: Mass Warfare and the Demand for Progressive Taxation." *International Organization* 64(4):529–561.

Scheve, Kenneth, and David Stasavage. 2012. "Democracy, War, and Wealth: Lessons from Two Centuries of Inheritance Taxation." *American Political Science Review* 106:81–102.

Scheve, Kenneth, and David Stasavage. 2016. *Taxing the Rich: A History of Fiscal Fairness in the United States and Europe*. Princeton, NJ: Princeton University Press.

Schultz, Kenneth A., and Barry R. Weingast. 1998. "Limited Government, Powerful States." In *Strategic Politicians, Institutions, and Foreign Policy*, ed. Randolph M. Silverson, pp. 15–49. Ann Arbor: University of Michigan Press.

Schultz, Kenneth A., and Barry R. Weingast. 2003. "The Democratic Advantage: Institutional Foundations of Financial Power in International Competition." *International Organization* 57(1):3–42.

Schumacher, Julian, Christoph Trebesch, and Henrik Enderlein. 2021. "Sovereign Defaults in Court." *Journal of International Economics* 131:103388.

Schumpeter, Joseph A. 1991. "The Crisis of the Tax States." In *Joseph A. Schumpeter: The Economics and Sociology of Capitalism*, ed. Richard Swedberg. Princeton, NJ: Princeton University Press.

Schwartz, Herman M. 1989. *In the Dominions of Debt: Historical Perspective on Dependent Development*. Ithaca, NY: Cornell University Press.

Scott, James C. 1998. *Seeing Like a State: How Certain Schemes to Improve the Human Condition Have Failed*. New Haven, CT: Yale University Press.

Scott, James C. 2017. *Against the Grain: A Deep History of the Earliest States*. New Haven, CT: Yale University Press.

Scott, John. 2003. "Transformations in the British Economic Elite." *Comparative Sociology* 2(1): 155–173.

Shaw, Stanford J. 1975. "The Nineteenth-Century Ottoman Tax Reforms and Revenue System." *International Journal of Middle East Studies* 6(4):421–459.

Shea, Patrick E. 2013. "Financing Victory: Sovereign Credit, Democracy, and War." *Journal of Conflict Resolution* 58(5):771–795.

Shea, Patrick E., and Paul Poast. 2018. "War and Default." *Journal of Conflict Resolution* 62(9): 1876–1904.

Sicotte, Richard, and Catalina Vizcarra. 2009. "War and Foreign Debt Settlement in Early Republican Spanish America." *Revista De Historia Económica/Journal of Iberian and Latin American Economic History* 27(2):47–289.

Sicotte, Richard, Catalina Vizcarra, and Kirsten Wandschneider. 2008. "The Fiscal Impact of the War of the Pacific." *Cliometrica* 3(2):97–121.

Sicotte, Richard, Catalina Vizcarra, and Kirsten Wandschneider. 2010. "Military Conquest and Sovereign Debt: Chile, Peru and the London Bond Market, 1876–1890." *Cliometrica* 4(3):293–319.

Silberman, Bernard S. 1993. *Cages of Reason: The Rise of the Rational State in France, Japan, the United States, and Great Britain.* Chicago: University of Chicago Press.

Skowronek, Stephen. 1982. *Building a New American State: The Expansion of National Administrative Capacities, 1877–1920.* New York: Cambridge University Press.

Slantchev, Branislav L. 2012. "Borrowed Power: Debt Finance and the Resort to Arms." *American Political Science Review* 106:787–809.

Slater, Dan. 2010. *Ordering Power: Contentious Politics and Authoritarian Leviathans in South Asia.* New York: Cambridge University Press.

Smith, Alastair. 2008. "The Perils of Unearned Income." *Journal of Politics* 70(3):780–793.

Smith, Joseph. 1979. *Illusions of Conflict: Anglo-American Diplomacy toward Latin America, 1865–1896.* Pittsburgh: University of Pittsburgh Press.

Sng, Tuan-Hwee, and Chiaki Moriguchi. 2014. "Asia's Little Divergence: State Capacity in China and Japan before 1850." *Journal of Economic Growth* 19:439–470.

Sobek, David. 2010. "Masters of Their Domains: The Role of State Capacity in Civil Wars." *Journal of Peace Research* 47(3):267–271.

Soifer, Hillel David. 2015. *State Building in Latin America.* New York: Cambridge University Press.

Sørensen, Georg. 2001. "War and State Making: Why Doesn't It Work in the Third World?" *Security Dialogue* 32:341–354.

Sprague, O.M.W. 1917. "Loans and Taxes in War Finance." *American Economic Review* 7(1):199–213.

Spruyt, Hendrik. 1994. *The Sovereign State and Its Competitors.* Princeton, NJ: Princeton University Press.

Stallings, Barbara. 1972. *Economic Dependency in Africa and Latin America.* Beverly Hills: Sage Publications.

Stallings, Barbara, and Robert Kaufman. 1989. "Debt and Democracy in the 1980s: The Latin American Experience." In *Debt and Democracy in Latin America*, ed. Barbara Stallings and Robert Kaufman, pp. 201–223. Boulder, CO: Westview Press.

Stasavage, David. 2011. *States of Credit: Size, Power, and the Development of European Polities.* Princeton, NJ: Princeton University Press.

Stasavage, David. 2016. "Representation and Consent: Why They Arose in Europe and Not Elsewhere." *Annual Review of Political Science* 19:145–162.

Stasavage, David. 2020. *The Decline and Rise of Democracy.* Princeton, NJ: Princeton University Press.

Stein, Burton. 1985. "State Formation and Economy Reconsidered: Part One." *Modern Asian Studies* 19(3):387–413.

Stern, Fritz. 1977. *Gold and Iron: Bismarck, Bleichröder, and the Building of the German Empire.* New York: Alfred A. Knopf.

Stone, Irving. 1992. *The Global Export of Capital from Great Britain, 1865–1914: A Statistical Survey.* New York: Macmillan.

Stubbs, Richard. 1999. "War and Economic Development: Export-Oriented Industrialization in East and Southeast Asia." *Comparative Politics* 31(3):337–355.

Subercaseaux, Guillermo. 1922. *Monetary and Banking Policy of Chile.* New York: Clarendon Press.

Summerhill, William. 2001. "Railroads and the Economic Development of Argentina, 1857–1913." Technical report, University of California, Los Angeles.

Summerhill, William R. 2003. *Order against Progress: Government, Foreign Investment, and Railroads in Brazil, 1854–1913.* Stanford, CA: Stanford University Press.

Summerhill, William R. 2005. "Big Social Savings in a Small Laggard Economy: Railroad-Led Growth in Brazil." *Journal of Economic History* 65(1):72–102.

Summerhill, William R. 2015. *Inglorious Revolution: Political Institutions, Sovereign Debt, and Financial Underdevelopment in Imperial Brazil*. New Haven, CT: Yale University Press.

Summers, Lawrence H. 2000. "International Financial Crises: Causes, Prevention, and Cures." *American Economic Review* 90(2):1–16.

Sunderland, David. 1999. "Principals and Agents: The Activities of the Crown Agents for the Colonies, 1880–1914." *Economic History Review* 52(2):284–306.

Sunderland, David. 2004. *Managing the British Empire: The Crown Agents 1833–1914*. London: Royal Historical Society.

Sussman, Nathan, and Yishay Yafeh. 2000. "Institutions, Reforms, and Country Risk: Lessons from Japanese Government Debt in the Meiji Era." *Journal of Economic History* 60(2): 442–467.

Suter, Christian. 1992. *Debt Cycles in the World-Economy: Foreign Loans, Financial Crises, and Debt Settlements, 1820–1990*. Boulder, CO: Westview Press.

Suter, Christian, and Hanspeter Stamm. 1992. "Coping with Global Debt Crises: Debt Settlements, 1820 to 1986." *Comparative Studies in Society and History* 34(4):645–678.

Suvla, Raafii-Sukru. 1966. "The Ottoman Debt, 1850–1939." In *The Economic History of the Middle East 1800–1914*, ed. Charles Issawi, pp. 94–106. Chicago: University of Chicago Press.

Suzuki, Toshio. 1994. *Japanese Government Loan Issues in the London Capital Market 1870–1913*. London: Athlone Press.

Svolik, Milan W. 2012. *The Politics of Authoritarian Rule*. New York: Cambridge University Press.

Swam, William L. 2009. *Japan's Economic Relations with Thailand*. Bangkok: White Lotus Press.

Sylla, Richard. 2002. "Financial Systems and Economic Modernization." *Journal of Economic History* 62(2):277–292.

Tait, Alan A., and Peter S. Heller. 1983. "Government Employment and Pay: Some International Comparisons." IMF occasional paper 24.

Tan, James. 2015. "The Roman Republic." In *Fiscal Regimes and the Political Economy of Premodern States*, ed. Andrew Monson and Walter Scheidel, pp. 208–228. New York: Cambridge University Press.

Tang, John P. 2014. "Railroad Expansion and Industrialization: Evidence from Meiji Japan." *Journal of Economic History* 74(3):863–886.

Taylor, Alan M. 1992. "External Dependence, Demographic Burdens, and Argentine Economic Decline after the Belle Époque." *Journal of Economic History* 52(4):907–936.

Taylor, Alan M. 2002. "A Century of Current Account Dynamics." *Journal of International Money and Finance* 21(6):725–748.

Taylor, Alan M. 2006. "Foreign Capital Flows." In *The Cambridge Economic History of Latin America*, ed. Victor Bulmer-Thomas, John Coatsworth, and Roberto Cortes-Conde, pp. 57–100. Vol. 2. New York: Cambridge University Press.

Taylor, Brian D., and Roxana Botea. 2008. "Tilly Tally: War-Making and State-Making in the Contemporary Third World." *International Studies Review* 10(1):27–56.

Taylor, James. 2015. "Financial Crises and the Birth of the Financial Press, 1825–1880." In *The Media and Financial Crises: Comparative and Historical Perspectives*, ed. Steve Schifferes and Richard Roberts, pp. 203–214. London: Routledge Taylor & Francis.

Tej Punnag. 1968. "The Provincial Administration of Siam from 1892 to 1915: A Study of the Creation, the Growth, the Achievements, and the Implications for Modern Siam, of the Ministry of the Interior under Prince Damrong Rachanuphap." PhD thesis, Oxford University.

Thak Chaloemtiarana. 2007. *Thailand: The Politics of Despotic Paternalism*. Ithaca, NY: Southeast Asia Program Publications, Cornell University.

Thane, Pat. 1986. "Financiers and the British State: The Case of Sir Ernest Cassel." *Business History* 28(1):80–99.

'tHart, Marjolein. 1999. "The United Provinces, 1579–1806." In *The Rise of the Fiscal State in Europe, c. 1200–1815*, ed. Richard Bonney, pp. 309–326. New York: Cambridge University Press.

Thies, Cameron G. 2005. "War, Rivalry, and State Building in Latin America." *American Journal of Political Science* 49:451–465.

Thies, Cameron G. 2007. "The Political Economy of State Building in Sub-Saharan Africa." *Journal of Politics* 69(3):716–731.

Tibebu, Teshale. 1995. *The Making of Modern Ethiopia 1896–1974*. Lawrenceville, NJ: Red Sea Press.

Tilly, Charles. 1990. *Coercion, Capital, and European States*. Cambridge, UK: Basil Blackwell.

Tilly, Charles. 2009. Foreword. In *The New Fiscal Sociology: Taxation in Comparative and Historical Perspective*, ed. Isaac William Martin, Ajay K. Mehrotra, and Monica Prasad, pp. xi–xiii. New York: Cambridge University Press.

Tomz, Michael. 2007. *Reputation and International Cooperation: Sovereign Debt across Three Centuries*. New York: Cambridge University Press.

Tooze, Adam, and Martin Ivanov. 2011. "Disciplining the 'Black Sheep of the Balkans': Financial Supervision and Sovereignty in Bulgaria, 1902–38." *Economic History Review* 64(1):30–51.

Topik, Steven. 1979. "The Evolution of the Economic Role of the Brazilian State, 1889–1930." *Journal of Latin American Studies* 11(2):325–342.

Tornell, Aaron, and Philip R. Lane. 1999. "The Voracity Effect." *American Economic Review* 89(1):22–46.

Tracy, James D. 1985. *A Financial Revolution in the Habsburg Netherlands: Renten and Renteniers in the County of Holland, 1515–1565*. Berkeley: University of California Press.

Tracy, James D. 2014. "Taxation and State Debt." In *The Oxford Handbook of Early Modern European History, 1350–1750: Volume II: Cultures and Power*. Oxford, UK: Oxford University Press.

Tunçer, Ali Coşkun. 2015. *Sovereign Debt and International Financial Control: The Middle East and the Balkans, 1870–1914*. New York: Palgrave Macmillan.

USAID. 2012. *Fiscal Reform and Economic Governance Project, 2004–2010*. Washington, DC: USAID.

Vandervort, Bruce. 1998. *Wars of Imperial Conquest in Africa 1830–1914*. Bloomington: Indiana University Press.

van der Windt, Peter, Macartan Humphreys, Lily Medina, Jeffrey F. Timmons, and Maarten Voors. 2019. "Citizen Attitudes toward Traditional and State Authorities: Substitutes or Complements?" *Comparative Political Studies* 52(12):1810–1840.

van de Ven, Hans. 2014. *Breaking with the Past: The Maritime Customs Service and the Global Origins of Modernity in China*. New York: Columbia University Press.

Vandewalle, Dirk. 1998. *Libya since Independence: Oil and State-Building*. Ithaca, NY: Cornell University Press.

Van-Helten, J. J. 1978. "German Capital, the Netherlands Railway Company and the Political Economy of the Transvaal 1886–1900." *Journal of African History* 19(3):369–390.

van Zanden, Jan Luiten, Eltjo Buringh, and Maarten Bosker. 2012. "The Rise and Decline of European Parliaments, 1188–1789." *Economic History Review* 65(3):835–861.

Verdier, Pierre-Hugues, and Erik Voeten. 2015. "How Does Customary International Law Change? The Case of State Immunity." *International Studies Quarterly* 59(2):209–222.

Vergara, Ximena, and Luis Barros. 1972. "La Guerra Civil del 91 y la Instauración del Parlamentarismo." *Revista Latinoamericana de Ciencias Sociales* 3:71–94.

Vestal, Theodore M. 2005. "Reflections on the Battle of Adwa and Its Significance for Today." In *The Battle of Adwa: Reflections on Ethiopia's Victory against European Colonialism*, ed. Paulos Milkias and Getachew Metaferia, pp. 21–36. New York: Algora Publishing.

Vignon, Louis V. 1893. *La France en Algérie*. Paris: Hachete et cie.

Viner, Jacob. 1929. "International Finance and Balance of Power Diplomacy, 1880–1914." *Southwestern Political and Social Science Quarterly* 9(4):407–451.

Vizcarra, Catalina. 2009. "Guano, Credible Commitments, and Sovereign Debt Repayment in Nineteenth-Century Peru." *Journal of Economic History* 69(2):358–387.

Vlastos, Stephen. 1989. "Opposition Movements in Early Meiji, 1868–1885." In *The Cambridge History of Japan*, ed. Marius B. Jansen, pp. 367–431. Vol. 5. Cambridge, UK: Cambridge University Press.

von Glahn, Richard. 2016. *The Economic History of China: From Antiquity to the Nineteenth Century*. New York: Cambridge University Press.

von Trotha, Trutz. 1996. "From Administrative to Civil Chieftaincy: Some Problems and Prospects of African Chieftaincy." *Journal of Legal Pluralism and Unofficial Law* 28(37–38): 79–107.

Vreeland, James Raymond. 2007. *The International Monetary Fund: Politics of Conditional Lending*. New York: Routledge.

Wagner, Gert, José Jofré, and Rolf Lüders. 2000. "Economía Chilena 1810–1995: Cuentas Fiscales." Technical report. Documento de Trabajo 188, Catholic University of Chile.

Waibel, Michael. 2011. *Sovereign Defaults before International Courts and Tribunals*. New York: Cambridge University Press.

Wakeman, Frederic. 1975. *The Fall of Imperial China*. New York: Free Press.

Wantchekon, Leonard, Marko Klašnja, and Natalija Novta. 2015. "Education and Human Capital Externalities: Evidence from Colonial Benin." *Quarterly Journal of Economics* 130(2):703–757.

Weber, Eugen. 1976. *Peasants into Frenchmen: The Modernization of Rural France, 1870–1914*. Stanford, CA: Stanford University Press.

Weber, Max. 1978. *Economy and Society: An Outline of Interpretive Sociology*. Berkeley: University of California Press.

Webster, Anthony. 1998. *Gentlemen Capitalists: British Imperialism in South East Asia*. New York: Tauris Academic Studies.

Weidemaier, Mark C., Robert E. Scott, and G. Mitu Gulati. 2013. "Origin Myths, Contracts, and the Hunt for Pari Passu." *Law & Social Inquiry* 38(1):72–105.

Weidemaier, W. Mark C., and Mitu Gulati. 2017. "International Finance and Sovereign Debt." In *The Oxford Handbook of Law and Economics: Volume 3: Public Law and Legal Institutions*, ed. Francesco Parisi, pp. 482–500. New York: Oxford University Press.

Weidemaier, W. Mark C., and Mitu Gulati. 2018. "Market Practice and the Evolution of Foreign Sovereign Immunity." *Law & Social Inquiry* 43(2):496–526.

Wesseling, H. L., ed. 1978. *Expansion and Reaction*. Leiden, Netherlands: Leiden University Press.

White, Harry D. 1933. *The French International Accounts 1880–1913*. Cambridge, MA: Harvard University Press.

Wibbels, Erik. 2006. "Dependency Revisited: International Markets, Business Cycles, and Social Spending in the Developing World." *International Organization* 60(2):433–468.

Wight, Martin. 1947. *The Gold Coast Legislative Council*. Vol. II. London: Faber & Faber.

Wilkinson, Steven. 2015. *Army and Nation*. New York: Oxford University Press.

Wilson, Constance M. 1983. *Thailand: A Handbook of Historical Statistics*. Boston: G. K. Hall.

Wilson, David A. 1966. *Politics in Thailand*. Ithaca, NY: Cornell University Press.

Wimmer, Andreas. 2013. *Waves of War. Nationalism, State Formation, and Ethnic Exclusion in the Modern World*. New York: Cambridge University Press.

Wimmer, Andreas, and Brian Min. 2009. "The Location and Purpose of Wars around the World: A New Global Dataset, 1816–2001." *International Interactions* 35(4):390–417.

Winkler, Max. 1933. *Foreign Bonds: An Autopsy*. Washington, DC: Beard Books.

Winn, Peter. 1976. "British Informal Empire in Uruguay in the Nineteenth Century." *Past & Present* (73):100–126.

Woodruff, William. 1966. *Impact of the Western Man: A Study of Europe's Role in the World Economy 1750–1960*. New York: St. Martin's Press.

Wright, Mark L. J. 2005. "Coordinating Creditors." *American Economic Review* 95(2):388–392.

Wynne, William H. 1951. *State Insolvency and Foreign Bondholders: Selected Case Histories of Governmental Foreign Bond Defaults and Debt Readjustments*. Vol. II. Washington, DC: Beard Books.

Wynne, William H., and Edwin M. Borchard. 1933. "Foreign Bondholders Protective Organizations." *Yale Law Journal* 43(2):281–296.

Yapp, Malcolm. 1987. *The Making of the Modern Near East, 1792–1923*. New York: Longman.

Young, Crawford. 1994. *The African Colonial State in Comparative Perspective*. New Haven, CT: Yale University Press.

Young, L. K. 1970. *British Policy in China 1895–1902*. Oxford, UK: Clarendon Press.

Yun-Casalilla, Bartolomé, and Patrick K. O'Brien. 2012. *The Rise of Fiscal States: A Global History 1500–1914*. New York: Cambridge University Press.

Zanetti, Oscar, and Alejandro García. 1998. *Sugar and Railroads: A Cuban History, 1837–1959*. Chapel Hill: University of North Carolina Press.

Zegarra, Luis Felipe. 2013. "Transportation Costs and the Social Savings of Railroads in Latin America: The Case of Peru." *Revista de Historia Económica/Journal of Iberian and Latin American Economic History* 31(1):41–72.

Zewde, Bahru. 2001. *A History of Modern Ethiopia, 1855–1991*. Athens: Ohio University Press.

Zhang, Nan, and Melissa M. Lee. 2020. "Literacy and State-Society Interactions in Nineteenth-Century France." *American Journal of Political Science* 64(4):1001–1016.

Zheng, Xiaowei. 2018. *The Politics of Rights and the 1911 Revolution in China*. Stanford, CA: Stanford University Press.

Zuo Zongtang. 1890. *Zuo Wenxianggong Zoushu Chubian* [Zuo Zongtang's Memorials to the Throne]. Vol. 59. Shanghai: Publisher unknown.

INDEX

The Princeton Economic History of the Western World

Joel Mokyr, Series Editor

Milton Keynes UK
Ingram Content Group UK Ltd.
UKHW030515301024
450210UK00002B/21